Ninety Miles and a Lifetime Away

NINETY MILES

AND A

LIFETIME AWAY

MEMORIES OF EARLY CUBAN EXILES

DAVID POWELL

For Erik Kirk—
Old friends are the
best friends.

David Powell—

UNIVERSITY OF FLORIDA PRESS

Gainesville

Publication of this work made possible by a
Sustaining the Humanities through the American Rescue Plan grant
from the National Endowment for the Humanities.

Frontis: Luis Cruz Azaceta, "Man Holding His Country," 1993. Acrylic, pencil, shellac on paper, 42" × 30". In the artist's collection. By permission of Luis Cruz Azaceta, New Orleans, Louisiana. Of this self-portrait, the artist says, "No matter where you go, you carry your roots—in this case, the island of Cuba. I keep on carrying the island with me, no matter where I go."

27 26 25 24 23 22   6 5 4 3 2 1

Library of Congress Control Number: 2021948936
ISBN 978-1-68340-257-2

University of Florida Press
2046 NE Waldo Road
Suite 2100
Gainesville, FL 32609
http://upress.ufl.edu

UF PRESS

UNIVERSITY
OF FLORIDA

FOR VICKI

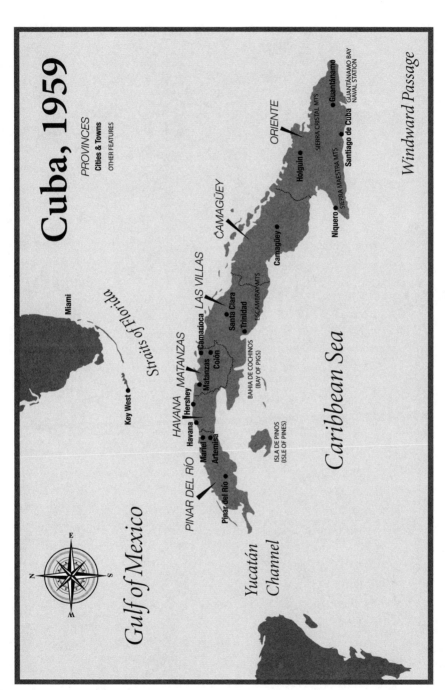

Map of Cuba, 1959.

CONTENTS

PREFACE

From 1959 through 1973, during the administrations of four American presidents, more than 600,000 Cubans came to the United States, most in two massive waves, as Fidel Castro turned Cuba's political, economic, and social order upside down and ended American domination of the island. Almost 250,000 Cubans came during the First Wave, from 1959 through 1962. Another 350,000 arrived during the Second Wave, from 1965 through 1973. The early refugees reached our shores mostly by air, and in daily numbers small enough that their coming usually was obscured by larger events of the Cold War. Some refugees first went to third countries and later migrated to the United States. Most came to the US without the required visas, but the government let them enter the country anyway.

The government created an assistance program for them unlike anything the nation had done before, featuring a buffet line of benefits that transformed the refugees' lives and America as well. Washington poured billions into it. Cubans also received preference under US immigration and naturalization laws. At the height of the Cold War, these policies were intended to demonstrate that liberal democracy and a free-market economy were superior to a totalitarian communist system. The government empowered the early Cuban refugees—the vanguard of a diaspora that has brought more than 1.4 million Cubans to the US since Castro assumed power—to become one of the most rapidly successful immigrant groups in American history. They in turn created a transnational community that enriched this nation economically and culturally and altered its political trajectory at a pivotal moment.

In 1975, after the end of the Second Wave, I moved to Florida as a reporter in the Miami bureau of the Associated Press. I witnessed Miami's wrenching transformation as this down-on-its-luck resort struggled to absorb the hundreds of thousands of Cuban refugees who had settled there since 1959. Some locals resented the changes taking place, like the prevalence of Spanish spoken in grocery stores. Having been raised in Texas and schooled in New York, I was not uncomfortable with the unfolding fusion of cultures in South Florida, but I began to understand the locals' hard feelings toward the newcomers. Many refugees did not intend to make the US their home, not at first. They wanted to retain their Cuban identity and return to their island. They called themselves exiles.

I learned about other facets of the Cuban exile experience when I transferred to the AP's statehouse bureau in Tallahassee. Lawmakers revised protectionist licensing laws so that Cuban professionals could resume careers and support their families. Cuban Americans won elections to Miami City Hall, the Florida Legislature, and the Congress. Before nationwide banking, banks from major financial centers like New York opened special offices in Miami as Cuban Americans helped to reinvent the city as a sparkling international hub for finance and trade. After becoming a lawyer in 1987, I traveled throughout Florida and got to know Cuban Americans in business, the professions, government, nonprofits, and the arts. I was struck by the deep passion for their native land as well as their sense of personal loss. But over time, like others, I took the Cuban Americans for granted, just another immigrant success story in America.

The idea for this book came during a casual conversation with friends in 2011 but, immersed in my law practice, I put it aside until one day a few years later. That day I went to discuss a real estate matter with Rick Fernandez, a high-ranking official for the City of Tallahassee. He had just returned from Cuba and described it as "the most amazing trip I've ever been on in my life." When I asked why he had visited the island, he said, "I went back to see my mother and my brother for the first time since I left in 1966 when I was twelve years old."

Rick's reply struck me like a thunderbolt. An engaging fireplug of a man, he told his story for almost one hour—parts of it are in these pages—and I was riveted. But as I walked away from his office, I wondered how many more people have stories like Rick's that are unknown except by a few intimates. What hardships did the early Cuban refugees endure? What history did they witness? What could others learn from their lives?

In April 2015, while practicing law, I began an eighteen-month exploration of the idea for this book. I read about Cuban history and the refugee experience. I attended a book-writing seminar at the Columbia Journalism School and enrolled in an online workshop on the practice of oral history. I studied the works of the Pulitzer Prize-winning interviewer Studs Terkel by comparing his interview transcripts and finished manuscripts. And I talked with friends who had lived this story. Interviews began in November 2016. At the end of that month, Fidel died. I took the news of his death as a sign that an era was ending. For me there was no turning back.

My goal for this book was not to write an account of the Cuban Revolution, or a history of the Cuban American experience, but to present the story of the earliest refugees who came to the US from Castro's Cuba and to do so through *their* voices. It is a story that shows America at its best—not without faults but as the imperfect land of refuge and opportunity that it has always been. For these Cuban Americans and others, their memories of the island and of exile are more than a chart to the course of their lives; their memories have shaped their identity. As the artist Luis Cruz Azaceta said in our interview, "I keep on carrying the island with me, no matter where I go."

My fifty-four narrators do not constitute a statistically valid representative sample, as in an opinion survey. For example, these pages do not include testimonies from the Cubans of color or Cubans of Jewish or Chinese descent who left the island in small numbers during that period. Still, these testimonies are valuable. Rarely do readers have the chance to hear Cuban exiles tell their stories in their own words, in English, with details about their daily lives or the historic events they witnessed. Because I want readers to hear their voices, I have kept my voice to a minimum.

When woven together, the most revealing passages from my interviews tell the larger story of the early Cuban refugees and illuminate common themes: most were subjected to degrading searches and confiscations before they left and arrived in the US virtually penniless. Extended families crammed into tiny living spaces while some worked at menial jobs that they once hired others to do. Many were taken aback by the rigid segregation in America despite their own homeland's history of racism, and the few refugees of color were limited in where they could live and work. Although the early Cuban refugees were overwhelmingly White, some Anglos denigrated them as "spics." But American Jews remembered the plight of European Jewry a few decades earlier and befriended them. Thousands went to college with low-cost "Cuban Loans" from the government. They made a new home in America.

All the Cuban American narrators left the island from 1959 through 1973.

Many are from what social scientists call the "1.5 generation," a term coined by the sociologist Rubén G. Rumbaut—born in Havana in 1950 and brought to this country in 1960—to describe migrants who arrived as preadolescent children, as distinct from "first generation" immigrants who came as adults and "second generation" native-born persons of foreign parentage. With their uncertain immigration status until the Congress in 1966 made them permanent residents on a fast track to citizenship, in today's political vocabulary we might have called some of them "dreamers" if they were without permanent resident status from an immigration visa and were here by the grace of the government. They remember their early lives in Cuba *and* coming of age in America.

I also interviewed a handful of non-Cuban Americans with insights into the story of the early refugees; for example, a foreign correspondent, a politician, and two historians. These narrators provide context for particular events or periods.

Using questions provided to the narrator in advance, I conducted each interview one-on-one in English in a quiet setting chosen by the narrator—a living room at home or a private office or conference room in the workplace—and recorded the conversation with a digital audio recorder. The typical interview ran for two hours. I conducted follow-up interviews with some narrators and allowed each narrator to identify specific parts of his or her conversation to remain confidential. Only a few narrators did so; those each chose only brief passages. A professional transcriber prepared a transcript of each recorded review, and I audited the result. Each narrator conveyed to me in writing, under copyright law, the world literary rights to his or her interview.

In editing the transcripts, I followed the polestar standard in the style guide of Columbia University's Center for Oral History Research: "The role of the transcript is to represent, first and foremost, what a speaker intended to say, as clearly as possible, in the text." I edited transcripts with these techniques: I cut crutch words, false starts, and reflexive phrases such as "well," "uh," "kind of," and "you know" and broke run-on sentences into smaller sentences. I deleted redundant words, phrases, or sentences and corrected grammatical errors but did not alter a narrator's word choice on any material matter. I gave each narrator an opportunity to review, edit, and correct the edited transcript before I chose passages for the book.

I chose passages that helped to tell the larger story, then omitted my questions and edited these excerpts for clarity and length, but only if the context was not altered. I added a few explanatory footnotes to aid the reader. I changed some verbs to the active voice and, to resolve ambiguities, changed a few personal pronouns; for example, "he" became "my father." These editing decisions were based on my judgment of how best to present these stories to a general audience in a readable format, true to the narrators' intent. The responsibility for doing so is solely mine.

In *The Unwomanly Face of War: An Oral History of Women in World War II*, the Nobel laureate Svetlana Alexievich calls oral testimonies like these "history through the story told by an unnoticed witness and participant." They are a time-honored way to preserve shared experience. But memory is fallible. As Studs Terkel says of his narrators in *Hard Times: An Oral History of the Great Depression*: "In their rememberings are their truths. The precise fact or the precise statistic is of small consequence." The testimonies from my narrators reflect this limitation. One narrator remembers Fidel in 1959, after the end of a two-year insurrection that ousted the dictator Fulgencio Batista, triumphantly entering Havana in a jeep. Another remembers him riding past cheering throngs atop a Sherman tank. Perhaps both are right. He could have changed vehicles as the procession made its way through the rapturous city.

We should be mindful of vagaries like these and read critically. We may want to ask why most Cubans chose not to leave in the First and Second Waves, like peasants in rural areas where full-time, year-round jobs were scarce. Experts may disagree with some narrators in their recollection of, or explanation for, what happened on the island and after their arrival in the US, as indeed they sometimes disagree among themselves.

Where a narrator asserted a verifiable historical fact, I tried to confirm it. For example, one narrator says that during the 1957 attempt to assassinate Batista in Havana's Presidential Palace, her father answered the telephone in Batista's personal office as he and others in the assault team searched unsuccessfully for the dictator. The historian Hugh Thomas confirms it in his authoritative *Cuba: The Pursuit of Freedom*. Where my research demonstrated that an event was remembered inaccurately, I omitted it from the book. Where I could neither confirm nor disprove a narrator's memory of an historical event—like how Castro entered Havana in 1959—I sometimes included the unconfirmed memory. As Studs Terkel said, these testimonies are the truths that *they* remember.

Finally, there is a nomenclature issue. Many Cuban Americans whom I interviewed call themselves "exiles." *Webster's Third New International Dictionary* defines "exile" as "forced removal from one's native country; expulsion from home." The word is derived from the Latin *exilium*, which means banishment. Thus the word carries a connotation of being cast out from a place by some authority.

In contrast, some Cuban Americans I interviewed call themselves "refugees," as did the US government. *Webster's Third New International Dictionary* defines "refugee" as "one who flees to a foreign country or power to escape danger because of his race, religion, or political beliefs." The word is derived from the French *réfugié*, which means "gone in search of refuge." Thus it carries a connotation of choosing to leave a place due to some threatening circumstance and seeking shelter or protection elsewhere.

I use these words interchangeably because both can apply. Cubans generally chose to leave their homeland starting in 1959 because they could not abide the sweeping changes made by the Castro regime, but they had to get the regime's permission to leave in the form of an exit permit. Once here, however, they could not return under express and de facto policies, enforced by the regime with rare exceptions until 1979, forbidding those who had opposed the revolution or accepted foreign citizenship from going back.

The Cubans who left their island starting in 1959 may have done so as refugees, but once here most of them considered themselves in exile, like the exile that Cubans of earlier generations experienced during the periodic upheavals of the colonial era and the early years of the republic. However, this exile would be different. It was a separation from their homeland from which they expected to return, as had those from earlier exiles, but ultimately did not.

These are some of their memories.

A NOTE ON NAMES

Cubans generally follow the Spanish custom of identifying a person by his or her given name, the father's first surname (*primer apelido* or *apelido paterno*), and then the mother's first surname (*segundo apelido* or *apelido materno*). Sometimes the two surnames are joined by the Spanish conjunctive "*y*." Thus Fidel Castro is known in Cuba as Fidel Castro Ruz after his Spanish-born father, Ángel Castro y Argiz, and his father's Cuban-born housekeeper, Lina Ruz González, later Ángel's second wife. In this tradition a woman typically does not change her surname upon marriage. Sometimes a married woman may append her husband's *primer apelido* to follow her own, joined by "*de*," or adopt a hyphenated last name with her *primer apelido* and her husband's *primer apelido*.

I follow the Anglo American tradition of identifying a man or an unmarried woman by his or her given name and his or her patrilineal surname, so Fidel Castro Ruz is called Fidel Castro. An exception: entrepreneur Vicente Martinez Ybor because, mysteriously, his *segundo apelido* was used to name Tampa's cigar-making enclave Ybor City. Another exception: the artist Luis Cruz Azaceta because he signs his work in the Spanish tradition. I identify a married woman by her given name, her patrilineal surname, and then her husband's patrilineal surname. An exception by request: Paulina García Orta, her name in the Spanish tradition. Another exception: Albertina O'Farrill, because she was known by that name as a noteworthy political prisoner.

NARRATORS

A

Thomas J. Aglio—Born in Boston, 1931. He is the retired executive director of Catholic Charities of Central Florida. In 1962 he managed a church-run camp for Cuban boys brought to the US without their parents in Operation Pedro Pan. He resides in Winter Park, Florida.

Silvia Morell Alderman—Born in Havana, 1952. Came to the US, 1960. She is a lawyer, specializing in environmental law. She resides in Tallahassee, Florida.

Arelis Duran Alvarez—Born in Holguín in eastern Cuba, 1951. Came to the US in Operation Pedro Pan, 1962. She is a retired claims agent for the Teamsters Union insurance and pension funds. She resides with her husband Luis in North Haledon, New Jersey.

Carlos Alvarez—Born in Havana, 1950. Came to the US, 1960. He was an All-American wide receiver for the University of Florida Gators from 1969 to 1971, and in 2011 was inducted into the College Football Hall of Fame. A lawyer and mediator, he resides in Tallahassee, Florida.

Luis M. Alvarez—Born in Havana, 1950. Came to the US in Operation Pedro Pan, 1962. He is an accountant and resides with his wife Arelis in North Haledon, New Jersey.

C

Cesar E. Calvet—Born in Havana, 1945. Came to the US unaccompanied, 1961, and was taken into Operation Pedro Pan. He is a retired banker and resides in Orlando, Florida.

Margarita Fernández Cano—Born in Havana, 1932. Came to the US, 1962. A retired librarian, she began the lending arts program for the Miami Public Library, and in 2009 received the Lifetime Achievement Award of the Cintas Foundation. She resides in Miami, Florida.

Alberto R. "Al" Cardenas—Born in Havana, 1948. Came to the US, 1960. He is a lawyer, political commentator, and former chairman of the Florida Republican Party and the American Conservative Union. He resides in Coral Gables, Florida.

Mario Cartaya—Born in Havana, 1951. Came to the US, 1960. He is an architect with his own firm and a board member of the Cuba Study Group, a nonpartisan organization that advocates an end to US travel and trade restrictions on Cuba and dialogue as a means to achieve reconciliation among all Cubans. He resides in Fort Lauderdale, Florida.

Angel Castillo Jr.—Born in Havana, 1946. Came to the US, 1960. He is a lawyer, specializing in employment law, and before that was a newspaper reporter and editor. He resides in Miami, Florida.

Gabriel Castillo (aka Gaby Gabriel)—Born in Niquero in eastern Cuba, 1952. Came to the US on a Freedom Flight chartered by the US government, 1966. He is a musician and entertainer at South Florida resorts and nightspots. He resides in Miami, Florida.

Justo Luis Cepero—Born in Matanzas in western Cuba, 1962. Came to the US on a Freedom Flight, 1969. He is a founder of a family-owned food-processing business specializing in Cuban delicacies. He resides in Tampa, Florida.

Mercedes Fernandez Collazo—Born in Havana, 1954. Came to the US on a Freedom Flight, 1967. She is a homemaker and retired bank clerk. She and her husband Mike reside in Tampa, Florida.

Miguel "Mike" Collazo—Born in Havana, 1953. Came to the US on a Freedom Flight, 1967. He is a retired sod-layer and laborer. He and his wife Mercedes reside in Tampa, Florida.

Luis Cruz Azaceta—Born in Havana, 1942. Came to the US, 1960. An artist in multiple media, he is represented in museums and private collections around the world, including the Metropolitan Museum of Art, the Museum of Modern Art, and the American Museum of the Cuban Diaspora. He resides in New Orleans, Louisiana.

Emilio Cueto—Born in Havana, 1944. Came to the US in Operation Pedro Pan, 1961. A retired lawyer, he owns one of the world's largest private collections of Cuban cultural artifacts. He resides in Washington, DC.

D

Andrés M. Duany—Born in New York, New York, 1949, and raised in Santiago de Cuba in eastern Cuba. Returned to the US, 1960. An architect, he is a founder of the new urbanism school of town planning. He resides in Miami, Florida.

Jorge M. Duany—Born in Havana, 1957. Emigrated to Panama in 1960 then lived in Puerto Rico until coming to the US mainland. He is director of the Cuban Research Institute and a professor of anthropology at Florida International University. He resides in Doral, Florida.

E

Eloísa M. Echazábal—Born in Havana, 1948. Came to the US in Operation Pedro Pan, 1961. She is a certified interpreter for the FBI and a retired administrator at Miami Dade College. She resides in Miami, Florida.

F

Rafael E. "Ralph" Fernandez—Born in Havana, 1952. Came to the US, 1960. He is a lawyer, specializing in litigation. He resides in Tampa, Florida.

Ricardo "Rick" Fernandez—Born in Guantánamo in eastern Cuba, 1954. Came to the US as an unaccompanied minor by way of Spain, 1966. An accountant, he is a former city administrator in Dallas, Texas, and Tallahassee, Florida. He resides in Tallahassee, Florida.

Isaac M. "Ike" Flores—Born in Deming, New Mexico, 1932. He is a retired reporter for the Associated Press and served as its resident correspondent in Havana from 1965 to 1967. He resides in Winter Park, Florida.

Pedro A. Freyre—Born in Havana, 1949. Came to the US, 1960. He is a lawyer, specializing in trade with Cuba and Spain. He resides in Miami, Florida.

G

Tere Castellanos Garcia—Born in Havana, 1951. Came to the US in Operation Pedro Pan, 1961, was raised in Puerto Rico, and later came to the US mainland. A planner, she is a senior executive with an engineering firm. She resides in Miami, Florida.

Paulina García Orta (aka Paulina Rodriguez-Muro)—Born in Colón in western Cuba, 1944. Came to the US on the short-lived Camarioca Boatlift, 1965. She resides in Miami, Florida.

Paul S. George—Born in Miami, 1942. He is the resident historian at HistoryMiami Museum and a retired professor at Miami Dade College. He resides in Miami, Florida.

Romualdo "Romi" González—Born in Havana, 1947. Came to the US, 1961. He is a lawyer and was active in efforts to reunite the Episcopal Church of Cuba with the American church, which was achieved in 2020. He resides in New Orleans, Louisiana.

Bob Graham—Born in Coral Gables, Florida, 1936. A Democrat, he served as a Florida state legislator from 1966 to 1978, as governor from 1979 to 1987, and as a US senator from 1987 to 2005. He resides in Gainesville, Florida.

H

Maribel Pérez Henley—Born in Mariel in western Cuba, 1964. Came to the US on a Freedom Flight, 1970. She is a paralegal in the real estate practice of a major Florida law firm. She resides in Miami, Florida.

Adolfo Henriques—Born in Havana, 1953. Emigrated to Jamaica, 1961. Came to the US, 1973. A banker, he is vice-chairman of South Florida's largest development company. He resides in Key Biscayne, Florida.

Ana Cowley Hodges—Born in Havana, 1949. Came to the US, 1960. She is a retired journalism teacher in the public schools of suburban Katy, Texas. She resides in Houston, Texas.

Isis Rivero Hoffman—Born in Havana, 1938. Came to the US, 1961. She is a retired hospital architect and administrator of Columbia University in New York. She resides in Key Biscayne, Florida.

J

Julian C. Juergensmeyer—Born in Paintsville, Kentucky, 1938. A retired law professor, he directed the University of Florida's Cuban American Lawyers Program from 1973 to 1976. He resides in Atlanta, Georgia.

L

Hector Laurencio (*née* Hector García)—Born in rural Camagüey province in central Cuba, 1945. Came to the US as an unaccompanied minor, 1961, and was taken into Operation Pedro Pan. He is a retired ophthalmologist. He and his wife Maria reside in Coral Gables, Florida.

Maria Galatas Laurencio—Born in Artemisa in western Cuba, 1950. Came to the US, 1961. She is a retired anesthesiologist. She and her husband Hector reside in Coral Gables, Florida.

M

Guillermo G. "Gil" Mármol—Born in Havana, 1953. Came to the US, 1961. A retired corporate executive and management consultant, he serves on the board of the Center for a Free Cuba, which advocates the continuation of US travel and trade restrictions on Cuba unless there is a peaceful transition to democracy there. He resides in Dallas, Texas.

Myriam Márquez—Born in Santiago de las Vegas in western Cuba, 1954. Came to the US, 1959. She is executive director of the News Leaders Association and a former executive editor of Miami's *El Nuevo Herald*. She resides in Miami Beach, Florida.

Henry Martell (*née* Enrique Martell)—Born in Havana, 1947. Came to the US, 1962, and lived in Puerto Rico until coming to the mainland. A retired automobile dealer, he resided in Coral Gables, Florida, until his death in 2020.

Marijean Collado Miyar—Born in Brooklyn, New York, 1947. Moved to Havana, 1952. Returned to the US, 1961. She is a retired lecturer in art history and ancient architecture at Miami area schools, universities, and museums. She resides in Coral Gables, Florida.

Ricardo "Dick" Morales Jr.—Born in Havana, 1938. Came to the US, 1960. He is founder and board chairman of a group of construction and development companies. He resides in Jacksonville, Florida.

Gary R. Mormino—Born in Alton, Illinois, 1947. He is scholar in residence at the Florida Humanities Council and a retired history professor at the University of South Florida, St. Petersburg, specializing in immigration and Florida. He resides in St. Petersburg, Florida.

Luis C. Morse—Born in Havana, 1940. Came to the US, 1960. A veteran of the Bay of Pigs invasion, he served as a Florida state legislator from 1986 to 1998 including a term as speaker pro tempore of the Florida House of Representatives. He resides in Miami, Florida.

P

Eduardo J. Padrón—Born in Santiago de Cuba in eastern Cuba, 1944. Came to the US as an unaccompanied minor, 1961. An economist, he served as president of Miami Dade College from 1995 to 2019, and in 2016 received the Presidential Medal of Freedom, the nation's highest civilian honor. He resides in Miami, Florida.

Edmundo Pérez-de Cobos—Born in Havana, 1946. Came to the US in Operation Pedro Pan, 1960. He is a retired executive of American Express in England, Hong Kong, Spain, Argentina, and Mexico. He resides in Coral Gables, Florida.

R

Nestor A. Rodriguez—Born in Havana, 1958. Emigrated to Spain, 1969. Came to the US, 1971. He has held management roles in various not-for-profits in South Florida. He resides in Miami, Florida.

Carmen Leiva Roiz—Born in Havana, 1936. Came to the US, 1960. After living in the New York metropolitan area and South America, she worked as a secretary, newspaper columnist, magazine editor, and television producer in Miami. She resides in Miami, Florida.

S

Diana Sawaya-Crane—Born in Havana, 1951. Emigrated to Venezuela, 1959. Came to the US, 1968. She is a retired senior advisor to a Florida governor and two attorneys general. She resides in Tallahassee, Florida.

T

Hilda Molina Tabernilla—Born in Havana, 1937. Came to the US, 1959. Her late husband was private secretary to President Fulgencio Batista, and the family left Cuba with Batista in 1959. She is a retired seamstress and retail saleswoman. She resides in Palm Beach, Florida.

V

Jose E. Valiente—Born in Bejucal in western Cuba, 1950. Came to the US, 1962. He is retired from his own accounting firm and resides in Tampa, Florida.

Julieta Navarrete Valls—Born in Havana, 1942. Came to the US, 1960. She is a retired international development consultant. She resides in South Miami, Florida.

Jose A. Villalobos—Born in Guanabacoa in western Cuba, 1938. Came to the US, 1960. He is a lawyer, specializing in government relations. He resides in Miami, Florida.

Marielena Alejo Villamil—Born in Havana, 1947. Came to the US, 1959. She is president of an economics consulting firm. She resides in Coral Gables, Florida.

W

Mercedes Wangüemert-Peña—Born in Havana, 1950. Came to the US, 1960. Returned to live in Cuba with her two sons, 1979, then returned to the US, 1980. She works at a shelter for homeless refugees and resides in Austin, Texas.

Z

Victoria Montoro Zamorano—Born in Havana, 1949. Came to the US, 1961. She is a real estate agent and photographer. She resides in South Miami, Florida.

COMPLETE INTERVIEW TRANSCRIPTS, specifying the date and place of each interview, are available at the University of Miami's Cuban Heritage Collection. Visit www.library.miami.edu/chc/.

INTRODUCTION

He remembers the day they left, June 27, 1960. The memory is still vivid.

They loaded the family car, a brown-and-white 1958 Oldsmobile sedan, with as many belongings as they could fit into it. Then they closed the door to their two-story three-bedroom cinderblock home in suburban Reparto Flores, a block or so from the rocky edge of the Gulf of Mexico, and set out on the early-morning drive to the Port of Havana and the ferry to Key West.

His father Licinio Alvarez had prepared in secrecy. He knew the risks, the barriers they would face as they made their way out of the country with all the possessions they could take in the car and a few pieces of furniture he had surreptitiously shipped to Miami. Licinio was the general counsel of an import-export company in Havana that engaged in the extensive commerce between Cuba and its number one trading partner, the United States, but he had gone to law school with Fidel Castro and feared the changes that Castro would make after gaining power.

Licinio had traveled to the US before, on business and family vacations. On this trip he and his wife Isola were taking their three sons, Cesar, thirteen; Arturo, twelve; and Carlos, ten; and their daughter Ana, five. They had visas to enter the US, but this journey would be different: they were leaving not for a vacation but to escape a terrifying revolution.

"It was a nice day, a typical day in June in Cuba," Carlos remembers. "It didn't feel hot because you have sea breezes in Havana. Probably the hardest thing was getting in the car—the first step in this unknown journey, not fully appreciating what we were doing—and moving away from the house, thinking, I may not see this again. That was hard."[1]

Fruit vendors at the port were setting up their stands with mangoes, papaya, and plantains. In the terminal the family's papers were checked, probably by armed militia or *milicianos*, against a list of persons not allowed to leave the country after the insurrection that had ended in sudden victory the year before. Then Licinio drove the car into the open-air vehicle hold of the SS *City of Havana*.

Built in 1943 at Newport News, Virginia, to ferry armored vehicles for amphibious landings during World War II, the ship saw action on only one day, June 6, 1944, off the coast of Normandy. After the war it was sold, renamed, and refitted as an automobile ferry by the West India Fruit and Steamship Company of West Palm Beach, Florida. In 1956 the company deployed the *City of Havana* to compete in the thriving US-Cuba trade.[2] The ship joined its five-vessel fleet that carried manufactured goods in loaded railroad cars from West Palm Beach or New Orleans to Havana and brought back fruit, vegetables, and refined sugar.[3] Painted white, the 456-foot-long ship carried up to five hundred passengers and 125 automobiles on each crossing of its scheduled three round trips per week. Round trip fares were $76.00 for an automobile and $23.50 per person.[4]

The Alvarez family rode an escalator up to the passenger deck to wait for inspectors to check the vehicles for contraband. "We had packed the car with everything that my parents thought could provide some money to start us off in the US," Carlos recalls, "clothes, silver, every piece of jewelry that my mom could possibly have hidden. All of that was in the car, but a lot of that wasn't allowed to be brought from Cuba. My brothers and I were carrying silverware in our pockets."

From the passenger deck they looked down into the vehicle hold of the big ship. They saw inspectors go from car to car. Sometimes these searches delayed the ship's departure by hours. "When they got to our car, they just went around it," Carlos remembers. "My dad had paid off somebody—which is not unusual in Cuba—so they didn't check it. That's where my dad's shipping business experience helped." With the formalities completed, the vessel's two oil-fired engines cranked into gear. The *City of Havana* pulled away from the terminal and steamed through the port channel, past the drab, weathered walls of the sixteenth-century El Morro Castle at the harbor's entrance, for the seven-hour, ninety-mile voyage to Key West.

As the *City of Havana* entered the Florida Straits, passengers settled into the air-conditioned lounge with food service and a bar. For ten dollars they could enjoy the privacy of a day cabin while the ship cruised along at up to seventeen knots.[5] Or they could just soak up the watery scene from the deck, spotting marine life in the Gulf Stream that courses through the straits, those warm waters that Hemingway so artfully described as "the great, deep blue river, three quarters to a mile deep and sixty to eighty miles across."[6]

"You looked out the railing," Carlos says. "I remember the flying fish that went by the boat. Every once in a while you would see something else. It was fun being on the ferry."

The weather was fair that afternoon when the ferry docked in Key West. The vessel would make its final voyage from Havana on October 31, 1960, its schedule already reduced from three round trips per week to only one as trade and tourism withered in a deepening confrontation between the US and Cuba.[7] Licinio Alvarez led his family down to the vehicle hold, got behind the wheel of his two-tone Oldsmobile, and drove off the ferry.

After the Alvarez family continued their journey to Miami on the Florida Keys' Overseas Highway, more Cubans followed, on the ferry to Key West or airliners to the mainland or by escaping first to other countries and later making their way to the US. The First Wave ended in late 1962. The Second Wave began in late 1965 and ended in 1973 as the US government chartered airliners to bring more Cubans into exile in an organized mass migration intended to reunify families.

Their story is best understood through the memories of those who lived it—doctors and laborers, seamstresses and lawyers, bankers and librarians, musicians and accountants, architects and journalists, artists and business executives, clerks and politicians, teachers and government officials, college presidents and homemakers. All are rememberers.

When they talk to children, grandchildren, and friends about their lives, these are the memories they share: of fear, suspicion, and betrayal as their tropical home vanished in an all-consuming revolution; of anguish, despair, and heartache at leaving behind spouses, brothers, sisters, parents, grandparents, aunts, uncles, cousins, and friends, not to mention homes, belongings, livelihoods, and for some part of their identity; of struggle, hardship, and indignity as they started life all over in a different language; and of generosity, opportunity, and hope in a new home ninety miles and a lifetime away.

1

HOME

Before the revolution, by objective measures, Cuba was one of Latin America's leading countries. It had the fourth-highest per capita income and the lowest cost of living.[1] Considering literacy, infant mortality, and life expectancy, it ranked among the best five.[2] It was among the first countries in the hemisphere with railroads, electricity, and telephones, and it had one of the world's highest per capita rates of car ownership.[3] Still, Cuba was a relatively poor country in comparison to the United States.[4] Prices outpaced economic growth, so living standards went into a slow decline. Cubans were not as well off economically in the 1950s as they had been in the 1920s.[5]

The island reflected Old World customs inculcated during four centuries as a Spanish colony. Extended families lived together. Upper- and middle-class households hired live-in maids, cooks, and chauffeurs, typically people of color, and even some working-class families had paid help.[6] A young single woman, when traveling or on a date with a man, was often chaperoned by her parents or a mature woman like an aunt.[7]

Even as Spanish traditions influenced life in Cuba, the country was shaped by its long and complicated relationship with the US. The nineteenth-century revolutionary José Martí called it "the colossus of the North."[8] Cuba was economically dependent upon one commodity, sugar, and one export market, the US.[9] The dollar was legal tender at par with the Cuban *peso*.[10] American influence saturated the island. Economically, culturally, and politically, Cuba was as much a part of America as it was possible to be without statehood.[11]

Ricardo "Dick" Morales Jr.

JACKSONVILLE, FLORIDA

Dick and his two brothers were raised in a family compound in Havana,
the sons of Ricardo Morales and his wife Maria. Ricardo earned degrees in
architecture and civil engineering from the University of Havana and became
a successful construction entrepreneur whose rapport with American business
and culture typified Cuba's upper class.

I was privileged in that I came into a family that had money, a well-to-do family, well connected. We didn't have sugar mills or a lot of land, but my great-uncle had a trading company. They were sugar bankers, brokers, and traders. They had offices in Havana and New York. When my great-uncle died, he divided his fortune between his brothers and sisters and his twenty-five nephews. Daddy was the only architect in the family, so when everybody inherited money, they all built new houses. Bank financing was not easy to get in those days. Dad said, "I got more than anybody else because I have my share, but I got a bit of everybody else's when I built their new homes."

Dad built a new house when he got some money. He bought a whole block. I had one grandmother on one corner, another in between us, and we had the other corner. In the back was one of my grandmother's sisters, one of her nephews, and a vacant lot. Mother was always wonderful. She took care of Dad, us, the house, and servants.

I tell everybody, when I grew up in Cuba, "everything was up to date in Kansas City."* We had a phone company that was unique in Latin America because it was great. It was part of ITT.† I remember as a child, we had dial phones all over the place because ITT used Havana as a trial for that. We had television stations. We had newspapers. We had this. We had that. And Havana: the city services, the sophistication, the theater, the good, the bad, the whole thing—unique. Mexico City was a lot bigger, but we always considered the Mexicans uneducated.

Cubans were very Americanized. We had bank accounts in New York. All the movies we saw were American movies. The clubs were organized American style. They had English names: Havana Yacht Club, Vedado Tennis Club, the Country Club of Havana, the Biltmore Yacht and Country Club. All the well-to-do families sent their

---

* From the song "Kansas City" in the 1943 Broadway musical *Oklahoma!* by Rodgers and Hammerstein.
† International Telephone and Telegraph of New York owned control of the Cuban Telephone Company.

kids to the United States for schooling, if they were so inclined. Even the not-so-well-to-do came during the summer to travel, and Americans came to Cuba. They were well liked. Everybody spoke some English. The business and professional classes in Cuba were *very* Americanized. Not the political classes.

Mario Cartaya
FORT LAUDERDALE, FLORIDA

Mario and his brother lived in Havana with their parents and their mother's parents and brother. Mario's father Ignacio was an accountant who embodied the sturdy commercial ties between Cuba and American corporations. His mother Leida taught kindergarten at Instituto Edison, one of the capital's leading secular private schools.

My father worked his way to becoming an accountant. He worked for Frigidaire for many years in Havana. Then he started his own company where he not only did accounting for Frigidaire and Sylvania but sold their products in his store.

My mother was the princess. There's no other way to put it. She came from a different side of the family, very cultured when it comes to education and the arts. All of them played instruments. She was the piano player, the beautiful blonde that everybody loved, the one that was always sweet and kind and talented and musical. Her life was based on a love of the arts.

Our extended family lived together. By that I mean the mother with her parents, and then the husband, all lived in the same house, with, of course, their offspring—us—and one of my uncles. I grew up in an old-fashioned Cuban family household, where music and the arts were an everyday event. From my father, it was business and accounting. It was an interesting mix.

My parents had a great life because we had built-in babysitters in my grandparents. My parents were *always* going out during the week. They played canasta at somebody's house. They went to restaurants. They went to movies. The same things we do today. For them life was good.

My father traveled to the Port of New Orleans several times a year to check on his imports. He logged Frigidaire and Sylvania appliance serial numbers onto his books. He then tracked the appliances from shipment to arrival in Cuba and documented what store they were sent to and the date they sold, so his books had all that information.

From the earliest days of their republic Americans coveted Cuba with its commanding location alongside the Western Hemisphere's most important trade routes, the Windward Passage from the Atlantic Ocean into the Caribbean Sea, the Yucatán Channel that connects the Caribbean to the Gulf of Mexico, and the Florida Straits from the Gulf back to the Atlantic.[12] In 1808 President Thomas Jefferson failed in his attempt to buy the island from Spain, but the American economic and cultural penetration of Cuba soon began.[13] Enthusiasts in both countries periodically promoted annexation.[14]

In 1898 the US intervened at the end of Cuba's three-year War of Independence.[15] The intervention, part of what Americans call the Spanish-American War, is remembered for Theodore Roosevelt's fabled charge up San Juan Hill outside Santiago de Cuba. That the "charge" was not on horseback but a grinding infantry slog up a lesser mound dubbed Kettle Hill typifies Americans' many misunderstandings about Cuban history.[16] The Americans would not even let Cuban freedom fighters participate in Spain's formal surrender.[17]

After an exhausted Spain ceded the island to the US, American troops occupied it, sparking resentment and protests.[18] The Americans undertook massive public works—roads, bridges, power plants, schools, waterworks, sanitation projects, and the like—to create favorable conditions for American investment.[19] To the Cubans' chagrin, the Americans kept many colonial administrators in office.[20] US troops left in 1902 only after Cubans acceded to US demands for a naval coaling station at Guantánamo Bay, which could control the Windward Passage, and the right to intervene in the affairs of the new republic, which remained in effect until 1934.[21] American presidents dispatched troops to protect US interests in 1906 to 1909, 1912, and 1917 to 1923. President Franklin D. Roosevelt in 1933 sent an envoy to orchestrate regime change, helping to oust strongman Gerardo Machado in order to bring stability.[22]

The Cubans had rid themselves of one colonial power but got another.[23]

Andrés M. Duany

MIAMI, FLORIDA

Andrés was born into a leading family of the island's second-largest city, Santiago de Cuba, in eastern Cuba's Oriente province. His father Andrés J. Duany—he went by Andrew or Andy—had followed his own father into business. They managed the family's vast landholdings and epitomized the affinity that many propertied Cubans had for the US.

The wars of liberation started in 1868 and ended in 1898. It was on and off, virtually continuously, all over the island.‡ Because of the instability, everyone wanted to sell land, so my grandfather picked up an *enormous* amount over the decades. When the American army arrived in 1898 and prevailed—actually, helped slightly—he became close to the viceroy, General Leonard Wood.§ There had been thirty years of warfare of the cruelest kind. Leonard Wood calms everybody down. He puts *everybody* to work rebuilding a country where you couldn't drink the water, where sewers were nonexistent, and the cesspools were flooding. People were dying. After thirty years of war it was like Year Zero in 1945 Berlin.

Around 1904 my grandfather had property that abutted the city of Santiago. He laid out a streetcar from the central plaza to his land at the edge of the city. There he planned the suburb of Vista Alegre. It's on a French pattern with three converging avenues, monuments on the squares, and buildings in the classical manner. It was state of the art for its time. It was very elegant.

After the War of Independence my grandfather was hopeful that Cuba would become an American state. He was an *anexionista* in the political divide. When his side lost, he was tainted, as usually happens in Latin countries. He then sees the second president of the republic is a crook, and the third president is a crook. He sees the promise of the wars of liberation betrayed. He was prescient, and he could see that the Cuban story wouldn't end well.

My grandfather wanted to leave Cuba as early as the 1920s, despite it being a prosperous period. He sold his plantations in 1927 and left for New York. But the company that bought the land went bankrupt in the Depression, and he got it back in the thirties. So he returned to Cuba. But there was still this tradition of speaking English and of being born in New York. I was born in New York, as my father was, to have the option of becoming an American citizen.

Many Cubans studied in the United States. My father told me that the most fun they had was taking the ferry from Havana and getting on a train from Miami with *all* the Cuban college and boarding school students, stopping along the way at Emory, at Vanderbilt, all the way to Yale. That's the reason the US was so familiar to the people of our class. Cuba really did seem like an American state.

My father graduated from Princeton in 1937, returning to supervise his father's plantation, Alto Cedro. The land included two towns named after the lawyers who

---

‡ Long after most Latin American countries freed themselves from colonial rule, Cubans fought the Ten Years War from 1868 to 1878, the Little War of 1879 to 1880, and the War of Independence from 1895 to 1898.

§ A Medal of Honor winner, General Leonard Wood commanded Theodore Roosevelt and his Rough Riders when the US invaded Cuba in 1898. Wood served as the military governor of Cuba from 1899 to 1901.

had protected them. There's a song about it.¶ My father lived in one of them, and my mother as a bride lived above the shed where the locomotive was stored. The sugar plantation was to be my father's life's work. So, when my grandfather sold it in 1949, 1950, my father felt betrayed. He returned to Santiago and became a developer. He developed about forty city blocks at Vista Alegre.

We lived in my father's development, Terrazas de Vista Alegre. The house was on two big lots, and there was an empty lot next door where we played pickup baseball. Just beyond it were dry yard shanties with very poor people, *campesinos*. We were among the wealthiest people in Santiago. As a child I interacted with some very poor kids, *shoeless*. It was shocking to run across the evidence of their poverty. You know, from "You don't have any shoes?" to "Your toilet is a can?" Yet we played baseball together.

Before it ended in 1902, the occupation imposed changes on Cuba's public finance and land tenure systems that enticed American land speculators to the island. They bought 60 percent of rural lands.[24] They acquired three-quarters of the ranches and swooped into mining, banking, utilities, and transportation.[25] The US Federal Reserve had offices in Havana from 1923 to 1938 and served as lender of last resort during a banking crisis.[26] Protestant missionaries established churches and schools to convert Cubans from Catholicism, which had been a pillar of colonialism.[27] While baseball was the island's main sport, Havana social clubs organized American-style football teams and played exhibition games against US squads.[28]

By 1920 Cuba had eighty foreign communities, mostly American farm settlements.[29] Corporations founded communities like Hershey, an American-style model town for a sugar mill and plantation owned by the Pennsylvania chocolate maker.[30] During Prohibition, Americans swarmed into Cuba to drink and party.[31] Gangsters followed.[32] The traffic went both ways. Wealthy Cubans kept assets in the US.[33] Middle-class Cubans took vacations there, especially after World War II.[34] By 1959 about sixty thousand Cubans resided in the US.[35]

¶ Alto Cedro, Cueto, Marcané, and Mayarí are mentioned in the song "Chan Chan" by Compay Segundo on the 1996 album *Buena Vista Social Club*. This Afro Cuban song celebrates the life of rural peasants called *guajiros*.

Romualdo "Romi" González

NEW ORLEANS, LOUISIANA

*Romi grew up in a religious family. His father Romualdo converted from
Catholicism to the Anglican Communion and spent twenty-five years as a
priest in the city of Guantánamo, seeking converts to a faith transplanted
from the US. Romualdo moved the family to Havana when he became the
highest-ranking Spanish-speaking Episcopal priest in the capital.*

Typical of the period, the Episcopal Church was making an effort to Anglicize Cuba.
That was part of their mood. The Episcopal cathedral, Holy Trinity, was in Vedado.[**]
My father was supposed to raise the number of members of the church in the Cuban
community because the cathedral in Havana was a British, American, and Canadian
enclave. We always had more services on Sundays in English than in Spanish. In the
provinces that would have been the other way around, except maybe in Guantánamo they would have had a contingent from the base.

They had a morning prayer in English and then a nine o'clock in Spanish for the
Spanish community. Then at eleven it was in English again. In the late afternoon it
was Jamaican because, of course, the American parishioners did not want the Jamaicans going to church with them. So those were the congregations they had and how
they were separated.

We had a school at the cathedral. That's where I went to school. It was about two-
thirds foreign and one-third Cuban. My mother helped with things there. One of her
sisters taught there. The principal was lay. I don't think there was any religious staff.
It was English until noon and Spanish in the afternoon. As soon as the bell rang at
three o'clock, we were running the streets in Spanish.

Havana is urban, so there weren't many places that we could do children's activities. We had a small playground in our school. We played baseball 365 days out of the
year. It was the only game. Our school had basketball goals in that little playground,
and we sometimes shot basketball, but it was baseball. We had a league of Americanized schools. It was a big deal.

[**] The Vedado district of Havana took its name from the Spanish *vedado* or "forbidden" because it was barred
from development until the late nineteenth century. It became one of the city's more affluent districts.

Marijean Collado Miyar

CORAL GABLES, FLORIDA

Marijean was born in Brooklyn, New York, when her parents lived in the city. Her father Pedro Collado studied at the University of Havana, but his studies were interrupted when President Machado closed the campus because of student unrest. Pedro became a commercial artist and political cartoonist. His wife Maria was a hairdresser.

My parents got married in 1943 and moved to New York, where my mother had a brother who owned a series of brownstones. My father had been invited by the group that Eleanor Roosevelt invited in 1938, and he had fallen in love with the United States.[††] So they both had connections to the United States and spent ten years in New York.

My father was always interested in politics. I remember him talking about El Machadato.[‡‡] Machado was very liberal and did a bunch of *really* good stuff. It's just that, like all of them, he didn't want to give up power. My parents came to the US because my father had become enamored of democracy, which eluded him in Cuba. He was a dyed-in-the-wool liberal until his dying day.

They lived in Park Slope, Brooklyn, in an apartment in one of my uncle's brownstones. My earliest memory is of going to the Metropolitan Museum of Art—it's still a favorite place—and to Prospect Park. Both my parents worked. My uncle had married a Norwegian, and I had four cousins next door that only spoke English. They *never* spoke Spanish because back then in the States you were supposed to assimilate. Names were Anglicized. Maria and Pedro became Mary and Peter. It was only when I was with my parents that I heard Spanish.

They went back in 1952. I was a sickly child in New York, and I gained a couple of pounds, so they decided to stay. I was five and a half. My mother went to work as a hair stylist at Havana's premier store, El Encanto. My father started a silkscreen studio to do political and commercial signage. He plunked himself into cartooning with several publications and joined the newspapermen's association.

I arrived in preprimary, but I did not speak Spanish, so I had to learn the lan-

---

†† In 1938 First Lady Eleanor Roosevelt welcomed five hundred delegates, including Pedro Collado and other Cubans, to the antifascist Second World Youth Congress at Vassar College in Poughkeepsie, New York.
‡‡ El Machadato refers to President Machado's violent and repressive tenure from 1924 to 1933.

guage. I remember struggling. I remember feeling isolated at recess. I was fine in class because the school was partly English. By first grade I knew the language. What I've said my entire life is English was my first language, but Spanish is my mother tongue.

Alberto R. "Al" Cardenas

CORAL GABLES, FLORIDA

Al and his sister grew up in Havana with their American-educated parents. His father Alberto was chairman of Banco de los Colonos, which was owned by and served big sugar growers to free planters from dependency upon commercial banks. Alberto and his wife Edith spoke fluent English and used it on family trips to Florida.

In the fifties there was a ferry from Havana to Key West. We came two or three times for vacation when I was a youngster: literally put the car on the ferry, traveled to Key West, and took the car throughout the various attractions in Florida.

There was no I-95, so you got to see Florida pretty well. We went to Cypress Gardens and Monkey Jungle—all those things that nowadays you see on the side streets and say, "Oh, my gosh, who'd waste their time there?" To us at that time it was a big deal.

To me the biggest thrill a young guy could have was to stay at a Holiday Inn or Howard Johnson's where they had like twenty-three rooms, all open to the outside, with a little pool. You'd park your car in front of it. That was a highlight, being able to hit that pool.

Cuba was a nation of immigrants.[36] Starting when Columbus claimed the island for Spain in 1492, fortune-seekers and others made it a favored destination.[37] Sugar and tobacco became mainstays of Cuba's economy in the sixteenth century, and their importance grew after a revolt by enslaved people in the French colony of Saint-Domingue, now Haiti, prompted planters to leave for eastern Cuba from 1791 to 1804. Enslaved people from Africa and the West Indies worked on Cuban sugar, coffee, and tobacco estates.[38] By the early nineteenth century Cuba had a Black majority, chiefly enslaved people.[39]

With the end of chattel slavery in Cuba in 1886 immigration picked up from Europe, the West Indies, and China, although many arrivals were indentured to plantation owners.[40] In 1900 American occupation forces built the Triscornia Detention Station across the bay from Havana.[41] Modeled after Ellis Island, it was the main processing center when 785,000 Spaniards arrived between 1902 and 1933.[42] More immigrants came from Spain during this period than in the entire colonial era under a policy called *blanqueamiento* or "whitening."[43] By the design of White elites, these immigrants helped to ensure the predominance of White Cubans in the twentieth century.[44]

Ana Cowley Hodges

HOUSTON, TEXAS

Ana was the oldest of six children in a well-to-do Havana family. Her father Luis Cowley was a neuropsychiatrist who ran a psychiatric hospital, practiced in a second one, and had a clinic. He had done his residency in Washington, DC. He and his wife Yolanda lived in a well-staffed midcentury modern house in Havana's posh Biltmore district.

In Cuba everybody was from somewhere else, one or two generations before. That's why when you try to make everybody be in a shoebox, you can't. As you can see from my maiden name, Cowley, my origins are in the Cotswolds. I didn't know my grandfather. His father's family, the Cowleys, that's where *their* roots come from.

My dad was raised by a strict, conservative mother, and he played by the rules. My grandmother died when I was five. Her roots came from the Barcelona area of Spain. My dad dressed up until the day he died. He was completely dressed to drink coffee at breakfast. For a long time growing up, you didn't come to the dinner table not dressed properly, much less barefoot. That was from my grandmother.

My mother was an only child, and her family was very Spanish. Her father was born in Asturias, and he was the oldest. He left Spain to seek adventure. My grandma says there was an arranged marriage, and "he didn't want to marry her, so he got me instead." He had horses and land and ranching, but he was a pharmacist, like the old days where you mixed the chemicals. My mom's mother was educated for those times. She was a teacher. When her husband died, she took over the books and ran his pharmacy.

Mercedes Wangüemert-Peña

AUSTIN, TEXAS

Mercedes is the older daughter of José "Pepe" Wangüemert, a writer, artist, and political activist. After meeting at Havana's prestigious Instituto Edison and marrying, Pepe and his wife Violeta lived in the Víbora district in the rambling home of Pepe's father, Luís Wangüemert, a prominent journalist and commentator on radio and later television. They had two daughters.

My mom's family is one of the original one hundred Spanish families in Cuba. They were landed gentry. After the Dance of the Millions and the market crash, they went bust.§§ My mom was the school queen, and my dad was the student body president. They had nothing in common.

I lived for about three years in an apartment with my parents, but the house that I remember is my grandparents' house. My mother and father lived there when they first got married, and we moved out when I was three. I spent the weekend with my grandparents most of the time and on school vacations.

Oh, my God, talk about the house. Each floor had a different house. It was a downstairs, and then upstairs lived my best friend, Hortensia, who's still my best friend. It was almost eighteen adults. There were four generations, also my grandfather's sister and her kids. They were all related. The house was one block long, and I had a tricycle. That's how I went around in the house. I was the most spoiled brat you could ever imagine.

The neighborhood had been built right after we gained our independence, and in it architects tried to define a new Cuban architecture. So, the architecture was very idiosyncratic. It had a lot of Cuban style to it, bright colors, but all very livable. The most outstanding thing about the neighborhood was that there was always a domino game going in my grandparents' side yard, and my father and grandfather played in it.

My grandfather was from the Canary Islands, and he had been in Cuba since the 1920s. All of his family eventually came because of political stuff. They were Franco exiles, and they all lived there, plus maids, cooks, servants, and chauffeurs. Then at different times, different people that were exiles from Franco came and stayed with us.

My grandmother was from Andalusia. She had been a singer and dancer, and she

---

§§ The Dance of the Millions was the boom-and-bust cycle of Cuba's sugar industry in the years after World War I, following elimination of wartime US price controls.

came to Cuba on tour in, I think, 1925. My grandfather was the arts editor of *Heraldo de Cuba*, and he went to review the performance for the paper and came back every night. Her aunt wouldn't let her go out with him. The next year she came back, and again my grandfather was there. Finally, her aunt let her go out with him, and he asked her to marry. She said yes and stayed in Cuba.

My grandfather's girlfriend—his mistress—used to call him *tío* Luís, and I used to call her *tía* Sara. It was very open to everybody in Havana. She never came to the house. Even when *tía* Sara went to Caracas a few months after I left, they continued the relationship by mail. She was so intelligent and so witty. And she knew everybody. She was who I wanted to be when I grew up. Always.

My grandmother knew about it. She wouldn't talk about it. She never left the house. Her social life was getting together with her girlfriends and playing canasta. It was a separate life from my grandfather. When I spent the weekends with my grandfather, on Saturdays I would be with him and *tía* Sara, and on Sundays I would be with my grandmother. I knew there was something about it that I couldn't talk about, so I didn't.

My grandfather had the reputation of being a freethinker. He was a hard-core communist. He's of that generation of European Jews that fell in love with Lenin and the Russian Revolution. They lived a very dogmatic life. My bedtime stories were tales of La Pasionaria.¶¶ Everybody who was anybody that was coming to Cuba would go through my grandfather. I got to meet people like Camus. It was truly an ideal childhood.

Cuba had a history of racial discrimination rooted in chattel slavery, but the wars of liberation promised change.[45] Revolutionary leaders like José Martí and Antonio Maceo pledged equality for Cubans of color in a new republic, and they played a decisive role against the Spanish.[46] But their aspirations were stymied by the US occupation. Americans openly discriminated against Cubans of color and reversed their gains.[47] Some hotels, restaurants, clubs, and schools did not admit them.[48] General Wood even halted the immigration of Blacks and contract laborers from China, favoring immigrants from Spain.[49]

During the early years of the republic, the Cuban Congress rejected a proposal to prohibit racial discrimination in jobs and public places. But Cubans of color did not forget the promises that were made to them. They formed the Independent Party of Color in 1907 to press their grievances without success.[50] The pent-up anger erupted in 1912 in an uprising that began with demonstra-

---

¶¶ La Pasionaria was the pen name of Dolores Ibárruri, a writer and leader of the Spanish Communist Party during Spain's civil war. When Madrid was under siege, she popularized the slogan "They shall not pass!"

tions and strikes across the island. US marines landed in Oriente to guard American-owned sugar mills as White Cuban volunteer forces crushed the protest and massacred Blacks. For decades after, Black leaders aligned themselves with those in power.[51]

The Constitution of 1940 prohibited racial discrimination, but some White Cubans practiced it anyway.[52] Some public and private places, especially those that catered to Americans, remained off-limits to Cubans of color. Still, racial discrimination was not as pervasive as in the Jim Crow South. Baseball teams were integrated with White and Black players, Cubans and Americans alike. In 1947 Branch Rickey held spring training for the Brooklyn Dodgers in Havana instead of segregated Florida so that his White players could get used to playing with Jackie Robinson and three other Black players that Rickey had signed.[53]

On the eve of revolution, more than one of four Cubans was Black or mixed-race, usually impoverished, and typically living in an unintegrated world.[54]

Angel Castillo Jr.

MIAMI, FLORIDA

Angel was the oldest of seven children whose family lived in a residential building in Havana's Vedado district. Their father Angel was a lawyer, representing American corporations. Their mother Graciela taught psychology and philosophy at a Catholic girls' school.

From early on I got to go around the city and see the different people that lived there. There was a vast amount of difference between the way that the middle class lived and everybody else lived. I remember the city being a busy place with people moving about, department stores, movie theaters, restaurants. Havana had that mixture of old and new, and a lot of different people. It was a bustling place with people coming and going. There were always strikes and things like that on the streets.

I grew up in an environment that did not have apartheid laws like in the United States, but in reality it worked out that the Blacks were in the lower end of just about everything. I did not feel I was living in a world of oppression and poverty, but some people were. There was a vast difference between the way the middle class lived and everybody else lived.

There was a juvenile prison called Torrens.*** This was something out of Dante.

*** The Juvenile Correction Center at Torrens was located on the southwestern edge of Havana.

Most of the inmates were poor young Black men that were kept in horrible conditions. We had a group of volunteers that used to go, maybe once every couple of weeks, ostensibly to teach catechism, but most of what we did was bring them things like toothpaste and soap. The inmates gave us messages for relatives. I then went to these poor neighborhoods, looked for somebody's mother, and gave her a written note.

Coming from a well-to-do family it was stunning to see conditions in this world that I didn't have anything to do with. Going to a Catholic school, where you're constantly being reminded of Jesus talking about the poor, it made a huge impression on me. There was a lot of inequality. That didn't seem right to me.

I'm glad I had the experience because it has helped prevent me from imagining, in a nostalgic way, a Cuba that didn't exist. I try not to have false memories. The people that say Cuba was this wonderful paradise—I mean, it had good parts, but a lot of it needed improvement. The question was how to achieve it.

Havana was one of the world's most glamorous cities. With the Gulf Stream coursing eastward past its harbor, Havana for two hundred years had been the staging area for treasure fleets that carried gold, silver, and other plunder from Spanish colonies back to the mother country.[55] The city became rich as a trading center for tobacco, coffee, sugar, and enslaved people and later from commerce with the US.[56]

Before the revolution the city was home to one-fifth of Cuba's 6.5 million persons.[57] It had a larger proportion of the national population than any other major city except London and Vienna.[58] Six times as big as Santiago de Cuba, Havana was what geographers call a "primate city," one so much larger than a nation's other cities that it exerts an outsized influence on the country and commands a disproportionate share of the wealth and opportunity.[59]

The city had thriving Chinese and Jewish communities. Most of the Chinese were descended from indentured workers brought from Asia to harvest sugarcane. Thousands lived in Barrio Chino, the largest Chinatown in Latin America. It was the birthplace of a unique fusion of Cuban and Chinese cuisines and the scene of some of Havana's most scandalous tourist venues. The Chinese gave Cuba the La Charada lottery that translates words into numbers one to one hundred with an image to illustrate each. It became popular in Cuba and later Florida as *bolita*.[60] Jews came to the island from Europe over the decades, especially during the thirties as they sought refuge from the Nazis.[61] They found social freedom and commercial success.[62] Both communities had an array of social and business clubs.

Instead of one center Havana had many, among them Old Havana, Vedado, Miramar, Biltmore, Víbora, and Marianao. The affluent lived in stylish art deco, neoclassical, and midcentury modern homes in fashionable neighborhoods far from where *norteamericanos* sought their pleasures.[63] The city had a sizzling nightlife of casinos run by sharp-eyed American mobsters and nightclubs with lavish floorshows that featured big-name stars and voluptuous showgirls.[64] Tourists flocked to world-famous watering holes like Sloppy Joe's and El Floridita.[65]

Carmen Leiva Roiz

MIAMI, FLORIDA

In 1957 Carmen married Juan Roiz, an accountant. She was studying law at
St. Thomas of Villanova Catholic University to follow in the footsteps of her
father Roberto Leiva, a prosperous Harvard-educated lawyer from central
Cuba's Las Villas province. Carmen enjoyed Havana's many diversions.

Havana was an adventure, big, exciting, fun. Woolworth's was a popular place to have lunch. It had a huge counter—*huge*! It was a big five-and-ten. "El Ten Cent." It was across the street from the main stores. We used to have lunch at Woolworth's then go shopping.

People used to play the lottery. There were vendors all over downtown Havana, and they sold *billetes*—you know, tickets. People would buy and pick their lucky number. La Charada was popular. Each number had a meaning. One was horse, two was a nun, three was sailor or butterfly. You would buy a lottery ticket and play the numbers. If you dreamed of a butterfly you played number three. It was played once a week.

When I was single, we used to collect for cancer. We went out with tins to pick up money. We went to the Floridita. We were a group of girls, and we were in heaven because we were having daiquiris. Then somebody said, "Hey, there's Ernest Hemingway!" He was at the bar—of course. He lived in Cojímar, but he was a fixture of the Floridita. He gave me a ten-dollar bill. He was very charming.

Friday nights was going to the movies. Almost every American movie played there. They had subtitles. After that we went to a coffee shop, El Carmelo, where everybody gathered.

If you went to a nightclub the casinos were one side. For those who liked to play there was roulette and baccarat and poker. On the other side was the band and or-chestra, the dancing. If you wanted to have a drink and eat and watch the show and dance, that was separate. Of course, the casino was the moneymaker.

There was Tropicana and Montmartre and Sans Souci. The Casino Nacional was at the Hotel Nacional. The Capri also had a casino and shows. Big stars would come and perform in the shows: Nat King Cole, Johnny Mathis, Maurice Chevalier, Sinatra. Big elegant shows—*big* elegant shows. I saw Nat King Cole at the Tropicana. We went to see Tony Bennett at the Capri.

Montmartre was one of the main nightclubs, and they had big shows there. The Havana Riviera was a major thing. The Mafia was not in your face. I remember seeing George Raft at the Capri Hotel.[†††] I close my eyes, and I can see him getting on an elevator.

Marielena Alejo Villamil

CORAL GABLES, FLORIDA

As a child, Marielena lived in Havana's Vedado district with her sister and her parents. Her father Raúl Alejo was a partner in a dairy owned by two families, dating back to 1890. Her mother Margarita worked as a secretary for an American company before she married Raúl.

My father was one of two brothers. His father died when he was eleven years old, and my grandmother took over the family business. My grandmother worked day and night in the 1930s to raise two sons. It was a large dairy, but it was only in Havana, it wasn't on the whole island. My father didn't inherit the dairy, but eventually he and his brother bought my grandmother's participation. Throughout the 1950s he ran the office, my uncle ran the dairy. The farm was outside Havana. If you look today at Google Maps, it's called Lenin Park. That was our farm.

My father and my uncle and an uncle of his were the partners. They invested all this money in new stables for the cows in 1958 because they wanted to grow the business. All their money, all their cash, was invested in the business. We had the office and the distribution in a three-story building that my grandfather built in 1921. On the first floor was a dentist. We had Trias, the florist; they're big here in Miami.

---

††† Hollywood actor George Raft played gangsters in films like *Scarface* and *Some Like It Hot*. In 1955 he became a greeter at the Capri Hotel casino owned principally by Tampa mobster Santo Trafficante Jr.

TropiCream leased a storefront; it was an ice cream and burger place. There were six apartments on top. We had the corner apartment. My grandmother had the middle one, and her sister and husband had one. It had a big porch.

Twelfth Street was an important street, right in the middle of Vedado. You could go up Twelfth Street to Cemeterio de Colón.‡‡‡ Every time they had a military funeral, it went by the front of my house. I remember seeing from the top, the funerals of the military men. Twelfth and Twenty-third was a big intersection in Havana. It still is. We had the movie theater. Then we had Woolworth's down the other side. I remember going there to eat the blue-plate specials. We had the pharmacy across the street. We had a little market. It was urban living.

My dad came from a family that had a family house. It had a big porch, a *huge* living room, a *huge* dining room, seven, eight bedrooms. Then there was a courtyard. That was my great-grandfather's house. It was five minutes away. That house was open for anybody in the family to come at any time and eat there, all the brothers and sisters and offspring. They had a table for twenty. You could have breakfast or lunch or dinner. We had parties there, Sunday dinners. There was a full-time cook. Because they had all this money from the dairy, they pooled it, and all expenses were paid by the family—the food and the upkeep and the cooks.

My mother was from a more humble family. My mom worked as the secretary to the president of Sears Roebuck. Then she met my dad. My grandmother didn't want her to marry him because he was a playboy—good-looking, with money, and everybody knew him. He was the only boyfriend she ever had. Once she married my dad, she stopped working.

My mom always had us in all kinds of activities. She tried to give us as broad an education as possible. We played guitar, we played piano, we did horseback riding on Saturdays. We did tennis classes, we did ballet, we did Spanish dancing. We had a French teacher who came to the house to tutor. English was very important to my dad. We traveled to New York and Canada, never Europe. My dad was very pro-American. We celebrated Thanksgiving when nobody celebrated Thanksgiving.

We went to the Casino Español, the Spanish Club.§§§ They had one by the beach and one in El Prado, the main street. The one in El Prado was only for men. Maybe once a year the wives were invited. My dad loved to gamble, so he went there every Thursday to play poker because gambling was legal in Cuba in the 1950s.

Everybody knew everybody. Maybe you weren't friends with them, but you knew

---

‡‡‡ Named after Columbus, the 150-acre Cemeterio de Cristóbal Colón features elaborate monuments and tombs. Among Latin American cemeteries, it rivals La Recoleta and La Chacarita in Buenos Aires in grandeur.
§§§ The Casino Español was one of Havana's preeminent private clubs, a vestige of Spanish colonial rule.

who was who. If they didn't know you, it's because you were a nobody. The same thing in Miami now. Havana was a small town. You ran in circles. It was very lively. If you had money and worked hard, you had a very nice life.

Havana's population had exploded during the Depression as sugar production fell by 60 percent and unemployed workers in the countryside moved to urban shantytowns that became the object of intermittent reform campaigns.[66] Three-quarters of *habaneros* rented.[67] Many lived in dusty neighborhoods with tenements, factories, and slums.[68] A typical tenement had one or two floors with an interior courtyard and shared facilities like toilets, showers, trash bins, laundry, and play areas for children. Each family had its own room. In older neighborhoods the poor lived in decrepit rooming houses.[69]

There was a chasm between the capital's affluent set and other Cubans, especially those in rural areas where most jobs were seasonal and roads, schools, and medical care were wanting.[70] More than half the island's homes had electricity, but only 9 percent of rural homes were wired compared to 87 percent in the cities.[71] Four-fifths of all rural dwellings were thatched-roof huts, and fewer than 3 percent had running water. Eastern Cuba, including unruly Oriente province, was especially impoverished.[72]

Jose E. Valiente

TAMPA, FLORIDA

Jose and his sister lived near Havana in the town of Rincón. Their father, also named Jose, was a nurse who worked at two jobs to make ends meet. Their mother Odilia bought clothes in Havana and resold them to neighbors out of their modest home.

Rincón was a little town, less than two thousand people, one kilometer long, probably five or six blocks wide. That's it! Everybody knew each other. But it had a famous church, San Lázaro.¶¶¶ Every December seventeenth that little town was overwhelmed by people going to the church, walking from different towns to Rincón, making pilgrimages. It was a sight to see.

¶¶¶ The church of San Lázaro in Rincón is the site of an annual syncretic celebration that honors both the Catholic saint Lazarus and the deity Babalú-Ayé of the Afro-Cuban religion Santería.

My father would go from Rincón to Rancho Boyeros, where the airport is. There was a mental institution there called Mazorra. He worked there from six to twelve, came home, had lunch, took a nap, then went to La Covadonga, a hospital in Havana. My father was an emergency room nurse at La Covadonga. It was a spread-out hospital, one huge compound with separate buildings. He worked there six days a week. I don't know how much money he made, but we were not wealthy by any stretch of the imagination.

One day a week he was off, and we always went to Havana, like lots of families, to go to the movies or to watch a show. Havana was so beautiful and so busy. It was a beehive of activity. My mother used to drag me to Havana with her, maybe once a month. Havana had a clothing section, all kinds of clothing and fabrics. We used to take the bus to Havana, then the bus back with all the stuff we bought.

We lived in a very poor house. It was wood, no insulation, no nothing. It was like a tube. You had the living room, my parents' bedroom, my sister's and my bedroom, dining room, kitchen, all in a row. The restroom was in the back, indoors.

I had a lot of boys and girls I grew up with. We used to play cowboys and Indians. We used to play in the streets. We used to make our own toys. We used to make up games. We played baseball. There was a field, not completely configured. We made up the bases. Whenever we got ahold of old baseballs, my father took white medical tape and created this beautiful baseball. The foundation of the ball was there, with strings inside it, but the cover was all torn up. He took the cover off the baseball and put tape all over it. We used that.

Cuba is a ferocious baseball country. My father would take me to the ball game in Havana during the season. The seats were packed. The professional Havana team was our favorite. I was a *habanero*. We had teams in our towns, and we used to play other towns. It got feisty. Cuban ballplayers always find a reason to fight or argue over something.

Miguel "Mike" Collazo
TAMPA, FLORIDA

Mike and his brother were raised in San Antonio de los Baños, a town west of Havana. Their father Miguel supported the family as a mason, but over the years he also picked row crops and flowers and worked as a clerk in a hardware store. Their mother Celia sewed dresses and suits in a garment factory.

My father built his house. It was a small house, block with a concrete slab. It had two bedrooms, a kitchen, and an unfinished bathroom with just a toilet. My grandfather on my mother's side used to live with us because he had tuberculosis. That was contagious, and my father didn't want us in the same place, so he built him a little house in the back. My grandfather stayed there until he passed away.

I went to school in my town. We were in the school six days a week, not five like here, every day but Sunday. We studied math, world geography, composition, and everything else. We started about seven o'clock in the morning and by nine, nine thirty we would get a fifty-minute recess. We went to lunch at twelve. We stayed there, and we worked all the way to five o'clock in the afternoon. On Saturday we went to school for a half a day, and after that we played.

The whole month of December we used for Christmas—decorations, doing all kinds of stuff. On Christmas, all the parents worked half a day. They decorated the street. Everybody would be cooking, doing a pig, doing soup. Everybody would come over and drink beer or wine and share. It was a good neighborhood. I loved it.

We believed in Los Reyes Magos on the sixth of January—the three kings, like in the Jesus story: Melchior, Gaspar, and Balthasar.**** That's when we'd get our toys. We used to believe as a kid you go to sleep early, you put your letter out, and the *tres magos* would come in that night. The next morning you would find your gifts, usually on top of the bed or in the living room. Most of it was clothes, pants, or things like that. Anything we needed they used to give to us.

The Constitution of 1940 set an aspirational goal of eight years of primary education for every child.[73] Teachers were adequate, but rural schools were crowded and didn't have enough teachers or supplies.[74] Only about 50 percent of school age children attended classes in 1953, a smaller proportion than during the twenties.[75]

Public schools were seen as unable to prepare Cubans for the future.[76] Consequently, Cuba had many private schools to serve wealthy, bourgeois, and working-class families.[77] One in three elementary students attended a private school.[78] Many private schools were run by religious orders and served only boys or girls, but others were secular and coeducational. If they could afford to do so, families outside the cities enrolled their children in elite boarding schools.[79] The wealthy sent their children across the Florida Straits to be educated in el Norte or "the North."[80]

**** Día de los Reyes Magos or "Three Kings Day" is known in English-speaking cultures as Epiphany.

Emilio Cueto

WASHINGTON, DC

Emilio and his sister grew up in Havana. After their father died in a car crash, their mother Carmen raised the two children, supported by income from rental properties and aided by an extended family and a devoted housekeeper that Emilio called his aunt Conchita. Emilio wanted to attend the Jesuits' Colegio de Belén in Havana, as his father had.

Obviously, I was destined to go to Belén. The death of my father put a plow in that plan, but the Jesuits gave me a scholarship. We started in grammar school and went all the way through high school. The boarding was mostly for non-Havana people. The school had a full-day session. I went in the morning, came home for lunch, went back to school, and came back in the afternoon. It was one of the largest schools in Cuba, about six hundred. We had eighteen buses, and the buses traveled the city four times a day. I loved the school, I loved the discipline, I loved the teachers. It was the best thing that ever happened to me.

Jesuits from Spain had opened the school, but by the time I joined my classes, there were many Cubans there. It was more progressive, they were more forward-looking, they were more *Cuban*. My teachers were laymen. There was no coed. It was just a boys' school, even for the teachers. Religion, of course, was taught by a priest. Religion was not only religion as a subject, but religion as a way of life. We were to be young Catholic leaders, to make Cuba a Catholic country, and I took it seriously. I was a very militant Catholic.

There was a schedule that had to be met with rigor. Mass started at 8:30, and it meant 8:30, not 8:31. Then the bell rang, and you went to recreation. You went in a line. We did not move alone like zombies. We were always in groups. You learned teamwork; you learned that you're part of something bigger. We had homework all the time; we had constant reviews. I got good grades and many prizes.

Cuba had a measure of anticlericalism in our history. When the educational system was developed there was great animosity against private schools. Our degree from the private school would not be recognized by the state, so we also had to take every exam by the public high school. We'd never met these teachers who came with their exams. The fact that the majority of us passed the *other* exam, some with great distinction, gives you an idea that our education was solid. Otherwise we would not have passed the exam by teachers we'd never met, with questions we'd never heard of, with a program we didn't totally follow. That is the best measure I can give you of the quality of the education.

It took a lot of my attention. Most of my friends were from school, not from the neighborhood, because in addition to going to school every day, we had to go there to Mass on Sundays. It was a full-time job. I don't remember playing much in my neighborhood.

Diana Sawaya-Crane
TALLAHASSEE, FLORIDA

Diana and her sister were raised in Havana. Their father Assad Sawaya emigrated from Lebanon in 1929 and married Cuban-born Hilda Morse, a biology teacher descended from an American expatriate. In 1955 Assad went to Venezuela for work but periodically visited his family. Hilda enrolled their daughters at a secular coeducational school in the Víbora district.

My sister and I attended Instituto Edison, a very good school in Havana.

It was a regular classroom with the old-style attached wooden desks and chairs. The desktop had storage space underneath. There was a piano, and I remember the teacher playing the piano and all of us sitting on the floor, singing with the teacher. They taught us how to stand in line. You had to extend your arm and put it on the shoulder of the kid in front of you.

I studied natural sciences, arithmetic, reading, Spanish, English, drawing, civics and moral teachings, physical education, and calligraphy. They taught the Palmer Method of handwriting. We had to do continuous loops and straight vertical lines within notebook lines without lifting the pencil from the paper. We had to do it over and over to get our hand trained for cursive writing. We were taught handicrafts like embroidery.

Outside Instituto Edison there was a fellow with a little cart selling snow cones. I looked for pennies so we could buy snow cones. There were two solid balustrades flanking the steps to the main school entrance. The balustrades had a flat area at the top and at the bottom, with an incline in the middle. I remember sliding down the incline when the teachers weren't looking.

Carlos Alvarez

TALLAHASSEE, FLORIDA

Carlos and his two brothers lived in suburban Reparto Flores with their parents and a sister. Their father Licinio was an in-house lawyer for an import-export company. Both he and his wife Isola came from farm families. They enrolled their sons at the Colegio de La Salle in Havana's Miramar district, one of many Cuban schools operated by the Christian Brothers order.

The school was run by Catholic teaching brothers, and it was superb. They emphasized academics and sports. We were taught mostly by brothers. They could hit a baseball and teach science. We were taught French and Latin and English. It was the type of school that, if you got out of line, you got hit. And you wouldn't complain to your parents because they'd hit you again. They knew if a brother had hit you, it meant that you had done something really bad.

It was extremely competitive. They graded everybody on everything, starting from the first grade. On a weekly and a monthly basis, you were given your report card, but you weren't given your report card in secret. The principal of the school would come and say, "Jorge DeValle." He would come up, and he was the best grade. Then the next name—that would be the second-best grade for that week. All the way to the end. In the yearbook it even has who was the last guy in the class.

I tended to be at the top, so I was enamored with the school. But my goodness, how did the last guy in the class feel? It wasn't seen as anything evil or degrading. I never thought, Gosh, my friend here was last, but it had to have had an impact to some kids.

Between 1902 and 1952 Cuba had fifteen permanent or interim presidents, two provisional governors imposed by Washington, and for five days in 1933 a dysfunctional five-member presidency known as the Pentarchy. Between 1933 and 1936, not counting the Pentarchy, seven persons went through the revolving door to the presidency. Several others served as interim presidents for a few days or weeks.[81] One hapless caretaker served for less than twelve hours.[82] These upheavals prompted out-of-power politicians to go into exile until the strongman of the moment left office and power shifted again.[83]

Fulgencio Batista, a lowborn but charismatic noncommissioned army officer, led disgruntled soldiers in ousting an interim president in a 1933 putsch known as the "Sergeants' Revolt." Batista aligned his troops with reformers and students, then elevated himself to army chief of staff.[84] For years he played kingmaker.[85] In 1940 Cuba tried to restart its republic with a progressive new constitution.[86] Positioning himself as a reformer in league with labor unions and the fledgling Communist Party, but also sympathetic to business, Batista was elected president in 1940 in what was regarded as the most honest election in thirty years.[87]

When his term ended in 1944, Batista yielded office, divorced his wife, remarried, and moved to Daytona Beach, Florida. His successors Ramón Grau and Carlos Prío of the Auténtico Party countenanced armed gangs and gave Cuba a government rife with graft.[88] Grau's education minister, José Manuel Alemán, notoriously took trucks to the national treasury in 1948 and made off with millions that he invested in Miami real estate.[89] Meanwhile, wealthy from kickbacks, with a fortune estimated at $50 million, Batista plotted his return to power.[90]

Hilda Molina Tabernilla

PALM BEACH, FLORIDA

Hilda and her sister lived with their parents in an apartment above a family-owned print shop in Centro Havana. Their father Armando Molina ran the business and served as a city councilor for the Auténtico Party. He and his wife Teresa sent Hilda to a school run by French Dominican nuns. Then she met a soldier, Francisco "Silito" Tabernilla.

My plan was to be a nun when I graduated. The nuns had a business college, joined with the University of Havana. I was planning to do that when I finished what we called *bachillerato*. It was like high school plus one year of college—five years. But God changed my plan. I met my husband. I married at fifteen years old.

My husband was thirty-three, the first child of three brothers. His father was in the military, so my husband entered the army as a soldier. He graduated first in the class and then had a course in tanks in Guantánamo Bay.

I met my husband at the Havana Swimming Club in Miramar. My parents were members and my husband too. I took swimming classes, and the teacher was a friend of my husband. One day the teacher presented me to him, and we started talking. The first time we went out was to an opera, with my mother. My mother was always there.

My parents knew he wanted to marry me, and that I liked him. In Cuba at that time, women married very young. My parents didn't want it for two reasons: because I was too young, and they wanted that I finish my education. No problem that he was a military man. The problem was that Silito's family was friends with Batista. That was a problem because the Auténticos were always against Batista. But my husband tried to come every night, even if only for half an hour, to see me and talk with my parents. So they agreed. We married on May 7, 1952.

My father-in-law was a friend of Batista's for a long time. There was a revolution in 1933. My father-in-law was a general in charge of La Cabaña, and he knew Batista as a sergeant.[††††] He knew Batista was going to improve the army, and he united with the revolution of Batista.[‡‡‡‡] He kept on in La Cabaña until Grau was president.

Grau sent a letter to my father-in-law telling him he had to retire. My father-in-law said, "Why? I didn't do anything wrong." At that time he had served seven presidents. Grau said, "Because you are a friend of Batista." My husband was a lieutenant, and my brothers-in-law were in the air force. They decided to stick with their father, so they presented their resignations and went to Miami. That was the first exile of the Tabernillas.

At that time Miami was nothing. My father-in-law bought a small house. They worked at different places. Batista was in Daytona. They kept that friendship. Batista knew Silito, of course, because he knew the family. Batista said he needed a secretary, so Silito started working for him in exile.

The coup was March 10, 1952. Batista did the coup because at that time Havana had a lot of guns. Grau permitted several armed bands, and by the time of Prío that got worse. Batista said they needed that coup because of fighting in the streets, but also for him to get power.

---

†††† At the entrance to Havana harbor, La Cabaña is one of the largest colonial fortresses in the Americas.
‡‡‡‡ General Francisco "Pancho" Tabernilla was one of the few officers to join the Sergeants' Revolt of 1933.

2

AFTER THE COUP

Batista's coup was a surprise in more ways than one. After all, he had been elected president in 1940 and, limited to one term, held elections in 1944 that were honest enough for the opposition candidate to score a surprising win. In 1952, lagging in his comeback campaign for the presidential election to be held on June 1, Batista rallied the army and struck overnight in March.[1]

Cubans were weary of the corrupt Grau and Prío presidencies.[2] An audit of government coffers showed that from 1946 through 1950, a total $164 million or $1.78 billion in today's dollars was not accounted for.[3] Batista canceled the 1952 election, disbanded the Congress, replaced military commanders, doubled soldiers' pay, and declared himself *jefé del estado* or "head of state."[4] He imposed his own "constitutional law" that promised elections but authorized suspension of the freedoms of speech, press, and assembly and the right of habeas corpus.[5] By his coup, Batista ended Cuba's renewed experiment with democracy under the 1940 Constitution after only three presidential elections.[6]

With assurances that Batista was against communists despite his earlier alliance with them, President Harry Truman recognized his regime.[7] American indifference to the sacking of constitutional norms alienated many on the island.[8] Students at the University of Havana protested the coup.[9] The head of the anticorruption Ortodoxo Party called for a march on Batista's headquarters, but Batista's khaki-wearing political police, the Servicio de Inteligencia Militar or SIM, arrested him.[10] SIM officers would apprehend and kill more in coming years.

Silvia Morell Alderman

TALLAHASSEE, FLORIDA

*Silvia was the younger child of Judge José Morell of Cuba's Supreme Court of
Justice and his wife Rosa Marie. José had been born into a modest family in
a thatched-roof hut in central Cuba's Camagüey province, while Rosa Marie
came from a well-to-do Havana family. José's friend President Prío in 1949
appointed him to a lifetime position on the high court's most prestigious
panel, the Court of Constitutional and Social Guarantees.*

Batista enacted something called a constitutional statute, and it replaced portions
of the Cuban Constitution of 1940. It took some of it, whatever was convenient, but
other parts were not taken. When that matter came before the Supreme Court, my
father said that the de facto government did not have the power to replace the constitution. Regrettably, the Supreme Court said he *did*.

The Cuban Supreme Court was different than the American one. It had a series of
chambers that handled different types of topics. Civil matters like contracts would be
reviewed in one chamber. Then you had the chamber for criminal law. The elite chamber was the chamber that reviewed matters involving constitutional rights. That's the
chamber in which my father served. The larger court had thirty-one justices.

So life continued under Batista, certainly repressive, but he did not have to pack
the court because the majority voted *with* him. My father was not removed because
his vote was in the minority. They didn't worry about him as long as they had the
votes they needed whenever they wanted. My father wrote quite a few dissenting
opinions. If the judiciary had stood firm Batista might have machine-gunned all of
them or maybe not. Maybe he would have backed off.

Cesar E. Calvet

ORLANDO, FLORIDA

*Young Cesar and his sister were raised in Havana by César Calvet and his
wife Mirta on the top floor of a three-story apartment building in Havana's
Marianao district. César had studied medicine at the University of Havana but
then abandoned his studies for a career in government.*

My father was doing pathology in the progression to become an MD. He did not finish but worked in the medical field his entire life. He was director of one of the subministries of the health department, right across from the military base, Camp Columbia.* My mother was a homemaker.

My father was from Sagua la Grande. Sagua was a big center for the railroads and also sugarcane. My grandfather had a soft drink factory in Sagua. He also had an ice factory. And they had properties, so they were well off. My mother was from the same hometown. Her father was an employee of the railroads for over fifty years and was chief of the railroad station in Sagua over forty years. I loved Sagua. I never really cared for Havana. Too big.

We enjoyed an incredible economic environment in Cuba. On the way to the airport in Rancho Boyeros was an athletic village. They had a dome for basketball games. Beyond that was Ford Motor Company, the assembly plant for Fords. It was a prosperous country. There was crime, but the police were strong.

We were different from a lot of people. We were called *batistianos*. We knew that Batista was a dictator, but unless you were doing something against Batista—if you were not involved in any counterrevolution—you enjoyed tremendous freedom.

In 1953 a firebrand lawyer and disappointed Ortodoxo office-seeker named Fidel Castro rebelled.[11] The son of an Oriente landowner, Castro had boarded at Belén and studied at the University of Havana.[12] He advocated civil liberties as well as social welfare for all Cubans and an end to foreign domination.[13] After the courts dismissed his lawsuit challenging Batista's legitimacy, Castro organized an insurrection to oust the dictator. His followers included his younger brother Raúl. Their targets included the Moncada Barracks in Santiago de Cuba.[14]

They attacked on July 26, 1953. Outnumbered ten to one, Fidel's rebels were quickly routed.[15] Seventy were summarily executed, horrifying the public, but the Castro brothers were spared when a Catholic prelate interceded on their behalf. Fidel represented himself in a closed-door trial and was sentenced to fifteen years imprisonment. In the infamous Presidio Modelo on the Isle of Pines, he read on topics ranging from Simón Bolívar to FDR's New Deal and smuggled out his impassioned courtroom argument that concluded: "*La historia me absolverá* [History will absolve me]."[16] It was widely circulated.[17]

Batista staged a sham presidential election in 1954 and won, unopposed.[18] A Cuban of mixed-race descent, Batista in time created a class of civil servants of

---

* Founded by the Americans in the Marianao district in 1898, Camp Columbia was Havana's main garrison with army headquarters, barracks, hospitals, sports fields, a radio station, and an airport, making it like a small city.

color, but his high position did not alter the prejudices of White Cubans. Some hotels, restaurants, and clubs still discriminated against Cubans of color. Even Batista could not escape prejudice. When he tried to join the Havana Country Club, he was blackballed.[19]

Under public pressure, Batista in 1955 pardoned sixty-five political prisoners, including the Castro brothers.[20] Once free, Fidel founded the Movimiento de 26 de Julio (M-26-7) or 26th of July Movement, after the date of his stillborn revolt. He went to Mexico to plan another insurrection and raised funds in New York, Miami, Tampa, and other cities.[21] With money from Prío he bought an aging yacht named the *Granma*.[22] On December 2, 1956, Fidel and eighty-one followers landed in Oriente, Cuba's historic cradle of rebellion.[23] Batista's troops killed many, and initially Fidel was reported dead.[24] But survivors were missing in the Sierra Maestra, the island's highest and most picturesque mountain range.[25]

Gabriel Castillo

MIAMI, FLORIDA

Gaby lived with his mother's parents in Niquero, a town on Oriente's southern coast. His parents had divorced, and his mother Celeste had moved to Havana in search of a better life. His father, also named Gabriel, was a soldier in Batista's army in the Niquero garrison.

Niquero was a prosperous little town close to the famous Sierra Maestra. You could see it in back of our yard. Each neighborhood had its own little grocery store. Peasants would bring fresh milk from the farms nearby. It had a population of a little bit under eighteen thousand, so everybody knew each other. Families were married to each other.

I had a wonderful childhood because I was raised by grandparents. All the children had grown, so I was in a house where I was the baby. By the time I went into first grade, I knew how to read and write, and I would read a magazine called *Bohemia*. I started learning about politics.

My grandfather was a tailor. His biggest sin was being part of a political machine. He worked for the Díaz-Balart family, for Rafael.† My grandfather was the one that

---

† Rafael Díaz-Balart belonged to an Oriente political dynasty aligned with Batista. His sister Mirta was married to Fidel until they divorced in 1955. Two of Rafael's sons, Mario and Lincoln, later served in the US Congress.

would get the votes around the area to get his candidate elected, buying groceries for the peasants.

The first image I have of my father was in full military regalia with two grenades on his chest. I asked years later, "Why was he dressed like that?" Well, because approximately seven, eight miles from my hometown, Fidel Castro and the expeditionary men landed in the *Granma*, and my father was part of the military operation looking for them.

He said, "We saw them. It looked like they were seasick. They'd been traveling from Mexico for a few days. Nobody gave us an order to shoot at them when we first saw them. They told us to come back to the garrison." By the time he got orders to go get them, they had entered into the hills. I think this is a myth, but they say Castro only had twelve men by the time they got in the hills—the others were killed—but that was the image.

The rebels attacked the town one time. We knew that could happen, so a lot of families dug trenches inside the house. Ours was in the kitchen. That was *very* scary. They came into town and started shooting. I could hear them cursing at each other. I thought we were going to see a lot of dead people on the streets. There were *none,* just a lot of firepower. It was the typical Cuban spirit.

Although Castro's whereabouts were unknown, the insurgency spread.[26] In the beginning much of the violence was from groups other than M-26-7.[27] Buses were torched, trains derailed, and bridges destroyed.[28] In Oriente, Batista's troops tried napalm, parachute drops, and aerial strafing against the guerrillas.[29] The regime's opponents turned up hung or shot to death.[30]

Isis Rivero Hoffman
KEY BISCAYNE, FLORIDA

Isis and her sister were raised in Havana's Vedado district. Their father Armando Rivero was the chief bank examiner at Cuba's Federal Reserve. Their mother Angeles did not have a formal education but enjoyed music and art. Angeles's mother lived with the family and managed the household. After graduating from a prestigious boarding school in Bryn Mawr, Pennsylvania, Isis studied architecture at St. Thomas of Villanova Catholic University.

My years in college were some of the best years of my life because they were carefree. You have to work hard, but you don't have responsibilities. You're with good friends. I thought we would all begin working with architectural firms in Havana. What happened was the revolution. It changed all of our lives.

My family was against Batista because he was a dictator. My family believed in democracy. They had seen a lot of upheavals with the government in Cuba throughout the years. My father was reserved about politics because, even though the Federal Reserve was sort of separate from the government, it had to do with the government. But my mother was vocal and very much against Batista. Batista would have these elections. My father would vote. My mother refused to vote. We had to be careful because you couldn't say things out loud, and sometimes we had to tell my mother to cool it.

The one thing Batista did: if you didn't do anything against him, he didn't do anything against you. But it wasn't a stable time. People were being murdered. His chief of police was a *disgusting* guy that killed anybody. It was not a pleasant time at all.

A major opposition group emerged from student riots that prompted closure of the University of Havana.[31] José Antonio Echeverría, a charismatic architecture student and head of the university's student union, founded the Directorio Revolucionario Estudiantil (DRE) or Student Revolutionary Directorate.[32] It sought to bring down the regime through terrorism and assassination.[33] Echeverría and Castro agreed on some joint aims but disagreed on strategy and tactics. Their organizations remained separate.[34]

In February 1957 a writer for the *New York Times*, Herbert Matthews, traveled into the Sierra Maestra for a clandestine meeting with Fidel.[35] The often-told story—probably apocryphal—is that Castro had only eighteen fighters at the time, so he got his tiny band to march past Matthews in a circle to persuade him that the guerrillas were more numerous than they really were.[36] Matthews guessed Fidel had 300 fighters compared to Batista's 30,000, but it was surely a fraction of that.[37] He famously reported that M-26-7 was "democratic and therefore anti-Communist," and in fact Fidel and Cuba's communists were at odds during this period.[38] Fidel's avowed program reflected the reform ideas of Cuba's moderate left.[39] For their part, the communists in 1957 dismissed Castro as a mere "adventurer."[40] Matthews's adulatory reports made Castro an international figure and, when published in *Bohemia*, electrified Cuba.[41] Highbrow American journals soon likened Fidel to Robin Hood.[42]

Three weeks after Matthews's dispatches, on the afternoon of March 13, 1957, the DRE stormed the Presidential Palace.[43] Leaving a cup of coffee on his desk, Batista fled to the top floor with his bodyguards.[44]

Mercedes Wangüemert-Peña

AUSTIN, TEXAS

By 1957 Mercedes and her younger sister were living with their parents in an apartment in Havana, but the children spent much of their time with their grandfather, the journalist Luís Wangüemert, and his family. Their father Pepe Wangüemert was active in the underground.

My father was very charismatic. He was a member of the Student Revolutionary Directorate. They were mostly in Havana and urban. His underground name was Peligro because he was fearless.[‡] He could get away with murder.

I knew that he was not like a regular father because he was always disappearing. Sometimes he would show up at my school and had his hair dyed blond, or he would grow a beard. I knew there was something weird, but I never knew what it was. He had a *Don Quixote* book that he always had with him. He had hollowed it out, and he carried a .45 in it. If I was a good girl I could carry it. That was a big thing, to carry that gun.

Then my dad died.

My father got killed in the Presidential Palace attack. The attack was divided into two sections, one going to the radio station and the other going to the palace. My father went to the palace. He made it to Batista's office, and Batista wasn't there, but the phone rang. It was the American embassy. He said Batista had been deposed, and Cuba was now free.

When they couldn't find Batista, he went downstairs and got everybody together to leave. He got killed by sharpshooters on the roof. Very few of them survived. The palace is now the Museum of the Revolution, and every time I've gone there and seen the stairs, there are bullet holes in the marble. Those were fired at my dad.

The day the attack happened I was pulled from school. When I got to my house,

---

‡ "Peligro" means danger in Spanish. In director Andy Garcia's 2005 film about the Cuban Revolution, *The Lost City*, written by the exiled novelist Guillermo Cabrera Infante, a rebel from a prominent Havana family uses the *nom de guerre* "Peligro."

my uncle was at the house, and he was very nervous. It was weird to go to my house because I would always go to my grandparents' house first. I was not allowed to answer the phone. I was not allowed to watch TV.

I didn't see my mom for about two days. We lived in a cul-de-sac, and I saw this hearse coming through the street, and it freaked me out. I was on the second-story balcony. I saw my grandmother get out, then my aunt. That was unusual because she didn't live in Havana. And my mother got out. They were all wearing black. By the time they came up, I knew. My mom started talking about José Martí. She asked me if I knew how he died. I said, "Yes, he died fighting for Cuba." She said, "Well, Mercy, your father has died fighting for Cuba."

My dad died in March, and my mom was gone soon after that. She started dating right away and living in the country. So that was 1957.

At the radio station Echeverría failed to rally the public when his microphone was cut off.[45] He died in a shootout with police while trying to escape.[46] Thirty-five DRE attackers were killed. Batista ordered the most violent crackdown yet. Four DRE gunmen holed up in an apartment on Havana's Humboldt Street were betrayed to police and shot to death. The head of the Ortodoxo Party was found murdered. Fidel renounced assassination as a tactic and dismissed the palace attack as "a useless expenditure of blood."[47] With the DRE decimated, M-26-7 became the principal opposition group.

M-26-7 had two wings, the *sierra* wing of guerrillas in the Sierra Maestra led by Fidel and the *llano* wing of urban fighters led by a young teacher, Frank País of Santiago de Cuba.[48] A gifted organizer with a keen sense of politics, País smuggled arms and supplies to Fidel's mountain redoubt, set up cells in cities, and brokered deals with rival underground groups.[49] Within M-26-7 he was the only person whose stature and leadership skills equaled Castro's.[50]

On July 30, 1957, Batista's police picked up País and a confederate on a street in Santiago de Cuba, took them to an alley, and executed them gangland-style. País was twenty-three years old.[51] Some 60,000 mourners attended his funeral—the city's population was about 180,000—then the city shut down for five days.[52] Thus within four months, Fidel's most important rivals for revolutionary leadership were martyred.[53]

Romualdo "Romi" González

NEW ORLEANS, LOUISIANA

Romi went to school at the Holy Trinity Cathedral, where his father Romualdo
was the highest-ranking Spanish-speaking Episcopal priest in Havana.
Romualdo and his wife and son lived nearby in the Vedado district. By now
their daughter Ruth was in college in the US.

You couldn't help but hear when they attacked the Presidential Palace. We were not far from there. I was playing ball. You could hear all the shots. I didn't know they were shots. I couldn't figure out *what* was happening. Then I heard my mother, and she called my ass home.

We were living at the corner of Fifth and First in Vedado. Two houses down from us we noticed these two women lived there. My mother would say, "What do those women do? They're always getting boxes of flowers." They were gladiolas. Of course, it was weapons. So we were in a very hot neighborhood.

Bohemia magazine stoked the fires because they published typical Latin American yellow press photos of everything—the young men who were shot in the Presidential Palace assault or in the aftermath. All that came out in *Bohemia*. We were all able to *see*, up close, what was going on. All of them published things about the torturing.

Toward the end of the Batista regime, anybody who was between like fifteen and twenty-five was presumed to be in opposition, so if you were caught at the wrong place at the wrong time, they'd beat the living daylights out of you. On occasion my father would have to get some kid, some of them friends of my sister, out of jail. Sometimes they would come to our house while waiting to get the next flight out. Some of them were pretty badly hurt. I remember one of my sister's friends came in, and you couldn't recognize him. One of his eyes was swollen shut.

If somebody's child had been arrested, some family member would come to the house, knock on the door, and say, "Can you help?" My father knew a lot of people in the Batista regime or through the embassies, and he would go see if he could get to them fast enough. Sometimes it would be too late. They would say, "He died," or "He tried to escape." It was very scary for us. And it accumulated.

You'd hear bombs every night. The nine o'clock bombings, we called them. They would synchronize bombings with the *cañonazo*—that's the cannon they shoot at nine o'clock from La Cabaña. You'd get bombs all over the city. That was a routine.

My father was against Batista. Church people could not justify what was going on. They secretly bought bonds to help the revolution. They suspected the worst from the Batista regime. Toward the end it got out of hand. The underbelly of the criminal element had taken over.

The money rolled in for Batista and his cronies. He created a government bank for loans to job-creating businesses—as long as he and his family got shares in the borrower. He took a 30 percent kickback on public works contracts.[54] His brother-in-law siphoned money from parking meters and slot machines.[55] The government was bloated with no-show jobs.[56]

The dictator made lucrative deals with Florida gangsters Meyer Lansky of Hollywood and Santo Trafficante Jr. of Tampa.[57] He induced them and the Hilton chain to build new hotel pleasure palaces with easy financing, tax exemptions, and guaranteed casino licenses.[58] Of course, Batista got some of the skim.[59] Fed up with corruption, business leaders like Bacardi President José "Pepín" Bosch made big donations to M-26-7.[60] Sugar broker Julio Lobo funneled money to Fidel and said later, "We didn't care who overthrew Batista so long as somebody did."[61]

Edmundo Pérez-de Cobos

CORAL GABLES, FLORIDA

Edmundo and his sister were raised in the Vedado district near Havana's Cemeterio de Colón. Their father, also named Edmundo, was an investor and their mother Maria a homemaker. The family lived in a compound with Maria's mother and the families of Maria's five siblings.

It was a bloodbath. Castro had urban guerrillas in Havana. They created tremendous insecurity in order for people to stay home. When bombs went off in movie theaters, in restaurants, in nightclubs, people would look at their watches and say, "Is it nine o'clock or is it a bomb?"

From my grandmother's house, from the third floor, you could see and hear the bells of the cemetery. It was almost nonstop. Who were they? This was 1958. Soldiers. They had gone to the Sierra Maestra, and they were being brought back dead.

The family sympathized with the revolution. Batista was a dictator who had converted us into a banana republic and allowed bad influences from the United States, the gangsters Meyer Lansky, Santo Trafficante. So, Batista had to go.

Castro was financed by the rich. It was the Bacardis. It was the Lobos. It was those huge fortunes that provided most of the money, together with the upper middle class, because the objective was to get rid of Batista.

The opposition's leadership was fragmented between Castro, leaders of other factions, wealthy contributors, and exiled politicians.[62] Fidel bobbed and weaved, always angling to come out on top in the end game. He entered into alliances with other groups then withdrew.[63] He was for nationalizing US-owned utilities then he wasn't.[64] He favored breaking up huge plantations to benefit peasants then he didn't.[65] He said and did the expedient.[66] The goal was to dominate the opposition groups, not arrive at a consensus with them.[67] Through his deft maneuvering, charm, and the deaths of other rebel leaders, Castro would become the central figure in the new order.[68]

Margarita Fernández Cano
MIAMI, FLORIDA

Margarita earned degrees in physics and chemistry from the University of Havana and was a regular contestant on a television quiz show. Her father Rafael Fernández was an architect best known for Havana's first art deco edifice, the Bacardi Building. He and his wife, also named Margarita, raised their daughter and son in the Vedado district. In 1956 young Margarita married Pablo Cano, an engineer whose passion was jazz guitar.

It was very hectic: people being killed and persecuted. Bombs exploded in garbage cans. There was tension. Castro was off in the mountains. He was going to bring down the dictatorship, and things were going to be good again. At the time I was pregnant with my first child.

My brother had studied law with Fidel at the university. He knew Fidel well. He said you couldn't expect anything from Fidel: He was kooky wooky, crazy, a megalomaniac. Everything bad you can imagine, my brother thought of him.

Pablo was never sympathetic with Fidel. I was the only one sympathetic. He was a young person and was offering so many wonderful things. Communism was not spoken of. I had a lot of hope. It was a wonderful fantasy. I was totally involved. I got money for him, not a lot, from friends who were students and worked with me. If it was found out that you were involved they put you in prison, so it was very secretive.

I was the only nerd in the family. Everybody who took the time to see him as he really was said, "You're crazy."

Julieta Navarrete Valls
SOUTH MIAMI, FLORIDA

Julieta and her twin sister Ana lived in a Bauhaus-style home in Havana's Miramar district. Their father Jorge Navarrete was a tax lawyer for large American companies, and their mother, also named Julieta, was a descendant of Spanish nobility. The twins had two older brothers.

We were not allowed to go to the movies or other activities because the guerrillas were placing bombs there. And we heard about the bomb victims. This was all around us, so everyone was concerned and scared. Groups of youngsters in our midst were involved in anti-Batista activities. Ana was more involved. What would I do? Carry leaflets or write on a mirror with lipstick, *¡Abajo Batista!* [Down with Batista!]

I was engaged to be married at the ripe old age of seventeen. He was five years older. He was taken out of the country by his family during the Batista regime and sent to study at Loyola University in New Orleans. He was blatantly *fidelista*, and his family was—rightly so—fearful for his safety because so many young people had been caught and tortured and killed.

He started working with the revolutionaries in New Orleans. They would give talks on Fidel and the Sierra Maestra and raise money to buy arms. They were going to take a boat full of arms to join Fidel. They were caught by the police in New Orleans, and the boat was confiscated as well as the weapons. They were reprimanded but were treated kindly by the authorities there. They never left.

The Eisenhower Administration tried to block arms shipments to the rebels all along but dealt a serious blow to Batista in March 1958 by halting weapons sales to his regime too.[69] Fidel declared "total war" and called for a general strike in April.[70] It fizzled, but Raúl opened a second front in Oriente's Sierra Cristal range.[71] Women played important roles as leaders and fighters.[72] They smuggled messages, gun parts, and radios in harnesses beneath their skirts.[73]

With his rhetoric, Fidel aligned himself and M-26-7 with the tradition of Martí and Cuba's epic wars of liberation.[74] Even his strategic plans and battlefield tactics summoned up memories of the nineteenth-century freedom fighters known as *mambises*.[75] While establishing M-26-7 as the leading opposition group, Fidel and his inner circle considered how they wanted to change Cuba.[76] In the parts of Oriente under their control, they set up schools and hospitals, imposed a legal code and tax system, and even had a foreign policy.[77] No doubt Fidel became accustomed to ruling by decree.

Andrés M. Duany

MIAMI, FLORIDA

In Santiago de Cuba, the wealthy Duany family knew Fidel's father Ángel Castro as a neighboring landowner in Oriente province. "He was a bit of a crook," Andrés says, "in the sense of continually moving the boundary into our property." Still, the Duanys supported Fidel's revolt against Batista.

I remember shooting. I remember it very well because it was so exciting.

We lived on a high point, and it went down to a river, and the next high point was San Juan Hill. The battlefield had been renovated with trenches, the way they do old battlefields. Quite a few nights we could hear shooting, and they used San Juan Hill. They would go to the nice, dry, prefabricated trenches. Both sides wanted to have activity, minor stuff, not so much kill each other as have small victories. We were taken into my parents' bathroom because it had marble walls, and presumably that would stop bullets. We'd sleep in the bathroom.

Paradoxically, Cuba had the *misfortune* to have leaders of its wars of liberation of such greatness, *not* dissimilar to our founders in this country: Carlos Manuel de Céspedes, José Martí, Antonio Maceo, the Black general. They were all killed, never having a chance to be anything except heroic. You couldn't make them up. They're all Hollywood characters. That set a standard of idealism that was unattainable. Martí,

Maceo, and Céspedes promised a *social* revolution. That's why the Black population joined them. But the social revolution didn't happen. The Americans came in. The ability to press that resentment by Fidel was enormous.

The tragedy of Cuba is that the wars of liberation caused people to *never* be satisfied with the subsequent governments that were never honest or idealistic enough. So, two things happened: You got a *completely* unstable twentieth century because no president was good enough. And second, Fidel said, "My revolution completes the unfulfilled promise of the War of Independence." That connection is totally underestimated by Americans, the extent to which Fidel continued the War of Independence.

By mid-1958, M-26-7 had about four hundred fighters in the field.[78] Among Fidel's ablest *comandantes* were three veterans of the *Granma* voyage: brother Raúl, a bushy bearded farmer named Camilo Cienfuegos, and an engaging left-wing Argentine physician named Ernesto "Che" Guevara.[79] In August Guevara took a column of fighters to Las Villas province in central Cuba to cut the island in half. Cienfuegos traveled with another column to open a front in western Cuba but then was directed to join Guevara in Las Villas.[80]

Rebels dominated one-third of Cuba's landmass in late 1958.[81] Their numbers increasing, M-26-7 fighters fought Batista's troops to a standoff at the ten-day Battle of Guisa in November, setting the stage for a rebel takeover of Oriente.[82] After years of mismanagement, the army was in collapse.[83] As Graham Greene put it in his 1958 novel *Our Man in Havana*, "the President's regime was creaking dangerously towards its end."[84]

As it did so, the Eisenhower Administration scrambled. One US diplomat described Fidel as "having wild ideas and varying from radical to liberal in his political philosophy."[85] US Ambassador Earl Smith, a financier and Republican fundraiser from Florida, was blunt: he called Castro a communist.[86] As it had with Machado in 1933, the US sent an envoy to press the dictator to resign in favor of a *junta* that would not include Fidel.[87] It was one of at least two US initiatives to prevent Castro from taking power.[88]

On December 31, 1958, the Las Villas capital of Santa Clara fell to the rebels. It proved decisive.[89]

Hilda Molina Tabernilla
PALM BEACH, FLORIDA

After they married in 1952, Silito and Hilda Tabernilla and her parents moved into a large house down the street from Batista's house at Havana's Camp Columbia. In addition to his army command, Silito managed the presidential office. He and Hilda soon had two children. They were confident that Batista would put down the insurrection.

We believed it. The problem was when the United States didn't want to sell us more arms. The only ammunition they could get was no good. My house was on a little hill, and I saw the airplanes from the Sierra Maestra with the soldiers wounded and hurt and the ones that died. It was horrible.

Batista helped a lot of people. If he was walking and you were there, he'd stop and say hello. Unbelievably charming, very charismatic, very nice person. At the same time, he liked intrigue. A complicated man. But if you talked with him, you liked him. He was always nice to me. Every time I had a baby, he came to the hospital to see me.

The night we left was the only night that I saw him totally different. He always had a party in the Presidential Palace for the New Year, December thirty-first, but that year he canceled the festivities. He went to the presidential house in Columbia. I had all my family in my house, about twenty-five people. Around 10:30 my husband sent one of his aides, who said to me, "The general wants you at 11:30 in the presidential house for business with the president, and it will be all the officials and the ministers and the wives."

When I got there the aide said, "Most of the ladies are upstairs, and the officials and some ministers are down in the office with the president." So, I went upstairs. It was my mother-in-law and about fifteen ladies, maybe eighteen. About five or ten minutes later Marta came, the first lady. Then five minutes before twelve o'clock came the service with coffee, a cup of coffee to everybody. Then immediately came the president with the top officials, generals, some colonels, marines, the *policia*, and my husband and father-in-law. Batista was very pale. When he took the cup and said, *"¡Salud!"* he was trembling. I never saw him like that.

Then he left, and the aide said to me, "The general said that you go home and prepare yourself, wake up the children, because we have to be in the airport at a quarter to two. I will come to pick you up. The general said don't bring any luggage or anything—just you and the two children." I said, "Oh my goodness! What's going on? I can't believe this." My husband didn't tell me anything.

When I got home, I said to my family, "I have to leave the country." My mother prepared a little luggage with clothes for the children, Gerber baby food, two spoons. One was three, and the other was two. I took my two children, then I left. Everybody was sad.

Batista gave my husband three lists for the three planes. My family was in the number two plane, all our family. I didn't see my husband until I was on the airplane, when he sat next to me. Everybody was silent. I was in shock—really in shock—for more than a month.

Henry Martell

CORAL GABLES, FLORIDA

Enrique Martell and his two brothers were raised in a family that was sympathetic to the insurrection. Their father Alberto was a diplomat and law professor at the University of Havana, and Fidel had been one of Alberto's students. Their mother Alicia was director of Havana's kindergartens.

That's one night I will never forget, December 31, 1958. My parents had a beach house in Playa Jibacoa. I loved that place, beautiful beaches. The guy who developed the place was Che Fernández. Che Fernández happened to be a senator for Batista. He always had parties there, and one of the parties was on that night. I remember it like today.

We're looking at five hundred, six hundred guests. Beautiful house right on the ocean. All the kids were running all over the place, getting in the pool. About 11:30 he stopped the band. He took the mic and said, "I just want to say goodbye. We're leaving. As we speak, Batista just resigned and is leaving the country." People started screaming and running out of there. The houses were up on the hill, and everybody went down to the docks. I'll never forget standing there and seeing seventy-, eighty-foot Chris Crafts, probably four or six of them. The whole family got on those boats, and they ended up in Key Biscayne.

Everybody was shocked. You had a lot of government officials going back to Havana, trying to see how they're going to get out. Others were happy. My father was pleased to see it, thinking we are going to have a democratic government.

We *knew* Castro. Very bright. Very rebellious. He was caught at the University of Havana with guns in his locker many times. My father said if Castro had applied his smarts the right way, wow, he could have been the greatest of the great.

With a fortune now estimated at $300 million, Batista fled to the Dominican Republic, while the Tabernillas' plane went to Jacksonville, and the third plane flew to New Orleans.[90] Men in tuxedoes and women in evening gowns frantically tried to get flights out of Havana before the airport closed.[91] Five hundred Cubans fled to the US in the first forty-eight hours.[92] Another three hundred took refuge in foreign embassies in Havana and later were given safe conduct out of the country.[93] The First Wave had begun.

Victoria Montoro Zamorano
SOUTH MIAMI, FLORIDA

Vicki and her brother and sister lived in Havana with their mother Albertina O'Farrill and a governess. Albertina had divorced her husband Rafael Montoro in 1956 while he served as Cuba's ambassador to Portugal. After the divorce Rafael stayed in Europe as ambassador to the Netherlands while Albertina returned to Cuba with their three children, governess, and a cook.

Being a divorced woman in Havana at the time, my mom was a little ostracized. I remember not being invited to people's houses because I was the child of a divorced parent. All her friends were diplomats because she had been in the diplomatic service. My friends were not Cubans. They were mostly the children of diplomats that were in Cuba.

My mom's family had been very involved in government and history. They were never sympathetic to Castro. They were not Batista fans, but my family had been very patriotic up to my mother's generation. The O'Farrills came to Cuba as slave traders. They made their fortune that way. There was a time in Havana when city blocks were owned by the O'Farrills. They married prominent social people because the O'Farrills had money. My mom was the last one with that name.

My dad was working for Batista, technically. My great-uncle Miguel Ángel de la Campa, who raised my mom—because my grandfather died when she was young—

had been minister of state.[§] That's where all the appointments came from. I'm sure a little bit of nepotism entered into it. But they were independent. They were great minds and respected. Batista had his muggers, but he also had some intellectuals.

We were all gathered at my great-uncle's for New Year's Eve. I remember my mother talking with him and my uncles. All the cousins were outside playing. Batista called my great-uncle to leave on the plane with him, and my great-uncle said, "I have done nothing wrong, I don't have to leave." So he didn't leave.

The next day we found out that my great-uncle had jumped over the fence. Behind him was the embassy of Chile. He went into the Chilean embassy. Of course, we kids had visions of the butler helping him over the fence. Then he left Cuba. The house was ransacked. We went by it later on. They put little flags in the yards of houses that the mobs were going to ransack.

The dictator's departure unleashed the furies. In Havana, rebels wearing black-and-red M-26-7 armbands had shootouts with soldiers of a private army that had supported Batista.[94] Cadres put up roadblocks to search for fleeing *batistianos*. Mobs smashed parking meters and slot machines, sacked stores, and set bonfires on streets. Police in powder-blue uniforms shot some looters, but the brown cars of the dreaded SIM were nowhere to be seen.[95]

Maria Galatas Laurencio
CORAL GABLES, FLORIDA

Maria and her brother grew up in Artemisa in western Cuba's Pinar del Río
province. Their father Lorenzo Galatas was a physician and the town coroner
and their mother Caridad a homemaker. Artemisa was a resistance hotbed.

The majority of my family on my mother's side was sympathizers of Castro. There were a lot of people in town working with the movement. My father knew a lot of them. They were neighbors and neighbors' kids. My father was not a sympathizer of Batista, but he was skeptical of Castro. He kept telling my mother, "This guy is a communist. I don't trust this guy."

---

§ Miguel Ángel de la Campa served Batista as foreign minister, attorney general, defense minister, and ambassador to several countries and the United Nations.

Even though my father was not a sympathizer, we hid people in our home. We had one person from the movement living in my house for three, four months or more. My father was able to do that because his brother was the mayor. My uncle would also aid those revolutionaries because he wanted to save these kids' lives. And they were kids.

When Batista left it was a joyful celebration because he was not popular. People had a *lot* of faith in Fidel Castro. He was charismatic. He was young, he was handsome, and he spoke eloquently, so people were *very hopeful* that he was bringing a better system to the nation. But at the same time they were joyful, there were riots because people were angry at the government.

There were shootings right in front of my home, people being shot. A scene happened in front of my home on January first. There was a soldier, no rank, just a soldier, and he was in a tank in the middle of the street. He was trying to stop people from rioting, and the people got on top of him, just to grab him out and, I guess, kill him.

My mother, who was a sympathizer of Castro, would not tolerate any such thing. She stepped out and started yelling to the mob, "Leave him *alone*! He's only a soldier, he hasn't done anything wrong. Leave him alone!" One of the people in the crowd grabbed my mom, threw her inside the house, and told her, "Stop it! You are the sister-in-law of the mayor. They're going to lynch you if you do that." My mother finally said, "You're right." She stayed inside. I don't know what happened to the poor soldier, but they took him away.

My father was trying to get my uncle out of the city so the same thing wouldn't happen to him. Even though he had aided members of the revolution, people go crazy when something like this happens. My mom and my aunts were home. They took us—we were kids—and hid us in a part of the house that would be secure. My mom was scared. When I heard the shots, I was scared. I will never forget that day.

Ricardo "Dick" Morales Jr.

JACKSONVILLE, FLORIDA

Dick completed three of five years of the bachillerato *secondary program at Belén then finished high school at Culver Military Academy in Indiana. When he graduated, he joined his brother Eduardo to study engineering at Rensselaer Polytechnic Institute in upstate New York. They went home to Havana in the summers and for holidays.*

I happened to be in Havana when Batista left because it was Christmas vacation. We were at a New Year's Eve party with a family that were bankers connected to Batista that had a beautiful party every year. It came as a shock to all of us. Dad's partners had relatives that were involved with the Batista regime that had to leave. We didn't have any problem. We were totally apolitical. No one came after us, so we stayed in Havana.

Close to my neighborhood, there were some wealthy people connected to Batista that the revolutionaries came after because they had been either members of the armed forces or the police or had been cabinet ministers. Some of them were neighbors. There were bullets flying all over the place. I lay down on the sidewalk and watched all that. There was shooting, and several houses were full of bullet holes, and people arrested. There were bullets all around me.

I never saw anyone get killed, but I saw them hauled off.

Castro knew change was afoot in late 1958 when Batista's commander in Oriente offered to surrender his garrison and join the rebellion, only to renege later. Still Batista's sudden flight caught Castro by surprise.[96] On his short-wave Radio Rebelde on New Year's Day, Fidel called for a general strike to freeze everything until his forces could take control.[97] The island came to a standstill.[98] That night, in a nationwide radio broadcast from Santiago de Cuba, Fidel declared to ten thousand cheering Cubans: "The revolution begins now. It will not be like 1898, when the North Americans came and made themselves masters of our country. This time, fortunately, the revolution will truly come to power."[99]

Castro named exiled Judge Manuel Urrutia as provisional president and dispatched Cienfuegos and Guevara to claim the capital.[100] When their unshaven fighters—they were called *los barbudos* or "the bearded ones"—arrived in Havana, they did not loot or pillage.[101] Fidel set off on a 600-mile *caravana de la libertad* or "caravan of freedom" from Santiago de Cuba to Havana, stopping along the way to charm ebullient crowds, accept the surrender of Batista's soldiers and ordnance, and embellish his legend.[102]

Then came Fidel's tumultuous welcome to Havana on January 8, 1959, magnified by television.[103] It was reminiscent of the liberation of Paris in 1944.[104] As delirious, flag-waving throngs proclaimed him Cuba's deliverer, he received a twenty-one-gun salute from two Cuban naval warships in Havana harbor as his procession passed along the Malecón seawall roadway and esplanade. He was thirty-two years old.[105]

Guillermo G. "Gil" Mármol

DALLAS, TEXAS

Gil and his brother were the sons of the trusted outside counsel to Bacardi President Pepín Bosch. Their father Guillermo had assisted Bosch when he served as Prío's finance minister. Their mother Gisela was a homemaker. The family lived in Havana's Miramar district.

My family was not *fidelistas*. Not *batistianos* either. There were some who took a strong line against both Batista *and* Fidel. They were crooks and thugs. That was not common. Bosch and the Bacardís were anti-Batista, as was my father, and members of the Bacardi family *had* supported Fidel early in the fight against Batista.

My father wanted something better for Cuba. For him the law was not like being a carpenter, putting up shelves because somebody needed them. It was that, of course, but it was more than that. He felt that the rule of law was important. The endemic corruption, which was not just Batista—Batista wasn't the only one, but he majored in it—that was part of it.

My father worked with a fellow named Aureliano Sánchez, who played a reasonably important role for a couple of moments in Cuban history.[¶] He had collaborated with Aureliano in the fight against Batista. Aureliano was ambitious personally but also aggressive. He believed in the direct approach, shall we say. My father used to drive him around Havana at night, to meetings while he was carrying a submachine gun in a violin case. That was with Batista. Aureliano despised Fidel Castro all the way through. So that influenced my father's thinking.

I must have been about six when Fidel rolled into town. I remember his arrival. It was quite a show: trucks rolling in, tanks rolling in with his *barbudos*. Of course, he had collected the tanks from Batista on his way to Havana. He had a few popguns is what he had. That's not what it looked like when he arrived. He put on a show. That was a big deal—it really was.

There was a national euphoria. Our family was in a different place. My father was wary about what was going to happen. His reaction was, Well, it is what it is. He didn't know what was coming. I don't think anyone did. Fidel did, but the rest of the country didn't.

¶ Aureliano Sánchez had served as Prío's education minister and foreign minister.

Emilio Cueto
WASHINGTON, DC

Emilio was in his fourth year of the five-year bachillerato *secondary program at Belén. He had not been active in the rebellion, but he was sympathetic to the cause and put his faith in the fact that Castro had attended two preeminent Jesuit schools, Colegio de Dolores in Santiago de Cuba and Belén in Havana.*

I remember the day Batista fled. One of my uncles had a car. He came to pick me up, and we took to the streets. I remember the smashing of the parking meters. It was a joyful day. The fact that Castro had gone to high school in Belén went with the teachings in my school about social justice and democracy.

I saw him enter Havana because I lived one block from Twenty-third Street. At that corner there was a house that belonged to the husband of my aunt Lolita. I sat on the veranda, watching Castro arrive in Havana, one block from my house.

He was riding on a military jeep. He waved. Everybody, *everybody*—I mean, the *entire city*—was waving. It was the climax, because he had been traveling the country, and it was incredible. People were *amazing*. I've never seen anything like that, except perhaps when I was in New York and the astronauts arrived, some tickertape Broadway parade. Being part of that moment in Cuban history made me proud. I was there, I saw that parade, and I felt very proud.

He continued down that street, and he passed by the main street that led to our high school. It was vacation, but there were boarding students in the school. There was a tradition that every graduating class had a banner, which identified the class. Fidel was the class of 1945. Some people from the high school picked up his class banner and brought the banner to the jeep, and he *kissed* it.

I was a *fidelista*. We thought we had a Catholic man—young, socially minded— who promised so much change. He promised democracy, that he would not stay a day longer than needed, that we'd have elections in eighteen months. He promised the whole program, political and economic, of a liberal democracy. Everybody was so hopeful. It was a momentous day. It was like, My God! One of us is now leading the country. What better omen, that he's one of us.

That night, flanked by aging *mambises* from the wars of liberation, Castro addressed forty thousand at Camp Columbia. He proclaimed his insurrection's triumph as the realization of Martí's quest for *patria*, national sovereignty and self-determination—"with all, and for the good of all."[106] With these rhetorical questions he exhorted the rival DRE to lay down their weapons: "*¿Armas para que? ¿Para luchar contra quién?* [Weapons for what? To fight against whom?]" In a scene that would become familiar, the crowd roared back: "*¡Armas para que! ¡Armas para que!*"[107] The DRE complied, leaving Castro's legions as the only armed force.[108]

As Castro put the crowd under his spell three white doves fluttered through the air, and one perched on his right shoulder. Later it would be argued whether the dove was a sign of providence or the stagecraft of a master propagandist.[109]

Everyone hoped for the best.

Pedro A. Freyre

MIAMI, FLORIDA

Pedro was the youngest of six children. Their father Ernesto was a labor lawyer for American corporations. He and his wife Concepción lived with their children in a family compound in Havana's Miramar district, along with Concepción's mother and the families of Concepción's two sisters. They celebrated late when 1958 ended.

Oh, my God! That night, we were out on the sidewalk. This was December thirty-first, and we were up until all hours. People would shoot guns in the air: *Tah-tah-tah! Tah-tah-tah! Tah-tah-tah!* My brother was sitting there, and a bullet landed—*pachew*—right in front of him. I'll never forget that.

The following morning, we woke up early. There were car horns, and bells were ringing in the churches. Then we opened up the balcony in the house, and we saw a car drive by with a twenty-sixth of July flag, which was black and red. There were mobs in the street: "*¡Se cayo Batista! ¡Se cayo Batista!* [Batista fell! Batista fell!]"

Midmorning, a group of Fidel guys go half a block down. One of Batista's ministers lived there, and there was a gunfight—a *gunfight*—right down the block. And the three boys are on the balcony, looking out. My mother says, "Get in here! You're going to get shot!" She made us dive under the dining room table.

We had a gated courtyard in the back, so we closed the gates. All the family cars were parked in the back. Either that day or the following day, some fighters with twenty-sixth of July armbands came and said, "We want to requisition a car. We need a car to patrol." They wanted my father's Jaguar because it had a sunroof. My father, who was the ultimate schmoozer, persuaded them to take my cousin's 1956 Chevy convertible.

I saw Fidel roll into Havana on top of a Sherman tank, a 76 mm, long-barreled Sherman. I know the models of the tank. And there he was. He was this heroic figure, with Camilo Cienfuegos next to him. They were going down—I forget if it was Calzada or Paseo. I was with my father. Everybody was *excited*. Here was this guy. That, I remember.

Then I saw his speech where the dove landed on his shoulder. I saw it on TV. He said, We're going to go back to the 1940 Constitution. I remember that speech, *"¿Armas para que?"* You know, we're no longer going to persecute people. It was a moment of glory. What I heard and what I believed was, It's a new beginning. All will be well now.

3

LEAVING CUBA

The firing squads began right away.

Guevara executed ten captured SIM snipers in Santa Clara on New Year's Day 1959 before hurrying to Havana to take command of La Cabaña.[1] As Fidel set off on his caravan across the island, Raúl entered Santiago de Cuba and held hundreds on "war crime" charges.[2] A bulldozer dug a mass grave, and after summary trials by rebel tribunals, the condemned *batistianos* were executed by firing squads. Seventy died in one day.[3] Never mind that the Constitution of 1940, which Fidel had pledged to reinstate, prohibited the death penalty.[4]

The orgy of killing mirrored the fallen regime's pitiless violence and lack of due process.[5] Victims' bodies were found in roadside ditches, dumped into abandoned wells, and shipped to their families in pieces.[6] Estimates of the dead from the two-year civil war varied. *Bohemia* published a list of 898 known dead.[7] Fidel later claimed that twenty thousand died.[8]

The thirst for revenge could not be slaked. More executions followed, but for most Cubans they did not overshadow the joy of Batista's ouster, not at first.

Andrés M. Duany

MIAMI, FLORIDA

In Santiago de Cuba the wealthy Duany family were fidelistas *and celebrated when Batista fled the country. For a time they were caught up in the excitement of the new order, especially the children.*

The revolution was framed as an epic: the landing of the *Granma*, the Sierra Maestra, Batista suddenly flying out. It was a drama. There was a story to be told, and as kids we *knew* that story. It was absolutely compelling. There was incredible glamour. There would be four guys, not much older than us, with beards and *guns*. It was like, "Whoa! So cool!"

We used to have American baseball cards that came in chewing gum packs. I remember Mickey Mantle. Then in the revolution, they were replaced with cards of the new heroes. You could paste the cards into a kind of newsprint comic book with the exciting history of the revolution. You bought them in stores. We stopped collecting Mickey Mantle to collect the *Granma* and Camilo Cienfuegos. I learned the history of the revolution through that.

Carlos Alvarez

TALLAHASSEE, FLORIDA

Carlos and his brothers continued to study and play sports at the Christian
Brothers' Colegio de La Salle in Havana's Miramar district. Their sister stayed
home with their mother in suburban Reparto Flores. Their parents had
different perspectives on the changes sweeping over Cuba.

To me it seemed like a lot of happiness for the first six months or so. Everything was touched by the revolution. It was a lovefest. Signs everywhere, constant news about Castro and the revolution. Castro was beloved, and his army was beloved. This was a rag-tag army, so they had all kinds of weapons and different-sized bullets. They started giving bullets to the kids as souvenirs, which was pretty damn cool. I didn't have a lot of bullets, probably seven or eight.

Between December 1958 and January 1959, there were a number of empty seats at school. I got to number one in my class because number one left. It was some kid I never would have surpassed. I would always have been number two in the class because he was really smart. In December he's there, come January there's an empty seat and at least two other empty seats. They left with Batista.

There was a group of Cubans who knew that when Castro came in, they would be either incarcerated or killed, or their lives would be destroyed. Some of them left with Batista. That was a small but significant group, a group in the ruling class. My family didn't think we were going to leave. Why would we leave?

My dad had a sense that Castro would not be good for Cuba. He went to law school with Castro at the University of Havana. He thought Castro would ultimately separate from the US. My dad predicted it, that eventually he'll tie himself to somebody who can help him with this big enemy—it could only be Russia—and he would turn to communism.

My mom was in love with Castro. It's funny because my mom is a conservative Republican, but she was very pro the revolution. It just shows you the way things were back then. My dad was very fearful of Castro, and it took him a while to convince my mom. That's how come it took us a year and half to leave.

That last year, after school we—the three boys—had to go to a private English class, which we resented because that was the time when we used to play sports. That was about six or seven months ahead of time. That should have given us an indication, that my dad wanted us to learn English. I didn't put two and two together.

Provisional President Urrutia named a cabinet with many well-known reformers but no members of rival groups like the DRE.[9] Fidel became chief of the armed forces and in February took over as prime minister.[10] The cabinet replaced the Constitution of 1940 with a "fundamental law" that vested lawmaking power in itself.[11] Fidel slashed rates for the American-controlled electric and telephone companies and in the Urban Reform Law of 1959, cut rents by up to 50 percent.[12] With the Auténtico and Ortodoxo parties in ruins, he exercised extraordinary influence on the Cuban masses.[13] Stickers went up on homes: "*Fidel, esta es tu casa* [Fidel, this is your house]."

The revolution created a sensation in the US. Castro was treated to fawning television interviews with Edward R. Murrow, Jack Paar, and Ed Sullivan.[14] In April 1959 he visited Washington, New York, Boston, Montreal, and Houston.[15] He hired a Madison Avenue PR expert to advise him on how to make a good impression but rejected the suggestion that the *barbudos* shave their beards and swap their olive-green fatigues for Brooks Brothers suits.[16] Fidel was greeted like a rock star anyway, drawing huge crowds.[17]

President Dwight D. Eisenhower snubbed Castro by arranging an out-of-town golf trip, so Castro met with Vice President Richard M. Nixon and members of Congress.[18] He promised to hold elections after implementing land reform, within four years, not the eighteen months to two years promised earlier.[19] He was asked repeatedly about executions—by then 521 had been put to death—and communists.[20] Fidel defended the executions and denied that communists had any influence.[21] Once back in Havana he sent pending "war crime" cases to civil courts and said the death penalty would be reserved for serious counterrevolutionary offenses.[22]

Emilio Cueto

WASHINGTON, DC

Emilio was near completion of his five-year bachillerato *studies at Belén. After Fidel kissed his Belén class flag during his triumphant entry into the capital, Emilio was in thrall to the revolution.*

As happens in most wars, some priests had gone to the mountains to tend to the spiritual needs of the rebels, and among those priests were two Jesuits. They arrived in school about the end of January, convened us, and said, "Cuba has been liberated by these people. Many are illiterate because they are peasants. You have the privilege of education, so we ask for volunteers to teach these rebels." I raised my hand.

My mother could not understand why I would volunteer to teach someone to read. This was an initiative the Church had taken. We were taught to be men in service for others. That's the whole key to education in the Jesuits.

Starting February fifth—it was my birthday—we went to Managua, a town near Havana. There was a military barracks where the youth of the revolution were camping. We would go every night to teach them how to read little revolutionary booklets. A school bus took me there. We'd eat. We would be home at ten o'clock at night. It was an early literacy program not to be confused with Cuba's famous literacy program later, spearheaded by the government.

These people had taken up arms to free Cuba. I thought the *world* of them. I felt compassion because we were learned people and these people were not. It was a great moment in my life. Then a month, two months into the thing, we were expelled because we were Catholics. I wasn't asking anything of Castro, I was volunteering to teach. All of a sudden, my services were no longer required. That changed my entire outlook toward the revolution.

Every day got worse and worse and worse. There was a trial for some aviators, and they were acquitted. Castro was so upset that he ordered a new trial.* Oh, my God! This goes against everything that law and order *means.*

---

* In March 1959 a rebel tribunal acquitted forty-three servicemen in Batista's air force of war crime charges. Enraged, Castro ordered another tribunal to "review" the case. The acquittal was reversed and the defendants were sentenced to prison for up to thirty years.

Myriam Márquez

MIAMI BEACH, FLORIDA

Myriam was the only child of Alberto Márquez and his wife Irene. They lived in an apartment above a café that Irene's father ran in Santiago de las Vegas, a town near the Havana airport. Irene's father had served as an army sergeant with Batista before the Sergeants' Revolt of 1933.

My dad had a taxi. He would also come on a ferry from Havana to Key West and drive up and buy cars in Palm Beach and bring them back on the ferry and sell them. He was a small businessman, eighth-grade education. My mom was a schoolteacher. She taught elementary school. My family was definitely more blue-collar to middle class.

My parents separated and got divorced in 1956, '57. Right after the revolution, they got back together. The revolution was starting the firing squads. There were very few tourists coming to Havana. My father looked around and said, "What do I do? What's my business?" The government hadn't taken over businesses, like they did my grandfather's eventually.

My *mother* says, "If we're getting back together, let's get out of here." I never asked her why. Maybe she thought they'd be under more stringent watch because her father had supported Batista. He knew Batista from the thirties, forties—the *good* Batista. He was leaning toward Batista. She just had a feeling. They came in May to see friends, checked things out, left, and then put it together and came in September 1959. They were among the first.

I remember that ride to the airport and my father dropping us off. I had to come with my mom. My mom came in as a student to learn English. My dad was still doing his paperwork. I had nightmares about it later, about being on a bridge with my father, and it was going to collapse. Now that's gone away, but I had them for a while.

My parents didn't think they were coming for fifty, sixty years. They thought they were coming for five or six months, and then it'll be over.

In May 1959 Castro handed down the Agrarian Reform Law that limited the size of some farms and ranches.[23] Only a corporation whose shareholders were all Cuban could own land, and landowners could not own sugar mills. Four US companies alone would lose 1.6 million acres of sugar plantations. The regime promised to pay owners over twenty years but at prices one-quarter of the land's value, and with a suspect funding source.[24] Most of the redistributed land was put in state-run cooperatives beset with startup problems so severe that they were soon converted into government-owned farms with the peasants working for wages.[25]

After land reform, the regime took a radical turn.[26] That summer Washington secretly began planning to oust Castro.[27] Havana's new direction was made clear by the October arrest of *comandante* Huber Matos, a hero of the insurrection. He resigned as military governor of Camagüey province to protest rising communist influence and was charged with being a counterrevolutionary.[28] At his trial, Fidel gave seven hours of "testimony." A military tribunal sentenced Matos to twenty years in prison.[29]

In November 1959 Fidel promised a rally in Havana to resurrect the drumhead courts for the regime's opponents. The crowd of 250,000 thundered: "*¡Paredón! ¡Paredón!* [To the wall! To the wall!]" The firing squads began again.[30]

Marielena Alejo Villamil

CORAL GABLES, FLORIDA

Marielena and her sister attended Havana's prestigious Ruston Academy, a secular coeducational school with instruction in Spanish and English. Their father Raúl continued to run the family-owned dairy, but he watched with concern as the revolution took root.

My dad spent two months looking at the books, so he could pay back taxes in order to help the Castro government. Then things got worse. Castro started agrarian reform. At school we tried to help. I remember getting money to buy tractors. At one point there were maybe five, ten tractors in front of the school, to help the poor people of Cuba. Every day was something new.

What affected us was the rental issue because my grandmother and her family had lots of houses and apartments. That was her income. Once they started tightening up, they started stepping on our toes. There was a lot of discontent, a lot of uneasiness, because nobody knew where Castro was going. This is December 1959, very early in the revolution.

We had a piano recital on December twenty-third. That night when we got home my dad said, "We're leaving tomorrow for the States, maybe until the end of the school year." They had planned it all. We had student visas. I couldn't say goodbye to anybody. Everything was very secretive. You couldn't trust anybody because anybody could report you.

The next day they packed the car, a four-door Chevy, we got in the car, and we went to the ferry. My grandmother, my mother, my sister, and I. My dad said good-bye. He went to the airport and got a plane to Key West. He didn't want us to go as a nucleus. We brought a car full of stuff: clothes, sheets, and pillows. Just basic things because we were only coming for four months to finish the year. So it was just a ferry ride, inconsequential. I was twelve years old.

Angel Castillo Jr.
MIAMI, FLORIDA

When the new regime allowed the resumption of air travel to Miami, Angel returned there to complete the 1958–59 academic year at a military academy. Then he rejoined his six siblings in the family home in Havana and prepared to complete his bachillerato *studies.*

There were four family units that were significant, my mother and her three sisters, who all were married and had children. One sister's husband was a lawyer who owned an advertising agency. Another's husband was a manager for General Electric. They met one night over dinner and said, "We've got to get out of here." Within a short time, all those units left. The fourth unit was the poor cousins. The head of that family was a bank clerk whose job was something that my father had made happen. They had some resentment against the middle class. He ended up supporting the government. So, there were those family divisions.

My father and mother were convinced that Castro was going to plant a communist government which was atheistic, anti-American, and they did not want to expose us, the seven children, to being indoctrinated in that system.

One day my father came home and said, "Everybody pack one suitcase. We're leaving." That was a surprise. I had this huge collection of baseball cards and comic books that I had to leave behind, which was a major tragedy. But we all packed one suitcase. This was right after Castro had announced the first confiscations. My father knew someone at the American embassy and was able to get nine visas and airplane tickets. He told us he had gotten them that day.

My father, two of my sisters, and I came on a Friday. The story was that if someone came, my mother would say, They just went to Miami for the weekend, and they'll be back on Monday. In fact, after we had gone and my mother was still there, someone *did* go by the house and ask where my father was. On Sunday my mother left with the rest of the kids.

My father's story was, We're going to be gone for about six months, there's no way the Americans are going to let Castro stay, and then we're going back. He arranged for a relative to stay in our house. In retrospect the guy that I am scared for is my father. Forty-three years old, he's about to hit the big time with his law practice. He has to leave everything, he speaks a little English, and he doesn't have *any* money in the US. I would have been scared to death.

The regime's new direction resulted in the resignations of five ministers.[31] Then Castro forced out President Urrutia and replaced him with M-26-7 veteran Osvaldo Dorticós, a longtime communist.[32] Guevara replaced the national bank president and became Cuba's economic czar.[33] By 1960 the last moderate minister was gone.[34] As he took refuge in a foreign embassy, the publisher of *Bohemia* declared, "The Cuban Revolution has been betrayed."[35]

Ranchers and tobacco growers in central and western Cuba resisted land reform.[36] Small guerrilla bands fought in the Escambray Mountains.[37] But Castro's political police, known as the G-2, foiled many plots.[38] The regime set up neighborhood watch groups called Committees for the Defense of the Revolution.[39] An armed militia in blue-and-khaki uniforms, the *milicianos*, assumed police functions like vehicle checkpoints.[40]

Jose A. Villalobos

MIAMI, FLORIDA

Pepe was studying law at St. Thomas of Villanova Catholic University when Castro came to power. His father, also named Jose but known as Lolo, was mayor of Guanabacoa near Havana for twenty years. To avoid arrest by the new regime, Lolo took refuge in the Brazilian embassy with three sons.

I stayed in Cuba for a year. I had three reasons: Number one was to fight the system. Number two was to finish at Villanova. Number three was to clear my family's name.

After Castro they would incite the students to shoot somebody. They would say, We have a firing squad for tonight. We want you, you, you to come to La Cabaña.

Some would go; some would not. Shooting people that you don't even know. I witnessed that. I compare the revolution to a ladder: You go onto the first step, then the second step, and they take the first step out. Then you go to the third step, they take the second out, so there's no way down.

There was not an exam to be admitted to the bar, you just were admitted to the bar. But in order to be admitted, I went to the Supreme Court to be sworn in. They would come one by one. They would say, "Do you pledge allegiance to the new constitution?" Everybody said yes. I said, "No, that's not the Constitution of 1940." Retroactive laws, confiscation, death penalty. They were not pleased. As I left, there were a couple of people that beat me up. I got my bruises, but I knew judo, so I was not the worst off—they were.

There was an organization of spies, and a friend in that organization would put weapons in my trunk. I was arrested once. I put my hands up, and they took my wallet out, and they took a letter that I had that said, "To all *compañeros: Compañero* Pepe Villalobos is a man of my absolute confidence, and he's authorized to wear weapons. Signed, Che Guevara." There was a whole bunch of twenty-sixth of July stamps. They honored it. I forged it!

I got arrested several times. They let me go. I was able to do a lot with my forged documents. I worked with any organization against the Castro government, but mainly with the Christian Democratic Party, not because of the Christian or the Democratic, just because they were against Castro. I came to the United States several times.

Finally, I came to the United States in January 1960. I did not plan to leave, but they had a poster to capture me dead or alive, so it was prudent to go. I went to get my ferry ticket to Florida, and my name was there, to arrest me. But I had friends that allowed me to pass. I took the boat to Miami to train, buy weapons, and go back.

Luis C. Morse

MIAMI, FLORIDA

During the insurrection Luis handed out leaflets opposing the dictator.
His father, also named Luis, was a high school mathematics teacher who
opposed Batista then became a ship's captain in the merchant marine. His
mother owned a dress shop where she let the DRE hide weapons. After Castro
took power, Luis enrolled at the University of Havana.

They reopened the university, and I started studying electrical engineering. Unfortunately, I started not liking a lot of things that were being said. They started insulting property owners. I was brought up to respect property ownership, to aspire to have your own home. When you start insulting people who owned their home or had more than one home so you could rent and have a business—which one of my uncles did—that to me was socialism. You couldn't express any doubt or critique of the government.

I started getting into brawls with the twenty-sixth of July people, with the Federation of University Students, which was being taken over by communist cadres, until one day there was a *big* melee at the university. The next day I got a call from a good friend. He was an officer in military intelligence. He said, "Luis, there's going to be an arrest order against you. If you can get out, get out quickly."

I had been coming to the States almost all my life, so I had a visa. I talked to my mother. The next day I was buying a ticket, and the following day I was on the plane.

My friend said, "Don't worry. I will go to the airport and make sure you get on the plane." And that's what he did. He went over to the security people. He said, "Let me see the list." He started leafing through it, saw my name, saw the paperwork, and he said, "I'll return it to you later." He kept it until he saw me get into the plane, and then he went back to security and said, "You're doing a good job." He saved my life.

Luis Cruz Azaceta
NEW ORLEANS, LOUISIANA

Luis was the older child of Salvador Cruz and his wife Maria Azaceta de Cruz. With Luis and daughter Sonia they lived in a blue-collar neighborhood near Havana's Camp Columbia. Maria had two brothers and a sister who lived in the New York metropolitan area.

My father was a mechanic in the air force for almost thirty-five years. The revolution came as he was retiring. He had to be out there, hustling to sell cigars, towels, shoes, gardening—wherever he could make a buck—because they didn't pay him retirement for a year. When they started giving the first checks, it was half the money that he was supposed to collect for retirement.

I went to commercial high school. The subjects were mathematics especially, because commercial is all accounting—shorthand, typing, preparing yourself to be a secretary or an accountant. They used to teach English, so we learned a little English. I started commercial high school because I wanted to help my father with the bills. He wasn't making enough money to support the family. But my ambition was to join the air force and become a pilot. That's what I wanted.

I started working in the biggest drugstore in Havana, cleaning floors. When the owner found out that I had graduated from commercial high school, he put me to work answering phones and doing other things. I was there for about six months.

A lot of the people working there were joining the militia. I was seventeen, going on eighteen, I felt the pressure. I didn't want to be with the revolution. I didn't want to do *any* of it. It was very negative in so many ways. I agreed that the Cubans needed agrarian reform and to educate the people in the country, no question about it. Those were good things that the revolution did. But what became of the revolution? It was an egomaniac controlling the country, thinking that he knew all the answers and never accepting the failures that they committed.

My parents and I decided that I should leave the country because of the pressure to be a militia guy. My uncle Carlos claimed me—he was working in a factory—and my aunt Sara.

I went to the American embassy, and the line was blocks and blocks. My uncle Manolo used to stand there for three or four hours not to lose my turn, my mother three or four hours, my father three or four hours—my whole family. Three days. And then trucks and cars coming around, screaming at us, "¡Gusanos! ¡Esbirros! ¡Traidores! [Worms! Minions! Traitors!] Go to the Americans! We don't want you here!"

I got my immigration visa because I was claimed with a job, working with my uncles Carlos and Pedrin. My mother gave me money to buy a suit to come to the United States. I had my aunt send an overcoat, very light, so I wore that. You couldn't carry anything. I had maybe a dollar in my pocket. I remember the plane was cold.

More than land reform divided Cuba and the US. The regime began to "intervene" companies by sending government managers to run them, ostensibly for the owners' accounts. Usually the takeover presaged expropriation.[41] After signing a commercial treaty with Moscow in 1960, the regime asked three Western-owned oil refineries in Cuba to refine Soviet petroleum. The oil companies refused, so the regime expropriated the refineries.[42]

The US retaliated by eliminating the sugar quota that guaranteed Cuba a share of the US market at prices above the world market.[43] Cuba then expropriated more US-owned firms, including sugar mills and the electric and telephone companies, as well as hundreds of Cuban-owned businesses, including marquee brands like Bacardi.[44] The US responded with a partial export embargo.[45] Cuba retaliated by expropriating more US firms.[46] Property expropriated from US citizens eventually totaled $1 billion or roughly $9 billion in today's dollars.[47]

On January 3, 1961, the US severed diplomatic relations.[48]

Alberto R. "Al" Cardenas

CORAL GABLES, FLORIDA

Al and his sister lived with their parents in an apartment building in Havana's Vedado district. The family sympathized with the revolution and cheered the arrival of the barbudos. Then the regime confiscated his father's bank and his grandfather's Texaco distributorship. Al's father planned for the family to leave but could get permission only for his wife, children, and other relatives.

Obviously, the family was traumatized. Everybody thought that the United States would never let Castro get away with this, especially because he was confiscating all of the powerful US interests, Hilton, Texaco, you name it. He confiscated all the social clubs. So, people left.

I came with my mother, my sister, my uncle, my aunt, their four children, and my grandmother and grandfather—my mother's parents—all of us on the same plane. I remember the week preceding it: a lot of errands, going to see family members, leaving things like fancy linen, utensils, and pots and pans. There was a lot of running back and forth, packing, people saying goodbye, and the sadness of it all. That I remember vividly. My family buried gold coins and jewelry in the back yard because everybody thought we'd be back in a few months.

My dad arrived a year and half after us. They were confiscating all the banking industry, and they wanted his expertise in the sugar industry and banking and finance. People with talent weren't allowed to leave right away. That's how long it took him.

With inflation rampant, its economic program flagging, and under siege from the US, the regime in 1961 abruptly ordered a currency exchange.[49] Cubans surrendered old *pesos* and got two hundred *pesos* in new bills signed "Che" with the rest supposedly credited to an account in a government bank. Holdings of more than ten thousand *pesos* were confiscated. Old *pesos* were declared worthless, so people went on spending binges before the exchange, though it was a challenge with so much in short supply as the economy sputtered.[50] The regime rationed meat, fish, pork, and consumer items like toilet paper, toothpaste, and soap.[51] Eventually the Cuban staples of rice and beans were rationed.[52] For some the economic changes and political repression coupled with the increasingly harsh conditions of daily life were too much. They left.

Guillermo G. "Gil" Mármol

DALLAS, TEXAS

Gil and his brother attended Havana's secular coeducational Lafayette School. Their father Guillermo was outside counsel to Bacardi President Pepín Bosch. After the regime expropriated the iconic rum and beer company, the Bacardi family left Cuba, but Guillermo stayed behind with his wife Gisela and two sons. He was back in the underground, this time against Castro.

It didn't take long for there to be scarcity of certain products, like Tide detergent. About the time those scarcities began, these young women would come by the house, and *they* would have it. You had the opportunity to purchase Tide from them and listen to them talk about how bad Fidel was. They were on Fidel's side. He controlled the warehouses, and he was looking to see what intelligence they could get. It was transparently obvious.

Che lived around the corner from us. One day someone tried to kill him. He went over the wall with a handgun, but it was one guy. Didn't get Che, but I think the gunman killed the head of his security. They shot the gunman in the gut. He was young and strong, so he leapt the fence again, ran around the corner into our building.

He made it up the two flights, knocked, and my mother opened the door. It's this guy with a hole in him. She let him into the house. She put him on the sofa. My mother was thinking what is she going to do with this guy who's bleeding on the sofa? She got a mop, under the theory that if she could mop up enough of the blood and close the door, maybe these guys would figure the gunman had not gotten in and go chase him someplace else.

They got there while she was mopping. They took him away, and they arrested my mother. My father was at his office, so they found him and arrested him. My father knew people in the government, and he got them to say, "Look, his wife was cooking dinner, and he was in his office when this guy walked up the stairs." They were locked up for a few days, and then the government said, "Okay, you're released." They stitched this guy up and tried him and shot him.

My father was going to starve to death if he didn't become a communist because all his clients were nationalized. The acting administrator of the nationalized Bacardi company sent him a letter telling him, Your services have been discontinued. Go away.

The more immediate matter was the cell he was working with. Two of the young women he was working with were picked up. They knew who he was. They didn't talk, but they each got twenty years. When they were arrested, he put my mother and my aunt and us on a plane.

My father always said, and I believed him, that he was never an architect of a particular operation. But he was involved in direct action—making things fall down. That was a good reason for him to leave and a bad reason for sticking around, which he did. If those two women got twenty years, the bid-ask for my father would be thirty on the low end and something more permanent on the high end.

He stuck around to do stuff for Bacardi for several months, and then he left.

Mercedes Wangüemert-Peña

AUSTIN, TEXAS

After their father died in the assassination attempt on Batista, Mercedes and her sister lived in Havana with their mother Violeta, who soon married into the wealthy and politically prominent Alemán family. The two girls often stayed with their grandfather, the journalist Luís Wangüemert, now editor of a newspaper for the regime.

I was glued to the TV. I watched everything. I had a hard time with the executions, but the trials, yeah, get 'em, get 'em! I wish every *batistiano* had gone on trial. I used to have fantasies of killing Batista while I waited for the school bus every day.

I saw Che regularly. My grandfather and he were good friends. I used to be with my grandfather all the time at El Carmelo. It was a restaurant, and the leadership, especially the intellectuals, met there in late afternoons and evenings, just to have talk-a-thons. You never knew who was going to be there. Che always sat with my grandfather and next to me. He was extremely nice and funny and sweet to me. He bought me chocolate malted milks, and we drank them with two straws out of the same glass.

Che reminded my grandfather the most of my father because they were both action intellectuals, and sickly. My dad had really bad asthma too. Che had my grandfather's sense of humor, very English, wry. He and my grandfather were always punning, which is rare in Latino men. Fidel was a Southern Baptist preacher—hellfire and brimstone. Che was suave and cosmopolitan.

Then the shit hit the fan in my family with the revolution.

In June 1959 the *milicianos* came into the house and started shooting. It was about 2:00 a.m. My stepfather was in prison for six weeks then he was released. They came back in December, right before Christmas. My mother asked me to entertain the *milicianos* because she and my stepfather were going to run away. I had the maids make coffee, I served it, and the *milicianos* kept asking where my mother and stepfather were. They had each gone to a different bathroom and climbed out the windows. I found out later that my stepfather had been trying to smuggle his relatives' money out of Cuba.

My mother and stepfather sought asylum in the Brazilian embassy and went to Miami. I stayed in the house with the nannies and cooks and my sister. My grandparents kept visiting. Then the militia came and kicked us out, each with a doll. That was it. During the week I would go to my grandparents' house on my mother's side. On the weekend I went with my grandfather.

The night before we left, I was told my sister and I were coming to the United States to be with my mother. I didn't want to go. I did not want to be with my mother. I felt abandoned by her. The following morning, my grandmother dressed me and spoiled me rotten. My grandfather and his girlfriend and my mother's parents and my aunt and two cousins—we all went to the airport. My grandfather had to carry me into the plane.

The Urban Reform Law of 1960 provided that no one could own more than one residence and transferred all residential rental property to the state, ending private rentals and private building. Renters made payments to the government and were promised deeds.[53] Because real estate was the principal investment for the middle class, some families lost everything.[54] The exodus accelerated. With dollars for foreign exchange in short supply, the regime limited the amount of money that departing Cubans could take with them to smaller and smaller amounts until no dollars could be taken out legally.[55]

Cubans wanting to leave needed an exit permit known as a *permiso de salida*.[56] The departure of doctors, engineers, and other professionals grew so serious that in 1960 the regime canceled all exit permits and forced their holders to reapply with an inventory of their assets.[57] Those leaving forfeited their property if they did not return.[58] Then the regime drew up a list of skilled professionals prohibited from leaving.[59] Castro denounced his departing countrymen as *gusanos* or "worms."[60] For many the most degrading experience was in the Havana airport's forbidding, glass-enclosed secure departure area known as *la pecera* or "the fishbowl."[61]

Maria Galatas Laurencio

CORAL GABLES, FLORIDA

Maria stayed with her mother and grandmother in the town of Artemisa in western Cuba's Pinar del Río province after her father Lorenzo, a physician and the town coroner, took his son and a nephew to the US. Then Maria's mother Caridad arranged for the rest of the family to leave.

My mother had to let the government know we were coming over. The moment they knew, they started coming to the house, harassing us. They sent someone to take an inventory: bedroom sets, television, all the medical equipment my father had, everything. It would have to be there when we left. If not, we would not be able to leave. We couldn't sell anything, we couldn't give anything away—nothing.

I remember going to Havana to the airport, my mother, my little cousin—the brother of the one that came with my dad—my grandmother, and myself. We went in *la pecera*. They took everything out of the luggage, looking for stuff. They took things that they said we couldn't bring. We were limited as to clothing we could bring. We were not allowed any jewelry. I brought my most precious thing with me in my arms, my doll. That was about it.

They took my mother, and they searched her. Then they took my grandmother and me to be searched. I think it was a bathroom because I was in one stall and my grandmother was in the other stall. They did a rectal and a vaginal exam on my grandmother. She was seventy, maybe sixty-something. It was women in uniform.

Carmen Leiva Roiz

MIAMI, FLORIDA

Carmen was studying law at St. Thomas of Villanova Catholic University. Because the campus had stayed open while the University of Havana closed during the insurrection, the regime invalidated prior course work at Villanova.[62] Then it reversed itself. Carmen and her husband Juan, an accountant, looked on with growing concern. They had an infant son.

I didn't think the way that Fidel Castro acted upon getting power was right. He ignored the constitution. Nothing was respected. Remember, I studied law. To me that was the essence, the basis, of a country. That bothered me *so* much.

I spoke with my father very seriously. I said, "You should sell everything while you can. Let's go to the United States and wait to see what happens here." He said I was crazy because nothing like I imagined would happen so close to the United States. It was a phase, and the *americanos* would do something. Finally, he realized I was serious. My husband agreed with me.

Those who were for Castro were *really* for Castro. I went to school with his sisters; Emma and Juanita were both in Ursuline. Emma was one year ahead of me. We were good friends. I went to her bridal shower a week before I left. I was surrounded by the upper echelon of the new regime. I looked around, and I said, Oh, my God, where am I? I'd better not say a *word* about leaving. I managed to get through it, and a week after that, I left.

I remember going to the airport with my husband, my nanny, and my son. My parents stayed behind. The nanny stayed behind. Everybody was crying. I went into *la pecera* with my baby, nine months old. I remember carrying only my wedding ring and my engagement ring, which was big. I was carrying my son, and I had it under his wraps. They didn't search me. We were leaving with a tourist visa to come see my aunt.

I wasn't happy about leaving Cuba. It broke my heart because deep inside, for some odd reason, I had the feeling that I was not going back. And I was right.

Of the Cubans leaving for the US, 94 percent were White, 1 percent Black, and 5 percent mixed-race.[63] They were predominantly urban. One study found that more than 60 percent of the refugees who left for Miami between 1959 and 1962 came from Havana with another 25 percent from other cities. By comparison almost 70 percent of the island's population lived in small towns or the country-side.[64] The US mainland was not the only destination for those leaving.[65]

Diana Sawaya-Crane

TALLAHASSEE, FLORIDA

Diana and her sister saw the milicianos *arrest neighbors. They lived with their mother Hilda, a biology teacher, and grandmother in an apartment in Havana's Víbora district. Their father Assad watched events unfold in Cuba from Venezuela, where he sold insurance.*

I remember my sister and I being on the balcony of the apartment and hearing shots. It was at La Cabaña. It was the *paredón*. As kids, we didn't know what was going on. My mother did, of course. She told us: "Get back in the house! Get off the balcony!"

Dad was still in Venezuela. Being outside of Cuba he heard things that people on the island were not hearing. He told my mother: "Look, this guy's a communist, so I am not going back, and you need to come to Venezuela."

Because the Venezuelan government had a shortage of teachers, it had a program to hire them from other countries. The Cuban government allowed its teachers to teach in Venezuela for one year, right after Fidel took over. Mom applied, and they approved her application. She stored everything, and we left to go to Venezuela, my mother, grandmother, my sister, and I.

We didn't take much. My mother was able to take a *few* things out, but this is before they prohibited people from taking anything out other than the clothes on their backs. We didn't have the problems that a lot of other people had because she was under a government contract, and we were not leaving as exiles. I remember going up the steps to the airplane, turning around and looking back at the airport and thinking, I wonder when I'll see this again.

Adolfo Henriques

KEY BISCAYNE, FLORIDA

Adolfo and his two brothers lived in Havana. Their father Charles, the son of a British subject from Jamaica, managed Cuban operations for Canada's Bank of Nova Scotia. When the regime nationalized US and Cuban banks it delayed confiscating Canadian banks. Scotiabank finally sold to the regime under duress in 1960, so Adolfo's parents made plans to leave.

Gradually people became more scared: scared to talk, scared to go out. There were gunshots all the time and blockades in many streets. The last few weeks we were in Havana, I remember not feeling safe. It was a very uncomfortable feeling.

My parents started trying to figure out how to get out of Cuba. My father was afraid to ask the Bank of Nova Scotia for a transfer because by the time we were ready to leave, the bank had been sold to the Cuban government. Finally, my grandfather went to the British consulate because as a Jamaican national—Jamaica was still a British colony—he was a British subject. The British consul told my grandfather: "Your son is entitled to British citizenship because of *your* birthright." We could leave Cuba with British passports, all of us—my father and mother and their under-age children on their passports, not our own.

We took some personal belongings to my grandparents' house for safekeeping. My mom's silver, china, things like that. It was December, so it was cooler. We'd put on jackets and stuff the jackets with whatever my mom wanted to take to her mother's house, get in the car, and go leave it there. Because there was this military outpost across the street from us, we had to be careful not to be seen taking anything out of our house. In my parents' minds we were going to leave the island, but this wasn't going to last long.

When we left you could still travel with what you wanted except money. We had large duffel bags in addition to our suitcases. I *still* have linens that my mom took out of Cuba.

I don't think my dad's family came to the airport. I remember my mom's parents being there. We were on one side of a glass enclosure and the rest of the family—who were staying behind—was on the other. We were leaving my grandparents, so I was upset about that. That's the first time I ever saw my mother cry, and I only saw her cry three or four times.

Finally, we were able to get on the plane to Jamaica. My dad had thirteen dollars in his pocket, that's all: five for himself, five for my mom, and one for each of us. That was all you were allowed to take out. He *had* wired money to the United States, but he had no access to it. He didn't know what kind of support he would receive from the Bank of Nova Scotia.

No job, three kids and a wife to feed, and he doesn't know where he's taking us.

Cubans bound for the US were not the first to seek refuge across the Florida Straits. Thousands had fled to Key West during the first rebellion against Spain, the Ten Years War from 1868 to 1878, to work in factories set up by Havana cigar makers.[66] Key West became the largest city in Florida.[67] In 1885 entrepreneur Vicente Martínez Ybor founded a new town outside Tampa, with its natural harbor and rail connections to northern markets, and moved his cigar factory from Key West. Other factories and thousands of exiles followed him to Ybor City.[68] Before the War of Independence began in 1895 ten thousand Cubans were in Key West and Tampa.[69] After the growth of Miami that city became the destination of choice for Cuban exiles.[70]

By any measure this exodus was different from the earlier ones. During the centuries of harsh Spanish colonial rule, the recurring wars of liberation, and the periodic political upheavals after Cuba's nominal independence, Cubans never left their island in huge numbers like they did after Castro took power in 1959.[71]

Margarita Fernández Cano

MIAMI, FLORIDA

Margarita and her husband Pablo, an engineer and jazz musician, stayed in Havana with their daughter. Margarita's mother had died, and her architect father had left Cuba to teach in Indiana. A fidelista, Margarita took a job working for her aunt, María Teresa Freyre de Andrade, a major cultural figure who had been chosen to run the National Library.

Awful things started to happen.

Fidel got enamored with the library. We had a space for exhibitions and lectures, and he practically took it over with his entourage. Then books started to be taken off the catalogue. All the George Orwell books were removed, *Animal Farm* and *1984*. Other authors were censored. The books were not burned, but you needed special permission to use them. Newspapers like the *New York Times* and magazines like *Time* and *Life* were removed. I got more and more worried.

I saw other things that worried me. Government agents would go into the house of a family that had left the country, confiscate their library, and bring the books to be processed. Only a few books were included in the collection.

The library staff was required to cut sugarcane on weekends. Untrained people having to go cut cane was ridiculous because not just anybody can go "*pow*" with a machete and cut cane. The cane had to be cut by people who knew how. I am allergic to grass. I didn't go. I did not receive the art and music department post I was promised because of my negative attitude. Instead they gave me the serials department in the basement. I knew they were punishing me for not cutting cane. Things like that began to change my attitude toward the revolution. Forget it!

Julio Lobo asked my father if I could come work for him at the Napoleonic Museum.[†] Father was a close friend of his. His daughters were my age and good friends of mine. I decided to quit the National Library. Working at the Napoleonic Museum with Julio was wonderful. Julio liked Fidel Castro. I remember him visiting Julio, I assume to discuss the sugar industry.

My second child was born in 1961. We decided we had to save the children, my grandmother, and my brother because the rest of the family was gone. No other decision was possible after we ended up in jail New Year's Eve for playing jazz.

My husband Pablo was playing with other musicians at the Hotel Capri. The New Year's festivities had ended. It was two o'clock in the morning, and the musicians got together and were playing. It was a jam session. A cordon of people surrounded the group and started chanting, "Go home!" and "Imperialists!" They were people that joined the Committees for the Defense of the Revolution and would go to the street where you lived and chant horrible insults. This became very common. My aunt María Teresa got us out of jail. That day was the breaking point.

It took us more than a year to get our papers. We sent five thousand dollars to my father in American hundred-dollar bills hidden inside greeting cards. I had removed the money from a safety deposit box at the bank in Havana. We kept the money hidden behind a mirror in my apartment. It took a year to mail all the greeting cards.

Finally, the government gave us permission to leave, the *permiso de salida*. They separated us into two groups: my husband, the children, and me, and my grandmother and brother, like two separate families. We were scheduled on two different flights, two different days. I didn't want that because what if something happened and one group stayed here and the other one comes over? I said, "No way! We're not leaving like that."

Another month went by, and they finally told us we could all leave together on the same plane to Miami. We left five days before the Missile Crisis. When they said we had entered into international waters, everybody started singing the American national anthem.

[†] The sugar baron Julio Lobo had one of the world's largest collections of Napoleonic memorabilia, which was later confiscated by the Castro regime and is now in Havana's Museo Napoleonico. Lobo entered exile in 1960.

Mario Cartaya

FORT LAUDERDALE, FLORIDA

Mario attended the progressive Instituto Edison, where his mother Leida taught
kindergarten. Mario and his brother lived with their parents and an uncle in
the home of his mother's parents. Then Guevara, the regime's economic czar,
summoned Mario's father Ignacio. Guevara wanted Ignacio's accounting ledger
of Sylvania and Frigidaire appliances imported from the US.

Che wanted to document all private ownership of business, American goods, and private lands. They were giving gifts to people loyal to the revolution, homes, appliances, cars—whatever they could confiscate. My dad was detained for two, three days because he would not turn over his ledger.

Che tried to convince him to be a good revolutionary: Times have changed. We are brothers in the struggle for a new Cuba. My dad said to Guevara, "You're not my brother. I have one. You're not even Cuban. You're Argentinian. Why would I do anything for you?"

Well, that was not the thing that you said to Che Guevara. Che got up and put his hand on his pistol, whether to scare him or shoot him, we'll never know. The man that escorted my dad from his cell stood between Che and my dad and told Che, "I know Ignacio well. Give me twenty-four hours, and I'll get you that ledger." Then he told my dad, "Ignacio, please give me the ledger because we're going to get it anyway, whether you're dead or alive. Please don't die."

My dad gave them the ledger, and they told him, "You're blacklisted. The next time you say something, who knows what's going to happen to you." My dad *had* to leave. He had no future in Cuba. He had a strong sense of right and wrong. The biggest fear was that he would be killed because they were killing anyone that spoke out against the revolution. They stood you against a wall, the *paredón*. And he was aware that staying would deny us the freedom and opportunities he wanted us to have.

My father gathered the whole family, my grandparents, uncles, aunts, everybody. He told me, "Mario, go up to your room." I could tell something big was about to happen. We had this modernist stairway, and I hid behind the bollards. I saw and heard the whole thing.

My father asked for permission for us to leave the country. He felt like he had to ask for permission to take us away because our family was close. Of course, everybody began crying. My grandfather is the one who finally stood up and said, "You have to do this. You have to leave"—[Mario pauses to control his emotions]—"to care for your family. You have to be alive for your family." His was the final decision.

Hearing what everybody was saying—"This is temporary"—I never worried about never seeing my family again. I *lived* with my grandparents. I saw them every day. My uncles and aunts were like my other parents. It's not like American kids that live with their parents and they see their grandparents once a month or once a year. I *never* imagined that I would never see them again. We'll eventually come back. The Americans would never allow a communist government ninety miles away, right? Well, I never saw my grandparents, aunts, and uncles again.

My father took us on a tour of the island so we would never forget it. We started in Valle de los Viñales in the west in Pinar del Río province and drove across the island through all the big cities.‡ We ended up in Santiago de Cuba where we attended Mass at Our Lady of Charity, not just for us in our new life, but also for the lives of those we were leaving behind.§ It was a way of saying goodbye to the island.

Then we left.

I remember my dad and my grandfather trying to contain their emotions. I'd never seen my grandfather cry. I saw him cry that day. My grandmother went into her bedroom and would not open her bedroom door. She was so distraught that it was difficult seeing her. You could sense that feeling of doom. There's no other way to put it. There was a sadness among the adults, a special look in their eyes, not of fear, but of uncertainty. I've never forgotten that.

Walking up into the plane, a militiaman stopped my mother, took away her wedding ring, and put it in his pocket. That's the corruption that was so prevalent in the early years of the Castro regime. The militia was untouchable. They could do *anything* they wanted. I remember looking at my dad, thinking, Please don't say anything, please don't do anything. I remember watching my dad bite his bottom lip in anger.

I remember getting on the plane and leaving. Once in a while you would hear a sniffle, but it was so quiet it was loud. When we landed in Miami, nobody got up fast. I remember thinking, Why is everybody so slow? Everybody realized that the moment they touched American ground everything would change.

---

‡   The Viñales Valley, a UNESCO World Heritage Site since 1999, is a karst landscape encircled by mountains with dramatic outcroppings. The valley floor is still used for growing tobacco.
§   The basilica of Our Lady of Charity in Santiago de Cuba is the most revered Catholic shrine on the island.

4

FIRST WAVE

Starting in 1959 the refugees arrived in Key West, Miami, and elsewhere on the mainland, by air and by water, making the US for the first time a country of first asylum for a mass of refugees.[1] Ship and ferry service from Cuba to the US ended by 1961, and so did direct air travel to New York, New Orleans, Houston, and other cities. Then refugees arrived from Havana by air only at Miami. At the peak of this wave, 1,800 Cubans arrived in Miami each week.[2] A wealthy few made comfortable lives right away. Most did not.[3] To this day many of them can remember the date they arrived.

Marielena Alejo Villamil

CORAL GABLES, FLORIDA

On December 24, 1959, the ferry from Havana arrived in Key West with twelve-year-old Marielena and her mother, sister, and grandmother aboard with their family's Chevrolet. Her dairyman father Raúl had taken them to the ferry terminal in Havana that morning and then gone to the airport. "When we got to Key West," Marielena recalls, "he was waiting for us."

We drove to Miami. We stayed in one of those little two-story motels on Brickell Avenue. There were no big buildings then. My dad said, "All the Batista people are in Miami. We'll go to Tampa so you can be with family." Because he did not stay with us. He went *back* to Havana. He still had the dairy. He would come every month. That's why he wanted us to be near family.

We got to Tampa on Christmas Day. My mom's cousin lived on Davis Islands.* There was a little hotel on East Davis Boulevard. We were there for a couple of days until they got an apartment by the port, right there on Davis Islands, two bedrooms, one bath. We lived on Davis Islands for many years.

Eight months later my dad was bringing us a dog. He got on the plane and instead of the plane taking off, the *milicianos* stopped it. They got him out and started asking questions: "What are you doing? Are you bringing money?" He wasn't. They searched him. They let him go. He got back on the plane, and he said to himself, This time they let me go. Next time they're *not* going to let me go. When he got to Miami, he called my uncle and said, "Don't stay in Cuba. Come on over but kill all the cows so you don't leave them anything." My uncle said, "No, no, he's going to fall. He's going to die." My dad said, "Fine, it's all yours. I'm not going back to Cuba." That was in August 1960.

His friends talked him into joining the brigade.† He went to Guatemala. We were in Tampa, my mother, my grandmother, my sister, and I. My mother received a monthly check from the CIA, I guess. She needed money, so she had two jobs. She worked during the day at a CPA office in Tampa. She was a secretary. At night she worked in the First National Bank of Tampa, clearing checks. We had only one car, and my mom would call when she finished. My grandmother would wake us up—"Go pick up your mom"—so we had to go out at two o'clock in the morning. My grandmother never worked.

We had up to six people staying with us because my mom's cousin came with her husband. Nobody complained about one bathroom for six people. Then friends sent their kids. We had kids staying in our house in 1960 and 1961, children of friends. They sent the kids, then they came. The mother of this one guy was a pianist, so she worked in Miami Beach in one of the piano bars. Her husband was one of the engineers for the Verrazzano Bridge.‡ Eventually they moved to Staten Island. So waves of people came. Slowly they redid their lives.

Everybody was hopeful that Fidel would not last. There had been so many revolutions and turnovers, so chances were that if things were going to be so bad, the US wasn't going to put up with it. Famous last words, right?

---

* Davis Islands is a neighborhood near downtown Tampa, created in 1924 by filling two mangrove islands with mud dredged from Tampa Bay.

† Assault Brigade 2506 was the US-backed military arm of the effort to oust Castro by invading Cuba.

‡ Built between 1959 and 1964, the Verrazzano Bridge connects Staten Island and Brooklyn.

Pedro A. Freyre

MIAMI, FLORIDA

Eleven-year-old Pedro stepped off the plane in Miami in October 1960. The youngest of six children, he traveled with his married sisters and their husbands and children. Then his father Ernesto, a lawyer, and his mother Concepción came with the rest of the family.

It was everybody in the family. We invited my nanny, Victoria. She was an Afro Cuban. We said, "You're coming with us," and she said, "No, I can't. They don't treat blacks well in the US, and I don't speak English at all." So, we left her.

About a week afterwards, my mother said, "This is your new school. It's St. Patrick's.§ Here's a quarter for the bus. Here's a quarter for your lunch. Get off at the bus stop. Walk a block to the church and tell them who you are." St. Patrick's was very different. It was boys and girls, which was distracting. It was a challenge to speak English only. I fell behind. We got beat up almost every day by the Irish kids, who called us "spics." And that's how it went.

It was an exciting moment because Kennedy was running for president, and he was Catholic. He promised to liberate Cuba, the first in a long line of presidents that have promised to do so and have not done it. We were very excited. A *Católico* was going to be president. We thought Kennedy was God.

We lived at Biscayne Boulevard and Twenty-second Street. We called it *la casa de las cucarachas*—"the house of the cockroaches"—because there were cockroaches all over. It was a wooden house. It was two stories, seven bedrooms, and a big porch. It used to be a guesthouse, and *everybody* lived there. Twenty-one people. Five babies. The milk was rationed for the babies. One of my uncles stole milk at night. When more family or friends came from Cuba, I got evicted since I was the youngest. I slept on the porch, and somebody took over my bed. It was a *very* cold winter, made colder by our perception.

Of course, my childhood memories are tainted by idealization and the *Camelot* effect—"it never rained till after sundown"¶—but in Cuba there was a chauffeur, there was a maid, there was a gardener, there was a laundress, there was a cook, there was the country club, there was the Havana Yacht Club, there was a vacation home in Varadero, there was a little yacht. We were upper class. It was a *very* nice life. Here, we were scraping by.

---

§ St. Patrick Catholic School is the parish school for St. Patrick Catholic Church in Miami Beach.

¶ From the title song of Lerner and Loewe's popular 1960 Broadway musical *Camelot*.

We ate in two shifts because there wasn't enough silverware for everybody. There was one sitting. You ate, you washed the dishes, and then the second shift came in. You got one portion, you ate it, and *that—was—it*. I never went hungry, but there were many times when I *wanted* to eat more and there *was* no more. So, the quality of life was crap.

For the first time in my life I watched my mother cry. When my sister died my mother didn't cry. But shortly after we got here, she was overwhelmed with, How do I keep the family safe and together? A number of the companies that my father represented in Cuba gave him a stipend, 100 bucks, 200 bucks a month, which went a long way. Then he got connected with a group, El Consejo Revolućionario, which was planning the return to Cuba.** Everybody had to find little jobs—in a gas station, in a grocery. We had to feed the family.

I remember watching my first commercial jet plane flying overhead, and I thought, Oh, my God, I'm in America now. We were *enormous* admirers of the US. Everything American was bright and shiny and perfect. *LOS AMERICANOS*, in capital letters. American technology was the best. American TVs were the best. American cars were the coolest. *LOS AMERICANOS* were larger than life.

We were told: "¡*Fidel robó todo!* Fidel stole everything, but we're going to get it back. We're going to take everything back, and the hell with them. That's what we're going to do. We're here temporarily." That made it palatable. "Put up with the adventure. Get beat up in school by the Irish kids. It's a story you'll tell later. We're going back and reclaim our birthright. Your father is taking care of it. *LOS AMERICANOS* are going to help us."

Some Cubans persuaded US consular officials to grant them immigration visas with permanent resident status, but that was only one out of every eight during the First Wave.[4] Most refugees came on temporary visas.[5] After Washington severed diplomatic relations with Havana, Cubans had to get a visa from a US consulate in another country or a visa waiver from the State Department or through an intermediary. Every workday brought requests for twelve hundred visa waivers, and most were approved after a security check, although many were not used.[6] By one account, the government eventually processed 700,000 visa waiver applications.[7]

Upon arrival in Miami refugees underwent a health check and further security screening. The government set up a processing center in nearby Opa-locka and detained some refugees while security checks were completed.[8] Cubans with

---

** The Cuban Revolutionary Council was the political arm of the US-sponsored effort to overthrow Castro.

visa waivers were admitted on parole, an elastic exception to US immigration law that had been used to admit 31,000 refugees after the Hungarian Uprising of 1956.[9] In fact, the parole power was the nation's chief tool of refugee policy until 1980.[10] Cubans whose temporary visas expired were allowed to convert their status to parole.[11] Except for those with green cards, the refugees' uncertain immigration status lasted until the Congress addressed the issue in 1966.[12]

For most refugees the central challenge was supporting their families. Some 37 percent of the First Wave claimed professional, semiprofessional, or managerial positions (doctors, lawyers, accountants, and the like), and 31 percent claimed clerical and sales occupations.[13] One barrier was professional and occupational licensing laws that required citizenship or passing an examination in English. One in four exiles spoke serviceable English.[14] Some found ways to resume careers, but many did not. Those without skills did the best they could.

Angel Castillo Jr.

MIAMI, FLORIDA

Thirteen-year-old Angel and two of his sisters traveled to Miami with their father, a lawyer. Two days later Angel's mother flew to Miami with the other four children. The two oldest daughters then went to live with relatives in North Carolina.

All we Cubans have two birthdays, the one when we were born and the one when we came to the United States. We came October 14, 1960.

My father did a lot of menial jobs. He worked at a place where they packed coins in little paper tubes. He sold smoked fish to bars, door to door. My mother ironed shirts at a commercial laundry. I delivered the *Miami Herald* at four o'clock in the morning, I went to school, and after school I delivered the *Miami News*. I gave all the money I made to my mother. We're all proud of our roles, but this story is so archetypal because it happened to so many people.

For part of that time my father went to Puerto Rico because one of my mother's sisters and her husband had established themselves in San Juan. He was able to open an advertising agency there. My father stayed with them while he looked for work, which he couldn't find. He sold Nestlé's chocolates door to door while he was there. So that period from '60 to '65 was full of uncertainty. You had to worry every day about how you're going to pay for groceries.

One Christmas my mother pulled me aside and said, "You're the oldest, and I don't have money to buy everybody a Christmas present." I felt so bad for my mother. She had credit accounts at all the major department stores in Havana. We didn't want for anything. I said, "I don't need anything." [Angel's eyes tear and his voice quavers.] She said, "I got this nail clipper from somewhere, and that's for you." [He pauses.] I'm getting tears in my eyes because those are things you're not prepared for as a child. [He pauses again.] I still have that nail clipper.

I don't remember my parents ever feeling sorry for themselves because their decision to leave, on behalf of their children, was *so* clear cut and so consistent with their own values. They both wanted to go back to Cuba. That's one of those things that they kept alive over the years. As I talk to my mother now her attitude is, How naïve were we that we thought we were going to be gone for only six weeks? But that was the mood of a lot of people.

Marijean Collado Miyar
CORAL GABLES, FLORIDA

On September 10, 1961, fourteen-year-old Marijean flew to Miami with her parents. Marijean had been born in Brooklyn, New York, when her parents lived there years earlier, before the family returned to live in Cuba. Her father Pedro was a political cartoonist for the satirical magazine Zig-Zag, *and her mother Maria was a hairdresser. Relatives met them in Miami.*

My father was detained at the airport. My mother and I were free to go. I remember going to my aunt's house and her taking me shopping for school, going to a supermarket, going through all these motions while worrying, What are they going to do with my father? He was detained for two days, maybe it was just overnight, but in my memory, it was two days that they kept him, maybe because he was a visible person. I never asked him. I never asked my father so many important questions.

My lawyer uncles were working as busboys. My father held out, with great dignity, to do what he had done. This was his moment because *Zig-Zag* was operational in Miami shortly thereafter and hired him.[††] Somebody wrote a book, and my father illustrated the book. So for the rest of his days he was able to work in his profession.

That's not entirely true. A fellow artist came to get him because the younger man

[††] *Zig-Zag* published in Havana from 1941 until the regime closed it in 1960. It reopened in Miami as *Zig-Zag Libre* and published until 1983.

had found a gig working at the Surf Club doing the settings for parties. Half the year, for the first three or four years, he would have a gig at the Surf Club, doing stage design. My mother went to work at Burdines, at the beauty parlor. She always got work. A few years later she was able to buy her own beauty parlor.

Happy as I was to be back because I was an American, I hated the first five years because we were poor. My parents got a one-bedroom apartment. I was sleeping in the living room. I would have to open up the couch every night. The worst thing was being a number in an American public school. I *hated* high school. I remember a lot of animosity from the faculty, not from the student body, but from the faculty. They were all Anglos. Miami was not Havana.

Miami was a village until the railroad arrived in 1896, but it blossomed during the Florida land boom of the 1920s and again during and after World War II.[15] Before the revolution about 30,000 Cubans lived in Miami.[16] Airlines made dozens of flights each day between Havana and Miami for round-trip fares as low as thirty-six dollars.[17]

The surge of Cuban refugees made Miami the nation's second-busiest port of entry, after New York, from 1960 to 1969.[18] At first they went to the original Cuban neighborhood near downtown's Gesú Church.[19] Over time they crowded into aging apartments and houses in La Sagüesera, a swath of Southwest Miami that included a rundown district now called Little Havana. Others went to blighted parts of Miami Beach and outlying areas like Hialeah.[20]

Paul S. George
MIAMI, FLORIDA

Paul's parents were of Assyrian ancestry and settled in Miami during the Depression. Born in Miami, Paul was raised in the Riverside neighborhood and now resides a few blocks from Southwest Eighth Street—"Calle Ocho"—in the Shenandoah neighborhood.

This was the heaviest concentration of Cubans. This is Shenandoah. The north side of Calle Ocho is Riverside. These neighborhoods were hit with so-called White flight in the 1950s because of the growth of suburbia. The Jewish population in these neighborhoods diminished significantly. In Riverside many apartments built during the great boom of the mid-1920s were thirty-five, forty years of age. They were affordable for these poor Cubans. It was close to downtown, lots of churches in the neighborhood. It was close to the hospital complex and the civic center, where you got unemployment checks and assistance. They would have been lost souls out in suburbia.

The Beach was interesting. Miami Beach was the winter haven of the western world in the fifties and into the mid-sixties. It was one great hotel after another. It was heavily Jewish. Mid Beach was too expensive for a refugee, so the predominant base for them was South Beach. It was decaying. You had old housing stock there all the way south to the tip. If an elderly Jewish widow could live there year-round on Social Security, probably without a cost-of-living raise, a Cuban family, working hard, could pack into a small room there too.

You saw the change right away in the churches. They were more casual in their approach to Catholicism—this was still during the Latin Mass—the way they dressed, the guayaberas. Women came to church with hair in pin curls. As Cuban-owned mom-and-pop businesses proliferated, they shopped at those places. Spanish was spoken downtown. Miami High went into double shifts. And the influx just accelerated.

These people considered themselves exiles, not immigrants. They weren't becoming Americans: We're just here temporarily. We love our country. It's paradise. Local people moved out to a new neighborhood. They were pissed off. They reacted in the typical American xenophobic way. They thought these new people were too loud, too clannish, too nationalistic. It was cultural. What they didn't understand was that some very entrepreneurial people came over—people who were skilled in whatever they did—and now they were adapting to their new environment.

Local government and private charities assumed responsibility for assisting the refugees, but they appealed to Washington for help. On December 2, 1960, President Eisenhower made the first federal commitment to the crisis with a $1 million grant.[21] After President John F. Kennedy took office on January 20, 1961, one of his first steps was to create the Cuban Refugee Program (CRP) with income maintenance, health care, job training and placement, surplus food, public school subsidies, and interest-free college loans.[22] Reflecting the desire for a Cold War propaganda weapon as well as the ideals of the liberal welfare state, the CRP provided the most generous benefits for migrants ever offered by the US government.[23]

About 70 percent of the refugees registered at the Cuban Refugee Emergency Center.[24] Cubans called it El Refugio. Registrants who met need standards got monthly subsistence income and other benefits. In Florida the subsistence checks totaled $60 per person or $100 per family.[25] In 1962 El Refugio moved to a seventeen-story Mediterranean revival building on Miami's waterfront. Built in 1925, it is now a national landmark known as "Freedom Tower."[26]

Maria Galatas Laurencio

CORAL GABLES, FLORIDA

After a harrowing experience in la pecera, *eleven-year-old Maria arrived in Miami on September 7, 1961, with her mother, grandmother, and a cousin. Maria's physician father had arrived four months earlier with her brother and another cousin.*

My father, my brother, and my uncle were dishwashers in a restaurant. My father and brother had rented this little bitty one-bedroom apartment in Miami Beach in the same building where my uncle was living. There were five or six families there from our hometown. You know how it is: one comes in, and they bring the rest.

Once a month we were given a package by the government that had Spam, peanut butter, oatmeal, canned food. We were thankful, but to us, especially the kids, that was disgusting. I remember having to eat Spam. Oh, my God! That was horrible. Spam breaded, Spam fried, Spam mashed. I swore I would *never* eat Spam again. The peanut butter, we got excited. We saw "butter." We knew that word. Oh, my God, butter! When we tasted it I nearly vomited, but we learned to do things with it. My grandmother used to do peanut butter ice cream, which was delicious. Once a month we would get an allowance, one hundred dollars for a family.

We moved to Hialeah because my father's sister came with her husband. They were the parents of the two cousins who had come with my father and me. We decided to live together in a home in Hialeah. My mother started to work in a factory, sewing. My father started to work in a chair factory, on the night shift. There were not many Cubans in Hialeah. Practically no one spoke Spanish. We didn't speak English.

I remember having to share everything with the whole family. We would buy one chicken, and that would be divided among—let me see, we were four on our side, and five—nine people. Living there: my grandmother, my aunt and uncle, my two cousins, my father, my mother, my brother, and myself. So, one chicken would be divided into nine pieces.

My father and my uncle bought an old car—I think it was a DeSoto. It had a hole in the bottom, in the back seat. We used to joke that that was the air conditioning. All nine of us would fit in there. The DeSoto would stop in the middle of the road, and we would have to push it. Our outings were to go to the airport to go up and down the escalators because for us that was fun.

We didn't last long in Hialeah. My father found a job as a physician in the city hospital in Beaumont, Texas. At that time, city hospitals were able to employ doctors who had not completed their licensure validation. We didn't know where Beaumont was. It didn't even appear on the map. He went to Beaumont in January 1962. A couple of months after that, we went to Beaumont. He was making seven hundred dollars a month. For us that was a fortune.

I will always remember my first Christmas in Beaumont. My dad gave me a bicycle for Christmas. I *adored* that bicycle. We were living in an upstairs apartment, so I left the bike parked underneath the stairs where the bikes were supposed to be left. The next day, it was gone. I cried and I cried and I cried. The neighborhood people heard about it. They all got together, pitched in money, and got me another bike. They knew that we were refugees and we did not have economic means. They wanted to show that not all Americans were like whoever stole the bike. I will never forget that. It was *so* wonderful.

One CRP imperative was to resettle refugees away from Miami.[27] Most refugees wanted to stay there, but the CRP worked with national organizations and local sponsors to find jobs and housing outside Miami and adopted financial incentives and penalties for resettlement.[28] By 1962 the largest numbers of Cuban refugees outside Florida were in New York, New Jersey, California, Texas, and Puerto Rico.[29] Refugee families eventually were resettled in all fifty states, the District of Columbia, Puerto Rico, and the US Virgin Islands.[30]

Ana Cowley Hodges
HOUSTON, TEXAS

On November 2, 1960, eleven-year-old Ana flew to Miami with her mother and three siblings. Ana's father, a neuropsychiatrist, and the other two children took another plane that day. On Thanksgiving Day the Cowleys learned that their home in Havana had been confiscated. "And so," she says, "we all sat down to Thanksgiving dinner in the United States."

We stayed with one of my dad's friends—I would have *shot* myself if a family of eight landed in my house—for a couple of weeks until we found this house. Daddy had not brought much money. We went from a house with all these maids, a chauffeur, and we were renting this two-bedroom house, *and* my mom couldn't cook worth a flip.

My mother knew she wasn't coming back the day she walked out. She kept saying, "Castro is trouble." My dad had this dream that he would go back in six months, but after the house was taken, he realized that was it. We didn't stay in Miami for that reason. Mom said she was not going to stay in a town where people had one foot here and one foot there. Because a lot of people were talking about when they went back. Mom said, "There's not going to be any going back. We might as well move forward." Daddy was only thirty-nine, so he was pretty young. My mother was thirty-four.

Daddy was getting interviews, deciding where to go. He had a professor when he was in medical school that was in San Antonio, but he had been at the Terrell State Hospital.[‡‡] He called Daddy. He said, "Come to Terrell. We need somebody to head that hospital at some point down the road." So we ended up in Terrell, Texas.

My mother cried the day we pulled into Terrell. We stopped at this 7-Eleven, and she just burst into tears. I remember her saying, "This is worse than a John Wayne movie." Didn't please her at all. Even though I was little, I could tell it was quite different.

My dad went in as a clinician but spent two or three months studying in New York. There were three exams that you took to renew your license if your medical school was accredited, and Havana's was. He was named head of that hospital four years later. At some time or another, there were like twenty Cuban doctors in Terrell. My dad kept bringing them in.

Andrés M. Duany

MIAMI, FLORIDA

Even though the Duany family of Santiago de Cuba had supported Castro's insurrection, the regime confiscated the family's lands. In October 1960 a relative took ten-year-old Andrés and his two siblings to the US, where the family had assets and long-standing ties.

What I remember is this: We left on Friday. I landed in the house of my father's best friend from Princeton in Sands Point, suburban Long Island, a nice, big, old house.

---

‡‡ Terrell State Hospital is a psychiatric institution in Terrell, a town thirty-five miles east of Dallas, Texas. In 1960 the town's population was 13,800.

That Saturday I went to Lord and Taylor and his wife got me loafers, khaki pants, a blue button-down shirt, and a madras jacket. I'd never seen any of this before. She dressed me up, and I buttoned the three buttons, and she said, "Andrés, we only button the middle one." That's how clueless I was. My mother came later, then my father. It was about two and a half years before the family was reunited.

We never lived in Miami, went straight to Long Island. It was an affluent place then. It was *so* American before the Vietnam War, in the sense that there was this complete confidence. The parents of my friends were World War II veterans, thirty-five or forty years old: Iwo Jima, aircraft carriers, Europe. They were heroes. They seemed to be tall, slim, fun, smoking, hard drinking, sexy wives, convertibles, Halloween, Thanksgiving, reading *Tom Sawyer*, playing touch football. It was a complete *Leave It to Beaver* world. That is supposed to be a myth, but you walked to your neighbors, the doors were open, the mothers were friends, the neighborhood kids were friends and went to the same schools, and the girls all seemed cute. Whatever it is, between 1960 and 1963, that existed, *exactly*.

I went from Colegio de Dolores, Spanish Jesuit, to Buckley Country Day School, coed. Absolute shock. But for some reason I was much more at home. I picked up English almost immediately because I'd been hearing it all my life. I began to do well in school. Two and a half years later, I won the spelling bee. I don't know why, but American education was a better fit.

Cuba was in the news, and people were well informed. Now they're clueless. I mean, what people think today of what Cuba was like and will be like—I can't even begin to correct them. But because of the Cuban revolutionary epic, they knew about Fidel, they knew about this, they knew about that—*Life* magazine, *Time* magazine, everywhere Cuba. So they knew exactly where I was coming from. They treated me between slightly exotic and completely normal.

When I graduated from eighth grade my parents decided to go to Spain. The savings that we *did* have weren't going to go far in the US. We could live well in Spain, so we moved to Barcelona. The Cubans were in Madrid.

It was Old Europe. It wasn't harmed by the war. It must have been as Europe was in the 1930s. I never really lived there. My brother and sister did. They had years before going to boarding school. I was supposed to go to Choate and Princeton, just like my father. Except for summer I was shipped overseas.

The vast majority of those in the First Wave were from the upper and middle classes, but the refugees included some working-class Cubans.[31] Laborers, fishers, and peasants who could not afford a plane ticket crossed the straits in small boats, sometimes fifty to one hundred each week. They were called *humildes* or "the humble ones."[32]

Jose E. Valiente

TAMPA, FLORIDA

Eleven-year-old Jose left his hometown of Rincón in October 1962 to travel to the US with his father, a hospital nurse. The family had applied for four exit permits, but the regime issued permits only for Jose and his father. They left eleven days before the Missile Crisis that ended commercial travel to the US. His mother and sister stayed behind.

We left October 5, 1962, which is my second birthday. I remember the day—the *day*—as if I was there now.

We got off the plane in Miami, walked into the airport, and I spotted a gumball machine. All kids back then loved chewing gum, and in Cuba there was *none*; it had disappeared. It required one penny to take a gumball out, and I asked my father, "Could I have a penny for a gumball?" He said, "I don't have a penny." Whatever Cuban currency we had, my father wanted it all to go to my mother and my sister. So we were *literally* penniless when we arrived in the US.

We went through El Refugio, where we got processed. It was like Ellis Island—rows of Cubans arriving every day, standing in line, waiting your turn to be called. They gave us one hundred dollars a month for three months, until my father got a job. From there they took us to the Tamiami Hotel in downtown Miami. The US put us up.

It was October, so the Giants and the Yankees were playing the World Series. I sat in the lobby, watching in black-and-white. We lived there for maybe a week. Then he contacted friends from Cuba who had a house in Miami. He and his wife and two daughters welcomed my father and me, and we stayed with them for three months.

My father landed a job in January 1963. The hospital my father worked at in Cuba was a sister of Centro Asturiano Hospital in Tampa. We had some friends in Tampa who had come over before us—a couple with no children—and she used to work at Centro Asturiano as an orderly. So, my father got a job as an orderly, cleaning all the crap.

We came to Tampa on a Greyhound bus, the longest ride I've ever experienced in my life. I thought we'd never get to Tampa. We stopped at every town on US 41. We finally made it, and our first home was the Ponce de Leon Housing Project. This couple had a unit there, and they illegally allowed us to stay with them. We slept in the living room. They eventually bought a house, and we went with them.

I didn't see my mother and sister for three years.

The First Wave arrived in a racially segregated America. Jim Crow laws in the South oppressed Blacks in many ways.[33] In Miami's early years, restrictive covenants prohibited the sale of residential property to Blacks except in a cramped section called "Colored Town," away from the waterfront.[34] When zoning ordinances to confine Blacks to specific neighborhoods came into vogue nationally, Miami enforced a "color line" to restrict where Blacks could live.[35] Even after the Supreme Court in 1917 invalidated a Kentucky racial zoning ordinance, many cities ignored the decision.[36] In Miami the county adopted countywide racial zoning in 1945, but the Florida Supreme Court struck down the ordinance.[37] Miami and other cities circumvented these rulings with ordinances that didn't expressly use race to zone neighborhoods but achieved the same result with other restrictions.[38]

Segregation spread across America in New Deal programs to foster homeownership. To evaluate applications for federal home loans, the government created color-coded city maps that fixed risk levels to reflect, among other things, an area's present or anticipated racial composition. Black neighborhoods had the highest risk assessment and thus the lowest creditworthiness. They were shaded red, a practice called "redlining." Banks based their lending decisions on these maps too. In Miami, the city's northwest was designated for Blacks.[39] Developers got loans from federal agencies to build housing projects, subdivisions, and entire suburbs, so long as they were segregated.[40] The government in 1937 financed a Blacks-only housing project called Liberty Town in redlined Northwest Miami. It became the nucleus for the vast Liberty City ghetto.[41]

Starting in the late nineteenth century, thousands of towns used local laws, police intimidation, or mob violence to drive out Blacks or keep them from moving in. These all-White "sundown towns" were in all regions. Persons of color could enter town during the day but not after dark, although some towns permitted live-in servants of color.[42] Florida had sundown towns, including Miami Beach and Palm Beach.[43]

By 1960 this combination of discriminatory practices resulted in Florida having the most highly segregated cities in America.[44] Of the tiny number of Black or mixed-race Cubans in the First Wave, most shunned segregated Florida and went to northern cities.[45]

Hilda Molina Tabernilla

PALM BEACH, FLORIDA

Silito and Hilda Tabernilla settled their family in a new one-story ranch-style home on a quiet street in Palm Beach, across from a wealthy Cuban exile friend. Silito, who had been Batista's private secretary and an army general, worked at a construction firm then taught at a military academy in West Palm Beach. Hilda raised their children and later worked as a seamstress and sales manager for posh Palm Beach stores.

In the beginning of the exile, sleeping in the garage we had about eighteen soldiers who left Cuba because they believed they would be killed. They came here. There was no work, no jobs, because it was bad in Florida, very slow. Everybody that came, Silito said, "You stay here until you find a job, and we will try to find a job for you with friends." Someone's friends were in New York, so they sent the people there.

The aide of my husband was a *cuarterón*, a captain—very intelligent, wonderful person.§§ His name was Boca. He came also. He stayed with us for two and a half or three years, until his wife came from Cuba. Both of them lived with us.

At that time, all the Black people had to leave Palm Beach by six o'clock in the afternoon. If there was a maid or a cook, they had to leave, and they had a pass. Some of the neighbors told the police that there was a Black man—a *mestizo*, so he was not really Black—so the police came one day. My husband explained that the man was his aide and didn't have work or any place to be. They said, "Tell him that after six o'clock, we don't want to see him on the streets." Can you believe that?

Boca went to New York because they had work there.

The refugees' adjustment to American life depended upon many factors, such as their social and economic status and life experiences in Cuba; their familiarity with the US before their arrival; whether they spoke English; whether they had assets in the US; whether they were White, Black, or mixed-race; whether they came as adults, adolescents, or children; where they settled; and their new circumstances. Adaptation was difficult for some but not others.

---

§§ In the racial classification system of Latin American countries with a history of enslavement, a *cuarterón* or "quadroon" was a person believed to be one-quarter of black descent and three-quarters of European descent.

Luis Cruz Azaceta

NEW ORLEANS, LOUISIANA

On November 19, 1960, eighteen-year-old Luis arrived at New York's Idlewild Airport, now John F. Kennedy International Airport, on a Cubana airlines flight from Havana. Leaving his parents and sister, he came to the US to escape the pressure to join the milicianos.

All my family was waiting for me. Just going across the Fifty-ninth Street Bridge and seeing the skyscrapers, the Empire State Building, I thought I was in a futuristic city. It blew me away. Right away, I loved it. And then my first snowstorm. I *loved* it!

We went to New Jersey. My uncle Carlos was living in Hoboken, so I went to live with him and his wife Gladys, who was like a mother to me. They had three children. I started working in a factory in Hoboken, making trophies. I came on a Friday, and Monday I was working with my uncles Carlos and Pedrin. They were terrific carpenters. What I did was help them, cutting wood. I was making one dollar an hour in 1960. We were working sixty hours a week.

Union City was close by. I became friends with a lot of Cubans in Union City. Bergenline Avenue was the hangout. A lot of stores started opening, owned by Cubans—restaurants, all different kinds of businesses. Yes, Bergenline was the place. It wasn't Miami, of course. Then we got into the union, and we all got fired. That gave me time to think. What was I going to do? What was going to be my future? I didn't want to work in a factory all my life.

My sister Sonia came in 1961. She went to live with Aunt Sara. My grandmother came in '62. Sara got separated from her husband. I left Hoboken and moved in with Sara and Sonia. We rented an apartment in Woodside, Queens. I was driving them crazy because the apartment was small, and I used to have an easel, and coming from work, I would paint. Something was driving me. That was around '63. I used to go to the park in Soho, making drawings. Then I found a job in a button company in the Garment District. I worked there as a clerk. I used to bring paintings to the factory. I sold a few to some of the coworkers.

Later we moved to a house in Astoria, Queens. We were expecting my parents to come over, and we needed more space. I started attending a high school in Astoria that was an adult center at night. They had classes in dance, drawing the model, that kind of stuff. One of the instructors saw me drawing, and after a few classes, he called me aside and said, "Luis, you have a lot of talent. Are you painting?" I said, "Yes, I'm making some paintings." "Can I see them?" I said, "I'll bring you a few." I did, and he said, "You've got to go to the School of Visual Arts."

His name was Andrew Pinto. I'll never forget him because he's the one that gave me the push. He said, "It's your destiny. You have the talent to do it. Why don't you attend classes at night, just to see if you like it?" So, that's what I did.

Carmen Leiva Roiz
MIAMI, FLORIDA

Carmen and her husband Juan flew to Miami on July 21, 1960, with their infant son. They took a train to an aunt's home in a New York suburb. With a degree in business, Juan looked for work. Twenty-three-year-old Carmen, who had earned a law degree in Havana, made a home for them.

My husband got a job immediately in a CPA firm in New Rochelle, New York, so that's where my exile began. I was lonely. I missed my home, I missed my family, I had no friends. I wasn't used to doing house chores. When I was in Cuba we had help in my house. I didn't have any help. I was on my own, handling a baby.

Winter was not easy. When March came, I was sick and tired of the snow. Then not knowing if I could go back. I was sad, wanting to go back to Cuba, calling my mother. She said, "Hold on, everything's going to change here."

Little by little they started pouring in. A Cuban family moved into the same building. It was a complex in New Rochelle. They had four kids, and the girl used to babysit for us so we could go out to the movies—rarely, because we didn't have the money. Then another Cuban family. I remember taking the train to Grand Central with my stroller and meeting my Cuban friends who were staying in the city. So, things started to change.

We moved to Connecticut in '61. My husband got a job with Eagle Pencil Company, and he became assistant controller for Latin America. My son was ill, and I had him in the hospital, but he overcame that crisis. He was born with cystic fibrosis, and it was not diagnosed until he was six. Then my daughter was born. My husband was doing well at work, and things began to take shape.

Those five years, I was a Connecticut housewife. We moved to a better house. I was driving, I had a station wagon, a dog, two children, and I lived in the country. I was master of my house. I had Cuban friends. I had American friends. My children were in school. I loved it. I was totally Americanized. It was the American Dream.

Alberto R. "Al" Cardenas

CORAL GABLES, FLORIDA

In the summer of 1960 twelve-year-old Al arrived in Miami with his mother and sister, his mother's parents, and other relatives. Because his father had been chairman of a large bank in Cuba, the regime kept him in Havana to assist as it took over the banking and sugar industries.

All the family members and friends who arrived in the United States came penniless. They would stay with us for two or three months until they moved into their own apartment. We boarded six or seven different families, most of them true family members, others who worked with my dad, or just close friends. Man, it was nonstop. I never slept in my own bed until I went to college. I slept on the living room sofa.

My mom started working when we got here. She didn't have any skill sets other than she was good at sewing, so she made veils. Women wore veils in those days. She made them during the week, and the sisters at the church let her set up a table, and she'd sell these veils in all six or seven masses on Sundays. That brought in a little extra money. So everybody got practical about our survival skills.

My dad was a proud person. Remember: he arrived a year and a half after us. I remember my mom having gone to the refugee center and coming home with all this information about foods that we could receive. My dad banged his fist on the table and said, "We didn't come to this country to take from it. They invited us in. We'll figure out how to resolve things." That was the end of that.

We moved to Fort Lauderdale where my dad got a job, going from the chairman of a bank to a bookkeeper for a small trucking company. My parents were guarded about it, but I never saw them sulking, feeling sorry for themselves. They adjusted, even though we were in very different financial circumstances.

Thanks to Catholic Charities, I went to St. Thomas Aquinas High School in Fort Lauderdale and graduated from there. I was a good athlete, so I played football, I was captain of the track team, and I worked hard. I mowed lawns, delivered papers, worked at groceries. I had to fend for myself because my family didn't have resources to give me money to go to the movies or to do this or that. I learned early on the gift of self-determination.

There were only maybe three Cubans in that high school. We were a novelty, and Fort Lauderdale in those days was truly a southern town. I never felt *physically* threatened because I was a good-sized athlete, but the insults and the bad jokes about my origin and all of that happened. I have friends who say, "I don't know how you put up with that crap, people insulting your background." I never thought about it. I had a pretty good screening mechanism where memories that weren't great just faded away.

The early Cuban refugees were resented for reasons other than being different. In Florida they got more generous public assistance checks than residents.[46] They competed for low-wage jobs, and African Americans in Miami felt particularly aggrieved about losing unskilled jobs to overqualified exiles.[47] Some locals disliked the changes sweeping over the city. Exiles opened businesses with Spanish names, and television and radio stations aired Spanish-language programs.[48] Apartment buildings posted signs that read, "No Pets, No Kids, No Cubans."[49]

Despite the penchant of many Cuban exiles for insisting erroneously that there was no racism in prerevolutionary Cuba, some White Cubans came with the prejudices that existed on the island.[50] The few Cuban refugees of color in Miami often did not feel welcome in Little Havana and ended up in African American neighborhoods.[51] As persons of color, they were not accepted by some White Cubans; as Cuban exiles they were not accepted by some African Americans.[52]

Cubans also brought their fractious politics.[53] As the exile community grew, the city experienced occasional arson, dynamitings, and Molotov cocktail attacks as factions jockeyed for primacy.[54] Exiles ransacked the Cuban consulate before it closed.[55] In December 1961 a Miami broadcaster called the refugees "houseguests who have worn out their welcome."[56]

Mario Cartaya

FORT LAUDERDALE, FLORIDA

On November 12, 1960, nine-year-old Mario got off the plane in Miami with his parents and older brother. His accountant father Ignacio had been promised a job by Frigidaire, but the company had closed its Miami office due to the recession. The company offered Ignacio a job in upstate New York, but he turned it down because of the cold climate.

We came with one hundred dollars. My dad began working, making minimum wage, in a commercial laundry. This is a guy who had an education, started his own business, and now he's washing and folding sheets, pillowcases, and clothes during the day, and driving the truck to deliver them at night to hotels in Miami Beach. He was working sixteen hours a day. It got to the point that I hardly saw him, so some nights he took me on the truck, and I fell asleep on the passenger seat. My mother was pregnant, and no one would hire her. We were very poor.

We went to Freedom Tower to receive free cheese, Spam, crackers, and pastries that were a week old. They gave us rice and oatmeal. Cubans don't eat oatmeal, but I learned to eat oatmeal. It became breakfast. I ate *picadillo* made with Spam.¶¶ It tasted horrible.

I started at Silver Bluff Elementary School in Miami. I remember how my first day of school bruised my ego. The teacher had a reading assignment where all the students would read from a book. I'm looking at this book, and I don't know *anything* these kids are reading. They were reading so fast. I could not make out a single word. Don't forget: it's 1960. There weren't that many Cubans in Miami. They had *no* idea what to do with a Cuban kid. In my class I was the only one. All my friends were Americans, so I *had* to learn English. Six months after arriving I spoke enough English to get by.

It wasn't until middle school when I began to hear "spic" a *lot*, because we moved to Hialeah. Hialeah was the Cuban side of the canal. Miami Springs was the American side of the canal, and I went to Miami Springs Junior High. You have a pocketful of Cubans going into a very Anglo school. The whole "spic" thing was something that I had a lot of fights over.

There were two bridges that crossed over the canal from Hialeah to Miami Springs. One was close to Ninth Street. I lived on Seventh Street. To cross the other bridge, you had to walk north about a mile and then walk back. Nobody wanted to take that bridge.

The second week, there's a bunch of Americans waiting at the bridge. We tried to cross, and we got into a big fight. We got beat up pretty good. The second day, same thing. After a week, I was hurting. I told the guys, "I'm not going over that bridge. I'm going to walk the mile and come back. There'll be a day when we can cross that bridge, but not today."

We met more and more Cuban kids who walked to the further bridge. Soon there's fourteen, fifteen. We looked at the closest bridge, and there were five American kids guarding it. *That* day we went over the bridge. We beat the *crap* out of them. After that it stopped.

American Jews recognized the plight of the Cuban refugees. It had not been many years since European Jews had fled a regime that confiscated their busi-

¶¶ *Picadillo* is a classic Cuban dish, a soft, fragrant stew of ground beef, tomatoes, peppers, raisins, and olives.

nesses and put them in concentration camps. Those refugees were met with official indifference or outright prejudice in many countries, most shamefully in 1939 when the US and Cuba refused landing privileges for more than nine hundred Jewish refugees aboard the German ocean liner MS *St. Louis*.[57] Now the United Hebrew Immigrant Aid Society and the Jewish Family and Children's Service assisted in resettling Cuban refugees. Perhaps more important, on a personal level many American Jews welcomed these strangers from the Caribbean.[58]

Isis Rivero Hoffman

KEY BISCAYNE, FLORIDA

Isis received an architecture degree in 1960 from St. Thomas of Villanova Catholic University. She got a job designing city parks in Havana but resisted the regimentation of Cuban life under Castro. On August 17, 1961, while her parents stayed behind with her grandmother, twenty-four-year-old Isis flew to Miami with her sister and her sister's two children. They took a train from Miami to New York.

There was a group of us from the university who got together in New York. We were friends from architecture school, not necessarily from my class. We would gather for lunch and do some networking. We were all looking for jobs. One day one of them said to me, "Go see this architect. He's an English architect, and he's been helping the Cubans."

I went to see this man. He was a very distinguished-looking man, and I presented my book, mostly things from school. Right in front of me, he picks up the phone and calls a friend. He says, "I have this *wonderful* young Cuban architect sitting in front of me. She's *terrific!*" He had met me ten minutes before. He's saying all these grandiose things about me, and I'm sitting there, very nervous, because this man doesn't know me.

He hangs up the phone and says, "I think you have a job. Go to this place. You can go tomorrow." They were experts in hospitals. The next day I went, they offered me a job at one hundred dollars a week. I had friends making *sixty* dollars a week, so one hundred dollars was a lot of money for me.

A few months later I went to thank this English architect, Jeffrey Ellis Aronin. He helped a lot of us get jobs. I said, "I would like to personally thank you for getting me a job. You're helping the Cubans, and I was wondering *why.*" He said, "I'm Jewish, and I know the plight of people who go from country to country. That's why I'm helping."

He was helping out of the goodness of his heart. It was incredible.

Carlos Alvarez

TALLAHASSEE, FLORIDA

The weather was fair on June 27, 1960, when the City of Havana *tied up at the ferry terminal in Key West. Ten-year-old Carlos, his two brothers, and his sister piled into the family's two-tone Oldsmobile with their parents for the drive to Miami on the storied Overseas Highway.*

The car was so loaded down it was hitting the ground. We took some stuff off and had that shipped to Miami, to one of my aunts. But I remember my father saying to us when the car came off the ferry, "You need to become Americans because we're never going back." It didn't faze me at all. Obviously we're going back at some point. I had all my friends there. I couldn't comprehend what he meant.

He had had it with the political system in Cuba. My dad was born in the twenties. He'd seen revolution after revolution, upheaval after upheaval, and what is he looking at ninety miles away? A country that has economic downturns, fights world wars, all of that and more, but stays together. There's no constant political turmoil like in Cuba. He had just had it.

That's why we didn't move to Southwest Miami or Little Havana. My dad didn't want any part of that. He put a down payment on a house in North Miami. Nobody in the neighborhood spoke Spanish. Nobody at my school spoke Spanish. Nobody anywhere near us spoke Spanish. We came here not as refugees. We had resident visas. We started a new school and a trip back to Cuba was never mentioned. The first day of school, that's when it hit me.

My dad got a job in Miami, obviously not legal. But in 1960 there was a recession in the US, so they downsized, and he didn't have a job. The savings were going down fast. My mom was an unbelievable seamstress, so she started making alterations: your hem needs to be taken up or something needs to be done with your pants, she can do it all. We started handing out three-by-five cards all over the neighborhood: alterations ta-da, ta-da, ta-da. My mom started getting customers, so my mom and dad thought, Maybe there's a business to this.

They opened a dress shop, and alterations were free. Both of them worked to-gether. Then from one storefront they expanded to two in the same shopping cen-ter. They were able to make a living off it, not a great living, but a living to keep us going without ever going hungry. Somehow my parents made it work.

Somebody had to take a chance, and it was two Jewish guys who said, "We'll give you a break on the rent and extend it out." They took a chance on my mom and dad. A lot of the Jews in Miami at the time—1960 is not that far away from the 1940s—when they saw the Cubans coming, they sensed something that they could relate to. To this day we are thankful for the Jewish community that helped us in those early days.

By the time Cuba halted commercial air travel between Miami and Havana dur-ing the Missile Crisis of 1962, almost 250,000 refugees had crossed the Florida Straits.[59] Most of them hoped for a return to Cuba on the wings of American power. And no wonder: for decades Cubans had lived with a fulsome American economic, cultural, and political presence on their island. They remembered the troops dispatched to quell disorder and the envoys sent to ease out strongmen Machado and Batista. Surely this crisis would end like the others.[60]

Silvia Morell Alderman

TALLAHASSEE, FLORIDA

On November 11, 1960, eight-year-old Silvia and her mother boarded a plane to Miami, where Silvia's brother was waiting for them. Silvia's father José was a regular dissenter on the Cuban Supreme Court of Justice. He resigned on November 12 and sought asylum in the Mexican embassy. Months later he rejoined his family in Miami for his fourth exile since 1932.

It was Veterans Day, and there was a parade in Miami that made it difficult to get around. My brother took us to a house that was full of people coming and going all night. It was some kind of halfway house. The people who lived there were exiles and were generous enough to open their home to people coming in. My mother and I slept on a cot in the dining room.

My brother came the next day and helped us find an efficiency apartment, not air-conditioned. My mother had a five-dollar bill and a letter of credit for $125. She must have shown this letter of credit to the people who rented us our apartment. The next business day she tried to go to the bank to cash it, and she went to the wrong bank, the poor thing. We had to walk home because she had used her last dimes on the bus. She got my brother to borrow a car and take her to the right bank. That's how she was able to pay the rent.

Including the house in Cuba, between 1960 and 1964 we lived in about eleven different places. We lived in the efficiency. Then my father came, so we moved to a one-bedroom unit in the same building. Then we thought it would be convenient for my brother to live with us instead of the hotel where he was a bellboy, so we got a two-bedroom place. When my brother went to the Bay of Pigs, we didn't need extra space, so we moved to another place.

Then three of my sister's kids came, so we had to have more room. We moved in with some friends who had a large house. From there, my father got some funds for two months' payment on a house in Hialeah. It was very cheap, so we moved there with the kids. When my sister came, there wasn't enough room, so we let them have the house and moved to another place. We wound up being taken in by a wealthy family who lived on Brickell Avenue. We lived there for a while, then moved into an apartment.

My mother was somebody who had servants. She was never a good cook until later. Washing clothes and all those things that ordinary housewives do—that was not something she was used to. And she slogged through all of it. She was an incredible woman. There's just no other way to say it. She did what had to be done.

Everybody believed that this was a short-term thing. There were some Cubans who had a mythical suitcase packed. Next year in Havana, that was the belief for a long time.

Mercedes Wangüemert-Peña
AUSTIN, TEXAS

Soon after Mercedes's father died in 1957 in the ill-fated attempt to assassinate Batista, her mother Violeta married Gustavo Alemán, but now the couple was in exile in Miami. Ten-year-old Mercedes and her sister lived in Havana with their grandparents. The girls were reunited with their mother and stepfather on December 1, 1960.

That night was rough because they had a one-bedroom apartment, a duplex close to Jackson Memorial Hospital. There were no covers; it was cold. The four of us had to sleep in a bed, covered with newspapers. My stepfather worked in a grooming shop. He left soon after that and went to Guatemala and joined the Bay of Pigs.

The Red Cross had given us a first aid kit that included a dictionary. I asked the neighbor next door—an American—if I could have her old newspaper, and I would get the dictionary and translate everything. I listened to the news. I learned English really fast.

I hated Miami. Everybody was a *batistiano*, 90 percent of them. They were the people that I thought were the murderers of my father, or if they hadn't done it themselves, their families had. There was this particular jackal named Ventura.[***] He lived two blocks from our house in Miami, and he walked his two Dobermans up and down the street. The first time I saw him, I peed in my pants.

When the first Cuban business opened, it was a grocery called El Oso Blanco.[†††] My sister, my mother, and I went there on the first day. My sister was adorable, like Shirley Temple. Some ladies started talking to her and asked what her name was. She said, and the ladies started screaming, "*¡Asesinas!*" you know, "Assassins!" They started throwing fruit and vegetables at us. My mother changed my last name after that incident at the market. She gave me my stepfather's name, Alemán. So that's the name that I went by at school.

We moved to Miami Beach right away. We were the first Cubans in our building. Everybody else was Jewish, from New York or Eastern Europe, a lot of Holocaust survivors. They knew what we were going through, for God's sake, especially the concentration camp survivors. And there were a lot of them in that building. They missed their grandkids, so I had fifty grandparents. My sister and I were the only kids in this building of wonderful old Jews.

There was one gorgeous old lady, Mrs. Rosenberg. She was very skinny. She had white roots, black hair. She wore spaghetti strap dresses with falsies and fuck-me pumps with no back to them, big skirts, and makeup. She always wore multi bracelets—bangles—on both sides. She spoke with a German accent. She really befriended me.

During the Bay of Pigs invasion, my stepfather was fighting and my uncle was fighting on the other side, and even though my grandfather was not fighting, he was right there. I was incredibly hyper and very sad. There were these candies called C.

*** Esteban Ventura commanded Batista's police in Havana. He was responsible for the Humboldt Street Massacre when four rebels were shot to death in their hideout after the 1957 assassination attempt on Batista.

††† El Oso Blanco or "the White Bear" was a small Cuban-style market on Flagler Street in La Sagüesera.

Howard's violet mints, and I loved them. She said, "Let's go get some little violets." When she was paying, she did something and her bracelets moved. I saw the numbers on her wrist. And I froze. I knew what it meant.

I asked her if the Nazis had done that to her. She was very upfront. She said yes. Then she told me: "And the reason I'm here is because every time something horrendous happened, I always put myself in some wonderful place, a beautiful moment that I had had before"—you know, some sweet moment in her life, emotionally. "I want you to remember that." That's all she said. She was telling me how she survived. And boy, did it come in handy.

We lived with everything in our suitcases. We were always making plans for what we were going to do when we got home. Because that's what always happened with exiles from Cuba. My plan was to recapture my life, this time with my grandparents. I wouldn't let anybody take me out of Cuba. Later on, after I got married and had kids, it was fun to figure out how to get them back there. It was my escape mechanism. It was my fantasy. I did eventually.

Figure 1. Edmundo Pérez-de Cobos, *center*, with his mother Maria and sister Elizabeth at their home in Havana, circa 1947. Photograph by permission of Edmundo Pérez-de Cobos.

Figure 2. Margarita Fernández, *seated second from right*, and friends at Havana's Montmartre cabaret, 1951. Photograph by permission of Margarita Fernández Cano.

Figure 3. Marijean Collado, *standing on right end*, and classmates in costumes for a carnival at St. George's School in Havana, circa 1955. Photograph by permission of Marijean Collado Miyar.

Figure 4. Mario Cartaya, *right*, and his brother Ignacio in the surf on the beach at Varadero, Cuba, circa 1956. Photograph by permission of Mario Cartaya.

Figure 5. Jose Valiente and his mother Odilia and father Jose outside their home in Rincón, Cuba, Christmas 1956. Photograph by permission of Jose E. Valiente.

Figure 6. Diana Sawaya, *left*, and her sister Hilda outside the Havana airport terminal in Rancho Boyeros, Cuba, as they prepared to visit their father in Venezuela, 1956. Photograph by permission of Diana Sawaya-Crane.

Figure 7. Tere Castellanos, *second row on stairs on left*, at kindergarten graduation at Havana's Spring Garden School, 1957. Photograph by permission of Tere Castellanos Garcia.

Figure 8. *Right to left*: Marielena Alejo, with her mother Margarita, father Raúl, and sister Maggie at their home in Havana, 1959. Photograph by permission of Marielena Alejo Villamil.

Figure 9. Silvia Morell and her mother Rosa Maria on Silvia's seventh birthday at their home in Havana, 1959. Photograph by permission of Silvia Morell Alderman.

Figure 10. Isis Rivero in the backyard of her home in Havana, dressed for a date, 1960. Photograph by permission of Isis Rivero Hoffman.

FOTOGRAFIAS
Titular—Bearer—Titulaire Esposa—Wife—Epouse

Hijos — Children — Enfants

Este Pasaporte es válido por cinco años a contar desde la fecha de su expedición.

This passport is valid for five years counting from its date. — Ce passeport est valable pour cinq ans á partir de la date de son emission.

2

FILIACION:
Personal description — Signalement

Nombre de los padres Licinio
Parent's names — Nom des parents
e Isolina Angela
Rosenda.

Lugar de nacimiento La Habana,
Birthplace — Lieu de naissance
Cuba.-

Fecha de nacimiento 1º Abril/1950
Date of birth. — Date de naissance.

Estado
Status — Etat civil.

Profesión Colegial
Profession or occupation — Profession

Estatura Color de la Piel trigueña
Height — Taille Complexion — Teint

Color de los ojos pardos
Eye's color — Couleur des yeux

Color del cabello negro
Hair color — Couleur des cheveux.

Barba
Beard — Barbe

Señas particulares visibles
Visible personal marks — Signes particuliers visibles.

Firma del titular
Bearer's name — Signature

X Carlos Alvarez

3

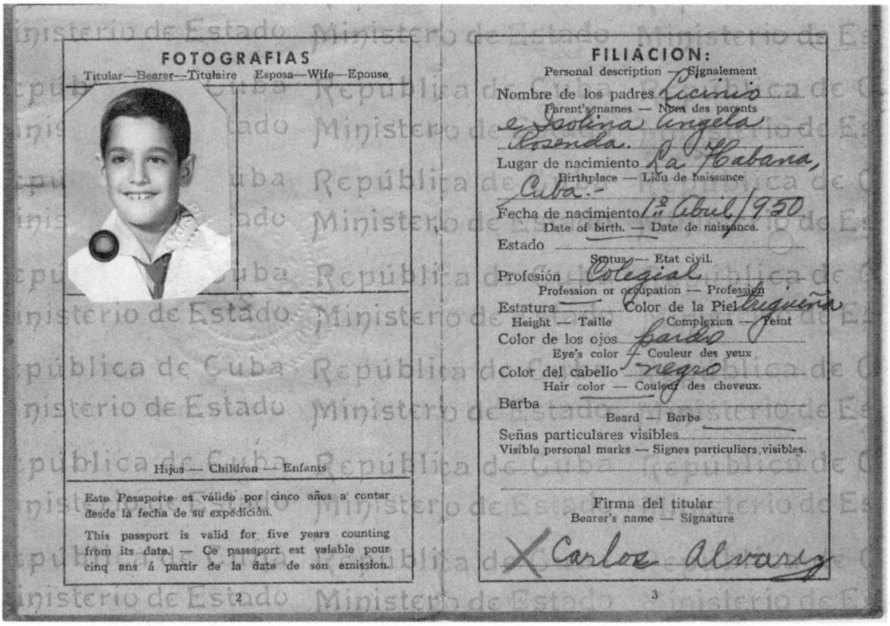

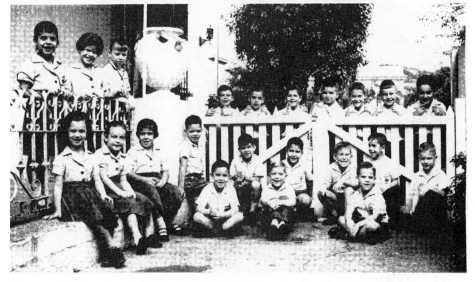

Figure 11. Carlos Alvarez used this passport when his parents brought him, his brothers Cesar and Arturo, and his sister Ana to the US on the ferry from Havana to Key West, 1960. Used by permission of Carlos Alvarez.

PRE-PRIMARY "B"
1st ROW: Enrique Paniagua, Richard Wolfe, Guillermo González del Mármol. 2nd ROW: Randee Falk, Susana Ríos, Marta Gutiérrez, Daniel Bethencourt, Guillermo Cabrera, Tomás Felipe Cabrera, Mark Bailus, Alan Paxton, Kevin Baker. 3rd ROW: Juan Andrés Salazar, Rubén Pérez, Rolando Bethart, Jorge Camacho, Manuel León, David Efron, Nabil El-Husseini. 4th ROW: Susana Prieto, María Hortensia Haget, Fedora Rodriguez.

Figure 12. Gil Mármol, *seated first row on the right end*, in a class photo at Havana's Lafayette School, 1960. Photograph by permission of Guillermo G. Mármol.

Figure 13. Mercedes Wangüemert, *left*, unveiled a portrait of her father José "Pepe" Wangüemert, at Havana's Instituto Edison, 1960; José died in the 1957 attack on the Presidential Palace. Standing, *back right*, is her journalist grandfather Luís Wangüemert. Photograph by permission of Mercedes Wangüemert-Peña.

Figure 14. Paulina García Orta, *center*, and two friends at the friends' beach house in Varadero, Cuba. Photograph by permission of Paulina Rodriguez-Muro.

Figure 15. Tom Aglio, *at right in suit*, with some of the boys of Operation Pedro Pan at Camp St. John in Switzerland, Florida, 1962. Cesar Calvet is in the top row, *second from left*. Edmundo Pérez-de Cobos is seated in the fourth row, *second from left*. Photograph by permission of Thomas J. Aglio.

Figure 16. Mercedes Fernandez, *at right in second row*, and her classmates with the Cuban and Soviet flags at a Havana elementary school, circa 1963. Photograph by permission of Mercedes Fernandez Collazo.

Ike Flores at Bay of Pigs 1965

Figure 17. Associated Press Correspondent Ike Flores at the Bay of Pigs, 1965. Photograph by permission of Isaac M. Flores.

Figure 18. Marine Corps Private Cesar Calvet during his tour of duty at the Guantánamo Bay Naval Station, 1966. Photograph by permission of Cesar E. Calvet.

Figure 19. Nestor Rodriguez, *back right*, with his father Nestor, mother Alicia, and sister Maria Conchita, at their home in Jaruco, Cuba, 1967. Photograph by permission of Nestor A. Rodriguez.

Figure 20. Maribel Pérez with her mother Hilda and father Juan in Mariel, Cuba, 1967. Photograph by permission of Maribel Pérez Henley.

5

CHILDREN WITHOUT PARENTS

As Castro transformed Cuba, the US began a clandestine attempt to replace him.[1] To foment discontent the CIA started a covert radio station, Radio Swan, on Swan Island off the coast of Honduras. In late 1960 Radio Swan broadcast nightly propaganda that the regime intended to abolish parental rights—the doctrine of *patria potestad* grounded in Roman law—and take Cuban children from their parents to be molded into revolutionaries.[2]

The regime never enacted such a law, but it employed a variety of tactics to bring young people into the revolution.[3] The Education Ministry in 1960 imposed a new curriculum in schools. Lessons included: "Q. What did Fidel Castro do? A. Fidel freed Cuba from the United States, which seized all our land."[4] Schools kept a record of each student's academic and ideological development to guide his or her education.[5] The authorities established an array of paramilitary organizations for young people. Membership was not compulsory, but the regime exerted pressure to join on children as young as five.[6]

Fearful parents began to send their children to the US. More than fifty Cuban girls were sent to a Catholic school in New Orleans in October 1960.[7] Other children traveled to the US with relatives or family friends or on their own with papers pinned to their clothes.[8]

Romualdo "Romi" González

NEW ORLEANS, LOUISIANA

American teachers and students were leaving the school at Havana's Holy Trinity Cathedral, so thirteen-year-old Romi was sent to the US on January 1, 1961, with his sister and baby niece. They lived in Alabama, where Romi's brother-in-law was a veterinary student. Romi's father, the cathedral's

highest-ranking Spanish-speaking priest, and mother stayed behind.

My father hadn't told me anything, but after our Christmas pageant at the school he told me to say goodbye to my classmates. I should have known it was coming because my father would not sign my permissions to join the neighborhood youth organization. Each neighborhood had one, and if you were going to play baseball, you had to be a member. I got that sign-up card and took it to him. He mumbled something about the Hitler Youth and put it away.

What most people worried about was you were going to have to do military service and go to their schools. Indoctrination systems were being put in place, and my father didn't want me to go through *that*. I had my Cuban passport, but I was a US resident. I'm sure the reason I got a green card was that the ambassador told my dad to get my ass out of there. My sister did too.

We went straight to Miami. My brother-in-law picked us up, and we drove to Auburn.

We spent the night there, and the next day his parents took me to Mississippi. I ended up in Itta Bena. That's outside Greenwood, Mississippi, about eighteen hundred people, and it has almost no claim to fame. It was a one-red-light town, railroad tracks across the middle. That's where the culture shock set in.

They had a cotton farm outside of town. A road ran past their house, and in every direction, there was nothing but cotton fields, rows and rows and rows up to the tree lines. You could not see the next farmhouse. There was nobody to play with. Well, there were other people, but they were Black or White sharecroppers. They wouldn't let me play with either one. That was Mississippi in 1961. It hadn't advanced much, not that it has now.

I went to Leflore County High School. Junior high and high school were mixed. There were kids in my eighth-grade class who had five o'clock shadows. They must have been sixteen, seventeen years old, and not very smart. I can't imagine what they thought about me. I never had anybody try to beat me up, but I had to do things like agriculture. Every day in the afternoon, they took us to castrate hogs, prune trees, drive a tractor, things that they do there.

Of course, we were segregated. That was a shock. In Cuba I played with all the neighborhood kids, whoever they were in color. We weren't told not to. That wasn't a part of the Itta Bena experience. That was the first time I was told not to drink water out of the "Colored" fountain. They still had "White" and "Colored." I said, "Is this different water?"

Within six months, my sister's husband finished veterinary school, and he had to do his internship in Lakeland, Florida, so she took me with them. I spent a summer there, running the streets. There were a lot of kids. My sister was pregnant again, and my mother came to visit. That was a treat. I ended up going to boarding school in Asheville, North Carolina.

My mother died the next year, when I was a sophomore. Back then breast cancer just wasn't a survivable thing. My father stayed until 1966, but he was terminally ill. He had cancer also. We couldn't go down there, so the British ambassador put him on a plane to Nassau, and from Nassau he came to New Orleans. He lasted about six weeks. He never left the hospital.

Julieta Navarrete Valls
SOUTH MIAMI, FLORIDA

The twin sisters Julieta and Ana Navarrete graduated from a Catholic girls' school in 1959 and were supposed to attend an elite New York finishing school. Instead their lawyer father and their mother enrolled them in a commercial art school in Havana to keep them close to home. Julieta studied fashion design. In June 1960 seventeen-year-old Julieta and Ana left for the US.

My father felt that we were in danger because of the rumors that the *fidelistas* were going to induct girls into the army. Also, because we were young and pretty. My parents were concerned about the *milicianos*. When we would go for a walk somewhere, we were invariably harassed. So he and my mom decided that the twins had to leave. I don't remember the explanation, but it was implied that this was temporary.

My younger brother Jose was in Dallas with his wife and baby. My older brother Jorge was going to get married and move to Dallas to study at SMU.* Ana and I were looking forward to the wedding; however, my parents decided that we were going to Miami and stay with one of the law firm partners and his family in Key Biscayne for a month or so, until Jorge moved to Dallas. Then the twins would be shipped to Dallas. So that's what happened.

My father said, "Twins, you have to get a job." One of his best friends and clients was the owner of the largest department store in Havana, El Encanto. Before we left,

---

* Southern Methodist University is a private research university located in Dallas, Texas.

he gave us a letter of introduction to Stanley Marcus at Neiman Marcus. I remember reading it: These are nice girls, the political situation is very unsteady, help them out. Ana or I called and got an appointment. Thank God we spoke English.

The day we were to go to Neiman's my sister got sick, so my sister-in-law came with me. We arrived at this magnificent office and were told that Stanley would not see us, his brother Eddie was going to meet with us. Eddie did the interview. He asked me, "What is your background?" I said I took a year of fashion design. He asked me, "Would you like to work in that department?" Talk about panic! I will remember and regret my answer forever. "No," I said, "I'd rather be a sales lady."

We didn't make much. Ana was placed at a desk where they sold gift certificates. I was sent to the men's department. I had never worked a day in my life. I had no clue of men's shirt sizes or anything else. Imagine this scared-to-death seventeen-year-old refugee kid. Stanley and Eddie Marcus were so fantastic to Cuban refugees. I know of at least three or four other Cuban women who were hired by Neiman's. We were the first.

About five months later my parents left Cuba with my grandmother. My mother and father left my grandmother with family in Miami and came to Dallas. I worked at Neiman's until I got married the following year and moved to New Orleans. Even my wedding dress was from Neiman's, bought at a fraction of the price.

An underground in Havana worked with the CIA against the Castro regime. James Baker, headmaster of the elite Ruston Academy, was involved.[9] Parents asked him to get their children out of Cuba by arranging scholarships to US schools.[10] The CIA wanted the children out, too, so parents would focus on the underground's work.[11] Baker went to Miami in December 1960 to raise money to bring Cuban children to the US and to establish a temporary boarding school for them. There he met a young Irish-born priest.[12]

Father Bryan Walsh ran the Catholic Welfare Bureau in Miami and had helped a few homeless Cuban children.[13] Walsh persuaded Baker that licensed child-placing agencies should organize care for the unaccompanied Cuban children Baker wanted to bring to the US.[14] Baker planned to get the US embassy in Havana to issue student visas for the children, and Walsh agreed the Catholic Welfare Bureau would assume responsibility for them in the US.[15] Corporate leaders agreed to pay for the children's airline tickets, although the US government later paid the children's airfare.[16] Thus was born the covert evacuation program now known as Operation Pedro Pan. It had two purposes—humanitarian and Cold War politics.[17]

The first two Pedro Pans arrived on December 26, 1960.[18] Fourteen thousand more followed.[19] More than half were adolescents, and two-thirds were boys.[20] Almost all were middle class.[21] Of the 14,000, about 8,000 went into group homes, orphanages, and foster care. Relatives or friends claimed about 6,000 as they got off the plane in Miami.[22]

Eduardo J. Padrón

MIAMI, FLORIDA

Eduardo's family celebrated when M-26-7 triumphed, but his father, a sales representative for a British pharmaceuticals company, and his mother watched with concern as the revolution turned radical. They put seventeen-year-old Eduardo and his brother Ernesto on a plane to Miami on July 21, 1961.

I had all these patriotic feelings. I was willing to become part of the militia. I was willing to become part of the literacy campaign. I put a sign in the door of my house, "*Fidel, esta es tu casa.*" That's when my parents began to worry.

Then I saw the revolution doing things that were not fair. They invaded homes and took things that were not theirs. I saw families being divided. I was very disillusioned. We never talked politics at home, but my parents kept an eye on me because they were concerned I would be persuaded to be with the revolution.

One day my parents got together with us around five o'clock in the afternoon and told us the next day we were going to the United States. They told us we had to stay in the house and to go to sleep. The plan was there all along, but we were not told until then because my parents were afraid that we would tell our friends.

My parents rushed to get us out because there was a rumor that Castro would announce *patria potestad*. They wanted to make sure we left before that law was implemented. That was probably one of the most difficult moments in my youth, because I just kept thinking, What does this mean?

Before we got into *la pecera* at the airport, my mother said something that has stayed with me forever. She said that no matter what happened, even if I had no food, I had to promise her I would go to college. She said, "An education is the only thing they will never be able to take away from you. Knowledge is power. It's worth every sacrifice." That has been my guiding principle and is responsible for who I am today.

We got to Miami late. Almost everybody was gone except the two of us and an older lady waiting for a niece. But you know the way things happen: She approached us. She said, "Aren't you the Padrón kids?" We said, "Yes." She said, "I know your parents." She identified herself, Rosa. She said, "Well, you cannot stay here." The niece never came, so she took us with her.

We were supposed to be part of Pedro Pan, but there was a break in communications. That's why there was nobody at the airport. Rosa knew my parents, definitely. Rosa saved us, she really did. It was supposed to be.

She lived in a duplex in North Miami. She had a small daughter. She said in the car, "We have to come in quietly because the owner lives next door. If they know I have two more kids in this duplex, they're going to kick us all out." My brother went to sleep, but I cried for three hours.

Two days later the owner realized we were there and told her to move. We had difficulty finding an apartment. We tried to get one close to downtown. Apartments had signs, "For Rent." When they saw us, they said, "It's already rented." I saw things I had not seen in Cuba. People had to sit in the back of the bus if they were of a certain color. But I also saw people who were very caring, very generous. Rosa took care of us as much as she could.

The minute we got to Miami, I realized I was Ernesto's father. I had to protect him and care for him. In twenty-four hours, I became very old. School was out, but I registered at Miami High and my brother at Ada Merritt School. I started delivering newspapers, doing inventory, washing dishes. On weekends I mowed lawns. The worst job was ironing at a drycleaner with no air conditioning in August. I still have the burn marks. But I went to school. I probably slept two to three hours at the most every day.

Eventually my parents came. It was '64 or '65. They weren't able to come together. The same company my father worked for in Cuba offered him a job in Colombia, so he took my mother and my brother to Colombia. I asked to stay. I wanted to live in the United States. I wanted to go to college here.

Operation Pedro Pan began in early 1961 as the Kennedy Administration was designing a refugee assistance program.[23] As part of it, President Kennedy created the Cuban Children's Program to care for unaccompanied children.[24] Never before had the government paid to care for refugee children.[25] So it was that Operation Pedro Pan and the Cuban Children's Program started at the same time, each a public-private partnership, each leveraged by the other.[26]

Ultimately Walsh's Catholic Welfare Bureau cared for 7,000 children from Catholic families. Three other voluntary organizations were under contract to care for children from other faiths, the Children's Service Bureau for Protestants and the United Hebrew Immigrant Aid Society and Jewish Family and Children's Services for those from Jewish families. Florida's welfare department took 700 children.[27] The government reimbursed caregivers $5.50 per day for foster care and $6.50 per day for care in group homes, boarding schools, and orphanages.[28]

Tere Castellanos Garcia

MIAMI, FLORIDA

Tere was the only child of Francisco Castellanos, a lawyer, and his wife Teresa, a school administrator in Havana. They sent nine-year-old Tere to Miami on September 20, 1961, with her eight-year-old cousin. She remembers her parents told her: "'You're going to the United States on a student visa. If anybody asks, you say that you're going to the United States to study, and we'll be there after.' I thought that was so fancy, going away to study."

At the Miami airport all the children who were by themselves were put in a big lobby. We were there for a while. Monsignor Walsh came in—he was a young priest then—with a big bowl of chocolate and Bazooka chewing gum. Those were two things I missed in Cuba.

My parents and my cousin's parents had agreed that we would not separate. But my mother had a good friend in Miami Beach with her husband. They had no kids, and they told my mother, "We can take her, but we can't take both." So, they called my name. They said, "You're going with so-and-so and so-and-so," Elvia and Nestor Miranda. They were wonderful people.

They registered me in Central Beach Elementary School.[†] They put me in a fifth-grade class for kids who did not speak English very well. When they thought you were ready, they put you in a regular class.

My cousin went to Matecumbe.[‡] He stayed there several weeks. We picked him up on weekends, and he came to the apartment. We slept on the floor, and he cried and cried. Oh, he *hated* it. He was not mistreated; he just missed his parents. He was sent to an orphanage somewhere. To this day he doesn't speak about it.

---

† The school is now Fienberg-Fisher K-8 School with an International Baccalaureate program.
‡ Camp Matecumbe was a Pedro Pan transient shelter south of Miami for up to four hundred boys.

My mother came eight days later, on my birthday. We lived in a little efficiency on Pennsylvania Avenue in Miami Beach. My mother worked cleaning houses. She had a sewing machine, and they would bring stuff that she would do at home. So that, together with what the government gave us, was how we got along. It was a very simple life. Nobody needed much, and nobody had much. I'm sure there were bad things, but I don't remember feeling bad.

My dad came three years after, '64. We got a bigger place. He started working with an air-conditioning business. They would break concrete to put in air-conditioning. In the evening he'd go to one of the hotels to wash dishes. Then a friend of his who had gone to Puerto Rico called him and said, "There's more opportunity here," so my dad bought a ticket to Puerto Rico. Eventually he got a job, and we went to Puerto Rico. That was in '64, '65.

The Catholic Church supported the social revolution in the Cuban countryside, with new schools, housing, and public works, so it did not criticize the Castro regime at first.[29] Then Archbishop Enrique Pérez of Santiago de Cuba—the prelate who had interceded to save Fidel and Raúl after the Moncada Barracks attack in 1953—warned that communism was "the new slavery."[30] Bishop Eduardo Boza of Havana inveighed against the regime, arguing that the revolution was not Christian because it was not just and ignored spiritual needs.[31]

Manuel Cardinal Arteaga of Havana and the archbishops and bishops in late 1960 issued a pastoral letter that deplored the rise of communism.[32] Priests were arrested for reading the letter at Mass, *milicianos* occupied churches and seminaries, and churches were bombed.[33] Fidel denounced the prelates as "fascists" and promised the "destruction of everything old."[34] In 1961 the regime expropriated one thousand private schools, many of them Catholic.[35] It expelled 135 Catholic priests to Spain aboard the ocean liner MS *Covadonga*, including Bishop Boza and 47 other Cubans who did not have Spanish passports or visas.[36] Before firing squads, many condemned prisoners proclaimed their faith by declaring, "*¡Viva Cristo Rey!* [Long live Christ the King!]"[37]

As more children arrived in Miami, Walsh organized a network of transient shelters and group facilities around Florida.[38] He re-created a Cuban *bachillerato* program in Miami for the first arrivals, but later the children attended public or parochial schools.[39] At the program's peak in October 1962, Walsh had a staff of three hundred—all but five were Cuban—to care for 1,500 children in Miami. Another 3,500 children were in thirty-five states.[40]

Arelis Duran Alvarez

NORTH HALEDON, NEW JERSEY

Arelis was the youngest of the three children of Miguel and Marta Duran, who lived in Holguín, where Miguel was an army veterinarian. On July 8, 1962, eleven-year-old Arelis and her brother went to Miami while their parents stayed with their oldest daughter and her family.

My parents heard they were going to separate children from their parents and indoctrinate the kids. They said, "Before they do that, let's send them ahead." They told us we were going on a trip. My parents thought we were going to come back within a few months.

They dropped my brother in Matecumbe. I remember the mosquitoes while I was waiting for him to get off the van. Then they took me to Florida City.§ It was late at night. They gave me milk, a Scooter pie—crackers with chocolate and a marshmallow in the middle—and an apple.

There were houses. There were four apartments in each, upstairs and downstairs. They were like little motels. My houseparent was a woman from Havana. Her husband hadn't arrived from Cuba, so she was by herself. She had three children, but only the little one lived with us. The other two were teenagers, a boy and a girl, and had to live outside the camp.

I cried almost every night for my parents at the beginning. I was a spoiled brat in Cuba. My mother used to bring me milk in a bottle, like a baby. While I was drinking the bottle, she was putting my socks and shoes on, to get me up to go to school. My childhood stopped.

I did the fifth grade. We had regular subjects—history, math, and science. We even had English. But the teachers were Cuban; the students were Cuban. We asked questions in Spanish, and we answered in Spanish. It was not like I learned English.

They used to buy us clothes twice a year. I had shoes with cardboard on the bottom because they had holes in the soles. They used to take us to the army-navy store, and I bought a skirt and a blouse. My girlfriends all got the same skirt, four of us. We wore orange and pink tops so we could be different.

Almost every other weekend they used to bring my brother to visit me or take me to visit him. We had a second cousin in Miami. They used to take us out some

---

§ Florida City Camp near Miami was a shelter for seven hundred girls and younger boys from 1961 to 1966.

weekends. When we got out, we called my parents in Cuba. They sent us money to save—it was not a lot—so when they got here they would have *something*.

I was in the camp for one year. My brother stayed in Matecumbe, then Kendall,¶ then Opa-locka.** By the time my parents came, I was happy. My parents wanted to take me out right away. I said, "Do you mind if I stay until I finish school?" They agreed, and the school agreed, so I stayed until June.

Operation Pedro Pan was thrown into disarray when Washington severed diplomatic relations with Havana. Its embassy shuttered, the US could not directly issue visas on the island.[41] When the State Department decided to grant visa waivers to Cubans, it gave Walsh unprecedented authority to issue waivers for children ages six to eighteen, although those seventeen and eighteen first had to pass a security check.[42] For much of the next twenty-two months, authorities in Miami *and* Havana honored confirmation of visa waivers on preprinted forms with Walsh's duplicated signature.[43]

Others helped the children to get out. Visa waiver papers were delivered through churches, relief organizations, the underground, and Western diplomats.[44] The British embassy in Havana issued student visas for Jamaica or the Bahamas. The Dutch embassy got children seats on KLM flights to Kingston.[45] Local managers for Pan American Airways and KLM became vital partners for anyone trying to leave Cuba.[46]

Hector Laurencio

CORAL GABLES, FLORIDA

Hector García lived with his mother Onelia "Nena" Laurencio and her extended family in the town of Calabazar near Havana. His father Anselmo García deserted Nena before Hector was born, so his role models were his mother's father and her brother Waldo Laurencio, a physician. On June 19, 1961, fifteen-year-old Hector was sent to Miami on his own.

¶ Camp Kendall near Miami was a Pedro Pan transient shelter from 1961 to 1963. The facility was the county's segregated home for Black children until the county integrated child welfare facilities in 1960.

** Opa-locka Camp was on the grounds of a former naval air station north of Miami. In operation from 1963 to 1966, the two dormitories and cafeteria and recreation building accommodated five hundred teenaged boys.

Eighty percent of my friends were in favor of the revolution. Maybe twenty percent were in the same boat that I was, against the revolution. You were not *allowed* to be neutral; you had to belong to the Committee for the Defense of the Revolution or whatever. I remember my friends joining the militia. Since we were not communists, we didn't belong to any of these things.

In 1961 my mother was sitting on the porch, and a guy from the Committee for the Defense of the Revolution walks up to my mom and says, "Nena, at the next opportunity, I'm taking Hector to jail." My mother said, "Why?" He said, "Because Hector was at the theater, jeering at the *comandante jefe*." My mother was worried.

The chief of Pan American was a close friend of the family, so he secured a seat for me on one of the flights. He traded that seat with G-2. He gave them three seats that *they* sold, of course, because corruption was rampant. I had my passport, and I had a permit to leave the country from my mother and hypothetically from my father. I always wanted to be a doctor, to emulate my uncle Waldo. I knew I couldn't become a medical doctor or go to a university because I was not a part of the system. So I was happy in a sense and unhappy in another. I was sad, leaving my mother, my aunt, my uncle, my grandfather, my grandmother, my friends, my school.

I was in *la pecera* for three hours, then the secret police sent me to a questioning room. The guy was trying to intimidate me. They kept me there over an hour, so long that the plane was ready to leave, but the chief of Pan American held the plane until they were through with me. He came into exile the next day, so I was quite fortunate.

I arrived about four o'clock in the afternoon. I didn't have *anybody* waiting for me. I had the telephone number of friends. I called to a policeman and said, "Sir, can you give me a dime to make a phone call?" That's why I'm not scared of anything, because when I arrived in the United States I literally had to ask, "Brother, can you spare a dime?"[††] The guy gave me a quarter. I called these people; they didn't answer. I was there, solo, by myself, at the airport.

This fellow comes and says, "What about you?" I said, "Well, I don't know. I'm here by myself." They put me on a bus, and I went to Matecumbe. I was there about a month. I didn't come as a Pedro Pan. I was recruited into the program just by the fact that I came by myself. The Catholics did this, for which I'm eternally grateful. It was amazing.

Then my aunt and uncle came. The government gave them a position as foster parents for Cuban kids. Dozens of kids would go through this home. On average,

---

†† The 1932 song "Brother, Can You Spare a Dime?" was a lament about poor workers during the Depression.

kids stayed there six months to a year. They didn't have their parents here, but they started coming.

My mother had to wait about two years. My grandparents came with her. Same flight, same plane, same everything. When my mother came, we moved.

Henry Martell

CORAL GABLES, FLORIDA

In late 1961 the lawyer and diplomat Alberto Martell and his wife Alicia
decided to send their son Enrique out of the country while Cuba went through
the throes of revolution. He remembers waiting, days before his fourteenth
birthday, for a courier on a lime green motorcycle to bring his papers. "When
everybody saw the motorcycle at somebody's house," he says, "they knew
someone was leaving. Sure enough, in December I got the exit permit."

I left on January 2, 1962. My parents and, I think, my mother's sister went to the airport. They stayed there. A lot of crying, and "Always write. Don't forget. Don't cry." I was scared.

When you got there, they put you inside *la pecera*. A speaker talks to you, calling you this and that and *gusano*. Then in the middle of the day they ask you to go to another room. They take your clothes off, completely, and try to figure out if you're taking anything with you. The only thing that I took was a Longines watch to try to sell here, but they kept it. Then they put you back in *la pecera* until about six in the afternoon.

From there we got into a Pan American Airlines plane, full. I would say 80, 90 percent were children, and 10 percent were adults and priests. [He pauses to control his emotions.] It was really emotional. All of a sudden, the pilot said, "We are out of Cuban airspace," and everybody started laughing. [His voice almost breaks.] It was a happy moment.

In order to get in, I had to stay with Pedro Pan. Once I was checked in, I was claimed the same day by my mother's cousin, Jose—we called him Chony—and Esther Femenia. They had two kids. They became my parents. [His voice almost breaks again.] I was one of the lucky ones, that we had this family.

The first day you're going to Freedom Tower to report, they give you some papers and a number, and you wait until they call your number. There used to be a park across the street from Freedom Tower, filled with birds. They called it Parque de las Palomas.[‡‡] There were so many Cubans that they said, "You can go to the Parque de las Palomas. We're going to call your number when we're ready." About the third day, they called me in.

I moved to San Juan, Puerto Rico, with the Feminia family. They were able to take out US dollars behind the lining of a coat. He had the distribution for Evinrude, Johnson, Jacuzzi, and Briggs and Stratton motors. He had that all his life; that was his business. When we moved down there, he was able to secure those franchises for the Caribbean islands.

I went to Catholic schools. Then I started working. I had a paper route and then merged with a Puerto Rican neighbor, a little older than me. I said, "Let's invest in a car. You drive, and I'll throw the papers from the back seat." We bought a Morris Minor convertible. Getting to throw from the car, we cut our time in half. We did well.

My parents stayed, seeking a way to leave Cuba. I stayed in Puerto Rico. We had letters, and some of the letters they would hold six, seven months before I got them. No telephone calls. I left in 1962, and I didn't see my parents until 1968.

Victoria Montoro Zamorano

SOUTH MIAMI, FLORIDA

Vicki and her brother and sister stayed in Havana with their mother Albertina O'Farrill and their governess. The Castro regime had dismissed Vicki's father Rafael as Cuba's ambassador to the Netherlands, so he had moved to the US to resume his medical career. In July 1961 Albertina reluctantly decided to send twelve-year-old Vicki and her siblings to the US.

My dad was living in New York. He had remarried. My mom—who hated him—wasn't thinking of sending us there. But then the searches started. I remember militiamen coming into the house at two in the morning. I never saw their faces. The three of us sat on the bed with our governess, Maretza, looking down at their boots. She was more a mother figure for us. She was Austrian. Maretza was a survivor of the Nazis, so she was familiar with this.

It was illegal to have US dollars. My mother had *two* linen closets at the entrance

---

‡‡ Parque de las Palomas or "Park of the Pigeons" was part of Bayfront Park and is now the site of an arena.

to her bathroom. She would hide dollars underneath the sanitary napkins. I remember, when I saw the boots, being afraid they were going to that closet and the sanitary napkin boxes.

My mother decided there was no place for us there anymore. I remember going to Old Havana and standing in line to get vaccinated. We were told we were going to visit my dad, who we hadn't seen in years. The three kids had one suitcase, and Maretza had her suitcase.

My dad was waiting in Miami with his wife. We went to Key Biscayne where he had rented a house. It must have been the second of July. The first two or three days we were here, it was the Fourth of July, and they started firecrackers. My brother, my sister, and I immediately ducked under the bed. I remember my stepmother coming in and saying, "Listen, those are firecrackers. We're celebrating the independence of the United States. You will *never*, ever have to worry about any of that again in your life."

My father bought a house in Hialeah for my aunt and grandmother and a house next to that one for us with our governess. He went back to New York because he had to work. He left us here for about a year, mainly because he thought my mother would come out, which she did in 1962. She came for my great-uncle's funeral. A lot of her friends who had had a lot of money, all of a sudden had no money. They were working. My godmother, who was one of the richest women in Cuba, was selling cosmetics in Burdines.

I remember my mother saying, "I'm going back to Havana because, first, my mother's there," which was true. I never saw my grandmother again. "I'm not going to be working here. That is going to blow over, and I will have kept my house, my servants, and my social life." That's what stuck with me. She was here for two months, then she went back. So, without getting into psychological scars, she chose to go back. It took me a long time to believe that there were philosophical reasons, other than she didn't want to go through what all the other Cuban women did.

The last time I saw my mother, I was twelve. The next time I saw my mother was the weekend of my thirtieth birthday. I didn't hear anything again until 1979. I mean, *nothing*.

Operation Pedro Pan accelerated with the clandestine assistance of socially prominent women led by Polita Grau, the niece of former President Grau, and her brother Ramón "Mongo" Grau. Albertina O'Farrill worked with this network. By one account, it revived the rumor about *patria potestad* in 1961 as part of a disinformation campaign.[47]

One hundred to two hundred unaccompanied Cuban children deplaned in Miami each week.[48] Walsh hired Jorge Guarch, a Cuban native who had moved to the US in 1949, to manage the arriving youngsters. The children were told to "ask for George" when they got off the plane.[49] The bilingual Guarch greeted them, handled the formalities, and shepherded them to waiting relatives or a transient center from which they could be sent to a foster family or group home.[50]

Edmundo Pérez-de Cobos

CORAL GABLES, FLORIDA

On April 7, 1960, fourteen-year-old Edmundo went to the airport with his parents for a flight to Miami on papers obtained through the Catholic Church. Before he entered la pecera, *his father whispered to him, "When the airplane takes off, look down at your country because you will never see it again." Three months later his father died in the Uruguayan embassy while awaiting safe conduct out of Cuba, so Edmundo never saw his father again either.*

When I arrived in Miami, I went through Immigration, no problem. I spoke a little English. A lady was outside the Customs door. Every time she saw a kid that could be Cuban, she said, "Pedro Pan?" You said, "Yes," or "*Sí.*" She took you someplace else, and you would be on a bus going to Matecumbe. To me it was the jungle.

It was temporary. I was sent to Orlando to Camp San Pedro.[§§] It had two buildings, one to sleep, the other to eat. Remember, there was no Disney World. Orlando was *very* small. An older Cuban couple and an Irish fellow used to take care of us. There wasn't much discipline. We became like in *Lord of the Flies*: from civilized, we became uncivilized.

Then we started Bishop Moore.[¶¶] We wore gray pants, white shirts, and blazers. I had just become fourteen. I was placed in junior year after a test. Although I could carry a conversation in English, my English was not up to par to study algebra or to go deep into Shakespeare. It was difficult. With time we realized we were not going to go back to Cuba as soon as we thought.

One day they said, "Pack everything because we're going to send you someplace else." The archbishop of St. Augustine had this *huge* farm on the St. Johns River where

§§ Camp San Pedro was a church-owned camp in Winter Park, Florida, and housed fifty Pedro Pan boys.

¶¶ Founded in 1954, Bishop Moore High School was the only Catholic high school in Orlando.

part was a summer camp for kids, full of trees with Spanish moss, full of snakes. It was Camp St. John in Switzerland, Florida.*** When we arrived, we met *another* bunch of kids that were already there. We went to Bishop Kenny.††† On occasion they would take us during the weekend to the city of Jacksonville. To us it looked old, sad, no traffic, no people on the streets.

That was when I saw the KKK in action. It was dark, and three or four of us decided to go to a little outpost about half a mile away. We were walking, and we passed what we later found out was the Ku Klux Klan. There was a burning cross and something going on. We figured that was not for us. This is the middle of *nowhere*, maybe thirty-five, forty minutes from downtown Jacksonville. When we came back, we told the people that were responsible for the camp. We described the garments, the burning cross. They said, "Oh, that sounds like the KKK."

All of a sudden, the people we knew in the Pedro Pan organization faded out, and Catholic Charities faded in under Thomas Aglio, a wonderful man from Boston.

Thomas J. Aglio

WINTER PARK, FLORIDA

Tom was a social worker at a Catholic hospital in Worcester, Massachusetts. In 1961 he agreed to set up an Orlando office for Catholic Charities, so he and his wife Margaret moved to Florida with their three daughters. Before he started, he was asked to manage Camp St. John. Tom went there in January 1962.

I was totally unprepared. I had little or no knowledge of the program. I didn't know any of the boys, not one. I had no three-by-five cards on them. It got to the point after two or three weeks that I forgot about starting the social agency in Orlando. I got so caught up in it.

The diocese owned a lot of property south of Jacksonville. They had a retreat. The manor was a big two-story building. There was a meeting room that was the cafeteria and a study hall. They had two dormitories. Another small residence was on the river. We had a junior Olympic pool. The boys used it a lot. We had baseballs and bats. They didn't have formal games, but groups of them would throw the ball, and they would throw a football.

*** Located south of Jacksonville, Camp St. John housed sixty boys at a time in 1961 and 1962.
††† Bishop Kenny High School is a coeducational Catholic high school in Jacksonville.

Camp St. John had been running for at least a year. Father Walsh was the head of the whole thing, and he was negotiating with bishops in dioceses all over. They were sending kids to Oregon, New Mexico, Texas. Miami couldn't hold them all. *They just kept coming.*

I didn't like anything about the camp. The kids needed to be loved, and they were not loved. They had two counselors, old Cuban men, one in each dorm. A chaplain said Mass, and the kids could go to confession to him, but the kids didn't like him because he was a Spaniard, and he had no time for Cubans. We had a cook. And we had a nurse half a day a week. That's all.

The chicken pox was *awful*. We had more than twenty at one time in our make-shift infirmary. There were waves of them. I went to visit the ones that were in the infirmary. It touched me a great deal.

Generally, the boys were from nice families, they were educated. Not all had gone to a private school, but many of them. They were neat and clean. They got along well. They got quiet at night. I don't think they cried themselves to sleep. When they first got there, they may have. Most of the ones we had were there because they had no one. They had the church. Oh, there was mischief. They would smoke. I would gently say, "You need to put that out because smoking's not permitted." I had one boy ask me why, and I said, "Can you imagine what it's like if we have a fire?"

And we *did* have a fire, on the grounds. Boy, if you ever wanted to see a group come together, they did. Those boys! I remember them finding carpets and burlap bags, beating the fire down. They beat that fire with brooms and sticks and got hot and wet and sweaty. The volunteer fire department did not put out nearly as much as they did. As soon as the fire was out, they were proud. *They* put out the fire. They were *one* then.

In June the archbishop came. I said, "This is no good. We need to close." He said, "*What?*" I said, "They don't belong in this environment. They need a home and a family, and we can find the homes and families." He bought it—*immediately*. Social workers did home studies because the state had to license the foster homes. It was the core of the middle of the state. I visited every one of those homes at one time or another. Some came and lived with the Aglios.

The camp closed around Labor Day. I made my farewell speech to them, *in Span-ish*. I looked out at all those faces, and they were stone. They did not want to go. The thought was going through my mind: They're all my friends who I love dearly, *all* of them. I *knew* those boys the last day. They couldn't stop hugging me. The separation was *so* traumatic for them. It was worse on them than it was on me. They were crying for each other.

Toward the end they began to call me Padre Segundo ["Second Father"]. Several still call me that, and they're, what, sixty-five years old. What did I say or do in less than a year with those boys that made them call me Padre Segundo? I was the boss of the camp, and yet to them I was becoming their second father. I *can't* grasp it. The biggest thing that I got out of it is that [his voice catches] I had the capacity to love a stranger—not a friend, a stranger.

There was nothing in the human sphere that could explain that whole thing, why I was called by the Holy Spirit.

Cesar E. Calvet
ORLANDO, FLORIDA

On June 11, 1961, fifteen-year-old Cesar left Cuba to stay with relatives in Miami Beach until another relative arranged a place for him at Camp St. John near Jacksonville. When the camp closed in August 1962, Cesar went to live with a foster family in Orlando, as did his friends Edmundo Pérez-de Cobos and Melquíades "Mel" Martínez.

I went to a home in the Rio Pinar Country Club in Orlando, June and Jim Berckmeyer, nice home, two cars. June was the number two person for the Florida Bankers Association. She was not doing this for the money; others were. Mel and I were supposed to be together, but I ended up with the Berckmeyers, and Mel ended up at a small house in Pine Hills, the Youngs. Nice people, nice Catholics, two teenagers. When I got my license, I had a car on the weekend. Mel lived far away, but we would go get him.

When the situation with Edmundo did not work out, Mr. Aglio came to see me. He said, "Do you think any of your neighbors would like to take Edmundo?" I went to visit Mrs. Berckmeyer. June said, "Cesar, let's go over and talk to Betty and Tiny." Betty and "Tiny" Labacz lived next door. Tiny was about six-five, six-six—huge man—retired army major. Betty worked as a nurse at Martin Marietta.[‡‡‡] Amazingly, they were willing, and then here comes Edmundo. He had a good home, good people because where he was before was a lousy situation. Edmundo would come over. He would sit down and talk with June. Of the three, I was probably the most difficult because I was hardheaded. Mel has always been a good politician.[§§§]

[‡‡‡] Martin Marietta Corporation owned an aerospace manufacturing plant and test site near Orlando.
[§§§] Republican Mel Martínez was elected a US senator from Florida in 2004 and served from 2005 to 2009.

We were accepted at Bishop Moore, but the education was difficult. We could talk, we could drive a car, go to the youth center. I could date, go to parties, and play football. I'm not that athletic, so I rode the bench, but I was part of it. They gave me a sense of belonging.

I graduated in 1964. Mr. Aglio came to the Berckmeyers' house and said, "Where can you go?" The Catholic Church was willing to buy my airline ticket. I called my uncle in New York, my mother's brother. He said, "Just come take care of your sister," because my sister left with another uncle and aunt in 1962, and they moved to New York.

I moved in with my uncle and aunt in Washington Heights. It was my uncle and aunt, their two kids, my sister, in maybe two-and-a-half bedrooms. I went to work for a community-owned savings and loan because I had to support my sister in a nuns' school. I was a teller. I started going to Bronx Community College two nights a week. I got different jobs at night.

When I moved to New York the idea was to get my parents out of Cuba. My uncle sent money to a friend in Mexico, and he bribed an official to get two visas to get my parents into Mexico. I repaid my uncle. I got them tickets to fly to Miami and then New York. That was in June of '65. It was quite a reunion.

Then I got my draft notice.

The children's evacuation did not become public knowledge until a Cleveland newspaper disclosed it in 1962.[51] *Miami Herald* reporter Gene Miller is credited with naming it after J. M. Barrie's fable about a boy who can fly and never grows up, made famous by the 1953 animated film *Peter Pan*.[52] The name stuck, but one irony is that Barrie's character led a group of "lost boys" without families. Another irony: many Cubans and Americans of good will created a program that turned the worst fears of Cuban parents—that they would lose control of their children—into a reality that for some lasted years.[53]

Some 141 agencies participated in the program in 110 cities in forty states, the District of Columbia, and Puerto Rico.[54] Most refugee children were well cared for; however, some suffered sexual or physical abuse, which sometimes went unaddressed despite complaints.[55] Only three died in the care of the Cuban Children's Program, and those three had chronic health problems when they arrived.[56] But exile presented emotional trials. Many children had suffered from seeing their Cuban schools closed. Some children felt abandoned when they entered *la pecera* in the Havana airport.[57] They were jolted again in the US when separated from a sibling or placed in a group home, orphanage, or foster home. Some called it a "double exile."[58]

Eloísa M. Echazábal

MIAMI, FLORIDA

Before her departure on September 6, 1961, thirteen-year-old Eloísa lived with
her parents and sister in Havana's district of Ampliación de Almendares. Her
father Ricardo Echazábal was the maître d' at the Comodoro Hotel, and her
mother, also named Eloísa, was a homemaker. Young Eloísa remembers when
the milicianos *intervened her Catholic girls' school and the nuns left.*

That was the straw that broke the camel's back because the schools began teaching communist doctrine. That's what made my parents and my aunts and uncles
decide we had to leave. They trusted Fidel. He used to say, "My revolution is as
green as the palm trees." And it was not green, it was red. They felt hurt, betrayed.
They *all* did.

My family learned about Pedro Pan through their contacts. My mother's family
was related to President Grau's family, distant relation. I remember my uncle taking
me and his son to Mongo's home. We had an appointment. When Mongo came out
to greet us, he had a little pad and a pen. He was a big guy. My uncle said, "I need
to get the children out of Cuba." He said, "Okay, what are their names?" He asked for
birthdates, and I don't remember what else. He wrote it down. "Okay, don't worry,
you'll hear from me in about a week."

My sister and I left together with three younger cousins. We caught the September sixth morning flight. I remember arriving at Camp Kendall. It was a dirt road. All
these young guys were lining up on the road. They were greeting the bus. A lot of
these kids were older boys making comments about wanting to go back to fight for
Cuba's freedom.

My father had arrived about a week before we did. He had a visa that was going
to expire, so he came. No job, no English. He was living in a room in Little Havana. He
was not at the airport, but he came to see us the next day at the camp. He talked to
the nuns, and it was decided we were going to stay. What was I going to do with my
father, together with my sister, in a small room?

We had to sleep in dormitories, in bunk beds. The girls' dormitories were run by
nuns. My sister and I were separated. Maybe ten bunk beds, five on each side, in my
dormitory, and the same in my sister's. The boys were in a separate building. During the day there were classes and activities. At night is when you heard everybody
crying.

We were there seven days. There was a blackboard on the wall in the reception area. Each day it had a new list of who was going where. My three boy cousins were sent to an orphanage in Richmond, Virginia. We were told we were going to Buffalo, New York. My sister was only eight years old and always followed me. Wherever I went, she went too. I was like her mom.

When we got to Buffalo, we went to an orphanage and another adjustment. The girls there were all American. It was difficult to relate to the girls since most of them had never had a family home before. My sister was placed on a different floor. All the nuns were Polish. They spoke English with a Polish accent. The nun on my floor was very nice. Every night after dinner she would teach me English. My sister and I were in the orphanage about two months.

I attended a parochial school. Slowly I started learning. I did pretty well in spelling, but they didn't teach me English specifically. There was no English-as-a-second-language teaching like now. I had to learn through osmosis. My sister went to school at the orphanage.

Then they transferred us to a foster home. We were in the foster home about seven months. Life in the foster home was no happier than in the orphanage. The foster family was a married couple and a daughter about a year or two younger than I. We had a social worker that came to visit us periodically. It was a nice family, but I did not feel warm and fuzzy. The lady of the house frowned upon my sister and I speaking Spanish to each other, even when we were in our shared bedroom. I always felt the daughter resented our presence. I missed my home and my parents. As in the orphanage, I cried almost every night.

My mother arrived in November. However, my parents decided to leave my sister and me in Buffalo, so we would finish the school year. I wasn't happy about that. My sister wasn't happy about that either. But we did what we were told. When we arrived in Miami from Buffalo, our parents came to the airport. I remember my father crying.

Operation Pedro Pan ended when air service between Havana and Miami halted during the Missile Crisis of 1962.[59] Thousands of Cuban children held visa waivers but could not leave.[60] Parents who had planned to join their children in the US were stranded too.[61] The Cuban Children's Program cared for refugee children through age eighteen until it disbanded in 1981.[62]

Luis M. Alvarez

NORTH HALEDON, NEW JERSEY

Twelve-year-old Luis left Havana on September 21, 1962, as part of Operation Pedro Pan, but his parents stayed behind with his older sister. His father Avelino Alvarez owned a bakery, butcher shop, and small grocery in the middle-class neighborhood of Jesús María and didn't want to abandon his business. His mother Elisa was a homemaker.

My father took me to the airport. Nobody else wanted to go. He wore dark glasses. He didn't want me to see him crying. We had a relative who worked at the airport. They had stopped going into the second floor to see the planes fly away. I remember the only person on that balcony was my father, waiting until the plane left, because our relative allowed my father to go up.

I had an uncle in the United States, but they didn't want me to live with my uncle. They knew somebody from Catholic Welfare was going to pick me up. They dropped the Matecumbe kids, and then we went to Florida City, thank God. Matecumbe was a jungle. They were sleeping in tents. In Florida City, we had houses.

The beginning was rough because you're separated from your family. After a year I went from Florida City to Opa-locka. Opa-locka was a base and had many barracks. We only used two to live in, and there were two floors. We had bunk beds. There was one barracks where the priests lived. My experience there was *very* good. They started sending kids to different places. They asked me if I wanted to go to New Mexico. I said, "No."

When we were in Florida City, we had Cuban teachers. We didn't learn much. I don't think they were prepared. Finally, we went to private schools. For grammar school everybody went to a Catholic school in Hialeah. Everybody in eighth grade was Cuban. Then I went to Pace High School.[¶¶¶] Some went to different schools.

The food was terrible. No Cuban food. I couldn't wait for friends of my parents to come pick me up. Then I would have black beans and rice and pork. I had two people that would take me out once in a while. My uncle had a friend. His wife was an excellent cook. My father had a friend who took me out. That's it. It wasn't every weekend.

My parents called once in a while. In Florida City we talked maybe once a month, but when I moved to Opa-locka, the phone calls were not as frequent. I never had a

---

¶¶¶ Monsignor Edward Pace High School is a coeducational Catholic school in Miami Gardens, Florida.

conversation with either of my parents about why they sent me here. It was: How are you doing? Are you okay? My only complaint was the food.

We had recreation twenty-four hours a day. I played a lot of sports. That's why I liked the camp, because I played everything. After a while, if I was playing baseball and I got a phone call from Cuba, I said, "Oh, shit, I've got to go answer the phone."

I spent almost four years there. My father could have left, but he didn't want to leave the business. He said he would never leave until they took his business away from him. Finally, they took the business. My father and my mother came over in '66.

A remaining mystery is why Operation Pedro Pan went on for almost two years when the two countries were such embittered enemies. The Castro regime had to know what was happening and allowed the evacuation to continue after it became publicly known. The regime's officials even honored Walsh's duplicated signature on preprinted visa waiver forms.[63]

The most plausible explanation is that Operation Pedro Pan served both countries' interests. For Washington, it initially helped Cuban parents in the underground by getting their children out of harm's way, and it served humanitarian and later propaganda purposes. For Havana, the departures helped to identify the regime's opponents.[64] At the time some Cubans believed that the Castro regime, desperate for foreign exchange, wanted the twenty-five US dollars paid for each child's airline ticket more than it wanted the child.[65]

The Pedro Pan story became the best-known tale about the early Cuban refugees, albeit one that did not always acknowledge the trauma suffered by some of them.[66] Decades later the tale resonated when a Cuban boy was found adrift in an inner tube near the Florida shore after his mother and others drowned while crossing the Florida Straits in a small boat.[67] The story of this five-year-old boy in 1999 revived memories of Operation Pedro Pan, triggered a custody battle that shook the exile community to its core, and changed America's political trajectory.

6

NO RETURN

On March 17, 1960, President Eisenhower approved a CIA plan to overthrow Castro, codenamed Operation Pluto.[1] It was straight from the Eisenhower Administration's well-worn playbook. The CIA in 1953 had joined with Britain's MI6 intelligence service in a coup to oust Prime Minister Mohammad Mossadegh of Iran, a nationalist who threatened British oil interests.[2] The agency, again at Ike's behest, in 1954 sponsored an insurrection that deposed the president of Guatemala, Jacobo Árbenz, whose leftist regime had expropriated 400,000 acres from the Boston-based United Fruit Company. Behind closed doors, Washington decisionmakers justified both covert actions to themselves as necessary in the Cold War against the Soviet Union.[3]

Operation Pluto called for a guerrilla insurgency with small teams, but CIA planners eventually switched to an amphibious landing by a US-sponsored paramilitary force of as many as three thousand troops on Cuba's southern coast near the city of Trinidad.[4] The "Trinidad Plan" required air support but, in the event of failure, offered the invaders ready escape to the nearby Escambray Mountains.[5] The recruitment of exiles had begun by then, and US-run training camps were open in Guatemala.[6] Those who enlisted were predominantly White, but Black and mixed-race exiles also joined.[7]

Soon after President Kennedy took office, the Joint Chiefs of Staff—despite their misgivings about it—told him that the plan had a "fair" chance to succeed. But Kennedy rejected the Trinidad Plan as "too spectacular."[8] Concerned that an invasion obviously sponsored by the US might provoke the Soviets into military action in Europe, the White House asked for a new plan with a "quiet landing" to downplay the American role.[9] The new landing site on the southern coast—at an inlet called Bahía de Cochinos or "Bay of Pigs"—became synonymous with colossal failure.

Luis C. Morse

MIAMI, FLORIDA

Luis went to Miami in June 1960 because his arrest had been ordered for brawling against pro-regime students at the University of Havana. His mother was still in Havana, and his father—also named Luis Morse—was at sea as captain of a Cuban merchant marine ship. Young Luis was en route to New York to stay with his uncle, but first he stopped in Miami.

I made contact with the people that were recruiting for the Bay of Pigs. The first, second day that I was here, walking in downtown Miami, I asked somebody, "Where are these offices?" The guy was a Cuban, and he said, "Oh, they're in that building over there." I was a walk-in.

I told them who I was, and they said they would get in contact with me. It took them a while to check me out with some of my friends in Havana. I was in New York a couple or three weeks. The guy that was in charge of recruiting said, "I am traveling to different cities where there are groups of Cubans, to recruit them. Right now, the people that are in the training camp are *building* the camp. You don't need to go there now because you're not going to get any training. As soon as training starts, you'll be on the first flight." So that's what I did.

From New York we traveled to Detroit, and from Detroit we traveled to Philadelphia. We traveled to Chicago. We traveled all over the place and met with different groups to convince them: We want you, we need you, to get our country back.

I got there in October. We were maybe a couple hundred. This was on the top of a mountain that had been bulldozed. They had built big concrete prefabs for different barracks and an esplanade for marching. There were two or three different shooting ranges: one for pistols and rifles; another one we would practice with mortars and 57-millimeter recoilless rifles. I learned how to shoot. Never had a rifle or a pistol in my hand before. Rained like hell.

They segregated us into black teams and gray teams. Gray teams were trained in intelligence gathering. Black teams were action teams. I was part of a black team. We did a lot of guerrilla training. The instructors were Germans, Swiss, Chinese. There were maybe a couple of Americans. The person in change was a Filipino. The theory was you were going to send the gray teams into Cuba. They would gather intelligence, identify targets, then notify base, and black teams would be sent to blow up, kill, et cetera; and then retreat to mountain ranges the gray team had identified. They would resupply us.

At some point, the philosophy of what we were going to do changed. The guerrilla thing was put aside, and they decided to do a conventional army thing. The thinking of a guerrilla fighter is intuitive and not doing things by the book. Now it went by the book. They brought in Americans—army, marines, I don't know what they were—to take over the training.

We had confidence that whoever was planning everything knew what they were doing. They didn't.

Silvia Morell Alderman

TALLAHASSEE, FLORIDA

Silvia's family was active in the US-sponsored effort to oust Castro. Her brother Jose "Kiki" Morell quit his job as a bellboy in a Miami Beach hotel to join the paramilitary force for the return to Cuba. After resigning from the Cuban Supreme Court of Justice to enter exile, Silvia's father became active on the political side of the plan to overthrow Castro.

My father was recruited to go on a tour of Latin America with other judges. They were seeking to expose to the rest of Latin America how the rule of law had been broken in Cuba. The purpose for the trip was consciousness raising and getting moral support, probably as a predicate for the Bay of Pigs invasion. The government was very involved and paid for the trip. There were several of them.

My brother went to train in Central America. He did it out of love for my father because he knew it meant a lot to him. All the boys of all the other gentlemen that were in the anti-Castro group were going. My brother was more of a party guy. If he had his druthers, he would not have been a part of that. But there was so much emotional pressure on him and his buddies—all of them—to go. He loved his dad, so that's why he did it.

The new plan called for strikes by B-26 bombers based in Nicaragua to control the airspace over a forty-mile-long landing zone. Up to fifteen hundred troops would land at three beachheads, Red, Blue, and Green. The immediate objective was to capture an airfield at Blue Beach, the town of Playa Girón, as a base for the brigade's planes.[10] If the invaders held the beachheads long enough, a provisional government of exile politicians would land, Latin American countries would recognize it, and the US could openly assist it.[11] In time an uprising was hoped for.[12]

The new plan was inferior to the Trinidad Plan. The Bay of Pigs did not have a deep-water port for supplying the invaders, now named Assault Brigade 2506 from the serial number of a recruit who died during training.[13] Castro had platoons of *milicianos* in the region.[14] There was no easy retreat because the mountains were far away, and inland from the beaches was the Ciénaga de Zapata, the impassable Zapata Swamp.[15] The new plan was codenamed Operation Zapata.

Castro was alerted by a story about the training camps published in a Guatemalan newspaper in October 1960.[16] The *New York Times*, *Miami Herald*, and *St. Louis Dispatch* followed suit.[17] So did *Time* and *The Nation* magazines.[18] Worse, Castro's spies penetrated the camps and sent films back to Havana.[19]

Not every exile taking up arms to oust Castro got involved with the brigade.

Jose A. Villalobos

MIAMI, FLORIDA

When Pepe left Havana to avoid arrest in January 1960, he followed his father, stepmother, and three brothers, while his mother remained. Before earning his law degree in Havana, Pepe had attended a military academy in Georgia. Now his aim was "to train, buy weapons, and go back."

I went to my father's house near Miami High. Then I got married, and I went to live with my wife in my father-in-law's house. I did a lot of things. I picked tomatoes, I worked on the docks, I worked at Jordan Marsh, a big store. They put me on the freight trucks. That was good because it was ten, fifteen trucks a day, so that made me fit. Then I went to work as a roofer. And training at night.

I worked with the Christian Democrats. They had a world organization. They used to have an armory, a place where you buy weapons. Each one of us would buy our weapons there—M1 rifles, boots, other weapons. Since I had training, I used to train a battalion. I did not work for the CIA because I thought it was infiltrated.

They wanted us to join with the Bay of Pigs. We thought the Bay of Pigs was not the right path, and because of the lack of knowledge of the people who were training the Cubans. There was a lack of communication. In addition, when you're training you don't take a picture and publish the picture if it's supposed to be secret training. Here, we had photographs in the newspapers showing people being trained in Guatemala. The Cubans were blinded by the fact that the Americans had never lost a war.

My suspicions were right, and I was not one of the victims.

The feints began before the landings. Sugar mills and other targets were sabotaged throughout Cuba, but the invasion went awry before it started.[20] Infiltrators sent to assist anti-Castro guerrillas were arrested.[21] A diversionary landing in Oriente aborted.[22] Air strikes began two days before the invasion, but Kennedy had reduced their number and Castro had dispersed his airplanes.[23] The strikes grounded much of Castro's air force, but a few fighters remained airworthy.[24] Forewarned, Castro ordered a nationwide roundup of suspected opponents. Thousands were detained in movie theaters, stadiums, and hotels.[25] There would be no uprising.

The night before the invasion, frogmen went ashore to place marker lights for the landing craft. *Milicianos* spotted them and opened fire.[26] Castro learned about the invasion at 2:30 that morning.[27] Concerned about a diplomatic furor if the US could not credibly deny involvement, Kennedy canceled follow-up sorties on Cuban airfields at dawn on Day One (April 17, 1961).[28] He had said publicly and told the exiles' political leaders privately that the US would not intervene militarily.[29] CIA agents and US trainers assured them and the *brigadistas* otherwise.[30]

Maria Galatas Laurencio
CORAL GABLES, FLORIDA

Maria's father Lorenzo, the doctor and town coroner in Artemisa in western Cuba's Pinar del Río province, had been skeptical of Castro, but Maria's mother Caridad was sympathetic to the revolution. "Sure enough," Maria says, "after Castro took power everything that my father had told my mother came true."

My father started to work against Fidel Castro. I guess he knew by communications with the underground that there was going to be an invasion from the Cubans that were out of the country. He started to gather medicines and medical equipment and guns and bullets, having it ready when the invasion came.

The head of the secret police, Ramiro Valdés, was our neighbor.[*] He lived two houses behind ours. His sister was close to my dad. When she came to visit, the dining room table was filled with medicines and bullets that were being packed to put in the garage. She never went past the living room.

When the invasion came, they started taking all the males into prison—in theaters, in stadiums, and everything. My dad *and* my brother were taken prisoner. My brother was only fourteen years old. They went to the movie house in town. My mother and I were left alone with all that stuff in the garage. My brother was let go in a couple of days, so he, my mom, and I started taking grocery bags to my grandma's home and my aunt's home and to the pharmacist that was our friend, trying to evacuate the garage before they came in to search.

When they were searching houses, Ramiro Valdés told the guys in the search, "Don't even bother to go into the doctor's home. I have been watching the doctor for months, and there's nothing going on there, so don't waste your time."

My father was held for a couple of weeks, then he was released to home detention. By that time my mom was on his side. She had realized what the Castro regime was.

Isis Rivero Hoffman

KEY BISCAYNE, FLORIDA

After graduation from architecture school at St. Thomas of Villanova Catholic University in 1960, Isis got a job designing city parks in Havana. Her father Armando still worked as chief bank examiner for the Cuban Federal Reserve. Isis and her sister were on their way to work on the morning of April 17, 1961, when they heard the news about the invasion.

My sister was the controller of the García Shipping Line.[†] It's the line that lent the ships to the invasion. Our architectural office had been moved to the Stock Exchange Building, a beautiful old cast-iron building with a center patio, right next to the port.[‡] Her offices were there too. Since we both worked in the same building, we went to work together.

---

* Ramiro Valdés, a veteran of the attack on the Moncada Barracks and the voyage of the *Granma*, served as interior minister and in other high-ranking positions of the Cuban government until 2019.

† The CIA leased cargo ships from the Ward-García Line owned by Cuban Eduardo García, including the *Atlántico*, *Caribe*, *Houston*, and *Río Escondido*, to transport troops and materiel to the landing zone.

‡ Opened in 1909, the five-story Renaissance-style Stock Exchange Building was also known as the Lonja del Comercio or Commerce Market. It served as Havana's stock exchange until 1959 and was restored in 1995.

The day of the invasion, we were going to work at 7:30 in the morning, and we heard on the radio that there had been an invasion at the Bay of Pigs, and that the García Line had lent the ships. My sister froze. She had *no* knowledge of this. The entire García family was in this country. She said to me, "What do I do?" I said, "If you don't go, it will look like you knew something about this, so you *have* to go to work."

Sure enough, they had intervened the building because of the García Line offices being there. Our handbags were searched by militia guys. I went to my office, and she went to hers, and the government had intervened at the company. Here she is, the highest officer in the company still in Cuba and not aware that the ships had been loaned to the invasion. I think they realized that she was caught by surprise.

When we went home for lunch, the bell rang. There were two people from the Federal Reserve, asking for my father. They weren't uniformed, but they were people who worked at the bank, who knew my father. Whoever didn't go to work that day they thought there was a reason they didn't go. My father had been home for about a month. He had had a bad bout of pneumonia. The men took him away. We found out later that my father's chauffeur went to the bank and said my father was fine. He had a little business on the side, and my father helped him with that, but he was a die-hard Castro supporter. He was envious of others.

For a week we didn't know where my father was. My mother sat in a dark room and didn't want to talk to anybody. He was in La Cabaña. His librarian at the Federal Reserve, who had been to the house to work with him once a week, was a communist. She wasn't a new communist; she was an old member of the party. She knew my father had been ill and was recovering. When she found out that my father had been put in jail, she raised hell until she found out which jail he was in and got him released. My father didn't go back to work.

It was a scary moment in Havana.

Emilio Cueto
WASHINGTON, DC

Seventeen-year-old Emilio also went to the Stock Exchange Building on April 17, 1961. He had completed his bachillerato *studies at Belén in 1960. Too young to enter the University of Havana at age sixteen, he audited law classes at St. Thomas of Villanova Catholic University and watched with alarm as the revolution turned radical. His widowed mother worried about him.*

The centers of my life were Catholic, anticommunist, and prodemocratic, so I was marked.

My father had a colleague, a dear friend. My mother begged him to convince me that I should leave Cuba. He invited me to lunch and said, "We think the best thing is for you to go to Spain." This must have been January of '61. The brother of my paternal grandfather had a place in a village near Asturias. The problem became how do you get a visa to go to Spain? By then the American embassy had closed. Everybody was trying to get a Spanish visa. The queue was incredible.

The mother of a close classmate was active in the regional organization of the Galician community in Cuba. She said, "What are you going to do in a little town in *Spain*? I have a better solution for you. I can get you to the US, where you will study in the university." She said, "Bring me the passport."

Life went on. Every day something would happen: Another communist would be in power; the conservative newspaper was shut down, and the others were closed. Everything was signaling that life would change for the worse. We got the exit permit at some point.

On April fourteenth, which was a Friday, my classes ended at six, and I arrived home. My mother said a Jesuit priest had called. Of course, you would not talk on the phone because we thought our phones were tapped. About 7:15 or 7:30, I walked to another home in Vedado, and there he was. I knew him. He said, "Here's your passport. You have a Jamaican visa." I would go in a plane to Jamaica. My instructions were to get off in Miami and just give my name. My name would be on a list of waived visas, and I would be allowed in.

I was told, "You're leaving on Monday morning," the seventeenth of April. "You go that morning very early to the Lonja del Comercio," a commercial building in Old Havana. "You go to the third floor to this travel agency. A lady named Teté will give you the ticket." We woke up in the morning and found out Castro had closed the *airport*. Castro sensed something on the fifteenth of April. He knows the invasion is pending. This is all happening that weekend on which I am supposed to leave on Monday.

Monday, I went to downtown Havana to see the lady with the ticket. The lady says, "The airport is closed, but here's your ticket. You probably won't go because the invasion is arriving." I got home, and it was pandemonium. My aunt used to work for a magistrate. He had been taken to jail, so my aunt was crying. I called a couple of friends, and their mothers said, "My son has been taken to jail." It was just *crazy*.

After Kennedy gave the stand-down order for follow-up air raids by the exiles' Nicaragua-based planes, Castro's remaining aircraft had air superiority.[31] The

Green Beach landings were canceled.[32] Castro's pilots sank the supply ship *Río Escondido*; the brigade's ammunition stock, communication gear, and aviation fuel went down with it.[33] With some of Castro's fighters still in the air and the aviation fuel gone, the brigade's airplanes could not use the Playa Girón airfield after it was secured.[34]

Kennedy reinstated the remaining air strikes for Day Two (April 18), but fog prevented the brigade's planes from attacking Castro's aircraft.[35] When US planes dropped supplies, they were lost in the swamp or at sea. By the end of Day Two, 20,000 Cuban troops with artillery and tanks had backed the 1,300 *brigadistas* up against the sea at Playa Girón.[36] Castro was determined to prevent the landing of the exiles' provisional government.[37]

The Joint Chiefs urged Kennedy to order US air strikes from the nearby carrier *Essex* on Day Three (April 19), but he refused. Castro's forces pushed toward Playa Girón from three directions, so Kennedy authorized the US Navy to evacuate the brigade. As Castro's forces closed in, American jets overflew the retreating brigade but were denied permission to fire on the Cubans unless fired upon.[38] A few *brigadistas* took to sea, but most fled into the swamp.[39]

Luis C. Morse

MIAMI, FLORIDA

When Luis joined the Second Battalion aboard the transport ship Houston *for the voyage to Cuba, he was surprised to find that his father, the merchant marine captain Luis Morse, was the skipper. Second Battalion was tasked with holding the village of Playa Larga at Red Beach and its road to Playa Girón while other units held the airfield at Blue Beach.[40]*

Our objective was to attack and hold for seventy-two hours. They would land a government in exile, and then at the end of seventy-two hours, the United States could participate, barefaced. So, we were supposed to hold.

The landing was a disaster. What the brains behind the invasion thought they had seen on the beaches as clouds were not clouds. They were reefs. Our little landing craft got their bottoms ripped in those reefs, and the landing craft that we had were Sears aluminum boats. Some arrived and were able to turn back and keep bringing back. It was a slow, slow landing.

Then the sun came up, and Second Battalion was all landed. We were supposed to take Playa Larga and hold. Suddenly we heard planes, we looked up, and there was a Sea Fury—not ours—and that Sea Fury made a beeline for the *Houston*, so my father veered off and tried to hide.[§] We lost sight of the ship because it was a small inlet.

The next thing we saw was a plane shooting rockets and a lot of smoke, a lot of explosions. The rocket went through the covers for the cargo hold and made a big hole in the bottom of the ship, so it was sinking. Dad aimed toward land and that gave time. The other battalion was able to get off the ship and reach safety. I thought Dad was dead. That was the worst moment of my life. I never felt so low.

The second day is when they started flowing in. There's only one road into that little town, Playa Larga, and there was swamp on either side of the road. We did not have to spread our fire. It was concentrated on the road, so we were able to hold off pretty well.

We got ordered to retreat to Playa Girón, the big town, and make a defense on the road from Playa Larga to Playa Girón. We held and held. We ran out of ammunition, totally. We got orders that we had failed. There were going to be no reinforcements, no nothing, and those who could, should try to reach the north shore or the mountains.

The brigade held for sixty-four hours.[41] Castro's forces captured 1,189 *brigadistas*. Casualties included 114 dead.[42] Castro's losses were believed to be 1,650 dead and 2,000 wounded.[43]

Pedro A. Freyre

MIAMI, FLORIDA

Pedro was too young to serve in the brigade, but his brother Tito and brother-in-law Alfredo "Cuco" Cervantes trained in Guatemala, and shipped out from Nicaragua for the invasion. Tito was a forward air controller; Cuco was in the infantry.

My brother Tito is one of the most courageous people I know, not because he's a daredevil. Quite the contrary: it's because he overcame his fears. Cuco went with him. They landed. They were betrayed.

My brother tried to escape, disguised as a civilian, but they identified him. There was a firefight, and two of the guys with him were wounded. Some *milicianos* were killed, and later they said, "He's a common criminal because he committed murder," so there was a moment where it looked like he wasn't coming back.

---

§ The Hawker Sea Fury was a British-made propeller-driven fighter.

My brother-in-law was shot in the leg. He was captured and put in a tractor-trailer. This is an incident that is burned in our memory. A hundred and fifty-six prisoners were put in there. They shut the doors. It took hours to get to Havana, and when they opened the door, there were a couple of inches of sweat and urine on the floor because of all that condensation. They couldn't breathe, and nine of them were asphyxiated. One of them was Cuco, twenty-six years old.

My sister Rosa Maria was a widow at seventeen with a six-month-old baby.

The Bay of Pigs debacle prompted several government studies to determine what went wrong. Two reports placed differing degrees of blame on Kennedy for his misuse of air power and the CIA for mismanagement, but the agency's defenders challenged those reports' impartiality.[44] CIA leaders blamed Kennedy. The CIA's official history of the fiasco was written later but kept secret until 1998, with the most sensitive portion withheld until 2016. It reflected Washington finger-pointing, but it also asked embarrassing questions about the agency's decisions.[45] To this day the invasion remains shrouded in controversy. One certainty is that Kennedy publicly took the blame for the failure, saying, "I am the responsible officer of the government."[46]

On the island the refugee exodus resumed.[47] Castro threatened to try the *brigadistas* before a revolutionary tribunal unless a ransom was paid in the form of bulldozers worth $28 million.[48] Washington opposed Castro's proposal because the bulldozers could be used for military purposes.[49] The ostensibly private committee negotiating with Castro then rejected his revised proposal for farm tractors worth $28 million plus "indemnification" for losses from the invasion.[50] Five *brigadistas* were executed for offenses while serving the Batista regime, and the few other *batistianos* went to prison.[51] The remaining *brigadistas* were tried en masse later and sentenced to imprisonment for thirty years.[52]

Luis C. Morse

MIAMI, FLORIDA

After the order to escape was given, Luis, Tito Freyre, and a few others fled into the swamp and changed into civilian clothes. After several days, most of that time without food or water, they had a shootout with milicianos, killing two. Luis was severely wounded in his left shoulder and lost consciousness. At first, Luis and Tito were held for trial on murder charges.

When I woke up, I was in a warehouse. A young guy was yelling at my face, "You killed my uncle. I'm going to kill you." I said, "Oh, shut up," and fainted again. The next time I woke up, I was at a first aid station and a nice nurse was telling me, "They have a TV crew there because they want to film you while they sew you up. They want to see you scream." She took a tongue depressor, broke it, and gave me the tongue depressor so I could bite on it. I was biting and making faces, but I wasn't yelling. Then I fainted again.

The next time I woke up, I was in the military hospital in Camp Columbia. They realized that the guys in the first aid station that had sewn me together had left an air pocket, and it was becoming infected, so they had to open it up, clean it, and resew the wound.

Castro started the talks about selling us back to the United States. He said, "You guys choose the people you want, and I will allow them to travel to the United States and negotiate with the United States to pay your ransom." All different groups selected, and the navy guys voted for my dad to be part of the group to go negotiate.

The day they were supposed to come to the States, my father told Castro, "Commander, I'm sorry, but I cannot go." Castro said, "Why?" My father said, "My son is on the list of the not-negotiable because of 'war crimes.' How can I be expected to negotiate for the rest of the brigade if I can't negotiate for my own son?" The captain who was with Castro said, "He's one of the two we are holding for trial." Castro overruled the captain.

My father was allowed to visit me because he was leaving. There I am in my room in the Camp Columbia hospital, and in walks my father, who I thought was dead. From the worst day of my life to the best day of my life, all in one month.

Afterwards we were put in with the rest of the brigade at Príncipe prison.¶ They did a trial. They condemned us to thirty years in jail. There was no torture, there were no guards coming in to hit us. Mostly it was bean soup, soups with parts of animals we didn't recognize. It wasn't good tasting, but it was a sustainable diet.

After the bulldozer talks failed, the *brigadistas'* families took the lead in seeking the prisoners' release. They formed the Cuban Families Committee.[53] New York lawyer James Donovan, who had negotiated the exchange of a Soviet spy for a downed American U-2 pilot held by the Soviets, agreed to assist.[54] Castro raised his demand to $62 million but let sixty sick or wounded prisoners go to the US to build support for the ransom.[55] As part of their lobbying campaign, the young infantryman Luis Morse and others appealed for help on television's *Ed Sullivan Show*. Luis also appeared on the game show *To Tell the Truth*.[56]

¶ Castillo del Príncipe in Havana is an eighteenth-century Spanish fortress that served as a prison.

Kennedy was determined to oust Castro, so the president in 1962 authorized Operation Mongoose, a covert program of sabotage and hit-and-run raids.[57] The CIA's Miami station, headquartered on the University of Miami's south campus, became the largest outside of Washington.[58] From afar Cuban exiles wondered if they would ever go home.

Diana Sawaya-Crane

TALLAHASSEE, FLORIDA

Eight-year-old Diana and her sister left Havana on November 6, 1959, with their mother and grandmother so they could join their father Assad, who had a job selling insurance in Venezuela. Their mother Hilda got a job as a biology teacher in the town of Coro. The family watched events in Cuba expectantly, waiting for Castro to fall so they could return.

Dad got a promotion to work in Mérida, a beautiful city in the Andes. The nearest place my mother could be placed was San Juan de Colón, a small town in the southwestern part of the country. Colón is an old town located on a plateau in a tropical rainforest, surrounded by mountains. It had a population of less than fifteen thousand people. Compared to all the concrete in Havana, Colón seemed like paradise.

We were the only Cubans. We were much taller than the other kids. We had different last names. We talked with a different accent, so we had to learn a whole bunch of new words. But I don't remember them treating us badly. And, of course, my mother taught at the high school, so when we started high school, *that* was difficult. My identity started to change in the sense that I was Cuban, but I wanted to fit in.

Dad decided to come back to Colón so he could be with the family. He started a poultry business. We moved to a house that had approximately an acre of land in the back. We had fifteen hundred to two thousand egg-laying hens. We had chickens that were prepared for sale to supermarkets in another city, not in our little town.

After we left Cuba, my cousin Luis Morse left. We know him as Luisito. You know, in Spanish, especially Cubans, we use diminutives, so there are "itos" and "itas," suffixes used to express affection. Luisito's dad, *tío* Luis, who was a captain in the Cuban merchant marine, jumped ship in Ecuador, and made his way to Miami. Luisito's mother and his sister came to the United States.

Our parents shielded us from the terrible events taking place in Cuba. The only memory I have related to the Bay of Pigs has to do with my grandmother. She was an expert in the needle arts. After lunch she would recline in her rocking chair next to the window in her bedroom, crocheting and listening to the radio.

After the invasion, many members of the brigade were captured, including our *tío* Luis and our cousin Luisito. As names were released, they were read on the Venezuelan radio. I recall my mother telling us to keep my grandmother distracted from the radio around a certain time in the afternoon. Later, I learned it was so that if the names of her captured son and grandson were read on the radio, she would not hear it. We knew what had happened, that our *tío* Luis and our cousin Luisito had been in prison, and that they were *heroes*. Thankfully, my grandmother never knew.

Our parents were very patriotic and instilled in us a sense of love and loyalty toward Cuba. We never became Venezuelan citizens, so they had to get the visas extended to stay there. Whenever we celebrated a birthday, Christmas, New Year's, or any important date, they played the Cuban national anthem on this little record player followed by the Venezuelan national anthem. We all stood, hand over our hearts, and sang. I remember both my mother and father tearing up. It was sad.

Adolfo Henriques
KEY BISCAYNE, FLORIDA

When seven-year-old Adolfo and his two brothers got off the plane in Kingston, Jamaica, with their parents on January 17, 1961, the family was carrying thirteen dollars. Their father Charles had managed Cuban operations for Canada's Bank of Nova Scotia before the regime took it over in December 1960. He and his wife Maria and their children had only the belongings they could carry.

A few weeks later, the bank offered him a job in Jamaica, at a lower level than he had in Cuba, because it was the only available job. He had to take a couple of steps down. He accepted any job he could get.

My parents realized that maybe this is going to take longer. We have to go to school and need a place to live. My dad's compensation limited our housing options, but we got fortunate. A coworker at the bank had a large home on the top of a hill. They took us in as boarders. It was a three-story house. I think they had eight servants. Breakfast, lunch, and dinner were prepared for you. You dressed for dinner every night.

After the first two years in Kingston, we moved to a home owned by the Bank of

Nova Scotia. Pretty much through the rest of the time that my dad worked for Scotiabank, they lived in one of the bank's homes. I did not have the experiences that many people did. We lived comfortably and well. I was lucky.

Jamaica was one of the "in-transit" points where Cubans would wait for their visas to enter the United States, Mexico, or wherever they were going. We spent a lot of time helping Cubans in-transit through Kingston. Many of them needed access to the bank. Money was wired to them from family in the United States or other places, and my father was one of the few people who spoke Spanish. There were *constant* trips to the airport to pick somebody up, going to what they called El Refugio, which was a Catholic-supported home where people stayed when they came to Kingston. My parents stopped by weekly and saw people they knew or met new ones. This continued for years.

My father listened to the radio every night, hungry for any information on Cuba and waiting for the end of the Castro regime, thinking, This can't last. Their *hope* continued to build every day, but after about five years, it was a less constant topic of conversation. We never asked when we were going back to Cuba.

For me Jamaica became home.

During the renewed negotiations to free the *brigadistas*, the US discovered in October 1962 that the Soviet Union had placed offensive nuclear weapons in Cuba. Kennedy ordered a naval "quarantine" to halt the buildup. The crisis ended with the Soviets withdrawing their missiles. In exchange Kennedy made a conditional pledge that the US would not invade Cuba and a tacit promise to withdraw obsolete US missiles from Turkey.[59] Cuban exiles considered Kennedy's no-invasion pledge a second betrayal.[60]

Castro and the Families Committee settled on a $53 million ransom of food, medicine, and cash, and the ransom was raised with help from the Kennedy Administration. Food and medicine makers donated the goods for a tax deduction.[61] When the first shipment reached Havana on December 23, 1962, the *brigadistas* began to return to the US.[62] They were flown to Homestead Air Force Base in South Florida for a reunion with their families at Miami's Dinner Key Auditorium. The last group arrived before dawn on December 25, 1962.[63]

President and Mrs. Kennedy welcomed the brigade at a ceremony in Miami's Orange Bowl on December 29, 1962.[64] After the brigade's leaders were briefed privately on the CIA's new clandestine campaign against the Castro regime, they swallowed their bitterness at Kennedy's decision not to provide US air cover and, at the ceremony, presented him with their battle flag.[65] His remarks to the forty thousand were greeted with chants of "*¡Libertad! ¡Libertad!* [Freedom! Freedom!]" and "*¡Guerra! ¡Guerra!* [War! War!]"[66]

Silvia Morell Alderman

TALLAHASSEE, FLORIDA

Silvia and her parents knew the long-awaited landings were imminent because her father, a former Supreme Court judge, was close to the exiles' leadership. "We knew it was taking place the night it was taking place," Silvia says. "I remember my parents pacing all night." Silvia's sister and her family were still in Cuba.

My sister and my brother-in-law and family had moved into the beach house at Varadero to get out of harm's way. My sister was at home with the kids, and a neighbor ran over and said, "Turn on the TV." They turned on the TV, and my brother was on TV with his arms over his head, walking in a group of prisoners. He was sentenced to thirty years in prison, and they were moved to the Isle of Pines. He was able to write to us for a while, but then the correspondence ceased.

We were given the news that the boys would be brought back to meet their families at Dinner Key Auditorium. They flew them into Homestead and then bused them up. We were there for a whole day as the flights of soldiers came in. Nothing. We knew he was alive because a friend of his had been let out early for medical reasons.

We went home, and the next day we came back and waited. And waited. And waited. He was on the last flight. They marched in and went across this stage as their names were called out, and the families met them after they stepped off this dais. It was quite a night. It really was.

Pedro A. Freyre

MIAMI, FLORIDA

Pedro had a privileged vantage point to watch these events unfold. After Castro's ransom proposal for the bulldozers died in an impasse, Pedro's lawyer father Ernesto became a central figure in the second negotiations for the release of the brigadistas.

My father became the secretary of the Families Committee. He was an *excellent* negotiator. He was one of the negotiators of the deal, and he met with Fidel Castro five times with that American attorney, Jack Donovan. He said Fidel Castro was *extremely* intelligent and a man of tremendous charisma. He recognized Fidel as his enemy, Fidel recognized him as his enemy, but they treated each other with respect. He said the Cubans changed positions a couple of times, but at the end of the day, they did what they said they were going to do.

My father was in Cuba in one of the negotiating sessions during the Missile Crisis. That was scary. We spent a week here thinking that it would be the end of the world or that we would never see my father again. It is astonishing after what happened that the negotiations went on. Cuba desperately needed the medicines. Finally, everything came to fruition, and it was Christmas Day 1962. We were at the Dinner Key Auditorium. I'll *never* forget that day. The brigade came. They were dressed in khaki uniforms. It was an incredible moment.

Just a few days after that there was an event at the Orange Bowl. President Kennedy came. I was there. I saw it. My father was on the grandstand with the president. Kennedy made a wonderful, beautiful speech, and they gave him the brigade's flag. He said, "I'll return it to you in a free Havana." We're still waiting.**

Many people thought he betrayed the brigade, that he chickened out. That feeling got exacerbated with the Missile Crisis because the sense was that he lost another golden opportunity. Of course, that was viewed through the lens of Cuban exiles, not through the American lens. We now know better. As an American, I certainly understand why he did it the way he did it. I think it would have been a *catastrophe* if they had invaded.

My mother, who was the realist, told my father, "You have to stop. You have to make a living for the family. *¡Esta cosa Cuba! La cosa de Cuba tiene que terminar* [This Cuba thing! The Cuban thing has to end]. I don't want to hear about Cuba. I don't want to talk about Cuba. These are bad people. I hate their guts. I'm worried about our family here. That's the end of it."

At that point we accepted that we were here for the long haul.

Kennedy racheted up the US isolation policy. He prohibited almost all imports from Cuba and almost all exports to the island.[67] The State Department tightened rules to prevent US citizens from traveling to Cuba.[68] The Treasury

---

** In 1976 the brigade's veterans won the return of their silk battle flag from the John F. Kennedy Presidential Library in Boston. It is now displayed in the Bay of Pigs Museum in Miami's Little Havana.

Department froze Cuban assets in the US and barred banks from transactions with Cubans.[69] Under US pressure, the Organization of American States (OAS) endorsed a hemispheric ban on travel to and financial transactions with Cuba.[70]

Castro allowed the ships and aircraft that delivered the ransom to bring 9,700 refugees to the US.[71] By one estimate, 150,000 Cubans wanted to leave.[72] But the Kennedy Administration did not allow a resumption of commercial air service to Havana.[73] Cuban refugees entering the US from 1959 through 1962 totaled 248,070.[74]

The First Wave had ended.

Carmen Leiva Roiz

MIAMI, FLORIDA

With their two children, Carmen and her husband Juan were settled in Connecticut, where Juan worked as an in-house accountant for a corporation. Carmen's parents remained in Havana and expected Castro to fall. So did Carmen and Juan.

My husband went into Manhattan to register for the invasion. They never called him. The invasion came, and nothing happened. I remember being glued to the radio, to the phone, calling friends in Miami. I had friends who went to the university with me that died in the invasion. It was devastating.

My parents left after the Missile Crisis. They managed to leave on an empty medicine ship that left from Havana with refugees. They had to leave everything. My father's bank account had been frozen. They stayed with us for a couple of months, but they didn't like Connecticut. They decided for them it was Miami. My father wanted to be with his friends. All his cronies were in Miami.

For some refugees the struggle went on. They formed paramilitary bands and raided by air and by boat but without real prospects for ousting Castro.[75] After Operation Mongoose was terminated for lack of success, the Kennedy Administration set up new covert initiatives that included attacks on power plants, sugar mills, and oil refineries.[76] Kennedy in 1963 clamped down on raids from

US territory to prevent attacks on Soviet ships.[77] Exile leaders denounced him for seeming to accept Castro's regime.[78]

In 1963 Castro made secret overtures to Kennedy about opening a back channel between the two leaders.[79] Kennedy tried to set up a line of communication that would minimize the risk of disclosure before his 1964 reelection campaign.[80] The president's chief goal was to stop Castro's export of revolution to Latin American countries, and he asked his advisors to "start thinking along more flexible lines" about Cuba.[81]

In a Florida speech on November 18, 1963, Kennedy warned Havana about Cuba serving as a base for "forces beyond this hemisphere" to subvert Latin countries. "This, and this alone, divides us," he declared. "As long as this is true, nothing is possible. Without it, everything is possible."[82] Privately Kennedy sent a more nuanced message to Castro through the French journalist Jean Daniel.[83] Castro and Daniel were in discussions on November 22, 1963, when they were told to turn on the radio.[84]

Paul S. George

MIAMI, FLORIDA

Paul graduated from Miami High School and enrolled at Miami's new community college, which opened as the First Wave began to arrive. Living in a neighborhood becoming known as Little Havana, Paul followed news of the Bay of Pigs invasion and the Missile Crisis.

There was a lot of optimism when news of the invasion came. Many people believed that Castro would fall or that he would be taken out. The exiles believed it. They went to the churches and prayed. I was at Dade County Junior College; today it's Miami Dade College. We demonstrated right over here on Cuban Memorial Boulevard. There was a lot of hope.

And just as soon as it started, it was over. It was a shock. Even more than that, heartbreak. Kennedy became suspect because the air support that they believed was promised wasn't there. A year and a half later, with the Missile Crisis and Kennedy's assurance that he wouldn't invade Cuba, he became the great villain in this story. There were people who just reviled him, even after he was assassinated.

Mercedes Wangüemert-Peña

AUSTIN, TEXAS

Mercedes witnessed her stepfather's homecoming with the brigade in December 1962 and attended the Orange Bowl ceremony with President and Mrs. Kennedy. In Spanish the First Lady told the brigadistas *that she would use their example to teach her two-year-old son about courage.*[85] *"The whole house came down," Mercedes says. "They couldn't stand him."*

I didn't get to spend too much time with my stepfather until we moved to California, which was about three weeks later. My mother's brother had moved out there. In Cuba, he had worked for AT&T, and they offered him a job in LA. Usually with Cubans, somebody establishes a beachhead somewhere, and others follow. Culver City was the beachhead.

My mother wanted to leave Miami because there was too much politicking going on—all the political feuds; you raised money to go back to invade, whether as guerrillas or to bomb. She just wanted a regular life. My stepfather wanted a regular life.

After we moved there, other people from the Bay of Pigs started moving there. Back then when one Cuban family moved to a neighborhood, everybody moved there. There were a whole bunch of them in that neighborhood, and our house became their headquarters. They would get together with my parents. Then we started hearing the stories about how they had been treated in prison. They were kept for days with the lights on, standing up, things like that.

The big thing was Kennedy got killed.

The day that Kennedy died, that night they all came to the house. It was an open house. Here I am in the living room, watching Walter Cronkite and crying my eyes out, and they're all sitting around the dining table, a house full of veterans, laughing, joking, having a great time, toasting Kennedy's death. For years I was sure *they* were the ones that did it.

For all but the most implacable opponents of the Castro regime, the failure at the Bay of Pigs and the resolution of the Missile Crisis meant one thing: they were not going home. It was a searing experience that they never forgot.

Marielena Alejo Villamil
CORAL GABLES, FLORIDA

Marielena stayed in Tampa with her mother, sister, and grandmother. Her dairyman father Raúl had learned to fly as a hobby in Havana and had many pilot friends. They talked him into joining the brigade as a flier. "I had no idea where he was," Marielena says.

My dad was a good family man. He insisted on coming to see us, so in March 1961, they let him get out of Guatemala. He came to Tampa. That's when I found out that he was in training. He had flown over Cuba in the bombers, throwing pamphlets and stuff. He stayed for a week or two or whatever it was, and he said, "Okay, I have to go back."

He came to Miami and got an ear infection. They wouldn't let him go back to Guatemala until it got cleared. Guess when he got cleared: April sixteenth, at the airport, waiting with three other pilots to go to the invasion. They never let him go. The ear infection saved him.

On April seventeenth he went back to Tampa, and the invasion started. When it was over, my dad said, "We have to look forward. We're going to be in this country the rest of our lives. By ourselves, we don't have a chance. If the Americans are not going to help us, nothing's going to happen. We're here, we're going to be here, and we're *never* going back to Cuba." That was his rationale. And he was right.

We just kept going. We had to work and go to school and have our life here. We had to survive. For *years* we didn't talk about Cuba in my house.

Mario Cartaya
FORT LAUDERDALE, FLORIDA

Mario and his brother went to school in Miami while their accountant father Ignacio worked in a commercial laundry. Their mother Leida delivered a baby girl and eventually went to work as a teacher's aide. The rest of their large extended family remained in Havana.

We thought about going back until the day I was sitting with my dad, watching the news of the Missile Crisis. It became apparent that no other invasion of Cuba would be allowed. My father said, "Looks like we're here to stay." That was 1962.

The first years were difficult years for us: tough years for my dad, worse years for my mom. For me, it wasn't that bad. I missed my grandparents and uncles, but I had school. I had baseball. I had my childhood to live. That wasn't the case with my dad or my mom. They had to provide and protect.

My father was a realist. He said, "I've got to begin turning my attention toward this being the rest of our lives. How do I take care of my family? Whatever money I save, I use it to bring relatives from Cuba or buy a house"—which we did, in Hialeah. The whole emphasis of our lives changed, and the way that we looked at ourselves changed, based on my father's realism. This was permanent. We wanted roots.

From my mother's viewpoint, it was tough. The realization that she would never see her parents again was difficult to accept. My grandfather got sick. He died without ever meeting my sister. Then my uncle got sick. He died. Finally, my grandmother got sick, and she died too. We couldn't speak with them. We couldn't visit them. We found out through letters that made their way to us in Miami through Spain. Losing her parents without ever seeing them again was *very* painful to my mother.

That was the beginning of my subconscious burying painful memories. I remember my father telling me, "Don't cry. You've got to be strong for your mom." I didn't let them down. I never cried until I visited Cuba.

7

LA REVOLUCIÓN

For those still on the island an even greater upheaval was to come.

The failure of the Bay of Pigs invasion enabled Castro to consolidate power.[1] He ruled out elections, aligned Cuba with the Soviet Union, and stocked up on weapons from Moscow.[2] Guevara eliminated any doubt about the regime's intentions when he said the Cuban Revolution would be characterized "by the possession by the people of the means of production."[3] In time the regime completed the nationalization of virtually all enterprises, including butcher shops, bars, and laundries.[4]

As Castro's radical program and police state took root during the sixties, more Cubans wanted to leave, including some who had originally stayed because of Fidel's promises. Many were working class or lower middle class and suffered hardships due to the regime's program and the US isolation policy.[5]

Isaac M. "Ike" Flores

WINTER PARK, FLORIDA

Born in Deming, New Mexico, the son of a laborer and a waitress, Ike joined the Associated Press while a student at the University of New Mexico on the GI Bill. By 1965 he was assigned to the foreign desk in New York and, fluent in English and Spanish, began seeking accreditation as the AP's resident correspondent in Havana. He got it and, leaving his family in New York, traveled to Mexico and then Cuba.

It took me about two hours to clear the airport. They went through everything, squeezing toothpaste out of tubes, opening my sealed tobacco tins—I was smoking a pipe at that time—and going through my luggage wholesale.

I got my first look at the Plaza de la Revolución where Fidel made his speeches: a giant statue of José Martí, the big caricatures of Che Guevara that you see on television. It was a totally new, eye-opening experience. The first or second thing to strike me was the propaganda spewing out of the radio and television twenty-four hours a day.

Everything had deteriorated—hotels, apartments, whole sections of Havana. The country was woefully short of construction materials—tools, paint, things like that. Everything was rationed, so there were long lines of Cubans with their ration books at *bodegas,* which are small neighborhood grocery stores. There was a very active black market.

This was the middle of 1965. By then, the *barbudos* had managed to screw up everything. Infrastructure was old and dilapidated because they had confiscated American and European companies that ran that infrastructure—the telephone systems, sugar mills, processing plants of all kinds. The Cubans tried to maintain that infrastructure, but they didn't have the spare parts, they didn't have the know-how.* Cuba was producing hardly *anything* that it needed in the way of consumer items. They did grow some foodstuffs they needed, but certainly not all.

You were lucky to get running water in your home, and you were a rarity if you got hot water. Electricity was in short supply. Neighborhoods would get blacked out from time to time. Sugar, rum, and cigars were almost completely off the market so that they could be exported and bring in foreign currency, which was badly needed in the mid-sixties.

The Soviet Union had a large presence. They were all over the port, unloading all kinds of materiel—heavy equipment, military vehicles, and large crates full of who knows what. The Soviets brought oil into Cuba. In return, they received Cuban sugar, a geopolitical presence, and a strategic military base in the Caribbean. The Soviets established their own colony in Havana. I saw them in bars and restaurants and nightlife places.

Cubans had their good times. There were restaurants if they could afford it. There were street parties, concerts, movies, and impromptu musical get-togethers. The Soviet Union brought in the Bolshoi Ballet. They and other Eastern Bloc countries sent athletes for sporting events to compete with Cubans. And there was always baseball.

---

* With so much infrastructure and industrial machinery on the island made in the US, Washington's trade embargo prevented the sale of spare parts for repairs to keep that equipment in operation.

Cubans had two leagues. Teams played each other throughout the year, and all of this culminated in a "world series."

There was a smattering of resistance at the University of Havana, but there were no known organized resistance groups. They were in exile. Small groups carried out sabotage in the countryside. These were isolated cases that posed no great threat.

The prisons were *overflowing* with political prisoners. I met with some of their relatives, and they told me what those people were undergoing and how they were being treated. You've got to realize the prison system was vast. In La Cabaña living conditions were *awful*. Prisoners received two meals a day and sometimes not that. There were vermin in the food and crawling all over their quarters. There were no showers. Isla de Pinos was no better.

The G-2 was a feared organization. You could say or do almost anything and get thrown in jail. They just picked you up. They could torture you into confessing to anything they wanted you to confess to. They used electrical prods, beatings, fists, clubs. I was told they would attach electrodes to the genitals. That's where a lot of prisoners came from. Others were caught in acts of rebellion. Most of them did not have trials. Castro had show trials for high-profile people.

I had restricted travel. I wanted to take a familiarization trip to Santiago, and eventually the foreign ministry came through. I was only there for a couple of days. Fidel had recruited people there to join his revolution, and I wanted to find out whether they still believed that way. There were many who believed that way despite the shortages.

I managed to get another trip out into the countryside. The rural people put up with all kinds of sacrifices because Fidel kept making big promises. And he *did* bring schoolhouses and teachers out into the countryside. He *did* bring a visiting doctor or a nurse into some of these villages, which they'd never had before. That kept them inspired and hopeful. It's hard for people from the outside to understand what the feeling was in support of Castro. There was dissension, but there *was* support.

It was always called the revolution. To this day it's called *la revolución*.

Castro's initial development strategy sought to elevate rural living standards. Some 150 new villages were built.[6] Camp Columbia was converted into an education complex for 10,000 students, including many of the 85,000 rural young people who got new scholarships.[7] Havana was allowed to become rundown as resources were directed to the countryside.[8]

The regime adopted an industrialization plan to reduce reliance on sugar, but the plan faltered due to mismanagement and the US trade embargo.[9] Sugar production plummeted from 6.7 million tons in 1961 to 3.8 million tons in 1963. Since sugar accounted for 90 percent of Cuba's foreign earnings, Fidel put off industrialization, reemphasized sugar, and got the 1965 harvest up to 6 million tons.[10] Still, per capita income fell 15 percent from 1959.[11]

Cubans of color were rewarded for supporting the revolution. The regime ended racial discrimination in public and private places and gave people of color new opportunities for jobs and education.[12] But it exercised iron rule through apparatchiks and the G-2.[13] Political commissars were installed in the military, factories, and schools. Cuba's prisons held an estimated 50,000 political prisoners.[14] By 1966 they included Polita and Ramón "Mongo" Grau and Albertina O'Farrill of the clandestine network that got visa waivers for Pedro Pan children.[15] Religious believers, gay people, sex workers, and dissenters for a time were confined in work camps.[16]

Gabriel Castillo

MIAMI, FLORIDA

Gaby's mother fled to Tampa with her father in 1959 after the regime discovered that he was active in the emerging underground. Gaby's father was jailed because he had served in Batista's army. He was later released and became a taxi and truck driver. Gaby lived with relatives in Niquero on Cuba's southern coast.

Everything was political. In a small town like that, we were outcasts. They said we were no good because we had family in the States. I realize now there was a lot of envy among people against other people's prosperity. I didn't see that back then because I didn't have the intellectual ability to decipher that feeling in people, but I felt it.

You lived with a lot of fear in '64, '65, '66. If you had a little bit of dissent about the system, you would go to jail for political deviation, for saying, "This is a crappy system." The Committee for the Defense of the Revolution made my family's life impossible. They were constantly asking questions. The neighbors told on you.

My mother was the one active in getting everybody out, along with my grandfather. They tried to get us out through Mexico, and they couldn't do it. They tried to get us out through Spain. They couldn't do it. There was another option, to be a *balsero*, a rafter, and leave illegally. Jamaica was south of Niquero. A few people had done that, and Jamaica back then would take Cubans and give them the opportunity to come to this country.

Operation Pedro Pan ended in 1962, but Cuban children were evacuated again after Castro imposed conscription for males aged fifteen through twenty-six. With no air transportation between Havana and Miami, children were sent to the US by way of Spain. Starting in 1966, by one report, ten to twelve unaccompanied Cuban youngsters arrived in Madrid each week.[17]

Little is known about this almost forgotten effort, and accounts of it are fragmentary. They indicate that Catholic prelates in Spain sponsored the evacuation through church agencies with financial support from the privately funded Foundation for Hispanic-American Exchange. Cuban youngsters in transit through Spain were cared for in hostels and monasteries until they left for the US or other countries or reached age eighteen.[18] At one point the effort was aided by the youth arm of the Falange party allied with the dictator Francisco Franco.[19]

Once a child was in Spain, the US Catholic Conference arranged a US visa and found a sponsor to assure that the child would not become a burden on American taxpayers.[20] Catholic prelates later persuaded the State Department to issue visa waivers for the children.[21] At least three thousand unaccompanied Cuban children are believed to have taken this escape route in the late sixties.[22]

Ricardo "Rick" Fernandez
TALLAHASSEE, FLORIDA

Rick grew up in the city of Guantánamo in eastern Cuba, the younger son of an accountant who worked at the nearby US naval station and as an intelligence operative for Fidel during the insurrection. Rick's aunt Miriam was an M-26-7 fighter. After Castro took power and veered toward communism, Rick's father Ricardo resisted the regime with acts of sabotage. He was sentenced to thirty years in prison. In 1966 Rick's mother Ilda decided he should join relatives in New York.

They wanted my brother Pepe to leave because he was over fifteen. I remember them saying that they couldn't do both of us. I was just twelve. I told them, "I don't need to leave. Whatever they want to hear, I'll tell them." But little by little I could see that it was happening because the paperwork started coming. We had to go to Havana for some paperwork, probably meeting with the embassy.

I went to see my father at Isla de Pinos. It was a long bus ride, then you took a ferry packed with people, so it was a whole day. Isla de Pinos was tremendously harsh. They would strip you and spread you open, humiliating you, just to visit. I remember feeling, Why are they *doing* this? My mother was getting my father's signature for me to leave. I remember him signing the papers and giving me the little speech about being a good man.

At first, I was going to the old La Salle school in Guantánamo. After Castro came, that went away, and it was just a normal public school. I was a good student until they found out I was going to leave, then all of that changed. You got treated differently. Nothing with the kids; it was the administration. That would have been the fifth or sixth grade.

It wasn't the worst of times—that came later—but it was tight. There was no meat to be had, not even chicken. Every once in a while, a piece of pork would show up on the black market, but it was rice, beans, and eggs. And beans, not all the time. If you didn't get beans, you got chickpeas. Those were rough times.

I remember being assigned to pick cotton. That was a day trip. The second time was to cut sugarcane. That was a week during time off. Almost everybody in the group I was with had put in their papers. They graded you on how much you cut. They gave you a hammock in a big tent, and that's where you slept. I spent a night there, and then I faked a stomachache. Miriam came and got me. Those papers couldn't come fast enough at the end.

My mother wanted a better life for me, and she couldn't go because she had to take care of my brother and my grandmother and grandfather. My brother talked it up as being an adventure. I think he convinced me.

I remember the long bus ride. My mother kept hugging me, and me hugging her back. It was August, so it was hot in the bus. We went somewhere—it must have been somebody's house—and we slept together. She hugged me all night long. The next morning, I remember the airport. There were a lot of people. I remember the plane being huge and jam-crowded. I had a black flannel suit, hot as hell, a white shirt and a black tie, and some underwear and shoes. I don't think I had ever worn a suit before. There wasn't a lot of emotion.

When we got to Spain, they took us up in the mountains. It looked like a ski lodge, and you could see snow on the peaks. We stayed there a couple of weeks and moved to El Escorial.† It's hilly, and the monastery sits on top. It's like a forty-five-minute train ride from Madrid. We weren't *inside* the monastery. There were buildings on the grounds, and they had a main hall to play cards or hang out, then a long hallway with rooms, like barracks. Your clothing and stuff were in cabinets. We didn't have much.

Ninety boys, all from Cuba and all under eighteen. I was the youngest. I would say most of them were fifteen. The ones who were seventeen, eighteen had been there a while and couldn't find a sponsor in the US. There might have been a few going to Central America. Once you became eighteen, there was a priest who had a small parish in Madrid that accepted these kids and tried to get them jobs and get them integrated into Spanish society.

The priests didn't have a big presence. They'd check on us, ask us to go to Mass, but it wasn't mandatory. There was one adult who ran the complex. Then he left, and they brought in another one days before I left. They were both Cubans. They kept all the records, made sure we ate and went to bed on time, and broke up fights. They fed us well, and there was always coffee and drinks. There was school, but nobody went. We played cards; we were canasta junkies. We played baseball. We'd hang out in town and chase girls. They had a huge library. I remember reading a lot of Spanish novels.

My uncle Harry in New York, my Irish uncle, a marine, flew to Madrid. I didn't know he was coming. One day we got a call, and he made arrangements for someone to come get me. It wasn't a common thing for any of us to have a visitor. Next thing, I was on a train for Madrid. Uncle Harry says, "Let's go to the US embassy," and he walks in like he owns the place. He was—he still is—an angel. Within two weeks I had my papers to leave.

I was in Spain three months, August 7 to November 15, 1966, most of it in El Escorial. It seemed a lot longer.

As he had with Kennedy, Castro in early 1964 sent a private message to President Lyndon B. Johnson proposing negotiations to address the two countries' differences.[23] Tenuous secret contacts between Washington and Havana continued through go-betweens for almost a year and defused two minor crises.[24] But Johnson kept the US isolation policy firmly in place. Alarmed by Castro's support for insurgencies in Latin America, the OAS recommended stronger

---

† El Escorial is a complex at the Royal Monastery of San Lorenzo de El Escorial, forty miles from Madrid. It is a UNESCO World Heritage Site.

economic sanctions against the regime.[25] For a time the hemispheric travel ban left Cuba with direct air service only to Mexico City and Madrid, among destinations in the West.[26]

Cubans who could not get an exit permit for Mexico or Spain took their chances.[27] Some swam miles to the US naval station at Guantánamo Bay despite patrols by Castro's coast guard.[28] Still more set out in small boats or makeshift rafts on the dangerous journey across the Florida Straits. Some were lost. Others were machine-gunned by Cuban patrol boats.[29] Despite the impediments, 30,580 Cubans arrived in the US in 1963 and 1964.[30]

By 1965 from seventy to two hundred Cubans fled the island every month in stolen or homemade watercraft or aboard US-based vessels that rendezvoused with refugees and spirited them back to Florida.[31] The publicity about desperate Cubans leaving the island embarrassed Castro just when he was seeking a role on the world stage with diplomatic initiatives and military adventures in Africa that eventually included support for insurrections in Angola, Congo-Brazzaville, Ethiopia, Guinea-Bissau, and Mozambique.[32]

Isaac M. "Ike" Flores

WINTER PARK, FLORIDA

As resident correspondent for the Associated Press, Ike covered the changes sweeping over Cuba. The regime reviewed his dispatches before transmitting them to New York, so he smuggled out the most sensitive ones in diplomatic pouches. He saw Fidel at mass rallies and public events but was never granted a one-on-one interview with Cuba's "Maximum Leader."

A guy named Paco Teira was assigned to me as a minder. That's what we called these people, minders. He spoke English and Spanish, and I spoke both languages. He allowed me to have pretty much free rein around Havana.

I found out that Fidel was meeting with the Swiss ambassador at a pizza joint in Miramar, La Costa Azul.‡ Fidel was a night owl. I showed up with my chauffeur, maybe midnight; I had a chauffeur and an ancient Cadillac. There were heavily armed guards, as you would expect. Paco was there, cooling his heels. He and I sat down on

‡ Swiss Ambassador Emil Anton Stadelhofer represented US interests in Cuba after Washington severed diplomatic relations in 1961.

a bench. Soon the ambassador walked down this curvy path and nodded at me as he went by to leave. We knew each other. Paco sent somebody in to tell Castro that the American correspondent was there. Fidel was curious, I guess, as to what the hell I was up to at that hour. So I was escorted up there along with Paco.

Fidel said, *"Oye, hombre* [Hey, man]." There were a lot of military people in fatigues, but these guys were at ease, eating and drinking, including Fidel. He said, *"Siéntate aqui* [Sit here]." Paco and I sat on a bench next to his. We ordered beers. I told Fidel that I wanted an interview. I told him he could explain some of these things that were unanswered, like the refugee problems. Fidel said, "Oh, I don't do that. What you will learn, you will learn with everybody else from my speeches. I tell everything that I want to tell, everything I know, in my speeches."

He was still a fairly young man. I had seen him at various places, but to meet him for the first time, he was an impressive figure, with that beard and cap, the fatigues and boots. He was personable, but charismatic? I wouldn't go that far. He liked people. He talked to people whenever he could, so I guess to Cubans he was charismatic.

Fidel was a big baseball fan. He wouldn't talk about anything else. The only thing he repeated was, "What I have to say you will learn with everybody else."

As he was about to leave and I was about to get up, he put his hand on my shoulder and said, *"No, quedate sentado* [No, stay seated]. I'm going to leave now." That's as close as he and I got. He said his next speech would have something of what I was after. Something was *happening*.

The day after my meeting with Fidel, I was called in by Ramiro Valdés, the czar of information. He said, "Just keep this meeting to yourself. Don't report it—if you know what's good for you," something to that effect. And I did. I mean, there was no hard information. I did go to see the Swiss ambassador. I said, "What was Fidel talking about?" He would go this far: "The topic of our conversation was refugees. They're getting on his nerves, and I think he's getting ready to do something." That's all he would say. Maybe that's all he knew.

Fidel made this big speech that astounded everyone, allowing Cubans to leave the country legally and allowing Cuban refugees in exile to go to Cuba to get their relatives. Fidel even provided a special port for them to use in a village called Camarioca.

Located a few miles from the beach resort of Varadero, Camarioca became the scene of a crash construction program after Castro's speech on September 28, 1965. The regime built a compound with dormitories, a cafeteria, and a playground for departing refugees and those coming for them.[33] As the crowds grew, housing was requisitioned in nearby hotels and apartments.[34]

Exiles hired hundreds of vessels—tugboats, shrimpers, sailboats, and run-abouts—for an evacuation reminiscent of Dunkirk. Some were seaworthy and helmed by qualified skippers; others were not.[35] The autumn voyage from Miami took eighteen hours, and bad weather in the straits often delayed the return from Camarioca.[36] The US Coast Guard stationed ships in international waters to escort returning vessels to Key West. The guard furnished life jackets, fuel, and engine repairs when necessary and took aboard refugees from overloaded watercraft.[37]

The Second Wave had begun.

Paulina García Orta

MIAMI, FLORIDA

Paulina and her sister were the daughters of a prosperous furniture merchant in Colón, in central Cuba's Matanzas province. After their father Santiago García died in 1958, the girls stayed with their mother Ofelia, who soon arranged for them to leave in Operation Pedro Pan. At the last minute, Paulina decided to stay.

My sister left November 13, 1961. I had a boyfriend in the underground who was caught October thirty-first. Those people—meaning Castro's regime—were so good at infiltrating every group in the underground. I don't know how they managed, but they caught *everybody*. I didn't want to leave until I found out the decision in Roberto's trial.

I used to go to La Cabaña every Wednesday for visiting. When I saw inside La Cabaña, that was not nice. They killed so many people, so many kids. The trial lasted about seven hours. It was a show. There were about sixty people. They were asking for five to be in front of the firing squad. The trial was finished in '62, and they committed Roberto to twenty years.

Time goes by. I started asking for visas for Spain, Mexico, but everything was failing. They didn't want anybody to leave. My mother said, "Oh, my God, we're stuck here." That was in 1965.

September 28, 1965, Castro said, "Everybody who wants to get out of here, they are allowed to go." They put speakers on all the blocks. It didn't matter where you lived, you listened. The phone rang. It was my sister in Miami: "This time you don't have an excuse. Everybody in Miami is looking for a boat. I'm going to get a boat, I'm going to give them money, and you're coming." That started in October. She paid a hundred dollars for each of us.

My sister sent the names and addresses with the boat. When the police got that report, they went to our house. They said, "You're claimed by somebody in the United States, and we have to inventory your house." They took inventory of everything, they put a seal on the door. We left *everything* on the table, the cash, the bank accounts, everything. You were only allowed three pieces of clothes. I couldn't take anything, no pictures, *nothing*.

We went to Camarioca on October twenty-third. We were four. My mother's sister and her husband came with us. They said, "Your boat is already here, but we have bad weather, we have to wait." Like they could care less if we died. They gave us an apartment with no furniture. We had two bedrooms, two baths, nice but empty. We had to sleep on the floor. The next day they called us for breakfast by microphone.

We left on October twenty-fifth, in the morning. The *Abell* was fifty-two feet with a little cabin in the bottom. There were thirty-two people, so the old ladies and the little kids were in the cabin. People like me—I was twenty-one—and the men were in the back of the boat. We were like sardines. The *capitán* was Cancio. When we were getting aboard, Cancio decided my luggage couldn't fit. A little bag for three pieces of clothes. I said, "Leave it. I'm going with whatever I have on." A lot of people had money, jewelry. I didn't bring anything. I was sad. I said, "I know I'll never come back."

I was outside, so I could see everything. Sunny sky. It was breezy, and the sea was choppy. You could see the whitecaps. A cold front was coming in. The Coast Guard was always behind us. Even though it was not an easy trip, we felt safe. When we got into the Gulf Stream, it was a rough sea. We got soaking wet. People cried.

Another thing that was scary: What am I going to find on this end?

Isaac M. "Ike" Flores

WINTER PARK, FLORIDA

Ike made the seventy-mile drive from Havana to Camarioca to see the impromptu boatlift as exiles streamed in from Florida and Cubans hoping to leave arrived from around the island.

The Cubans were overwhelmed at Camarioca. There were thousands coming and going into this little fishing village. The first word that comes to mind is bedlam.

The exiles who had a little money had motorboats. Others had sailboats. Everything in between. They would put ashore in and around Camarioca. There was a wharf. Some of the motorboats would use that because there were fuel pumps, so they would refuel.

All the exiles were primed to seek out relatives. They would telephone over these bad connections. Days would go by before you got a connection. Sometimes they would leave somebody on the boat and go inland and seek out their relatives and bring them back. Neighbors would tell neighbors, and word got around.

Some had spent days traveling to Camarioca. They hadn't slept. They hadn't eaten. Some people were overjoyed. Other people were desperate. Some claimed they didn't have enough to eat, didn't have clothes they wanted. A lot of them didn't have jobs. They had been fired because they had asked to leave the country.

All they wanted was to get on the boat. They wanted out.

The State Department saw Castro's announcement as a propaganda ploy that could be turned into a US advantage.[38] President Johnson soon declared that "those who seek refuge here shall find it."[39] Swiss Ambassador Stadelhofer agreed to mediate between the two countries to establish an orderly evacuation. The result was a Memorandum of Understanding (MOU), the first accord between Washington and Havana since Castro took power.[40] Its stated purpose was to reunify families.

The MOU created an "airbridge" across the Florida Straits with chartered airliners paid for by the US government. Those without relatives in the US were at a disadvantage in getting seats on the planes. The MOU gave first priority to "immediate relatives" of refugees in the US: parents of unmarried children under age twenty-one, spouses, unmarried children under age twenty-one, and brothers and sisters under age twenty-one. Also eligible were other "close relatives" of refugees in the US. The regime refused to allow the departure of draft-age males and skilled personnel.[41] It also rejected Washington's proposal to release political prisoners.[42]

Agreement in hand, Castro halted the boatlift on November 9, 1965, stranding several thousand Cubans at Camarioca. US-chartered vessels later brought them to Key West.[43] In all, 4,993 Cuban refugees crossed the straits from Camarioca in late 1965.[44] On December 1, 1965, the first chartered DC-7 left Varadero for Miami with seventy-five refugees.[45] In time the airbridge became known as Los Vuelos de la Libertad or the "Freedom Flights."[46]

Miguel "Mike" Collazo

TAMPA, FLORIDA

Mike grew up in San Antonio de los Baños near Havana. His father Miguel was a mason and also worked in a hardware store. His mother Celia worked in a garment factory.

In early 1960 my father did the paperwork to come to the United States. As soon as he turned in the paper, the government took him out of the hardware store because he was not with the revolution. That's what they used to say: "You're not with the revolution." You could not work any place because everything belonged to the government. From then on, you were on your own.

From 1960 to 1967, when we got out, we just tried to survive. We used to go to farms, pick corn, bring it home, and make grit because the food started coming up short. My father went to Oriente to do some work in construction for people he knew. They paid him under the table. He sent that money to my mom, and my mom took care of the home. He worked there about a year, year and a half until he got tired and said, "I cannot be without my family any longer," because it was far away, from one end of the island to another.

I was a seventh grader in Cuba. After the seventh grade, to be able to graduate to high school, you had to go to a camp. They said, "Volunteer," but it wasn't volunteering. Either you go and you pass, or you don't go, you don't pass. Since we were going to get out of the country, my mom kept telling me, Don't go. I repeated seventh grade two or three times in Cuba.

A friend of my father over here had a company, Raúl Leon. The guy claimed my father to bring him to the United States. He went through that about four or five years, and then they changed that, for a friend to claim a friend. The only way you got out was if you were family.

This lady who lived around the corner came earlier than we did. She moved to Miami and found somebody with the same last name that we had, to claim us as family. He had a big factory. I don't remember his name; I know it was Collazo. You had to turn in all that paperwork with the new name. I was fourteen and nine months. They did all this paperwork in a hurry, so I was able to get out of the country before I was fifteen.

We went to my father's brother and stayed there six days before we got out.

Cuba compiled a list of immediate relatives wanting to leave, and the US compiled a list of refugees who claimed family members on the island. The Swiss then prepared a joint list of immediate relatives eligible to leave and claimed by family in the US. That became the "A" list for the airbridge. Another list included lower-priority close relatives.[47] Washington later sent a "supplemental list" of 120,000 Cubans claimed by exiles in the US.[48] Using these lists, Cuba prepared an embarkation list for each flight.[49] The regime determined dates of departure by a lottery with a unique number assigned to each family on the lists.[50]

Those leaving took only a few changes of clothing, if that, and nothing else. They had to pay all debts, replace worn-out household appliances, and turn in ration books.[51] As before, they lost jobs and forfeited homes, cars, and bank accounts. Renters had to pay two months' rent in advance. And there was a new requirement: male heads of household and sometimes their spouses were assigned to agricultural work camps until departure. They lived in thatched-roof barracks with no walls, a dirt floor, and little sanitation. They were ridiculed as "Johnsons."[52]

The chartered airliners flew from Miami in a 195-mile-wide air corridor designed to prevent Cuban and US air defense alerts.[53] The identity of each refugee on an embarkation list was checked for "derogatory information" in US records. If none appeared, the refugee was preliminarily approved to enter the country. US immigration and health inspectors flew to Varadero on the first flight each day and checked refugees before they boarded a plane, then the inspectors flew back to Miami on the second plane of the day.[54]

Justo Luis Cepero

TAMPA, FLORIDA

Justo and his brother were raised in Matanzas on Cuba's northern coast. Their father Alejandro Cepero began selling his mother's homemade tamales on the beach in Varadero as a teenager and over time parlayed his earnings into two bodegas. Alejandro and his wife Marta Rosa decided to register for the Freedom Flights.

Once we put in for the lottery to come to the United States, they took the stores. They did an inventory of everything we owned to make sure we didn't give anything away. And by God, when you left, everything they inventoried better be there, or you didn't get to leave.

They put my father in a concentration camp to work until his lottery number came up. My mom was the glue that kept us together. I remember my grandmother and my mom listening to the little radio, and they read these lottery numbers out on Saturdays or Sundays. If they read your number, then you knew that you've got so many days to get your affairs in order. Of course, you can't leave with anything.

We left as a family. It was my father, my mother, my grandfather, my grandmother on my mother's side, my brother, me, and my uncle—my mother's brother. It was September. It was hot. I had so many mosquito bites from waiting in that Varadero airport that they thought I had chicken pox. I remember my parents telling us we're going to a better place where sidewalks walk by themselves. You don't get only one toy for Christmas; you get *more* than one toy. That's what I remember them telling us about coming over here.

Mercedes Fernandez Collazo
TAMPA, FLORIDA

Mercedes and her two brothers lived with their parents in Havana's Marianao district. Mercedes stayed with her grandparents in their home across the street from her parents' small house. Her father David Fernandez was a mechanic and bus driver, her mother Elvira a homemaker. They decided to follow Mercedes's paternal grandfather to the US.

It was bad, very bad. Everything was restricted, even food. We had little cards that would tell you your ration for the month. You had to take your card, and they would give you so much rice, like five pounds. Everything was in shortage, so if you wanted to get something, you had to run to a store and make a line.

When you became a teenager, they would make you volunteer, but it wasn't volunteering. They would make you go to a camp. You would leave your parents and go there and sleep there and *work*. They made you cut sugarcane. You *had* to do it. I never got to go, thank God. They took my father's job. So, my father would have to get bottles and go sell bottles. He had to do things like that to live until we came because they wouldn't let him work. His job had to be under the table. We had other family that helped us out.

In September 1967 I turned thirteen, and in December we came. It was hard because I had to let my friends go. I didn't understand, but I was happy to come, in a way. I didn't know anything about politics, but they would say, "Over there, we're going to have everything." They knew it was going to be a better life for us.

We all came together. It was my mom, my dad, my two brothers, and my mom's parents. It wasn't easy. My grandfather was the one asking for us. He lived in Tampa. The airport was small. They checked all your papers, and they gave you bad looks. I could only bring three dresses, wearing one, two in the suitcase. I had a blue one. That's the one I remember. Two pair of shoes, the pair that I was wearing and one in the suitcase, and some underwear. That's it.

Some Cubans continued to escape through Mexico and Spain. Both countries required transit visas for those traveling on to the US. Obtaining one from Mexico sometimes required a bribe.[55] By 1966 hundreds of Cubans were stranded in Mexico, unable to meet US visa requirements. The State Department allowed them to be paroled to relatives in the US.[56]

Spain gave Cuban refugees temporary financial assistance, the only other country to do so.[57] Eighty thousand Cuban refugees went to Madrid from 1961 to 1972 in the hope of getting a US visa, and by 1972 one thousand arrived every month. However, a 1968 change in US immigration law slowed the issuance of visas to refugees in third countries. The US embassy in Madrid issued only four hundred visas each month, so Spain became a bottleneck. The average wait was twenty months.[58] Finally, the US allowed Cuban refugees in Spain to enter the US on parole based on an affidavit of support and a health certificate.[59]

Nestor A. Rodriguez
MIAMI, FLORIDA

Nestor and his sister were raised in the town of Jaruco in western Cuba. Their father, also named Nestor, was an accountant at the sugar mill and plantation in the nearby model town of Hershey. Their mother Alicia was a teacher and a classically trained pianist. In 1962 Nestor's parents applied for exit permits.

I must have been four or five when the militia came to the house and took my mother's piano outside because we had presented our papers to leave. They said, "You can't teach piano anymore." The neighbors were yelling, "*¡Gusano!* [Worm!]" They yelled, "*¡Paredón!* [To the wall!]" That piano stayed outside for two nights. Luckily, it didn't rain. We had to get someone to help us get it in. My mother continued her piano lessons.

I felt my environment becoming more hostile, especially in school. Teachers asked, "Why are your parents leaving, why are they *gusanos*? Do you pray at home? And if you pray, do you pray to God or to Fidel? If you get sick, God will not bring medicine. It's Fidel that *allows* you to have that privilege." The overwhelming feeling was fear and rejection.

My father was sent to a hard labor camp in the countryside. They never said, "You're going there because you're being punished." They said, "You have given up your right to work and to your house and to your property, therefore, the revolution needs you to be here to fulfill that need." They called it volunteering.

My father came home every forty-five days to spend one night with us. He wouldn't talk about it in front of me. We knew he was skinny, that he was upset, that it wasn't a nice place to be. I only heard about it later. The food was horrible. He did menial work, like working the fields. He had to work in a sewer up to his waist in sewage. So read between the lines, look at the symbolism: You belong in the sewers. You're leaving us behind because you want a better life. Well, we're going to show you what the revolution thinks of *you*.

As a family, we never lost faith that we would leave. Spain was one option. I remember the conversations about Costa Rica and Venezuela or the Freedom Flights. The ideal would have been to come to Miami directly. That never happened for us. The first available opportunity was Spain. We left in '69.

We arrived in Madrid in the winter. We were met by my parents' friends from Hershey. They had rented us a modest apartment. My father got a job in an American freight company. They needed someone to translate between the Americans and the Spaniards. He spoke English, so he was able to do that. My mother started giving piano lessons. In about four or five months we moved to a larger apartment. I went to school, my sister went to daycare. It was the first time that I experienced another world away from the repression of revolutionary Cuba. Even though this was Franco time, to us it was night and day.

The most significant observation was the abundance of goods, the ability to eat what you could afford. The smell of fried potatoes in olive oil, or window shopping, or knowing that the Prado museum was there, and you could go look at Goya paintings; that the composer Joaquín Rodrigo was playing a concert. He wrote the *Concierto de Aranjuez*, the famous guitar concerto. I had a clear sense that you can't take for granted what you have.

The conversation was always, Should we stay here? Do we like it enough? My parents did, and I did too. My sister was too little. But we also said, The opportunity is in the United States, and our family is there. We had to claim my maternal grandparents who had stayed in Hershey. We couldn't have done that from Spain.

My father's sister is the one in the United States who "claimed" him. That's the term. She raised the money for it. She's the one who did all the paperwork. It took twenty months to get the American visa. It seemed like an eternity.

More than 350,000 Cubans registered for the Freedom Flights. Surprised by the number wanting to leave, the regime stopped accepting applications in May 1966.[60] When it announced in 1973 that the airbridge was ending, thousands went to a government office in Havana to get a seat on one of the last flights and reportedly staged a near-riot when denied one.[61]

Isaac M. "Ike" Flores
WINTER PARK, FLORIDA

Just as he reported on the Camarioca Boatlift for the Associated Press, Ike covered the emotionally charged departures of the Freedom Flights until his Havana assignment ended in 1967.

The airlift could bring many more refugees than Fidel ever thought possible. The Swiss embassy had to approve all documents. The Swiss ran a consular section in the old American embassy building in Havana. They did the processing for these people on the Freedom Flights.

They had special buses for people who were boarding the Freedom Flights. They ran from a gathering place that would pick up these people who were leaving. They were searched as they got off the buses. I saw this process. You couldn't take money out of the country. You had no passport. You had this special visa that had been given to each member of a family, and you had to show that upon boarding. All these people had been vetted by the Cuban government.

Cubans have big extended families, so their departures were heart-wrenching. The Cubans often were leaving relatives behind, not through bad intentions. It just *was*. They were *persona non grata* to government agencies, but they were courageous to their friends, neighbors, and relatives.

Yet they were joyous departures. Say, one family was leaving. Their neighbors would come to the airport to see their departure. They were happy during this procedure but unhappy afterwards. I remember talking to a few people after the flight left, and they were crying to lose their neighbors, their friends, their relatives. Some were sorry they hadn't done the same thing.

Maribel Pérez Henley
MIAMI, FLORIDA

Maribel was raised in western Cuba's port city of Mariel. Her father Juan Pérez and his nine siblings and their families lived in a large house with Juan's parents. The men worked in the family's adjoining bakery, while the women cared for the home and children. In 1965 Juan's parents and five siblings and their families left for the US. Juan, his wife Hilda, and Maribel stayed due to a paperwork problem.

They took the bakery as soon as my grandfather left. Because the bakery and the house were together, we got to stay in the house. They let us live in a room. The communist brothers of my father stayed there too. We were living with enemies.

It took my parents two years to get our approval. As soon as my father started the paperwork, he was taken to the camp to work. My father must have been late twenties, early thirties. He would be in these camps in the middle of nowhere, cutting cane. He cut himself with a machete, and they wouldn't take him to a hospital. It was a very hard life.

He would spend months there. It wasn't like they were making money; it was a work camp that they had to go to in order to get out. They had to use whatever they could find to sleep on the floor, and then they cut cane all day. They were hardly fed, so they were trying to kill snakes or whatever they could find to eat. They had a curfew; they couldn't be wandering the countryside.

I remember him showing up at the house. He would bring big bushels of bananas or whatever he could find because my mother didn't work a job. She washed people's clothes and ironed. That's how she maintained me. I remember seeing him for a weekend. Then he went back.

Military men showed up at our house and told my mother that our paperwork had been approved. They took an inventory. Everything that my father and mother had stayed in that room. They taped up the door with red tape, and that was it. My mom and I were standing in the street. Whatever you're wearing, that's all you're taking. We didn't take *anything*. We had a week. We had nobody except my mom's brother who lived in Artemisa. He picked us up, and we went to pick up my dad. My dad was in Pinar del Río. He didn't know that we could get out.

We arrived in the middle of the night. I remember that *extremely* well. The *miliciano* didn't want to let him go until the next day because my father had to turn in his boots. I started crying. I told the *miliciano*, this man dressed in green fatigues, "Please let my father go." I guess he felt sorry for the little kid crying and crying. He finally let him go.

The men that were there started bringing out crackers and *leche condensada* [condensed milk] to feed me. The little bit they had they were giving to me. After I became an adult, I understood what was going on. That meant so much to me. It's like it happened the other day.

We drove back to my uncle's house in Artemisa. He lived on a farm, and he knew he wasn't going to see his sister for a long time, so we celebrated *veintiquatro de diciembre*—you know, Christmas Eve. He killed a pig; we had a party.

We got to the Varadero airport. They told my parents we couldn't leave because we didn't have the smallpox shots we needed. My parents had theirs, but I didn't have mine. This is the day we were going to leave, December 22, 1970. They told my father, *"Ella no puede irse* [She can't leave]." These were Cubans, *mean* Cubans. One little paper, and they're not letting you out. They said my *parents* could leave, and I could follow. Well, that wasn't going to happen.

My father threw a fit. I remember my mom telling him, "You go, and we'll follow." He said, "Absolutely not!" I don't know what they did, but they took us into this room, and they gave all three of us these shots. It happened on the spot. We were put in a room, waiting for the plane. We were moving closer and closer to the American side. The feeling was there. Finally, we left. Everybody was happy. I imagined that my parents had this weight lifted off of them.

Gabriel Castillo

MIAMI, FLORIDA

*After years of waiting, Gaby and his grandmother got permission to leave on
a Freedom Flight. His parents were divorced; his mother had come to Tampa
with her father in 1959, while Gaby's father remained in Cuba. Gaby lived with
relatives in Niquero.*

I remember the excitement of leaving. By that time, from what I had seen as a teenager, I didn't want to stay in Cuba. A lot of adults that I knew had been put in jail for no reason, not kids my age but their parents, maybe grandparents.

We were on the "A" list since I was a minor, and my mom was asking for my release from Cuba. Since my grandmother was my caretaker, she came with me. My father drove us to Havana. When we left, his father—my other grandfather—said, "Give me a hug because I'm never going to see you again." I never saw him again.

I thought we were going to leave from the airport in Havana, but no, you go to Havana with your documents. We reported to an old mansion that the revolution had taken from some rich man. I was with my grandmother, just her and me. My father accompanied us. They thought since I was going to be fifteen on June sixth—this is March eighteenth—that they were not going to let me go.

My grandmother was in her sixties. They interviewed her in a room, and she was, my God, she was a housewife. I don't know what they asked her, but she was in there for a while. I guess they were doing that to every adult. They did not interview me.

When we got to Varadero, I started seeing guys with brown hair and light eyes, and I asked, "Are those Americans?" "No, those are Swiss." At the time I didn't know that the Swiss government was acting as an intermediary. We got off the bus. Everybody had smiles on their faces. The Swiss said, "Come this way." They served us breakfast. To have ham and eggs, it was a delicacy. And orange juice! We had not seen that in *years*. Soon after that we were on the plane. It was one of those old planes, but to me it was a brand-new thing.

We didn't leave with anything but the clothes we had on. And what I had on—you'll laugh. I had on this blue three-piece suit custom made in Niquero. It was 100 percent wool. With a white shirt. Because we were going to the North. It's called el Norte. It's *frío* [cold]. In *March*? In *Florida*? Give me a break! That was the only thing I had. My grandmother said, "You don't take anything off until your mother sees you." Oh, my gosh! That I remember. It was hot!

And then worrying about my grandmother being sick. Never been on a plane before. Neither had I. I was the one that got airsick. They had little bags, you know.

We left Cuba on March 18, 1966. As the plane was leaving—this sounds so romantic—there are royal palms all over Cuba. I used to read a lot of José Martí's writings. He said, "*Las palmas son novias que te esperan.*" It means the palms are girlfriends that wait for you. I looked at the palms as they were getting smaller, and I said, I will never see you again. Everybody was happy. People were clapping.

They say Spain is our mother country. Hell, no! The United States is our mother country.

8

SECOND WAVE

When Castro announced that anyone who wanted to go to "the Yankee paradise" could do so, telephone traffic between Miami and Havana spiked 800 percent.[1] Initially the US government discouraged the boatlift by fining boatowners and impounding vessels.[2] The flotilla just grew, so the focus of the Coast Guard's mission shifted to escorting the returning boats to Key West.[3] There the new refugees were questioned before being bused to a reception center in Opa-locka with immigration, health, and customs inspectors, and then to Freedom Tower.[4]

Paulina García Orta

MIAMI, FLORIDA

On October 25, 1965, twenty-one-year-old Paulina and her mother arrived in Key West with thirty other Cubans aboard a boat returning from Camarioca. Paulina's sister Ofelia had come to Miami four years earlier and was living with an aunt and uncle. She had arranged passage across the straits for Paulina, their mother, and another aunt and uncle.

We made it to Key West about six o'clock. It was getting dark. They took us to a little dining room with chairs, waiting to be interviewed—interrogated, actually. In the meantime, a lot of ham, cheese, bread, milk. We were hungry for anything. People were eating like no tomorrow, anxious for all the things that you didn't have in Cuba. In those times there was *nothing*.

They put another vaccine here. [She gestures to her shoulder.] Then there were three little cabins that you go in on your own and explain the reason why you were here. It took us until about one thirty or two o'clock in the morning because they had to classify *everybody*.

They took us that night in those little navy buses to Opa-locka. A lot of people were there waiting for friends. They all banged on the windows, but we had to be cleared by ourselves, not with any family there. We had a place to sleep, a place to get a shower. We were treated first class.

The next day we had *café con leche, pan, mantaquilla,* [coffee with milk, bread, butter], water. Everything was in English. I was lost, so they directed us what to do— shower, breakfast, chores. At nine o'clock, we took the bus to Freedom Tower, filled out papers. My cousin was living in Boston, so my aunt and uncle wanted to go to Boston. They did the paperwork, gave them clothes, bought the airplane ticket to Boston.

There was a lady sitting on the table beside everything that you fill out: who you are, if you wanted to be relocated someplace else. I said, "No, my sister is here. We're going to stay in Miami." I was sure I didn't want to live in cold weather. "Well, if you stay in Miami, we don't have any help for you." In other words, they couldn't do anything, just release us with a paper. They gave you another paper to go to the Social Security office to request a number.

My mother and I got out of Freedom Tower about five o'clock. My sister was waiting outside. My uncle was making *arroz con pollo* [rice with chicken], and a lot of people were gathering. It was a small celebration. They were living in a nice house in the same block as the Orange Bowl. We stayed there for two months until my mother, my sister, and I rented a small apartment across from the Orange Bowl.

I started working in the City National Bank on November twenty-fifth, at night. My sister was supervisor for data entry. You know how they perforated paper tapes for the computer. I was there for two years. Since I started at City National at five o'clock, I went to apply for the English Language Center. I said, "I want English classes." I stayed there six months.

So to me it was a soft landing. I never expected it to be as easy as it was.

The Johnson Administration did not wait for the conclusion of negotiations on the MOU to prepare for the airbridge. The CRP had been winding down, but now it added staff.[5] The government leased an old air force officers' billet at the west end of Miami International Airport as a shelter for 450 refugees pending resettlement. They called it "Freedom House."[6]

US officials initially estimated that 50,000 Cubans would cross the air-bridge.[7] When the MOU was announced on November 6, 1965, the official estimate reached 100,000.[8] Others put the number higher.[9] But no one knew: as an open-ended, government-run evacuation of refugees from a foreign country, the Freedom Flights were unprecedented.[10]

Gabriel Castillo

MIAMI, FLORIDA

Thirteen-year-old Gaby was on the "A" list because he had been separated from his mother since 1959, when she and her father came to the US. They claimed Gaby and his grandmother, who arrived in Miami on March 18, 1966.

My grandfather, my mom, her brother, and another brother were waiting for us. They were crying. When they saw me with my three-piece suit, they all laughed, but they were dressed in suits too. This is back in suit-and-tie days.

We went to the famous Freedom Tower. Another bus. A lot of happy people there. Not a big crowd, but it was a busy place. Families being put together again. Since we were leaving Miami, they gave me and my grandmother seventy-five dollars apiece, which we thought was a great gesture of generosity. We were being sponsored, but they still gave us money.

The family joined us again at Freedom Tower. My grandmother went to Tampa with my grandfather. He was a tailor in downtown Tampa. I didn't go to Tampa. By the time I got here, my mother had married a doctor. She was living in Sanford—Seminole County—with her doctor husband. He was a pathologist for the local hospital. He was Cuban. They had met through friends in Tampa four years before I came. He was a cultured man, showed me etiquette. He gave me a lot of information about this country because he had been here since the mid-1950s. I had never been to a restaurant in my life.

They decided I should go to a summer camp so I could be immersed into the English language. It was a Catholic summer camp. I met kids that were in Peter Pan. It was all in English. For a couple hours in the morning, they just taught English, on a seventh-, eighth-grade level. And a lot of physical activity. There was a lake and swimming pool and basketball. It was a great adventure.

I was put back almost two years in Sanford Junior High. I started in the sixth grade. I was doing algebra in sixth grade. I should have been in the eighth grade. The guy said, "No, it's going to be better for you if you do this because of the language barrier." As little as I was, I became part of the basketball team. I was a guard because I was quick.

The impression that I got from Sanford for the rest of the United States was, oh, my gosh, they were the friendliest people in the world. They would take me into their homes, and they would get a glass and say, "Glass. Water." In three months I could understand *every* word in English that was being spoken to me. Those kids and their parents went out of their way to teach me the language. I felt welcomed.

President Johnson had to balance the desire for a Cold War propaganda victory over Castro with the political costs in Florida, which even then was a presidential swing state. Florida Governor Haydon Burns demanded "immediate and mandatory resettlement" outside the state.[11] Labor and civil rights leaders argued that more Cuban refugees in Miami would mean unfair job competition for workers, especially African Americans.[12] The voice of the city's Anglo establishment, the *Miami Herald*, warned that more refugees would burden the local economy, and a *Herald* columnist groused, "We're up to our armpits with Cuban refugees."[13]

Johnson dispatched a team of high-ranking officials to prepare a plan to address local concerns.[14] They promised that 80 percent of the new refugees would be resettled elsewhere within seventy-two hours.[15] The Johnson Administration soon showered the city with increased school subsidies, small-business loans, unemployment funds, and money for medical facilities, low-cost housing, and water and sewer improvements.[16]

Miguel "Mike" Collazo
TAMPA, FLORIDA

After waiting seven years, fourteen-year-old Mike, his brother, and his parents arrived in Miami on September 10, 1967. No one in the family spoke English. Since there were no relatives in the US to claim them, a stranger in Miami named Collazo did so. A good friend of Mike's father who owned a sod-laying business in Tampa, Raúl Leon, helped too.

When we got there we were happy because we were in the United States. They sent us to an office to check us out, names and everything. They filled out all the paperwork for Social Security and where we were staying. Then they gave us a shot and sent us to a room with four bunk beds, and we stayed there until somebody came and got us.

I will never forget: I cried. I told my father, "Now what are we going to do? Where are we going to live? Because we don't have anybody here, no family." We left everything: house, clothes, friends, everybody. He told me, "Don't worry, you'll make new friends. We are going to be alright."

The guy who claimed us came to meet us. He was a real nice man. My father appreciated what he'd done. And the friend of ours, the one who got him to claim us, she was there too. We were allowed to get out for so many hours. She took us to her house to eat and then took us back. Leon came from Tampa to make sure everything was ready for us to leave. They gave us an airplane ticket to Tampa.

The first two weeks we stayed with Leon. My father started working with Leon right away, so he was making money a week after he was here. He used to do rolling to press the sod down. Then we rented a house in West Tampa. The rent was sixty bucks a month.

They put me in the eighth grade in West Tampa Junior High. Two teachers spoke Spanish. They gave you a test to see how you do, and I passed everything. But I only stayed there for a year. My father got cataracts; he got blind in both eyes. I had to pull out of school to help my mom because my brother was too young. My mama used to work in a factory that made clothes. She made like fifty dollars a week, so she needed help.

I went to work for Leon. I did it for about two years. I worked in the field picking up sod for a year. Getting up at three o'clock in the morning, going home 1:30, two o'clock every day, just to make eighty, ninety bucks a week, which was good in those times.

A friend got a Baptist church to operate on my father without charge. I went back and did eighth grade, and I did ninth grade. When I was going to tenth grade I decided to work instead of going to school. I told my father, "I prefer working," which I regret. But I don't regret it, because it made me a man, with responsibility.

Upon arrival the new refugees went through document checks; baggage inspection, if they had any; a health exam; clothing distribution; and an interview with a resettlement agency. They were questioned by US intelligence agencies about conditions in Cuba.[17] Those over age fourteen were fingerprinted, photographed, and asked for biographical details for a further security check.

If a refugee was denied entry, the government arranged passage to another country of their choice.[18]

Registration with CRP was still voluntary, but most new refugees did so.[19] In the First Wave, resettlement was based on job and housing availability outside Miami. Second Wave refugees were resettled where they had a relative, and they were expected to find a job.[20] Those who refused resettlement were denied financial assistance.[21]

Once refugees resettled, volunteer agencies helped them find jobs, housing, and food.[22] Those who met state eligibility standards for public assistance—the aged, blind, disabled, and families with dependent children—received benefits with reimbursement by Washington. The monthly subsistence income for needy registrants in Florida was increased in 1971 to $86 per person and $246 per family.[23]

Justo Luis Cepero
TAMPA, FLORIDA

On September 26, 1969, six-year-old Justo arrived in Miami aboard a Freedom Flight with his brother, his parents, and his mother's parents and brother. They had waited years to get out. Justo's father Alejandro had relatives in Tampa, so the family went there.

We moved into my father's stepbrother's house for a couple of days until we were able to rent a house in Ybor City. None of us spoke English, not a word. We lived in Ybor for two years.

My mom started working in a clothes factory. My father got a job with Sexton Valenti.* He was a sorter. He also worked as a carpenter. He made tables, desks. He worked at the carpenter shop during the day and then the night shift at the tomato company. He was offered a managerial position, but he declined it because he said he wasn't going to stay there long. He was going to make his own business.

We started making tamales so he could take them to the jobs where he worked and sell to people during lunchtime. No label, no nothing. He started getting orders. When he saw the tamales were working, he took them to bars and stores. He said, "If you sell one tamale, you charge fifty cents. Twenty-five cents is for me, twenty-five

---

* Sexton Valenti is a fresh produce wholesale company in Tampa.

cents is for you." So the store made money. Whatever they didn't sell, that's what we ate at night.

We would do it in the house in Ybor City. Everybody had something to do. So when my dad left, he could drop ten tamales here, fifteen tamales there, take twenty to his job. After the job, he came back to the house, picked up another ten or fifteen, and went to his second job.

We moved out of Ybor, and my father bought a house. The orders got bigger and bigger. It got big enough to where my father dropped his second job, the tomatoes, and just kept the cabinetry, which was a higher-skilled job, so they paid him more, two-something an hour. My mom eventually dropped her job and dedicated more to the tamale operation. And that's the way the tamales started.

As the first of their families to arrive in the US, children evacuated by Operation Pedro Pan filled out forms to claim their parents, making the youngsters anchors in a family migration chain.[24] When the Freedom Flights began, families were reunited. The wards in the federally funded Cuban Children's Program dropped from five thousand to five hundred within six months.[25] For some children, being reunited with parents after years apart was a challenge. Many of them had matured and begun to assimilate.[26]

Luis M. Alvarez
NORTH HALEDON, NEW JERSEY

Luis had arrived in Operation Pedro Pan in 1962 and was finishing four years in the government's Cuban Children's Program. He was at Camp Opa-locka on the grounds of a former naval air station, and a reception center for those on the Freedom Flights was also on the grounds. Luis's father, who had owned a bakery, butcher shop, and bodega in Havana, and his mother arrived in 1966.

In Opa-locka we had a great time. All I did was play sports all day, go to school, and that's it. Didn't have to worry about anything, everything was given to us. One of the things that they made us do was to file an application to claim our relatives.

When I left in '62, my father still owned the business. He could have left, but he didn't want to leave the business. They took the business eventually. Then he got sick, and his doctors told him, "If you want to see your son again, you'd better leave." He had cancer. I never knew my father was sick. They never told me.

My parents came in March of '66. When they came, they had to go to Opa-locka. They opened a barrack to interview them, and whatever they did in there. That day they arrived, I had a school basketball game, and I couldn't miss the game. Through the fence, I saw my father and my mother, inside the barracks, and we waved.

I went to the game that evening. I told my friends, "Listen, if you go in there to see your parents, when you see my parents, tell them that I'm trying to talk to a priest to see if I can get them out the next day." When they asked about me, somebody said that I was playing a basketball game. I never heard anything. I saw them the next day. The next day they got out, and my father's friend got us an apartment in Miami, and that's where we lived for a month.

Since we had an uncle in New York, they said, "New York will take you, and they will give you welfare, but not Florida. We cannot help you here." So we came to New York. We lived in Manhattan maybe two, three months.

New Jersey was cheaper than New York, and my father and mother got work in New Jersey. My mother sewed in a factory. My father tried to get a job in a bakery. There were Cuban bakers that he knew from his business in Cuba. My father would work three months, then he would get sick, so on and off. He had to stop working.

We lived in Union City, a six-apartment building on Bergenline Avenue. That's where most of the Cubans lived in the late sixties. A lot of Cubans were coming there. Big change from Cuba. Different climate, different atmosphere, very dense. I was going to Marist High School in Bayonne. I would have loved to stay there, but we couldn't afford it. The next year I went to public school in Union City. I had to work because my father couldn't work.

My father passed in May of '69, and then one day I had an argument with my mother, and everything came out. She told me, "You hurt your father when we came. You went to play your stupid basketball game." My father never accepted me playing sports. He never understood that, here in the United States, it's normal if kids play high school sports. My father had—which I never realized—a short life to live. One of the things that I regret is that I didn't pay attention to my father's illness. I was dating, and I had to work.

Even as the Freedom Flights brought Cuban refugees across the Florida Straits with a bureaucracy's methodical regularity, other refugees crossed the Atlantic from Spain.

Ricardo "Rick" Fernandez

TALLAHASSEE, FLORIDA

Thirteen-year-old Rick arrived at New York's John F. Kennedy International
Airport on November 15, 1966. After three months at a monastery in El Escorial,
Spain, where he had been sent by his mother and his imprisoned father, Rick
came by himself on a flight from Madrid on papers arranged by his uncle Harry.

My aunt Elba and uncle Harry lived in Queens, and my aunt Lilly and uncle John lived in Bridgeport, Connecticut. They were all there. It was late at night. Everything I had, I left, except for one pair of underwear. I got a handkerchief signed by a bunch of the guys. That's basically what I brought with me. The next thing I know, I'm on my way to Bridgeport, with my little thing of underwear and cold as shit. It was the middle of November. They had a coat for me, so that was nice. I put on my coat, and we headed to Connecticut.

I spent a week or two in Bridgeport. I didn't like it. It was very industrial. There were no Spanish-speaking people other than my aunt. Then I went to Harry and Elba, and I was so happy. They have two children. Two-bedroom apartment in Woodside, Queens, right next to the train tracks, on the fourth floor. It was a living room, two bedrooms, and a tiny kitchen, so the three kids slept in one bedroom and my uncle and aunt in the other. I was there probably five years.

Uncle Harry paid for all our stuff. He was working two jobs. He was working on Wall Street. Then at night he was working in the rail yards in Long Island City, so he'd come home, have a shot of something—you know, a good Irish man—take a shower, go to bed, then he was up and out with his suit on.

The next school day my aunt took me to Junior High School 125, about ten blocks away. I didn't speak a word of English, and they're trying to figure out where to place me. They asked me some mathematical questions in Spanish, and I answered. They placed me in a section with real smart kids, which is one of those lucky breaks. About half the kids were Cuban, so it was Cuban and Jewish in our class and one girl from India.

It wasn't a bilingual school. It was totally English. The math I was learning in seventh grade here I already knew. It tells you that they teach mathematics in Cuba earlier than they do here. They put me in Spanish 1. But it was English for the histories and these kinds of things. For the first three months I just faked it. Everybody knew what the game was.

But in about three months, I was pretty fluent. There wasn't any formal training. I watched *I Love Lucy*. My aunt liked it, so whatever she put on I watched. Uncle Harry's family lived upstairs on the fifth floor, his mother, his father, and his two sisters. They're all Irish. I spent a lot of time with them, playing cards. Everything was in English. I think that did it.

The group I hung out with in junior high school was primarily Cuban and Jewish. After school there was a different group that I ran with, Irish, Puerto Rican—a true melting pot, that area of Queens at that time. I missed my friends, so I always wrote letters. All they ever wanted was, Hey, can you send us a real baseball? And, of course, I missed my family.

One of my classmates was Judy Fox. We were like brother and sister. She knew what I was going through, and she said, "Hey, my dad needs somebody to help him." This was ninth grade or so. I went to work for them, Murray Fox and Edie Fox. By the time I was finishing high school, Harry and Elba wanted to move upstate to get better schools, and I didn't want to go. Murray and Edie said, "You come live with us." I lived with them from then on.

I worked at their store, my parents' store, a Jewish family store. In the front we sold housewares. In the back, we had a yarn store where all the ladies would sit and knit or crochet all day and gossip. Even when I had class, I didn't go to class or I dropped in and came right back. We'd work until eight, nine o'clock every night and then go out to eat. They were family.

I never paid for room and board. Murray never paid me. It was always, "Hey, I need twenty bucks." "Yeah, just take it." It always worked that way. He was the most liberal person I know. They were really pushy on education, especially Edie. I went through college living there, totally out of the goodness of their hearts. You don't realize how unusual that is until you get out into the world.

Nestor A. Rodriguez
MIAMI, FLORIDA

After twenty months in Madrid, thirteen-year-old Nestor, his sister, and his parents received permission to enter the US. They arrived in 1971, almost nine years after they filed papers to leave their home in Jaruco, near the model town of Hershey.

We arrived in Miami late that night. I forget exactly the moment, but family was here. I remember the weather. It was June. Humid.

Miami was *nothing* like it is today. It was purer, in a sense, very similar to the post-cards. There was something different about Miami that I picked up. It had to do with the weather. The landscape looked like Cuba, the palm trees and coconut trees and the beach. It was very similar to Cuba, and that was comforting. But I also felt very detached and concerned as to what it was going to be like here and concerns about survival.

We went to my aunt's house. There were four of us. We had other relatives, so I ended up living with my mother and sister at one of my grandmother's sister's, while my father stayed with his sister. Then he was able to get an apartment and buy a car. We rented a little one-bedroom efficiency in what's now called Little Havana. We lived there for about a year, year and a half. Then we moved to a three-bedroom apartment.

My father started to work in accounting for a couple of companies. My mother started to work at a factory building airplane parts, and then at night she went to Barry University and got three degrees, her bachelor's and two masters. She learned English and taught piano at home. My mother was more ambitious; she wanted to teach school.

I learned some English in Spain, but I had to learn it when I got here. Sister was four when she arrived here, so she immediately picked it up. My mother was in school, so she got home late, but my sister and I were glued to the TV.

I went to a series of schools. I was put behind one year because of my English. I went to Miami High in 1975, graduating in '77. I finally felt comfortable enough with my language skills to be sociable. A lot of it had to do with my participation in marching band and in concert band. I became very involved with the music club, and I was pianist for the chorus.

My maternal grandparents arrived here when I was at Miami High. They were the love of my life, my grandparents who lived in Hershey. We claimed them. They got out pretty quickly, probably two years. They came from Spain also, so they lived in Spain for a little bit, three months. They got here, and we settled them in.

Progressively my parents did better. My father was able to buy a house in '76, ' 77. My senior year in high school he bought a townhouse in Sweetwater. That became our home.

As the Cuban diaspora unfolded during the Second Wave, some refugees who had settled elsewhere in earlier years made their way to the US mainland or territories like Puerto Rico.

Diana Sawaya-Crane

TALLAHASSEE, FLORIDA

*Diana and her sister Hilda lived with their parents in the small town of Colón,
Venezuela. Their father Assad had emigrated to Cuba from Lebanon many years
before but left for work in Venezuela in the 1950s. The family reunited there in 1959.*

Once my parents realized there was no going back, they decided to send us to the
United States, where their families were living. We were both in high school. Our
parents considered this country to be the land of opportunity with the best form of
government in the world and the best educational system.

They contacted Dad's sister, from the Lebanese side of the family. She and her
husband were retired. They lived in Maine six months of the year, and the other six
months they lived in St. Petersburg. She came to visit us in 1965 or 1966. She didn't
speak Spanish, and we didn't speak much English, but she could speak Arabic with
my dad. She probably went there to check us out and see if it would work out for us
to come live with them.

To come to the United States, we had to go through many steps to get student
visas. My sister came in 1967 to go to St. Petersburg Junior College. She did not speak
English fluently, but she learned it quickly. When she came, SPJC was not requiring
foreign students to take an English proficiency test. It was instituted the following
year. Foreign students whose first language was not English had to take the test to
enroll in universities or colleges.

When I came in 1968, it was *such* an overwhelming experience. I was sixteen years
old, and I had just graduated from high school. I remember leaving from Caracas on
August 15, 1968. Hilda had returned to Venezuela for the summer, so she and I flew
to Miami and then to Tampa. I had never been to the US. I remember getting off the
plane and walking down the stairs. I thought something was *very* wrong because it
was *so incredibly hot*. It was like an *oven*.

St. Petersburg seemed like a movie set because everything was so *clean* and so
perfect, and the houses looked so *beautiful*. They looked like dollhouses. It was sur-
real. All I could go on was the movies I had seen. I guess that was my idea of what it
would be like.

We arrived at our aunt and uncle's home. They lived in this bungalow, and my
aunt and uncle were not there. They were still in Maine, but Hilda had the key. There
was no food in the house, so my sister and I walked to Publix because we didn't have

any transportation.[†] And *that* was—oh my gosh! *What* an experience! *To walk into Publix!* I was *overwhelmed*.

I had never seen *so* much food and *so* many choices and *so* many different things. It was *unbelievable*, just the abundance. The vegetables and fruits looked so *beautiful*. Not a *spot* on them. So many *boxes* of wonderful stuff. We bought a lot of food. Luckily for us, the manager let us take the grocery cart back to the house because we were walking.

I had taken the test in Venezuela. I think I got five out of one hundred. I enrolled in an adult education center in downtown St. Petersburg. It didn't help. I took the test in December and failed. Hilda went to St. Pete High School and asked the principal if I could enroll as an audit student to enable me to interact with English-speaking people and learn the language. They said yes. I went to St. Pete High for several months, until I took the test and passed.

I was accepted at St. Petersburg Junior College, late 1969 or 1970. There were hippies on campus, antiwar debates, and demonstrations. It was very different. But the students I met were accepting of foreign students. We met very kind people who helped us along the way.

Adolfo Henriques

KEY BISCAYNE, FLORIDA

Adolfo and his two brothers excelled at their schools in Kingston, Jamaica, where the family settled after leaving Havana in January 1961. Their father Charles had been the Bank of Nova Scotia's top executive in Cuba, but he took a lesser position with the bank when he and his wife Maria took the family into exile in Jamaica.

In November of 1966 my dad was transferred to the Dominican Republic as general manager of the Bank of Nova Scotia. I got to the Dominican Republic a year after they had civil unrest that resulted in the United States sending troops.[‡] There was still a US military presence, but eventually they left. The three years that we spent there were good years for living in the Dominican Republic.

---

† Publix Super Markets is a chain of grocery stores based in Lakeland, Florida.
‡ President Johnson sent US troops to the Dominican Republic in 1965 to quell a leftist revolt against the ruling military junta and thus prevent "a second Cuba" in the Caribbean.

My brothers and I were enrolled in an American high school. I was at a more advanced level in Jamaica than in the Dominican Republic but was introduced to subjects like US history, world history, and government. Sciences, math, and language skills, I was ahead of the game. I was number one in my class in the Dominican Republic through high school. I finished high school there. That same year, my dad was transferred back to Jamaica to run the bank's operations there.

I came to the University of Miami. My high school paid the application fees for me to apply to other schools because I scored well on the SATs and I had great grades. I got into every one of them—Boston, et cetera—but Miami was it. My brother was coming to school here. My parents wanted us close. I spent one year at the University of Miami.

I wanted to study medicine. I realized it would be easier to get into medical school in Jamaica, so I enrolled at the University of the West Indies and stayed in Jamaica for a couple of years. Along the way, I realized that I did *not* want to study medicine. My older brother had finished an accounting degree and was getting his master's. That's what I ended up doing.

I got reaccepted at the University of Miami, but my kid brother was coming to a small school in the middle of Florida called Saint Leo.§ I ended up coming to Saint Leo, and I finished my undergraduate degree in business and accounting there in 1974.

Jorge M. Duany

DORAL, FLORIDA

Jorge's father Rafael—a member of the prominent Duany clan of Santiago de

Cuba—resigned his job as a Havana television producer and director in 1960

and found a new job in Panama City, Panama. Then he sent for his wife Mirtha

and two sons. Jorge, a distant cousin of Andrés Duany, was three years old.

My father had to reinvent himself five or six times. I don't think he had a definite vocation. He had been a swimming coach. He had worked for the family business in Santiago. He had studied radio broadcasting in the US. He was a theater director. He had all kinds of occupations.

Television was one of the areas in which the Cuban revolutionary government intervened more quickly. He resigned his position at the TV station in Havana, found another job in Panama, and left by himself. There were six months, nine months, be-

§ Saint Leo University, located in Central Florida, was the first Roman Catholic college in the state.

tween his leaving and the rest of the family leaving, which at that point was only my mother and my older brother. We settled in Panama on December 26, 1960.

My mother was a teacher by training. She didn't want to leave. She initially identified with Fidel and the revolution. It was a difficult decision because she left her mother, two siblings, and the rest of the family. My father wouldn't talk about politics. I never had any conversation with him about what he thought about the revolution. Clearly he wasn't sympathetic to it.

My brother and I went to a Jesuit school, then we moved to La Salle. My mother was teaching Spanish there, but then she became pregnant, and they let her go. For some reason they decided that my mother was not fit to be teaching while she was pregnant.

We were sent to study in the Panama Canal Zone.[¶] It was a missionary Catholic school. It was a standard American school, like anywhere else in the US, for Americans in the Canal Zone and for some Panamanians and others who spoke English. Most of the teachers were American. My parents wanted me and my brother to learn English.

Each morning we took a van with six or seven students. We'd go to the Canal Zone and come back every day. It was like an American military base. There was a clear boundary between the Canal Zone and the rest of the city. It was very tense and divided. It was difficult for me because I looked like an American, and it was not the best place to look like a *gringo*, especially in the 1960s, because there were riots at the border of the zone.

I didn't know much English. I had an interpreter; the teacher assigned me a girl who was Panamanian. She helped me with my homework and translated for me because I didn't understand what was going on in the classroom. I didn't do well my first semester. The second semester I did much better. That's where I picked up most of my basic English. At some point we got a green card.

In 1966 my father lost his job. He went to Puerto Rico, which is the reason the family moved there. We always lived in the San Juan area. We first lived close to my father's work. He would walk a few blocks to Miller International, which was a producing company for TV in Puerto Rico. He did that for a number of years. We went to school nearby.

I lived in Puerto Rico from '66 to '75, until I came to study in the States.

The Cuban Refugee Center told exiles if a relative was on an approved list for the Freedom Flights, but they did not know when the relative would arrive because flight assignments in Cuba were random. Most refugees did not know their departure date until just days before leaving. Spanish-language radio sta-

---

¶   The Panama Canal Zone was a 553-square-mile unincorporated area that was granted by Panama to the US in 1904 to facilitate construction and operation of the canal. It reverted to Panama by treaty in 1979.

tions in Miami broadcast a list of names of the day's arrivals, and the *Miami Herald* printed the list the next morning.[27]

For exiles in the US, the chance for family members to leave—through third countries or on the Freedom Flights—created a frantic rush to bring out loved ones. When relatives arrived, after years of waiting, there was a celebration and then the reality of life in exile.

Mario Cartaya

FORT LAUDERDALE, FLORIDA

Mario and his brother lived with their parents in suburban Hialeah. An accountant by profession, their father Ignacio worked long hours at a commercial laundry until his health faltered. Next he sold Bibles and then got a job as a bookkeeper. Their mother Leida got a job as a teacher's aide and, after earning her certification, a teacher.

Most of the money my father saved was spent in bringing family members from Cuba. They came out through Spain—that's how my grandmother and her sister came out—or through Mexico—that's how my mother's brother, his wife, and his son, came out. My father brought as many family members as he could.

You could buy a human in the late 1960s. The cost was $5,000 per person, payable to the Cuban government, and that included the airfare. That was a lot of money. You also had to pay for the hotel in the transfer country until their visa to the US was approved and they could arrive here legally. That was the process, flawed but effective. My father paid for it all.

Myriam Márquez

MIAMI BEACH, FLORIDA

Myriam and her parents were among the first refugees to leave Cuba in 1959, and they left behind many family members. Myriam's father Alberto sold cars, and her mother Irene worked at a hat factory in Miami. Eventually Alberto and Irene divorced, and she remarried. As conditions deteriorated in Cuba and the regime allowed emigration, relatives began to arrive.

My mother was having a crisis because her parents were there, and she wanted to bring them out. She was sending them money through Mexico. Calling Cuba was an experience because you had to go through a third-party line, and you had to wait until they called. It could be two to three days. If you missed that call, you had to start the whole process over again.

My aunt, my mother's only living sister, went through Venezuela to come to Miami. Then my grandparents came on the Freedom Flights. They got here in '70 because my sister had just been born, my sister from my mom's second marriage. It was a huge deal. They took them from the airport to a holding area, and there was a fence there. My mom's emotion when she saw her aging parents coming out—and they had aged a *lot*—that was big.

They lived with us, and we made room in our house. We also had an older cousin who had come about six months before them on the Freedom Flights. To make room for all these people, my stepdad took this big wide family room, split it in half, put up a wall, converted one side into two little bedrooms, and over here was what was left of the family room. Typical Cuban house.

I remember going to different homes to welcome the next person who came, people that were friends. This was very rudimentary. People were just getting lives together, so you would go to a house or an apartment. They would have *pastelitos*, and they might have *croquetas*.** They'd have old Cuban songs playing. There were record companies in Miami that were producing records that had been over there.

They would talk and talk and talk, telling how bad it was.

Luis Cruz Azaceta
NEW ORLEANS, LOUISIANA

Six years after he entered exile in November 1960, twenty-four-year-old Luis was living in Queens, New York, with his sister Sonia and an aunt. He worked at a button factory in Manhattan and attended art school at night. He worked to bring his father and mother out of Cuba. They arrived in 1966.

We tried to get them out through Jamaica, Canada, for all those years, but they couldn't get out. It was not allowed. Then they opened the doors. We saw the op-

---

** A *pastilito* is a meat-filled puff pastry. A *croqueta* is a bread-crumbed fried roll with a filling of meat, fish, cheese, mashed potatoes, rice, or a vegetable.

portunity, so we got them here. They came through Miami as refugees. I got a lawyer. He did all the paperwork.

They spent two or three days in Miami. Then they came to Kennedy, where the whole family went to receive them—everybody, all my aunts, my uncles, they all came. That was an experience, seeing my father on the escalator with a *very* long coat. It was very emotional to see my mother. They came with nothing at all.

We all lived together in Astoria, my aunt Sara, Sonia, and I and my parents. My father started working in a factory in Queens. We didn't want him to do that, but he said, "No, I have to make money." He was old. After retirement, to start working again in a factory. Imagine that!

They used to send the workers in a factory to get coffee, get *pan con mantequilla*, you know, bread and butter. He started buying *panacillos* from the bakery, which were much better.†† He would open them and put butter in there, and that's what he would sell to the workers at the factory. He was always looking to make an extra buck.

I was able to go at night to the School of Visual Arts, and I liked it a lot. But I said, "This is not enough. I've got to go during the day." I quit the button company and went to work at the NYU library, in '67. My first year during the day I won a competition in an exhibition. They gave me a partial scholarship.

I was working part-time at night, getting up around six o'clock in the morning, going to school at eight, leaving around three to four o'clock, going to the library to work part-time, going home and doing homework, sometimes until three o'clock in the morning. I did it for four years.

As the Freedom Flights continued with clock-like precision, both sides had reason to regret the agreement to organize the evacuation, and for the same reason: no one expected so many Cubans to clamor for a seat on the aging propeller-driven planes that ferried them across the straits. One refugee woman gave birth to a daughter in midflight.[28]

The airbridge created social, political, and fiscal issues in the US. In 1968, after racial disturbances in Miami's Liberty City ghetto, the *Miami Herald* called for an end to the Freedom Flights, arguing that Cuban refugees got more assistance than impoverished Americans.[29] The *Herald* also argued that the airbridge undermined the US isolation policy intended to bring down the Castro regime.[30] Eventually the newspaper advocated a phase-out of the CRP.[31]

A Senate committee voted in 1971 to keep funding the CRP but to stop funding the flights.[32] However, opponents backed down after Florida's sena-

†† A *panacillo* is a small round or oblong loaf of bread.

tors and the Nixon Administration successfully argued that it would be unfair to halt the airbridge before all the Cubans who signed up for it—and consequently lost their jobs—were brought out.[33] By the time Washington began to phase out the CRP in 1978, American taxpayers had spent $1.3 billion—more than $7.8 billion in today's dollars—to assist Cuban refugees.[34]

Mercedes Fernandez Collazo

TAMPA, FLORIDA

Thirteen-year-old Mercedes, her two brothers, her parents, and her mother's parents arrived on a Freedom Flight on December 23, 1967. Mercedes's father David, a mechanic, and her mother Elvira, a homemaker, took the family to Tampa, where David's father lived.

When we got to Tampa we went to our grandfather's house. I think it had three bedrooms. We were seven people. I laugh about it now, but it wasn't funny. We lived with him about two weeks, and he threw us out. He was used to being by himself. My father rented a house in South Tampa. We had three bedrooms. My parents had one bedroom with my brother—I don't think he was even three years old—then my brother and I had a bedroom, and my grandparents.

My father's uncle had a gas station where he was the manager. He talked to one of the guys, and they gave my father a gas station so he could run it. Since he was a mechanic he ran the gas station. My mother would be the cashier, and my father pumped the gas. She pumped the gas when he was busy being the mechanic. He managed different gas stations for years.

I was thirteen. I was an age that I wasn't a kid, and I wasn't a woman, just in-between. I went to Madison Junior High. In Cuba I had just graduated from sixth grade. They placed me in eighth grade because I was able to do eighth-grade math. I didn't know how to speak English. In about a year I picked it up from being at school, from watching TV. I still have my accent.

There was one Cuban student. She helped me out. Whatever she was doing I would sit with her. When the teachers said something, she translated because I didn't know how to speak English. I took whatever she took. But in a year I was able to do my own thing. I liked home economics, learning how to cook, to make your own dress. Everything was so fast.

Then I went to Plant High School in South Tampa. I had pretty good grades, considering that it was hard. I was getting through a language barrier. I tell you, it just flew. I was going to school, and then I met my husband. I graduated in June, and I got married in February. My parents had to run to the courthouse and sign for me because I was seventeen.

The Second Wave refugees were from lower economic rungs than those in the First Wave.[35] By 1973 only 6 percent of all Freedom Flight refugees had professional, semiprofessional, or managerial occupations; 9 percent were skilled workers; 4 percent semiskilled workers; 3 percent service workers; 2 percent farmers and fishers; and 64 percent children, students, and "housewives."[36] The average age was 47.5 years.[37] As a group, they were older, less educated, and more female than the First Wave.

Most Cubans of Chinese or Jewish descent left the island by the end of the Freedom Flights, and most settled in New York or Florida. Again, Cubans of color were the most underrepresented racial or ethnic group.[38] Of 1971 arrivals only 2 percent were Black and 4 percent were mixed-race.[39] Their numbers were limited by the fact that the Freedom Flights were reserved for those with relatives in the US, and so few Blacks and mixed-race Cubans had gone in the First Wave that few Cubans of color on the island had relatives in the US to claim them. In addition, Black and mixed-race persons were leery of the US with its history of racial discrimination. Most of those who came settled in northeastern cities.[40]

The new refugees had one thing in common with the First Wave: they arrived with no money.[41]

Maribel Pérez Henley
MIAMI, FLORIDA

Six-year-old Maribel arrived on a Freedom Flight on December 22, 1970, with her parents. They left behind four of her father's siblings who were with the revolution and their families. They joined her father's parents and five siblings and their families in Miami.

For me the plane ride was amazing. It was in the morning. My parents were elated. As soon as I walked into the plane, I could smell toys. Don't ask me why, but I smelled toys.

We sat down, and the stewardess gave us food—*real* food. It was sandwiches, something to drink. I ate part of my sandwich, and I'm there folding it with a paper towel to save it. Because food was scarce. I was sickly in Cuba and underweight. She comes over and says, "Why aren't you eating?" She spoke Spanish. I tell her, "I'm saving it for later because I want to make sure I have something to eat." She goes, "Oh, no, no, no, no. You have to eat all of it. Where you're going, you're going to have a lot of food." I remember her bringing me another sandwich.

We arrived here right away. They put us on a bus, and we were taken to Freedom Tower. We went through some lines and some rooms. We saw all these different people trying to help us. We had to show them all these papers. We didn't have luggage. It was just us with the clothes we were wearing, so there was nothing to inspect. We were in shock, all three of us, because it was a strange place. It was chaotic. My parents left with paperwork to get help, Social Security, that kind of stuff. It was night when we got out. We were picked up by my grandfather, my grandmother, my aunt, and my uncle.

We lived with my aunt and uncle. It was a one-bedroom apartment. I arrived on December twenty-second. It was two days from Christmas. I walked into a room *filled* with toys. My aunt never had kids, so *I* was her kid.

We slept in the living room. My aunt and uncle worked in a garment factory. They were afraid they would get kicked out of the apartment because there were no children allowed. At that time that was very prevalent. I wasn't allowed to go outside. I said, "Oh, my God, I came to this country to be hidden." I never went outside until we moved. My mom did not work.

It didn't bother me that I couldn't go outside. I had all these people providing for me. I had clothes, I had shoes, I had food. I was hidden, but I had all these things. I was in heaven. So, it was fine. We were navigating through a place where we didn't know what was going on.

My father is a go-getter. From being a baker, he went to construction. He realized he wasn't going to be a baker here, but he wanted to have his own place with his wife and myself. He saved money and bought himself one of those little Falcons. Finally, after a year, year and a half, we moved, and I started first grade. Age-wise, I was a year behind because I was here for a year and didn't go to school. I didn't have problems. I loved school.

I went to school one day, and a week later I was speaking English. Like a fluke of nature, I learned English immediately, and I *didn't* have an accent. To the point that I was handling all the administrative stuff of the family: all the Social Security appointments, all the Medicaid appointments, all the citizenship appointments. You name it, I was doing it.

We moved like ten times before we finally settled in Hialeah.

As extraordinary as they were, the Freedom Flights began in 1965 just as the US stepped up its military involvement in Vietnam, re-directing the nation's attention from a Cold War conflict in the Caribbean to a shooting war in Southeast Asia. The American combat role ended on March 29, 1973, one week before the airbridge closed.[42]

When the last Freedom Flight taxied to a halt on April 6, 1973, some 260,561 Cuban refugees had crossed the airbridge. US officials estimated that another 30,000 Cubans wanted passage on the Freedom Flights.[43] Others said it was more. In all, Cuban refugees admitted to the US from 1965 through 1973 totaled 345,481.[44]

The Second Wave had ended.

9

SETTLED IN AMERICA

The national commitment to help the early Cuban refugees weather a short-term crisis became a national commitment to help integrate them into American life. The government gave grants to colleges for retraining programs and refresher courses to prepare refugee doctors and teachers for licensing examinations.[1] Programs assisted dentists, optometrists, social workers, and other occupational groups.[2] Courses at fifteen colleges trained Cuban professionals to teach Spanish in US schools.[3] Florida lawmakers eliminated the citizenship requirement for a professional or occupational license, authorized licensing exams in foreign languages, and directed licensing boards to implement programs to prepare Cuban refugees to take them.[4]

As the refugees spread throughout this vast country, they saw its wonders and its faults.

Silvia Morell Alderman

TALLAHASSEE, FLORIDA

When the government withdrew funding for the political arm of the effort to oust the Castro regime, Silvia's father had to find another way to support his family. A former judge on the Cuban Supreme Court of Justice, José Morell was not licensed to practice law in Florida.

There was a program at Kansas State Teachers College, now Emporia State University, to train Cuban professionals to become teachers in American schools. We had to eat, you know. We left for Kansas on February 14, 1964. The people in Emporia were *very* welcoming. The Cubans who came to that program were curiosities. Everybody wanted to talk to them. They assigned sponsor families to connect with us. The whole community took in the Cubans.

In August we moved to Chadron, Nebraska, a little town in the northwest corner of Nebraska where my dad got a job as a college professor. It is beautiful rolling hills and pine trees. The population was five thousand. That was a shock because we were used to Havana and Miami. Chadron had two stoplights, and one of those was a flashing red light. That's where I grew up. If people ask me, "Where are you from?" I tell them, "Chadron, Nebraska."

We were the only Cubans for hundreds of miles. I had the sense that I was different, even though everyone was welcoming. I made good friends. There were boys who said, "Go back to Cuba." Those kids did not do well after they got out of school. On the whole, it was a wonderful experience. We traveled back to Miami enough that we stayed in touch.

We learned the hard way there was segregation in America. My father's sister and her husband followed us into the program at Emporia the following year. They were both lawyers. My uncle was of mixed-race parentage, a very light mulatto. There was this terrible phrase in those days about how somebody could "pass for White." My uncle was like that.

While they were there, we did one of those trips to Miami. I remember going into a restaurant with them in Memphis, and all eyes were on us. They seated us. Some of those White ladies in Memphis were all freaked out. We finished our food quickly and got out of there. After that we ate in hotel rooms or in the car. That was shocking. We didn't have things quite like that in Cuba. I'm sure there was discrimination but not so blatant.

I began to experience what it was like to be an American: cheering at football games, eating apple pie, being a part of the pep club—all the things you do when you're a teenager. I had a marvelous college experience in Chadron. That's where I got my undergraduate degree. I felt very American. I had melted into the pot by that time.

I graduated from Chadron State when my father retired from teaching. We moved to Florida. I had the dream of going to law school.

In 1966 the Congress addressed the immigration status of the early Cuban refugees. Before then immigration law required Cuban refugees on temporary visas or visa waivers to go to a US consulate in a foreign country if they wanted a green card that was a prerequisite to citizenship.[5] About 75,000 Cuban refugees did so.[6] Granting the Cubans a special path to citizenship was considered and rejected by the White House as early as 1963.[7] But with so many Cuban refugees in the country on parole,[8] and up to 4,000 more arriving monthly on Freedom Flights,[9] the Congress passed the Cuban Adjustment Act of 1966, and President Johnson signed it.[10]

The statute allowed a Cuban who entered the US with or without a visa after January 1, 1959, and remained in the country for two years, to ask the government to "adjust" his or her status to permanent resident.[11] The two-year requirement was later reduced to one year.[12] More important, the adjustment was retroactive up to thirty months, thus cutting by as much as half the normal five-year wait time for permanent residents to apply for citizenship. The hope was that granting Cuban exiles permanent resident status and a shorter path to citizenship would enable them to rebuild their careers, support their families, and tie them to the US.[13]

The government set up a Cuban Adjustment Center in Miami to process applications.[14] By the end of 1974, 200,000 refugees had applied for citizenship. By 1980, 55 percent of eligible Cubans in the Miami area were citizens.[15]

Angel Castillo Jr.

MIAMI, FLORIDA

The oldest of seven children, Angel attended Miami Military Academy for part of his high school education before his family left Havana in October 1960. In Miami his lawyer father worked as a door-to-door salesman and other menial jobs while Angel attended Edison High School.

The thing that changed my life was they had one of those college information nights, and this woman from Stetson University came. I had never heard of the school. Stetson in those days was a Baptist school, which is something I have *nothing* in common with. My guidance counselor encouraged me to apply because my friends were going to Miami-Dade Community College or wherever they could go.* I applied to Stetson, and they admitted me but with no financial aid.

I wrote them back and said, "I would like to attend, but I don't have any money."

---

* Founded in 1959, the two-year Dade County Junior College became Miami-Dade Community College. It is now the four-year Miami Dade College with eight campuses and 165,000 students, many of them immigrants.

Incredibly, they wrote back and said, "Okay, you can have this scholarship, this loan, and you can work in the cafeteria." I didn't have a great record in high school, but they were very generous. So that's how I got to go to college.

My parents were humiliated that they didn't have the money to send me to college. My mother would occasionally mail me a five-dollar bill when I was in school. I couldn't afford to make long-distance telephone calls or come home for the holidays.

That lasted until they moved to Los Angeles in '65. California passed a law to require the teaching of Spanish in public schools. They didn't have enough teachers, so they sent recruiters to Miami. Here, there was this pool of lawyers and doctors and people who couldn't practice their professions, so my father and a number of his lawyer friends were recruited.

They moved to Los Angeles. Everybody moved but me because I was attending Stetson. They went to school at night at Mount St. Mary's College. My father, at this late point in life, obtained a master's degree in Spanish literature. My mother also got that degree.

Once my father and mother moved to Los Angeles, that's when their life became normal again. They were able to buy a house. My father taught Spanish in seventh and eighth grade in a Black school in Compton until he died from heart disease in 1976 at age fifty-nine. My mother ended up working for a bank in the back office until she retired.

I had a great time at Stetson. My degree was issued in '68. I had no idea what I wanted to do. I went to the *Miami Herald*, and I said, "I used to deliver this paper, I just got out of college, and I'd like to get a job here." That was my start in journalism. I did that for almost ten years, until I decided to go to law school.

I've heard a lot of stories of people who ended up in Chicago and all these cold places, but what I picked up about Cubans is that they're *survivors*, they're entrepreneurial, and they get ahead. I have felt blessed and grateful that we have had those opportunities and those drives.

The challenges for refugee lawyers were particularly vexing because the legal systems of the two countries differed.[16] In 1973 the Florida Supreme Court authorized the University of Florida and the University of Miami to offer special courses to prepare qualified refugee lawyers to take the bar exam.[17] The court also removed the citizenship requirement for a license to practice law.[18]

Julian C. Juergensmeyer

ATLANTA, GEORGIA

*Born in Kentucky, Julian was a law professor at the University of Florida in
1973 when he was asked to lead the university's Cuban American Lawyers
Program. He had trained in France in the civil law systems of Europe and Latin
countries like Cuba. Those systems were fundamentally different from the US
legal system based on England's judge-made common law.*

The biggest thing is the reliance of civil law lawyers on codes—civil code, commercial
code, criminal code, civil procedure code, all based on the Napoleonic Code. Cuba had
all codes, most of them closely inspired by Spanish codes. Cases are relatively unim-
portant in civil law, so the big task was to transition Cuban lawyers from a code orientation to a case law orientation. They weren't used to reading cases. The idea we came up
with was to build on the Cuban lawyers' civil law background rather than treat them as
nonlawyers and start from scratch. It was a good theory, but frankly it didn't work well
because we needed to use UF professors, and few had any civil law training.

The University of Miami did a program, but they didn't fill the need because of
the cost, and they wanted to keep it small. The Miami program was able to do theirs
mostly at night during the week, but ours was all day Saturday and all day Sunday.
UF felt that we had to make the program more generally available. Our tuition was
small compared to Miami. It was set up as a one-time event. We had several entering
classes. We graduated 314.

We did the bar exam topics, only in English—you know, the first-year courses:
property, torts, contracts, business organizations, civil procedure, criminal procedure. It wasn't a degree program; it was a program to qualify them to take the Florida
bar exam. We tried to prepare them for practicing in the States as well as passing the
bar, so it was more than tutoring.

There were elderly people in the program and some quite young. There was
a big range in terms of whether people had had a successful practice in Cuba or
whether they'd only recently been admitted to the bar or had worked in industry,
never practicing law even though they had a degree. Quite a few Cuban lawyers in
Miami were working as consultants with firms. A lot of them had adjusted totally,
spoke excellent English, understood the lectures. Then there were a lot who were
not adjusting well, were having financial difficulties, were unhappy, their English
not as good as it needed to be.

There was a good bit of controversy over whether they should have some sort of degree, and there was a lot of controversy over whether they should be considered UF law graduates. As it turned out, all they got was certification to take the bar. A lot of them never came to grips with that, and as a result were disappointed. A relatively small number passed the bar.

Carmen Leiva Roiz
MIAMI, FLORIDA

Carmen received a law degree from St. Thomas of Villanova Catholic University but never practiced before she, her husband Juan, and their infant son left Cuba in 1960. Carmen's husband got corporate jobs in Connecticut, where they had a daughter, then in Peru, Cleveland, and Brazil. Their son had been diagnosed with cystic fibrosis.

I loved Brazil. I would have lived there all my life. I had a *beautiful* huge house. It was a wonderful time of my life, until my husband became ill with multiple sclerosis, and the company dismissed him. They didn't give that reason; they gave another reason. The day that he was diagnosed, I was sitting in that living room. I looked around, and I said, "I cannot support this life. I have to go to work." I came to Miami—where else? My parents were in Miami. I needed the support of my family and my friends. That was 1972.

I went to the University of Miami. There was a program for Cuban attorneys, and I took it. That was every evening. I wanted to become a lawyer and support my family. One of the prerequisites of that program was to have practiced law in Cuba, which I didn't meet. But they waived that prerequisite for some people. It was a good course; I did well. I finished in '75.

I took the bar the first time. I had a lot of problems on my hands, and I failed. When I tried to pass the bar exam again, they told me I didn't meet the requirements of the program that I took because I hadn't practiced. They didn't allow me to take it again. That was the bar examiners.† I appealed—nothing. It was very frustrating.

I was *drained*. I had a husband in bed, unable to move; a son going in and out of the hospital; a teenage daughter; and two elderly parents who were my salvation. My parents took care of my husband, feeding him, bathing him, everything. Thank God for my parents.

---

† The Florida Board of Bar Examiners, an administrative agency of the Florida Supreme Court, regulates the admission of lawyers to practice law in Florida, including the bar exam.

My first job was at the Coca-Cola Bottling Company. I was an executive secretary, and I couldn't type. I did everything. One day the phone operator didn't show up, and they asked me if I could go to the switchboard. I had no idea what I was doing. I transferred calls, they went the wrong way. I remember Lucille Ball doing that on *I Love Lucy*, and I was doing the same.

My son Johnny died in 1980. He was twenty. My husband died eight months after. That was the worst crisis of my life.

By then I had left the bottling company, and I was working for a needlepoint place in Coconut Grove. I saw this ad asking for a writer for a magazine. I sent in my résumé, so they asked me to write something. When they received my sample, they loved it. I learned the craft, and I was very happy. Then I learned that the *Miami Herald* was opening a Spanish newspaper, and they were looking for journalists. I needed the money, so I sent my résumé. I got the job. While I was doing that, I applied at another magazine, and I got a job. I loved working on the magazines.

Only 14 percent of the refugee lawyers who took the Florida bar exam in July 1975 passed, far below the overall 90 percent passing rate. The Florida Supreme Court in 1976 and again in 1979 denied requests for oral examinations and for reduced grading standards and other dispensations for refugee lawyers seeking bar admission.[19]

While parents struggled to feed, clothe, and shelter their families or re-establish interrupted careers, their children adapted to their new homeland. Miami's public schools pioneered bilingual education for Spanish-speaking pupils.[20] Those brought to the US before or during their formative years—sociologists call them the 1.5 generation—learned English faster and adopted American ways.[21] Many had the same experiences as their contemporaries in the Baby Boom generation.[22]

Cesar E. Calvet

ORLANDO, FLORIDA

In March 1966 Cesar received his induction notice from the Orlando draft board. He was in New York, working and studying part-time at a community college. His parents had just arrived from Cuba. Cesar returned to Florida and was inducted into the Marine Corps. He never went to Vietnam. His overseas assignment was a forty-five-square-mile base closer to home.

The company that I was with deployed to Guantánamo. That was '66, so I spent my twenty-first birthday and Christmas and New Year's in Cuba. To the Americans, it was lousy. For me, I was home. It was a very good feeling.

The marines do the protection. The navy's not going to run the mortars or the infantry. That's the job of the marines. Most of the time I was in a position called Suicide Ridge, which is one side of the base. We were not in the hills; the Cubans were there. Then there's the side where the airstrip is. The barracks are there, you've got a fence. And that one, you are *right* next to the Cuban side.

When we landed, we went to Suicide Ridge in an emergency. The sergeant came and said, "The lieutenant wants to see you," so I went to the lieutenant's bunker. He said, "I understand you're from Cuba." I said, "Yes, sir." I was the only Cuban, navy or marine, on the base. He said, "I don't want you to get any ideas about visiting your relatives." I said, "Lieutenant, with all due respect, sir, they would shoot me before they shoot you. I will be armed when I am on the hills." He smiled and didn't say anything after that.

There were a lot of civilian jobs to be done. Maintenance, everything. There were a few Cuban workers there. I don't know how many trucks came in every day that took people across.‡ Then you had people who requested asylum in the US. There was housing for those who were no longer going back to Cuba. They even had a place in the woods to have cockfights. Some of them eventually came to the States.

We had to stay with the military, but I talked to the Cubans at the end. They had a bar where their housing was. I ended up a couple of nights going to their bar. The Cubans on the base were proud of the fact that I was in the marines. They said, "You're a *marine!*" They'd heard about the marines.

I was at Guantánamo for six months.

Carlos Alvarez

TALLAHASSEE, FLORIDA

Carlos, his brothers Cesar and Arturo, and later his sister Ana attended a parochial school in North Miami. Their parents brought them to the US in June 1960 with green cards and from the start wanted them to become Americans. They were the only Cubans in their neighborhood.

---

‡ Cuban workers commuted to the base daily, but in 1961 the navy began to hire Jamaican contract workers. In 1964 Castro cut off the base's water supply, prompting the navy to install a desalination plant and to fire many commuters and hire more Jamaicans. Some 300 commuters declared themselves exiles and stayed on the base.

We were short of money, so Cesar decided to get a *Miami Herald* route. Then Arturo got a route next to Cesar's. We lied about my age, and I got a route next to Arturo. All three of us had paper routes next to each other. I was so small that I could not ride a bike with all the papers, so I ran my route and my dad would leave the papers every block, which helped me a lot because that got me in great shape. It was every day, 365 days a year. Ended up working that way for three years.

Cesar had a friend who said, "There's a Boys Club near here, and kids play sports. Maybe you guys would want to go." So we went to the Boys Club, and that changed everything. That got us back into sports.

I was mediocre in basketball, but I was good in baseball because that's what Cuban kids play. Then football came along, and I didn't want to play. I didn't understand the sport, but all the kids moved from sport to sport. They said, "You ought to try it." I thought, This is the ultimate American sport. If you want to be an American, you've got to play football. That's why I decided, Yeah, I'll play football. This is my key to being an American. This will get me my red badge of courage, I'll be an American. I went out for the team.

I was the fastest kid, so they made me the quarterback because they had the quarterbacks run all the way to the outside. The plays were simple, and I enjoyed it. A number of times I slept in my football uniform.

The first time I ever touched a football in a real game, I scored a touchdown. It was the first game of the year. We got the kickoff, and the first play was a sweep around the end. I got the ball, and I was sweeping around the end, like typical pee wee football. I don't know where their players went, but there was nobody there. So I kept going. Except I was still new to the game, I didn't know when to stop. I went all the way to a chain-link fence after the goal line, maybe thirty yards, and I touched the fence. I turned around, and all the kids on my team jumped on me, and I started jumping around. I was just beside myself. Oh, gosh, to this day I laugh about that.

We beat the hell out of that team. That sold me on football. I liked that it was physical, and I thought it was the key to being an American. Of course, the second game we played a good team, and we got the hell beaten out of us.

By eighth grade I was really into football. I played baseball and basketball until I got into high school, and in high school I played football and basketball. I dropped baseball because baseball interfered with spring football practice. I sometimes wish I had stayed with baseball. Certainly from an injury standpoint, it would have been better.

I didn't know anything about football scholarships until my senior year when I broke through athletically, in terms of body strength and everything else you had to be. I was a running back. After my second game, I was leading the county in rushing, so Vanderbilt offered me a scholarship. At that time, once they recruited you they couldn't take that scholarship away, so it was four years, all paid. My dad was thrilled. Then I got offers from Florida, LSU, Georgia, Georgia Tech, Miami. FSU did not offer me a scholarship. We had a coach from FSU, and because I had had a basketball knee injury the year before, he thought my knee wasn't good enough.

I thought, I'm not strong enough to be a running back or take that punishment. In college I want to play wide receiver. And Florida—really all the schools—told me they would try me out as a wide receiver. I also wanted to move away from Miami. My brother Cesar had started at the University of Florida. So I thought, Yeah, Florida, especially with my brother Cesar there and Arturo headed there for my freshman year.

It's funny the way it played out because we never lost to FSU when I played, and it was always *the* game for Florida players. It was the perfect place for me. It worked out really well.

Gabriel Castillo

MIAMI, FLORIDA

Gaby arrived with his grandmother on a Freedom Flight in 1966. His parents had divorced in Cuba years before, and his exiled mother claimed him. After a few years in the Central Florida town of Sanford, where he was set back two grades in school, Gaby and his mother moved to Tampa near her parents.

Tampa is where I finally encountered some rejection. I started Plant High School in 1969. The Cuban descendants with last names like González, Pérez, there was a certain rejection. I was a newcomer. It happens every time. Cubans reject the ones who are coming in now because they're newer. That's what happened in Tampa. It would've gone on if I would've paid attention to it.

My mother was a single woman, surviving, bartending. When they had the draft she said, "I took you out of a communist country because I didn't want you to serve the military. I don't want you to serve the military here. If I have to send you to Canada, I'm going to send you to Canada." I said, "Mom, if I have to go, I've got to go." Luckily, Nixon put in the lottery.[§]

---

§ The US military draft switched to a lottery system in 1969 after decades of relying upon a classification system that included deferments for college students, medical specialists, and others.

I hung out with the hippies and the musicians and the long hairs. I was a garage band rock musician, playing drums. I should've graduated in 1970, but it was 1972. Then I went a couple of years to Hillsborough Community College, associate of arts degree, but I didn't go on. I became a full-time musician as a twenty-year-old. I did gigs in Chicago, Pennsylvania, Georgia. And that's how I became what I am today—a professional non-famous musician.

I went through the regular cycle of my generation. I had my encounter with drugs and alcohol combined. I became sober October 18, 1984, through AA and a higher power of my own understanding. I would not trade the worst day of my life now for the best one that I used to have before October 18, 1984, when I saw a different way of living.

I was tired of being tired. I started thinking, What am I doing? One image that came into my head and into my heart was my grandfather. He came here almost seventy years old. He started all over again. He was a tailor. No English, just, "Good morning. Thank you. Good night." I said, If he started again at seventy, I can start again at thirty-two.

Some young Cuban Americans began to search for their identity. Students of Cuban heritage who were influenced by the civil rights and antiwar movements formed the Antonio Maceo Brigade in 1977 so young exiles could visit the island to explore its revolutionary project. Some became disillusioned as they saw conditions on the island and the regime's totalitarian ways.[23] For many, their parents considered it a betrayal.[24]

As they grew, young Cuban Americans navigated their way between America's changing social mores and the Old World customs that had shaped lives in what their parents and grandparents fondly remembered as *la Cuba de ayer* or "the Cuba of yesterday."[25]

Rafael E. "Ralph" Fernandez
TAMPA, FLORIDA

Ralph and his mother left Havana in January 1961. His father, an engineer who directed the laying of telephone cables all over the island, had gone weeks earlier. The family settled in Puerto Rico but in 1962 moved to Tampa, where Ralph's father got a job with the telephone company.

We had a cousin in Philadelphia. She had been in the United States prior to the revolution. She came to visit and introduced herself. She said, "I know a Cuban girl in Philadelphia who's moving to Tampa, and she is the prettiest thing. She's a princess. And now that I have met my little cousin, he's going to be her prince." She goes back to Philly and tells my father-in-law, Roberto Sanchez, who is a pharmacist, "I met the prince for the princess."

They moved to Tampa three or four months later. This would have been in 1965, 1966. I had just turned fifteen. I was a year younger than my class, so I was in the tenth grade. I was dating a cheerleader, and I was set in my American ways.

Roberto is a sociable guy. He invited my parents to their house. The next morning I said, "Hey, did you meet the princess?" My dad said, "Let me tell you about that princess. That's the prettiest thing I've ever seen. I cannot believe she's fourteen. She looks twenty." I was a real cheater and rat, so I called her, "Hey, you want to go out?" She said, "I'll ask my dad." He got on the phone and lit me up: "What kind of disrespect?"

A couple of weeks later we end up in some ball game at Jesuit. I tell my dad, "You see that girl in the stands? Who is that? Everybody's talking about her. Nobody's ever seen this girl." My dad said, "This is Roberto Sanchez, and this is Rebecca." I'm in shock because she *did* look twenty, and she was very pretty and super sweet. Her dad said, "My daughter cannot date. She's chaperoned, but you can come with us to a little party tonight, a Cuban get-together."

I'd never been to a Cuban function in my life. People with chaperones, the old ladies sitting around, all that. We went there, and she and I hit it off. On the patio there, I said, "Look at the stars. You and I are going to get married, and we're going to have two little girls." She looked at me and said, "Are you okay?" That's when we began.

Ana Cowley Hodges
HOUSTON, TEXAS

Ana and her five siblings, all younger than she was, grew up in Terrell, Texas, about thirty-five miles east of Dallas, after their family's arrival in 1960. Ana's father Luis, a neuropsychiatrist, worked his way up from a clinician to director of the state mental hospital in Terrell.

Terrell was so provincial. I just wanted to blend in. I wanted to wear blue jeans. My mother said, "You're not going down that route." I wasn't *allowed* to wear blue jeans, which was very upsetting when you're growing up in a town like Terrell, Texas.

The first time I wore blue jeans, they were blue jean cutoffs, and that was because I was in drill team. We were practicing routines in the summer at the stadium, and I *had* to wear them. It took me *forever* to get on the drill team. My dad said he was not raising a can-can girl. I had to beg. I couldn't wear a two-piece swimsuit for a while.

My parents didn't think it was a good thing if I "fit in." I know that sounds snooty, but my mother did not want me to "fit in." I snuck the car out when I was fourteen, just like any of them. But my parents wouldn't let me date unless I had a chaperone, which they felt, You'll thank us for it as you get older. Well, *that* doesn't work in Terrell. I couldn't date my freshman year, but I don't think anybody wanted to ask me out. They were scared of my dad. My dad was an imposing figure. You had to meet him first like if you were in the Old World. People didn't do that in Terrell, Texas. I finally got to go out.

My mother was very keen on the idea that I was not going to the local nearby university because that's where *everybody* from Terrell went—which is where I wanted to go because that's where my friends went. It was not even a choice. She said, "There's life after Terrell, Ana."

My parents thought education was awesome. As long as we were going to school, my dad said, "I'll pay the tuition." And he did. I went to the University of Dallas because it was Catholic, and then the nuns and I didn't see eye to eye. That's when I went off to the University of Texas.

The thing was, Terrell wanted to define me, and I allowed Terrell to define me in the views of the kids I went to school with, thinking I was naïve because my parents kept me so sheltered. I walked out of Terrell to the University of Texas—well, even at the University of Dallas—and I got to define me, as opposed to people pigeon-holing me.

From the CRP's establishment in 1961 the government made need-based college loans for refugee students. What came to be known as Cuban Loans were modeled on those available for citizens under the post-Sputnik National Defense Education Act of 1958, although Cuban Loans had more liberal need criteria than federal student loan programs for citizens.[26] This was an extraordinary benefit for Cuban exiles that was not available to other refugees.

A Cuban refugee could get a loan for one thousand dollars per academic year. Larger amounts were available for those in graduate and professional schools. Repayment was to begin one year after graduation. At first the loans were interest-free but later required 3 percent interest.[27] If the student became a teacher, the government would cancel up to half the loan.[28]

The sum of one thousand dollars per academic year for a college education may seem minuscule today, but in the 1960s—depending upon the private or public school—it covered from one-third to virtually all of the average annual cost of a student's tuition, room and board, books and supplies, and other expenses.[29] By 1971 some 11,600 refugee students had taken out Cuban Loans.[30] More did so later. Many Cuban Americans who became leaders in business, the professions, government, nonprofits, and the arts went to college on Cuban Loans.

Jose E. Valiente

TAMPA, FLORIDA

Jose and his father arrived in October 1962, days before the end of regular travel between Havana and Miami due to the Missile Crisis. Jose's mother and sister arrived by way of Mexico in 1965. Jose's father, a nurse, worked at a Tampa hospital while his mother was a seamstress in a garment factory.

In my family it was not whether you're going to college, it's *where* you're going to college. My father got me here for that reason. "Whatever we have to do, we'll find it, but you and your sister are going to college." That was set in their minds, that *we* were going to college, because they knew that was the ticket—to get a college degree.

I graduated from Hillsborough High School in 1969. The University of South Florida had just opened. Since I was good in math, I said I want to be an accountant. Math has nothing to do with being an accountant, but I didn't know that. I knew USF had a great accounting department, growing university, right here in Tampa. I did well enough to be admitted. We couldn't afford for me to go anyplace else.

I don't know where it came from, but the Cuban Loan was introduced. That was God-sent. I worked. My father paid some. But ninety-nine percent of my tuition, everything, was paid from the Cuban Loan. I financed my entire college career with a Cuban Loan. I graduated in four years and paid the loan back with interest after I started working.

Mario Cartaya

FORT LAUDERDALE, FLORIDA

Mario studied hard at Miami Springs High School and played on the baseball team. His accountant father had progressed from working in a commercial laundry to working as a bookkeeper, while his mother resumed her career as a teacher in the Miami schools.

Every penny my father saved he used in bringing family from Cuba. Even though I was a real good student taking advanced classes, I had prepared myself for never attending college. How could I afford college?

I'm in my civics class, and my teacher says to me, "Mario, you are too smart not to go to college. They have something called the Cuban Loan that you can apply for. They also have a Head Start Scholarship. If you go to school in the summer, they'll pay your tuition, and if you get a B or an A, they'll give you a scholarship—half-tuition. *And* with the Cuban Loan, you can pay the other half. With the money that's left over, you can buy supplies." It was like the parting of the Red Sea. I was going to college after all.

I went to Miami-Dade Community College at first. I went to school thanks to the Cuban Loan and the Head Start Scholarship. Then I filled out applications to attend architecture school at Cornell, Tulane, the University of Florida, and the University of Tennessee. Cornell accepted me. Tulane accepted me. Florida accepted me. Tennessee did not.

I went to the University of Florida, and I fell in love with the people there. It was probably the best decision I've ever made. When I finished, I was a rare double-degree in architecture and building construction. I left Miami as an insecure Cuban American. I came back a different person, open-minded, educated, understanding the American system and American culture. Going to the University of Florida was life changing.

The hallmark of the early refugees was their industriousness. Cubans revived Union City, New Jersey, and by 1970 owned a majority of stores on bustling Bergenline Avenue.[31] Cubans created sugar plantations in South Florida's Everglades Agricultural Area.[32] They staffed Miami's garment industry.[33] For a time the city tried to issue business licenses north of Calle Ocho only to English speakers, confining the newcomers to Southwest Miami.[34] However, by the 1970s Cubans owned twenty thousand businesses throughout the city, car dealerships, radio stations, *bodegas*, and more.[35] The first Cuban-owned bank opened in 1974 in two trailers in Little Havana.[36]

To finance their ventures, they got "character loans" from Cuban-born bank officers who remembered their borrowers' success on the island.[37] Even though the vast majority of exiles were considered White and many had enjoyed privileged lives in Cuba, they benefited from civil rights protections and affirmative action policies aimed at helping racial and ethnic minorities.[38] They got loans from the Small Business Administration (SBA) far in excess of their share of Miami's population. From 1968 to 1980, 46 percent of SBA-loaned dollars in the county went to Cuban American and other Spanish-language firms compared to only 6 percent for African Americans. By 1987 more than 10 percent of Cuban Americans in the county owned a business, while fewer than 2 percent of African Americans did, and the exiles' firms were bigger in terms of sales and employment.[39]

The connections that the refugees made with exiles throughout Latin America helped to re-create Miami as an international trading center.[40] By 1979 more than 60 percent of Cuban families in Miami owned their homes, one-third of Miami's businesses were Cuban-owned, and 90 percent of the construction industry in the booming city was controlled by Cubans.[41] The exiles' rapid success was unprecedented, no matter where they settled.[42]

Henry Martell

CORAL GABLES, FLORIDA

After leaving Cuba in 1962 without his parents, Enrique settled in Puerto Rico with family friends. His older brothers later went to Florida, but his parents could not leave until 1968. As a teenager Enrique got a job at a motorcycle shop in San Juan. When he became a naturalized US citizen, he changed his given name to the anglicized Henry.

I started working as a mechanic on weekends until my brother Pedro claimed me. He had moved to Miami. I moved to his apartment the day after he got married. I stayed with them for about a year and a half. I went to Miami High School for my senior year, and I flunked English, so I couldn't graduate.

I moved to Jacksonville with my brother Alberto. I took English in Joseph High

School. I went at night because by then I had a job as a mechanic for Porsche and Volkswagen. I took the English test. I was able to finish, but it was hard.

I met my wife, and we got married. I started buying used Volkswagens. We were in an apartment, and my wife's father offered me his garage to fix the cars. I worked at the dealership as a mechanic, bought some cars, put them in his garage, worked on them until two, three o'clock in the morning, and saved money. Then I became a certified Porsche technician. From there I was service manager, parts manager, then I talked to the owner and said, "I want to sell." That's where the money is. In 1971 I was the number one Volkswagen-Porsche salesman for the Southeast. Everybody was stunned. My goal was to have my own dealership.

I spent about ten years at that store, then a group from Pennsylvania was opening a Lincoln-Mercury store in Jacksonville. I moved with them. I was the sales manager. From sales manager they offered me the general manager position, which I accepted. That store was number two in the nation in profits. I spent twenty years with them. They grew to twenty-five dealers throughout the East Coast. I became vice-president of operations and ran all the dealerships. I used to be on a plane from Jacksonville on Sundays and come home on Fridays.

After about twelve years, that got old. I was going to buy the dealership in Jacksonville. In the meantime, General Motors and Ford called me. They knew how I operated dealerships. One didn't know about the other. They said, "Henry, would you like to move to Miami?" I said, "Of course!" So, I opened up Buick-Pontiac-GMC and Ford-Lincoln-Mercury in Doral, right across from each other. I had two here and one in Jacksonville. Later sold the one in Jacksonville and kept the two here.

Justo Luis Cepero

TAMPA, FLORIDA

Based on their experience running two bodegas in Cuba, the Cepero family grew their tamale-making business. Their factory was a toolshed in the backyard of their home in West Tampa. Later they got a real plant and expanded into other foodstuffs. Justo and his brother went to school and helped with production.

We started making tamales under the Catalina brand, taking them to stores, little Spanish markets, some Spanish restaurants. Eventually we built a freezer in the back where we froze the product. My father always taught us the business came first. Everything else was an offshoot of the business; this is what you've got to take care of. He was the brains of the outfit.

He finally decided that we needed to sell tamales in Miami. All this time we'd been selling product just in Tampa. There were only so many Cubans here. If you want to expand, go where the *Cubans* are. We didn't have a truck, so my father bought a used Chevy Super Sport. Every Friday we'd rent a U-Haul about 11:30, go to this freezer, fill the U-Haul with tamales. Not a refrigerated truck. Leave at one or two, get to Miami at seven o'clock in the morning, and start distributing the tamales.

This went on for about a year and a half. The U-Hauls got bigger and bigger. On the way back, we needed to bring raw materials because in Miami the raw materials were cheaper. He saw there was a market here for the stuff from there. So little by little we built a distribution of hams, cheeses, stuff like that. As soon as *that* started happening, we moved.

I would get up, say, five o'clock in the morning and go to work. Come 7:45, 8:00, I would go to high school, come back to work. Other people would go to the beach, and they couldn't wait until summer. Me, summer was just a ten-hour job.

My father had challenges going to banks, the people not understanding him just because of the language. We tried to get a loan so we could buy property. They would ask for stuff, and we didn't know what they were talking about. Until we met Braulio Lombardia, the president of People's Bank. At that time, bankers had relationships with people. Now they don't.

My father went to Lombardia and showed him what we were doing, showed him what we drove and where we lived. We weren't living luxuriously because we were all living in a three-bedroom house. No Cadillacs, no Lincolns. Everything went back into the business. We showed him where we were renting. He saw we were busting at the seams. He saw that my father was a hard-working man, and we were a close family unit. Since Lombardia saw that, he had no problems, just, "Here you go, Mr. Cepero." He was the one who generated the funds so that we could keep growing.

I dropped out of college for a couple of years, but the hounding of my father *and* my mother was so much that I had to go back to college and finish. My mother said, "This doesn't last. Anybody can come and take it away from you. Just look what happened in Cuba. We had stores; they took it away. But what your father had as far as business knowledge, they couldn't take that away."

Some early refugees entered business or the professions, but more had modest vocations. Women often found work faster than men, hiring on as waitresses, seamstresses, hairdressers, and domestics. They played a central role in exile communities.[43]

Margarita Fernández Cano

MIAMI, FLORIDA

Thirty-year-old Margarita and her husband Pablo Cano arrived in Miami on October 17, 1962. They brought their son Pablo and daughter Lisi. Margarita had worked at Cuba's National Library. Her husband was an engineer and jazz guitarist.

My husband immediately found a job as a jazz musician, jamming at a night club. He was making a good salary. The owner was a Jewish gentleman who was wonderful and knew a lot about music.

I was offered an interview for a job as a librarian at the University of Miami and on my way by bus, I had to transfer. Across the street was the Miami Public Library, so I thought, Oh, my God, the library! Why don't I go see what's available there? That same day I was able to talk with the director, who offered me a job. I started working at the library the second of January 1963. I owed my job to a bus transfer.

First, I was in the circulation department. It was a great experience. I think they were testing me to see if I knew the Dewey Decimal cataloging system. I did well, and they promoted me to the art and music department. Here, my life changed, and I changed the library by creating new services and the start of an interaction with the local art scene.

My husband started working for the education department, and he was recording special music for children using local recording studios. He thought, Gee, it would be great to have my own recording studio. With investors, he raised the money to build Climax Recording Studios. He started producing and recording local and internationally renowned artists.¶

I created a whole new experience for the library. My ideas had been developed in Havana from a correspondence with the Louisville Public Library in Kentucky. They had given me all the information on how to start a lending art program. I wrote to them again and told them I was now in Miami, and I wanted to start a lending art program at the Miami Public Library.

¶ Founded by Pablo Cano and bassist Orlando "Papito" Hernández, Climax Recording Studios in Miami produced records for such artists as Celia Cruz, Julio Iglesias, Jose Feliciano, and Gloria Estefan.

We started getting donations of original prints—Picasso, Warhol, and Lichtenstein as well as other important artists from the 1960s. We built a collection. People could check out framed artwork. Then we started art exhibitions in the branches. All the libraries had ugly stuff on the walls while others had nothing.

I stayed at the library for twenty-nine years. By then the library had a collection of art worth millions from donations. Going to the library and working there did not feel like a job.

Miguel "Mike" Collazo

TAMPA, FLORIDA

After dropping out of high school in tenth grade, Mike went back to work as a sod layer in booming Tampa. In 1972 he married Mercedes Fernandez nine months after she graduated from high school. He was eighteen; she was seventeen.

I got married in 1972. I went to a little easier job, Hav-A-Tampa cigar in Ybor City. I worked there for four years because my father was working there. He went to Hav-A-Tampa because it was lighter work. It was not in the sun all the time. It was a good job, picking up all the tobacco, big piles, and carrying it to the ladies who roll so they can make cigars. But it was not a paying job. It was only sixty-five dollars, sixty-seven dollars a week.

About a year, year and a half after I got married, we needed more money. My wife wasn't working, she got pregnant, so I decided to go with the sod because it was more money. You make $100, $110. I've been working for sod companies ever since.

At Leon Sod I was just a laborer. I laid it, and then I started doing like a crew chief. I had four or five guys, but I did the same thing, laid sod, drove a forklift and the flatbed. After that I went to Cura Sod for seventeen years. I was a supervisor of three crews. I usually handled the north side of Tampa. I used to lay a million, two million square feet a month. That's a lot of sod. I used to make $60,000 a year.

When the recession came, I got laid off. It was October 2008. After we came back from vacation, that's when that bad situation started about houses not selling, people turning in houses. It was a nightmare. They gave me two weeks' notice and goodbye, you're on your own. I was without work for about six months.

Cuban Americans turned to social, civic, and cultural institutions of their own making. Havana private schools like Belén for boys and Sagrada Corazón for girls were reestablished in Miami.[44] Clubs called *municipios*, based on Cuba's 126 prerevolution townships, connected hometown friends through musical and historical programs.[45] The Cintas Foundation of New York, created with a bequest from a wealthy Havana industrialist and diplomat, made grants throughout the US to architects, visual artists, and writers of Cuban heritage.[46]

Luis Cruz Azaceta

NEW ORLEANS, LOUISIANA

Luis finished his studies at the School of Visual Arts but kept his job in the library at New York University. He married, moved to Staten Island, and the couple had a son before the marriage ended. Through it all Luis worked to express himself through his art as part of New York's neo-expressionist movement.

I got a grant in '72, I think $10,000. It was the Cintas Foundation. Cintas helped a lot of artists, not only painters and sculptors, but writers, musicians, and playwrights. I got two grants from Cintas and three from the National Endowment for the Arts in ten years. Do you know how hard it is to get a grant? Thousands of artists apply. It's prestigious that you win a grant like that.

My first show with a blue-chip gallery, on Fifty-seventh Street in 1974, was paintings dealing with the subway. I found the subway to be extremely violent. I noticed that people didn't get involved. I couldn't comprehend that. They were violent paintings—body parts, people reading the paper while other people are killing each other. I wanted the paintings to be shocking. That started my career.

The first major museum to buy my work was the Metropolitan Museum of Art. The curator of twentieth-century painting, William Lieberman, saw my work in a group exhibition and got interested in my painting called *The Dance of Latin America*. Wow! You're talking about the most important museum in the United States. *That* was amazing.

The first ones who started buying my work were Jewish. They still do, more than the Cubans. My biggest collectors are Jewish. They understand the work. Cubans said, Oh, his work is too violent. They wanted me to paint palm trees and Cuban landscapes. They started buying my work when I became well known, not before.

My work has always been socio-political. Even though I do abstractions, they're socio-political. A work of art has to have content, not only beauty. You have to have both to be able to transcend. That's what I try to do, to make it universal. You've got to use your imagination. That's what an artist does.

I try to use all my experiences in my art. No matter where you go, you carry your roots, in this case, the island of Cuba. I keep on carrying the island with me, no matter where I go.

There was a dark side to the emerging Cuban American community.[47] Cuban gangs trafficked in cocaine and heroin.[48] Armed groups whose hit-and-run raids had failed to oust Castro turned to terrorism. They bombed embassies, firms that did business with Cuba, and the FBI field office in Miami. A bomb exploded on a Cubana airlines DC-8 in midair over the Caribbean Sea, killing seventy-three persons.[49] After seventy-five prominent Cuban exiles in 1978 entered into discussions with Castro to search for common ground in a series of meetings called *el diálogo* or "the dialogue,"[50] two *diálogueros* were assassinated.[51]

The terrorists were abetted by the virulent rhetoric on Miami's Spanish-language radio stations, where commentators denounced those deemed insufficiently anticommunist as *traidores* or "traitors."[52] Some Cuban Americans supported the terrorists by contributing money to them.[53] However, most turned to conventional politics to address their grievances, especially after the Congress in 1975 expanded the Voting Rights Act to protect language minorities and require bilingual elections in communities like Miami.[54]

Alberto R. "Al" Cardenas

CORAL GABLES, FLORIDA

After Al graduated from Fort Lauderdale's St. Thomas Aquinas High School, he took out student loans and worked his way through community college and Florida Atlantic University in Boca Raton. Then a nun from his high school helped him get into law school at Seton Hall University in New Jersey. Politics was in his blood.

We lived through the Bay of Pigs invasion. The number of people my family knew who had died or been incarcerated—a lot of pain associated with that. That affected my thinking a lot. By the time I got to law school, I had become a member of the Young Republicans. I ended up running for and getting to be chairman of the Ocean County, New Jersey, Republicans. I recruited a lot of young people and worked the streets. I won by one vote.

In the meantime, my dad died, and my mother didn't want to move from Miami where the family was. I had a younger sister I didn't want to be without *some* mentorship, so I changed my plans and came to Miami. That was 1975.

I got called by some friends in the national Young Republican movement saying, "How'd you like to be Ronald Reagan's field director?" I ended up doing that, and I met a lot of people in a hurry. The Republican National Committee and Republican Party of Florida got fond of me. These guys talked me into running for Congress against Claude Pepper, who was seventy-eight, and I was twenty-six or something. I said, "I still owe student loans, and this guy's an icon."**

I ran for Congress in '78 as a conservative Republican. I did a massive voter registration drive. I did a lot of things to, for the first time, build a Republican Party in Miami. But we fell short. I didn't win in a district that I would have easily won ten years later.

I was ready to practice law, but they asked me again to get involved with Reagan in 1980. I was a big fan of Reagan. The Cuban community really cemented around Reagan. We had little use for Jimmy Carter. Decent guy, but we didn't agree with him. Reagan came to Miami, said all the right things, embraced the Cuban cause. He was very good on his rhetoric, and everybody fell in love with the guy. This time we were successful.

The 1980 general election that swept Ronald Reagan into the White House had important consequences for Cuban Americans in Miami. The county in 1973 had made Spanish an official language.[55] Cuban Americans started winning local elections.[56] Those events heightened concerns among Anglos about the aspirations of these Spanish-speaking newcomers.

In 1980 voters adopted an ordinance to prohibit county business from being conducted in a language other than English.[57] The "English-only amendment" accelerated the Cuban Americans' political activity in heavily Democratic Miami.[58] By then more Cubans lived in Miami than any other city in the world except Havana.[59] The slogan for their voter registration campaigns: "Vote So That They Respect Us."[60]

** Democrat Claude Pepper served in the US Senate from 1936 to 1951 and represented a Miami district in the House from 1963 until his death in 1989. He was widely known as a champion of Social Security.

Bob Graham

GAINESVILLE, FLORIDA

The son of a dairyman and Democratic politician, Bob was born in Coral Gables in 1936. After graduation from the University of Florida, he earned a law degree from Harvard in 1962 and went home to get into politics. Bob served as a state legislator, governor, and a US senator.

There were significant blocks of people who wanted to keep the Cubans from voting because they thought it would threaten their political influence.

The resistance was from individual officeholders and political parties and institutions, plus from people who thought of themselves as "real" Americans and saw these large numbers of people who didn't speak good English threatening to take over political institutions. The English-only amendment was a symbol of this "us" versus "them," that if you didn't speak good English, you weren't a person who should be allowed to be a full participant in the political life of the community.

The numbers got to be so large that you couldn't call any place a democracy where it was difficult to vote for such a high percentage of people that were, for most purposes, politically like the rest of the population. The language used in the ballots wasn't keeping up with the numbers of people who spoke a specific language.

There were several reasons why they tended to enter politics through the Republican Party. One of those reasons was that they identified Democrats with people who had tried to keep them out. The Republicans smartly moved to fill that void. It gave the Republicans a surge of loyal voters. They contributed to Florida being Republican probably a decade earlier than it would have been, but for the Cubans.

I developed a strong friendship with Cubans after my return to South Florida from law school until I ran for governor, which was about a fifteen-year period. It wasn't hard because I found the Cuban population to be people that I had a rapport with. They were an important part of my early political career.

The other epochal event of 1980 was the Mariel Boatlift. Unrest had been increasing in Cuba, but Fidel was frustrated that Washington would not allow Cubans to immigrate and thus relieve the pressure on his regime. Following a small group of asylum-seekers, more than ten thousand Cubans flooded the

Peruvian embassy compound in 1980 to seek passage off the island. As he did in 1965, Fidel decided to allow disaffected Cubans to leave. Exiles could bring boats to fetch relatives, this time from the port of Mariel west of Havana.[61] The Third Wave began.

From April to October 1980, 125,000 Cubans were ferried across the Florida Straits in another ragtag flotilla that made for dramatic visual reports on the nightly television news.[62] It was a surprising demonstration of popular discontent with life in Castro's Cuba.[63] The government housed the new refugees in the Orange Bowl, tent cities under a Miami freeway, and elsewhere.[64] Eventually many were transferred to military bases outside Florida.[65] The Congress authorized public assistance for those who met need standards, but the new refugees did not receive the same generous government benefits as the early refugees.[66]

The label *marielitos* was originally intended as a pejorative.[67] Many were young men, skilled or unskilled workers, with Cubans of color a much higher percentage of the arrivals than in earlier waves—70 percent of the *marielitos* were working class, and only 7 percent had a college education. Sensational news reports swept the US that the Third Wave included many criminals and patients from mental hospitals. In fact the US government classified less than 2 percent as serious felons.[68] Others had been convicted of offenses that were not crimes in the US, some under Cuba's *ley de peligrosidad* or "law of dangerousness," used to detain addicts, dissenters, gay people, and vagrants.[69]

Maribel Pérez Henley

MIAMI, FLORIDA

Maribel and her parents arrived on a Freedom Flight in 1970, rejoining her grandparents and five siblings of her father Juan. The other four siblings were with the revolution and remained in Cuba. Then Juan's brother Jose came on the boatlift.

If you remember the stories, when you got to the port to pick up *your* family, the government put people on the boat that had nothing to do with you. In order to get your family out, you had to bring these people. Jose was institutionalized, and they must have let him loose.

My grandparents got a telegram that Jose was on one of those boats. My father, my mother, my aunt, my uncle, and I drove down to Key West. You could see the boats arriving and people getting off. We found out that he had arrived, but he was taken to Ohio. He was there for a couple of months. From Ohio they finally flew him here. We picked him up at the airport and brought him home—no holding period or anything like that—and he went to live with my grandparents. But he wasn't right, there was something wrong with him.

At that time people with mental disease were locked up. He had received electroshock over there—all the horror stories that you hear about, this poor guy went through. Mental disease was something that the family didn't talk about. It was hidden. It wasn't like now, that we try to make them more adaptable to life and live a quality of life with their impairments. If he had been born *now*, he would have been treated, and he would have been a productive member of society.

Jose lived with his parents for many years. Didn't work a day in his life. He felt that the family owed him, and he didn't want to work. The brothers were not going to support him. They helped him, but after a while, "you need to get a job," and he didn't want to do that. Once his parents died, he lived on his own, and then he disappeared. Easily ten years that we haven't heard from him. We don't know if he's homeless, we have no clue.

10

HOME

The Mariel Boatlift resulted in a rift between the early Cuban refugees and those who came in 1980 and afterward.[1] Some early refugees were reunited with relatives who had stayed behind to give the revolution a chance, only to decide later they would have better lives in the land that Cubans call La Yuma, after a 1957 Glenn Ford western, *3:10 to Yuma*, one of the last Hollywood films to circulate on the island before the US trade embargo.[2] But the domestic controversy over the *marielitos* damaged the reputation of Cuban Americans. Anglos in Miami saw the boatlift as further deterioration of their once-placid city.[3]

That feeling grew when the Fourth Wave brought 33,000 *balseros* or rafters in August 1994. Castro opened the door for them at the nadir of Cuba's economic crash after the dissolution of the Soviet Union.[4] To resolve the crisis, President Bill Clinton agreed to strengthen an agreement that Reagan had entered with Havana to tie up loose ends of the Mariel Boatlift. The revised migration accords of 1995 ensured legal immigration for 20,000 Cubans annually, not counting immediate relatives of US citizens.[5]

Clinton also adopted the "wet-foot, dry-foot" policy that continued to allow entry into the US for an undocumented Cuban refugee who reached a port of entry on dry land but required those found at sea to be returned to the island unless they met the legal standard for asylum.[6] The policy remained in place until it was rescinded in 2017 by President Barack Obama as part of his initiative to restore normal diplomatic and trade relations with Cuba.[7]

Ten percent of revolutionary Cuba's population eventually left for the US.[8] Social scientists found the Cuban American community cleaved between the early and later arrivals.[9] In one view, the early refugees shunned the newcomers and thus impeded them in their efforts to succeed; moreover, the newcomers had lower levels of education and fewer marketable skills.[10] Despite the early refugees' vaunted "economic miracle," by 2010 the average household income for all Cuban Americans was below that of other Latin American immigrant groups, and the poverty rate was above the national average.[11]

Jorge M. Duany

DORAL, FLORIDA

After earning degrees from three prestigious universities on the mainland, Jorge returned to San Juan as a professor at the University of Puerto Rico. In 2012 he was named director of the Cuban Research Institute at Florida International University in Miami.

I was always interested in questions of identity. Migration has been a way to focus on issues that are personal to me as well as to other people like me, and others who are not like me. By looking at migration, especially within the Caribbean Basin, I've been interested in what happens when people move from one place to another, and they enter into contact with other people who are different, and how they define themselves. Rather than look at the question as my own personal history, I tried to expand it and to understand other people's experiences.

What did the Cubans do when they established their economic foothold in Miami, how did they do it, and to what extent did it benefit others who came later, the *marielitos* and other Latinos? There are all kinds of theories about that, but I do think there's a split in the history of Cuban migration before and after 1980.

I've noticed the change in attitudes myself, but not just with Mariel. It began with Mariel because those who came in 1980 were so different from earlier refugees. They thought about Cuba and the US in a different way, mostly because they were born or raised after '59, so they had no memory of prerevolutionary Cuba. There was no *Cuba de ayer*, as it's called in Miami. Many were Black, working class, young, and single. A large percentage were gay. These characteristics separated the Mariel exodus from previous waves.

As the migration continued—especially after the rafter crisis in 1994—nearly 717,000 came from Cuba until the wet-foot, dry-foot policy was abolished by President Obama. It's the largest, most complicated, and most diverse wave of people who have moved from Cuba to the United States since 1959.

These are the people who most want to travel to Cuba, send money to the island, call their relatives on the phone, and oppose the embargo because that comes in the way of maintaining their connections with relatives on the island. Most also supported Obama's policies of engagement with Cuba. Most members of the earlier waves, to which I belong from a chronological point of view, still want to keep the hardline policies against Cuba.

Some early refugees who were resettled elsewhere eventually moved to Miami. One 1978 study found that 40 percent of the county's Cuban exiles had relocated from other parts of the US.[12] The draw was family or the booming economy or the familiar climate or the Latin culture that gave the city its charm.[13] They were joined by newcomers from other Latin countries.[14] By 2015 Miami, Miami Beach, Coral Gables, and Hialeah had Hispanic majorities, mostly Cuban Americans. Indeed, the foreign-born were now more than half the county.[15]

One might think it was preordained. Almost from its inception Miami affected a Spanish colonial ambiance. The decorative tiles in Freedom Tower, built during the Florida land boom of the 1920s, were imported from Cuba. Entire Cuban villages were stripped of red-tile roofs to adorn bungalows in Coral Gables.[16] As Cristina García mused in her 1992 breakthrough novel *Dreaming in Cuban*, "All the streets in Coral Gables have Spanish names—Segovia, Ponce de Leon, Alhambra—as if they'd been expecting all the Cubans who would eventually live here."[17]

Marijean Collado Miyar
CORAL GABLES, FLORIDA

After Miami High School, Marijean enrolled at the University of Miami and worked in the library. Because she had been born in Brooklyn while her parents lived in the US years earlier, she did not qualify for a Cuban Loan, so she borrowed from another student loan program.

I ended up going four years to the University of Miami. I mentioned that my father was liberal. I have followed in his footsteps, proudly so. When the Students for a Democratic Society came to campus, I went to a rally, and two of my Cuban friends picked up my chair and took me out. I just wanted to taste every flavor politically.

When I graduated, I was adamant that I was going to New York for graduate school.

I remember going on September 1, 1969, staying with my aunt and uncle in Brooklyn for a couple of weeks and meeting friends in Manhattan. Those were happy years. I got a master's degree in art history at Hunter College. And I got married in December of 1972 to the gentleman who is still my husband. He's a full-fledged Cuban, very different experience from mine. He came out the year before I did. He was in banking.

In March of 1974 we moved to Mexico. He became the youngest field representative for Bankers Trust. I worked sporadically. I put together a catering business. I did several things. I've been working since I was fourteen. We lived in Mexico for ten years. And then Miami. I lived away from 1969 to 1983.

I got a job teaching art history at Belén, and I did that for fifteen years. At one point I taught ancient architecture at the University of Miami. I've had one too many health issues, so I retired from Belén in 2000. Then I embarked on a career as a museum lecturer, the range of Western art history, from ancient to modern.

You know, none of us who came into exile have any right to talk about the Cubans who stayed behind and what they did and didn't do, because it was horrific. Our parents did a very good thing with starting all over again.

Eduardo J. Padrón

MIAMI, FLORIDA

When Eduardo's family reunited and left for Colombia, he stayed in Miami. "I saw more possibilities here than to start something new in Colombia," he says. After he graduated from Miami High School, he wanted to go to college but got rejected by elite universities. "I got the message," he says. "The message was that I had not been here long enough—did not have enough knowledge of the language—to be able to succeed in these schools."

Someone told me there was this college called Dade County Junior College. It had opened a couple of years before. I went there, and they changed my life. I found professors who would stay longer in their offices so when I finished my classes they could drive me home. Miami Dade College saved me.

I never planned to be an educator. My idea of the American Dream was to become rich. I wanted to make a lot of money. I studied economics, thinking that it would prepare me to become rich. I did well, all the way through my PhD. It was a good time in America when I finished. I had a job with the DuPont Company in Wilmington, Delaware, which at that time was the largest corporation in the world. It was a great job for a recent PhD. I went back to Miami to tell my former professors the great news. The reaction was shock that I would work for a corporation and not come back and pay my dues.

They gave me the famous guilt trip, which went on for three weeks. After a lot of thought, I said, "Okay, you're offering me this teaching job. I'm willing to do it for one year and one year only. I'm going to pay my dues, but after that year, I'm going to make money." I started there making about one-fourth of what DuPont had offered me. Halfway into that year, I knew that's what I wanted to do for the rest of my life. I found my calling. I realized that money is not everything in life. I have enjoyed that ride ever since.

Miami Dade has been the saving grace of the Cuban exiles and others. It's hard to find a household in Miami-Dade County that has not been touched by this college, especially the immigrant community. We all came through here, and we all say the same thing: Miami Dade was the bridge for us to succeed. So, if I sound passionate about this place, this is why.

Andrés M. Duany

MIAMI, FLORIDA

After his family relocated to Barcelona, Spain, Andrés was sent to the Choate School by his father, who had worked in the family's plantation and land development business in Santiago de Cuba. Then Andrés went to Princeton University, where he met his future wife and business partner, Elizabeth Plater-Zyberk.

I didn't originally intend to study architecture; I wanted engineering, but I hated it. After two days I switched to architecture, and that was it. Real estate development was in my blood.

It was the old Princeton, and it was hard. I was exhausted, so I took a year off to study in Paris, where I actually *did* learn French. Then I attended Yale graduate school. Elizabeth, whom I had met in Princeton, also came to Yale, by chance, and we got together. We graduated in the recession of 1974. There was no chance of finding work in the Northeast. We didn't even try. Architects in New York were doing park maintenance.

In those years there were two places that were not in recession: Texas, because of the high oil price, and Miami, which was receiving refugees from one of the leftist governments of Latin America. There's always one. So there were jobs. I was offered a teaching position at the University of Miami. We stayed, and eventually Lizz and I married, bought our house, and built this practice.

I thought Miami was horrifying, a town full of Cuban hysterics. My family held that Cuba was bad news. In Miami, as far as my parents were concerned, we would just breed back into trying to return. When my sister graduated from Princeton she married in Miami. My brother came here too. My parents remained in Spain for years but then came over. It is ironic that the family ended up in Miami after all, every one of us, including my grandmother. We got here twenty-five years after the revolution, and we stayed.

What happened here, there was a social reversal. The people who had money didn't have to work—*for a while*. Always it runs out. There wasn't enough for a lifetime, but you didn't have to work at the beginning. The ones who didn't have any money got to work the next day: washing dishes, becoming sheetrock contractors, becoming developers, working in the gas station, *buying* the gas station.

What I've been able to observe here—this isn't statistically so—is that those people who constitute the Cuban society of Miami *now* are wealthy, self-made. Doesn't mean they weren't educated. The grand old families that didn't have to work generally are kind of broke now. Within one generation, that will be gone.

Cuban Americans clustered in twenty enclaves around the nation, making them one of the most geographically concentrated immigrant groups. These enclaves were in eleven states and the District of Columbia.[18] Miami became the capital, with three exiled Cuban presidents—Machado, Prío, and Carlos Hevia, who served as president for one day in 1934—interred in a cemetery on Calle Ocho.[19] The flourishing city reflected Cuban Americans' idealized memories of a homeland that no longer existed.[20]

One hundred thousand Cuban Americans lived in Union City, New Jersey, and surrounding Hudson County, but "Havana on the Hudson" began to change in the late 1980s as the early refugees moved to the suburbs or retired to Florida.[21] No matter where they lived, Cuban Americans migrated to Miami almost as if they were going home.[22]

Arelis Duran Alvarez

NORTH HALEDON, NEW JERSEY

Arelis met her husband-to-be Luis at church in Union City and learned he was a Pedro Pan too. They had been at Florida City Camp at the same time but never met. They married and worked to bring Luis's relatives from the island. Eventually they bought a vacation home in Miami Beach.

The Cubans down here think they still own Cuba. It's different up north. We're Cuban and we're patriotic, but not like in Miami. Maybe it's the closeness to Cuba. The Miami people—I won't even say Florida because the majority live in Miami—are like the old type of Cuban.

New Jersey, we have accepted the American way more. When my husband comes to Florida, he speaks only Spanish to everybody in the gas station. Not up there. Completely different. All the Cubans started moving out of Union City to the suburbs. A lot came to Miami because of the weather.

By 2017, 1.4 million foreign-born Cubans lived in the US, and another 1 million claimed to be of Cuban descent. Two out of three lived in Florida, mostly the southeastern part of the state.[23] Bolstered by social, civic, and educational institutions of their own making, exiles in Miami venerated their native land's national character or *cubanidad*, the concept of "Cubanness." For some it was more than a cultural touchstone; it was a source of ethnic pride in Anglo America.[24]

Marielena Alejo Villamil

CORAL GABLES, FLORIDA

After high school in Tampa, Marielena went to an all-girls Catholic college in New Orleans, partly on a Cuban Loan. She spent a year in Madrid, earning a master's degree from the language school of Vermont's Middlebury College, also with a Cuban Loan. Then she moved to Miami and eventually took a teaching job, so the government forgave half her Cuban Loans.

I was not in the Cuban milieu here in Miami in the 1960s, I was in Tampa. In Tampa you mingled, and you got into American society, or Tampa society—the Italians and Cubans from the turn of the century. I went to school in New Orleans. I was still on my student visa. I called my dad and mom on Sundays at eight o'clock—collect. That's the only time I spoke Spanish. I was a regular college student. I was very conservative. I didn't like hippies. All my dates were Americans. All my friends were Americans. *I* was American.

When I came to Miami it was culture shock. It was like day and night. Since there were so many Cubans, everything was Cuban-oriented. People in Miami are totally different from the rest of the Cuban community because of the numbers and the power. Cubans here got involved in politics. They became executives and good businessmen. They made a lot of money. It was another world, a different mindset. The Americans couldn't last in Miami. They were not part of that group.

I only became more Cuban when I moved to Miami.

Tere Castellanos Garcia

MIAMI, FLORIDA

After a short stay in Miami when she came to the US in 1961 in Operation Pedro Pan, Tere and her parents moved to San Juan. She earned an architecture degree from Tulane, then returned to the University of Puerto Rico for a graduate degree. She married and moved to Miami in 1979.

My children were born here. I want them to know where they came from.

I have to tell you, I search for my Cubanness now. I want my kids to preserve it. When they were small, I remember being in the car with them and teaching them the Cuban national anthem. Those are things that are very important to me. [Tere pauses to control her emotions.] Because ultimately, that's who we are. And I want to make sure they know the story. [Her voice catches.] When my father died in Puerto Rico, when my mother died, when my father-in-law died, in their funeral Masses we always had the Cuban flag covering them.

Over the years I developed more of a Spanish accent in English than I used to have. The more relaxed I become, the more the accent comes out. Technically, I could have lost it, but I keep it. It's an ID of sorts. Even though I *think* in English, there's no question that I turn to Spanish. It's my go-to.

I picked up my Cubanness once I came back here.

In November 1999 a five-year-old Cuban boy was found lashed to an inner tube almost within sight of the Florida shore. His mother and eleven others drowned while crossing the Florida Straits in a small boat.[25] Immigration officials granted temporary custody of the boy, Elián González, to a great-uncle in Miami. Then, with the regime's support, the boy's father came to the US and asked for Elián while the courts addressed myriad legal issues. When the great-uncle refused to relinquish custody, Clinton's Justice Department in April 2000 had officers in body armor take Elián at gunpoint from a Little Havana home that was surrounded by angry protesters.[26] By then the boy had become a symbol of both the exiles' unyielding opposition to the Castro regime and Havana's unyielding opposition to Washington.[27]

Eventually the boy returned to the island.[28] Cuban Americans rioted.[29] They staged a one-day work stoppage in Little Havana.[30] More important, they cast the *voto de castigo* or "punishment vote" in the 2000 presidential election. Democrat Al Gore won less than 20 percent of the votes from Florida's Cuban Americans, down from Clinton's 35 percent four years earlier. Republican George W. Bush won an estimated 50,000 more Cuban American votes in Florida than the Republican nominee in 1996.[31] When the US Supreme Court halted the Florida recount of the 2000 presidential election, Bush won the state with a 537-vote margin.[32] With Florida decisive in the Electoral College, Cuban Americans were indispensable to Bush's victory and thus changed the nation's course.[33]

Alberto R. "Al" Cardenas

CORAL GABLES, FLORIDA

Having labored in the political trenches for the GOP for decades, Al was chairman of the Florida Republican Party during the 2000 presidential election. He was deeply involved in the campaign and the battle over the Florida recount.

I lived through that process. The president got a very significant Hispanic vote. When his father ran for president, the Cuban American vote was two-thirds of the Hispanic vote in the state. When the *son* ran for president, it got down to 53, 54 percent. That was still huge. So the president got over 40 percent of the Hispanic vote in the state. If you ask me, Was that one of the main reasons he won by 500 votes—absolutely!

It didn't matter whether you were a Democrat or Republican in the seventies or eighties, you felt the same way about everything. Now we have competition—at least in the Hispanic community—between Republicans and Democrats. Hispanics who are Democrats truly feel differently than Republicans about a whole array of issues.

By attempting to block Elián's return to his father, Cuban Americans put themselves starkly at odds with prevailing public opinion.[34] Miami was condemned as "an out-of-control banana republic within the American body politic."[35] The controversy's underlying issues and outcome even divided Cuban Americans.[36]

Guillermo G. "Gil" Mármol

DALLAS, TEXAS

Gil graduated from the Christian Brothers' reconstituted La Salle High School in Miami. With financial aid, he earned a bachelor's degree and MBA from Harvard and joined a management consulting firm. Later he became a senior manager of a Dallas technology company. The Elián González controversy resonated with him, as it did with many Cuban Americans.

I was outraged that they sent him back. That one hit me hard.

Once time goes by and you think about it, it becomes less annoying. You could make a case that the kid had lost his mother, he should be put back with his father—who, of course, hadn't shown much interest in him as a kid. But it felt hard, particularly the way it was done, that whole SWAT team. That torqued me off. Turned me off Janet Reno pretty bad.* She gave the speech when I became a naturalized citizen. She gave a good speech, so I always had a soft spot for Janet. No longer.

Pedro A. Freyre

MIAMI, FLORIDA

With a Cuban Loan and scholarships, Pedro worked his way through college and earned a law degree from the University of Miami. He took a corporate job before entering private law practice. Following his father's example, he became a spokesman on Cuban affairs for the Greater Miami Chamber of Commerce.

---

*   Attorney General Janet Reno was state attorney for Miami before joining Clinton's cabinet. She was in charge of the Justice Department when the boy was returned to Cuba.

I was a hardliner. I was very involved in the whole Elián González baloney. I saw that kid being used by the Cubans and by the Miami guys. I also saw a *horrific* miscalculation on the part of the Miami Cubans, the leadership here. They put all their cards on that bet. It blew up in their face.

They didn't understand the US mentality. You cannot go to an American and say, "Keep the kid away from his parents." His mother died. It was a tragedy. But he had a father. The father obviously cared about the kid. "Well, it's a communist country." So *what*? It's his *father*.

We became obnoxious. We were looked at as these crazy people.

What is the ethos of the exile experience for us? The ethos is the sense of loss, the mythology of exile, which is very beautiful. You're pure because you left. But more than anything else is a sense of honor and achievement. You *have* to achieve. Because you lost all this, you are called upon to be better than anybody else. You cannot be second best. We had that inbred: You have to show people that you came from a great family in a great country that was *stolen* from you. You have to do great things.

I think it's unethical and thoughtless to make people in Cuba suffer because we have this mythology. We lost. We're the South in the Civil War. The Yankees came. They burned Atlanta, they marched to the sea, and they took our plantations. *Tough patooties!* Deal with it.

The rise of Cuban Americans as a political force in Florida corresponded with the state's increasing influence in national elections. Of the most populous states, Florida was the fastest-growing presidential swing state. From 1980 to 2020, it switched between the Republicans and the Democrats four times, 1996, 2000, 2008, and 2016. Only Ohio, which consistently lost population on a relative basis, switched as many times as Florida. And Florida's political clout mushroomed. Based on population changes, Florida gained more votes in the Electoral College during this period than any other state, adding twelve to rise from eighth to tie for third. Only California and Texas came close, each adding ten votes, to rank first and second, respectively.[37]

The Cuban Americans' importance in shaping the politics of Florida reflected their significance in many fields.[38] They led the remaking of Miami from an aging resort for northern "snowbirds" into an international center for trade and finance, now handling more than one-third of all US trade with Latin America.[39] Miami became the crossroads between Europe, North America, and Latin America and the Caribbean.[40] The foundation for the early refugees' success was the economy they created for themselves in South Florida, with help from the government.[41] In the climactic televised speech of his 2016 visit to Havana, Obama said, "In the United States we have a clear monument to what the Cuban people can build—it's called Miami."[42] It may have been hyperbole, but there was enough truth in it.

Hector Laurencio
CORAL GABLES, FLORIDA

Hector García graduated from Miami High School in 1966. He changed his last name from García—the surname of the father who had abandoned him and his mother in Cuba—to Laurencio to honor his grandfather and his physician uncle Waldo Laurencio. While studying medicine at the University of Salamanca in Spain, he met and married fellow student Maria Galatas. Eventually they settled in Miami to practice.

Take any country in the world—name it, I don't care—and take away people who are professionals, and highly skilled labor, and decent people who do not agree with totalitarianism, and people who own businesses—put them together in a place, how do you expect they're going to do?

When you are a refugee from a political system, that creates a bond. When I had to go to a pharmacy, I didn't go to an American pharmacy. I went to the little *Cuban* pharmacy. If I would have a sandwich, I didn't have an American sandwich. I had a *Cuban* sandwich. If I was going to drink coffee, I would not drink American coffee. I would have *Cuban* coffee.

That's one of the main reasons we were successful. We created our own free enterprise economy.

Gary R. Mormino
ST. PETERSBURG, FLORIDA

Born in Alton, Illinois, Gary earned his doctorate in history from the University of North Carolina, Chapel Hill, and later won tenure at the University of South Florida. His areas of expertise are immigration and Florida.

The Cubans were lucky—seems a strange word—but they immigrated during the Cold War. They had everything working: A Democratic Congress. There weren't many immigrants in America at that time, so you didn't have a lot of competition. Plus, these people were not typical immigrants. Most immigrants don't come with middle-class values, certainly not the first waves.

You had *massive* amounts of government assistance, housing allowances, educational assistance. Times were flush. This was a prosperous period in America. We weren't generous with Mexicans in the West; they also had middle-class values and were espousing the American Dream and achieving success. Even if you look at Hungarians in the 1950s, not even close. Without a doubt, Cubans acquired most-favored immigrant status. Most people don't talk about that.

Give me a better example of an immigrant group than Cubans. Jews in New York City, clearly impressive. Irish in Boston, although it takes a lot longer, and more political success than economic success. Those two cities are also very different. In Miami the slate was clear. Throughout the 1950s Miami had been the number one tourist attraction. But by the 1960s, Miami was not the tourist magnet that it had been. There were troubling signs. If ever a community needed a jolt like Fidel, it was Miami.

The aftershocks are still being felt today. Just name the category that Cubans have not transformed: economics, politics, culture, language. It's hard to appreciate their economic clout, but it's huge. And it doesn't stop at the county line, if you look where Cubans live now. It's a profound influence on Florida agriculture. Florida was not a big sugar state before the 1950s. Big Sugar is essentially a reaction to Fidel.

It's hard to imagine Miami-Dade County, now Broward and Palm Beach, and even the politics of Florida, without the revolutionary takeover. Florida matters now, politically. When they arrived in 1959, Florida was insignificant. A lot of tourists came here, but there were no national figures. As late as 1940, Florida was the smallest state in the American South.[†] Now it's surpassed New York. Are you kidding me? Without the Spanish-speaking immigrants, Florida would be a middle-sized state now.

Maybe the greatest effect would be demographics, that it's not *just* Spanish-speaking Cubans anymore. My God, two-thirds of the families in Miami speak Spanish at home now. There's nothing like Miami, and all from those initial boat and plane rides.

US policy on travel and remittances to Cuba has been a political weathervane. President Jimmy Carter in 1977 ended the Kennedy-era restrictions on US

---

† Of the forty-eight states in 1940, Florida ranked twenty-seventh in population, behind Texas, North Carolina, Georgia, Tennessee, Kentucky, Alabama, Virginia, Louisiana, Mississippi, West Virginia, Arkansas, and South Carolina.

passport holders traveling to Cuba and the ban on spending dollars there.[43] Since then Republican presidents have tightened restrictions to block tourist and business travel,[44] and Democratic presidents have relaxed them to allow it.[45] Even restrictions on Cuban Americans visiting relatives on the island have been subject to policy zigzags.[46] Those who have gone compare their lives in the US to what their lives would have been.

Nestor A. Rodriguez

MIAMI, FLORIDA

After arriving from Spain in 1971, Nestor and his family settled in Miami. He earned a music degree from the University of Miami and, after a job with an airline, worked for the now defunct Florida Philharmonic Orchestra and other not-for-profits. In 2016 he visited Cuba and reflected on what his life would have been if he had not left.

I would have been very disappointed. I would have been extremely . . . limited. The suffering would have been more intense, especially growing up. I'm a gay man. I'm not a militant gay. I am now more out because my parents are not here. I grew up with parents who were not accepting of homosexuality. I wasn't in the closet per se, but I never had a conversation with my parents about my homosexuality.

Just thinking of my teenage years in those forced labor camps or "volunteering" to do agricultural projects and then going into the military by force, I don't know what type of life I would have had. I'm sure I would have found survival mechanisms the way you do everywhere. But I'm very pleased that I didn't have to live there. The record of gay rights in Cuba is mixed. I can tell you that from personal experience and testimonies of people I know. They are not welcomed. It's not a society that celebrates gay culture because it's a society that doesn't celebrate the *individual*. That's the type of government that exists there.

When I started to say to my parents, "If I ever go back"—it was like, What do you mean you're going back? Part of me didn't want to disrespect my parents. When they both died, I went back, but I went back without any expectations. I had an aunt there who was ninety-nine years old, I had cousins, and I wanted to talk about music projects with people in the music business.

I don't know my father's side of the family, but on my mother's side we keep pretty close. I stayed with them. They are revolutionaries, with a twist. They are highly educated. We share a lot of things that have nothing to do with the revolution; they have to do with our family, our grandparents, music. I went with a lot of respect for them. I didn't go there to judge them or to disagree with them. When you go to Cuba, at least in my experience, you talk about the reality without blaming anybody.

The one thing I learned when I went back to Cuba: I am from there, but I don't belong there.

Myriam Márquez

MIAMI BEACH, FLORIDA

After high school Myriam attended Miami-Dade Community College and later earned a degree in journalism from the University of Maryland. After a stint covering the statehouse in Annapolis, she returned to Florida as an editorial writer for the Orlando Sentinel. *In 2002 she and a colleague received permission from Havana for a reporting trip to Cuba.*

I was there twenty-eight days with a journalist visa. They follow you everywhere, and they don't try to hide it. They want to freak you out.

I only stayed in hotels a couple of nights. I stayed in rooms I was renting because I wanted to get a sense of the people. Every room I walked into had cement bags because anytime anything happened, it was hard to get cement, and they needed to plaster stuff. Buildings were crumbling.

I visited my mother's cousins out in the countryside. One of them had been a teacher who became the head mistress of the school. Her husband is a true believer. I said, "I think everything would have turned out better if Castro had focused on building up Cuba. Instead, he wanted to take on the world, and Cuba suffered from it." He nodded his head. He couldn't say it. I thought, Okay, we made a connection. You're trying to be respectful of *their* history.

I had an American prism going in. My parents had always said, "Cuba had the third-highest GDP in the Americas. It was the United States, Argentina, Cuba. Our radio and television were extraordinary for the Americas. We were leading the way in so many areas." Of course, I wasn't thinking of the American influence. I was thinking, Because we're *Cuban.*

I had meetings with officials. I said, "There are areas of Havana that look like Beirut, that just got bombed. What is that?" They said, "Well, we're a third-world country." I was like, Oh, my God, that's how they think of themselves: third world. I said, "You're comparing yourself to Haiti? El Salvador? Why? Look at what was before." That was my conversation with *them*.

I realized I'm *not* a Cuban American, I'm an American Cuban, so much more Americanized. Even though I've had this full, rich, Cuban experience in Miami, it's not what *they* had over there. I learned that when I went there for a month. It was eye-opening.

They never let me back in. I tried three times.

Not all Cuban Americans have gone back to the island. Some object to anything that might indirectly assist the regime. Or they cannot bring themselves to visit a country from which their parents brought them at great hardship. Others believe that engagement with the Cuban people is the only realistic way to break down the walls between the two governments.

Maria Galatas Laurencio

CORAL GABLES, FLORIDA

After getting his medical license validated, Maria's physician father moved his family to tiny Kirbyville, Texas, to practice. Maria graduated from high school there, then went to medical school in Spain, where she met and married fellow student Hector Laurencio. Eventually they settled in Miami, where both entered practice. They have not returned to Cuba.

If the system changes and becomes a democratic society, then I would *love* to go back. But not as long as it's a totalitarian dictatorship, not as long as the communists are there. First of all, I do not like not being able to express myself. Second, it would be sad for me to see what the country has turned into, to see the people, the way they are, hungry. And third, I wouldn't want *one penny* of mine to go to those criminals. I feel that if I go there, that is what I'm contributing to.

I don't see any advantage in the United States wanting to get closer to Cuba. The only way that I would see that would be *if* they gave something in return—and they haven't. We knew they wouldn't. So why give them the benefits? Why continue to sustain the system if they do not want to change?

The only thing Obama did that was good was when he gave his speech, he didn't hold back. For the first time Cubans heard an American president. He didn't bow down to the system. He spoke his truth.

Emilio Cueto
WASHINGTON, DC

Seventeen-year-old Emilio left Havana through Operation Pedro Pan on April 26, 1961, days after the Bay of Pigs invasion. With a Cuban Loan, he earned a bachelor's degree from Catholic University in Washington. Then he earned a master's degree from Columbia University and a law degree from Fordham University. He returned to Cuba ten times to see his mother before her death. A retired lawyer and renowned collector of Cuban memorabilia, he travels to the island frequently.

Every time I go, I take the road that goes to my school. I can follow every step along the way, and I recognize every single home. I remember my classmates descending from the buses to their homes because Havana hasn't changed. The first time I went, I said it couldn't possibly be. I mean, what happened to the city? *Nothing* happened. Havana has been so neglected. The changes were in the countryside.

I understand when you say, I'm not going there, it hurts, or I don't want to contribute to the regime. Those I understand. On the other hand, that position doesn't seem to have any impact on Cuba's future. If you abandon the possibility of dialogue, you're not part of the solution.

The Cuban family has been separated. I am committed to dialogue. Some of my books have been published in Cuba. Very few people have been able to accomplish that. I think I have provided a connection between the past and the future—the Cubans there and the Cubans here. I think it's a productive way to engage and to show that Cuba should be a higher value than the politics we each have.

Julieta Navarrete Valls
SOUTH MIAMI, FLORIDA

After Julieta married, she had two children and moved to South America for her husband's work. When the marriage ended, she moved to Washington, DC, and worked for Partners of the Americas, a not-for-profit spinoff from the Alliance for Progress aid program for Latin America. That led to other international work focusing on people-to-people initiatives, including programs in Cuba.

When I went back to Cuba in 2003, I went with a group from DC. It was basically a bunch of old people doing tourism. I went to see my house and take pictures, and it was *devastating* to see how decrepit it was. It was even missing the front door. Of course, it all came back, going to my house and remembering what this building was and so on. For the first couple of days, I was in shock.

On the third day I was walking around, and I was approached by two women, not really beggars, but they saw me as a foreigner. The women had little kids and a baby. One of them asked me, "Can you buy me some milk?" They wanted powdered milk. There was a little grocery nearby, and I said, "Okay, come on." I must have paid close to fifty dollars for two boxes of powdered milk. I gave them the milk, and one of them put her hand in her pocket, took out a penny, and said, "This is for you, so that you will not forget us."

I went back to the hotel [her voice breaks] and faced the wall and cried.

The Elián González controversy revived interest in Operation Pedro Pan and the Cuban Children's Program. It was a poignant story, so reporters sought out now-grown Pedro Pans for retrospectives.[47] Yale historian Carlos Eire wrote an award-winning Pedro Pan memoir, *Waiting for Snow in Havana*.[48] Florida City Camp was designated a historic landmark.[49] Usually overlooked in the celebration about the Pedro Pans was the emotional price that some of them paid for the separation from their parents and for their lost childhoods.[50]

Edmundo Pérez-de Cobos
CORAL GABLES, FLORIDA

Edmundo's widowed mother arrived in Miami in 1963, but he remained with his foster family in Orlando and completed his freshman year of college there before joining his mother. He worked his way through the University of Miami then got an advanced degree in management. Now retired, he reflects on his parents' decision to send him to the US at age fourteen, alone.

This is something very difficult to talk about and relay. It would be very difficult to write about the *feeling* of misplacement: What are all these people doing with me? What are their plans for me? What's going to *happen* to me? Why me?

I never blamed my parents. It was the best thing they did. It took a lot of courage, of not being selfish, to send a kid to another country, to something that was virtually unknown. You can imagine how scared they were that I would be sent someplace *else*, where they would *really* lose control. At least I was under the control of the church.

As for what the United States has done with Cubans—remarkable! Back in '60 and '61, when parish priests said, "We have kids that need a home. Take a boy, take a girl," people got up, went to the rectory and said, "I'll help, I'll take one." I have lived and worked in seven countries. That doesn't happen anywhere except the US.

Eloísa M. Echazábal
MIAMI, FLORIDA

After their Pedro Pan experience in Buffalo, New York, Eloísa and her sister were reunited with their parents in Miami in 1962. Eloísa graduated from Miami's Notre Dame Academy, then worked for an airline and a bank, earned bachelor's and master's degrees, and worked as a college administrator. Now she considers what her life would have been in Cuba.

It would have been terrible if I had stayed. I would have had to deal with the mandatory indoctrination. I would not have been able to continue going to church as I was used to and would have had to live with other things the communist government was imposing on all. My whole *life* would have had to change.

I am very fortunate to be an American. We are all very fortunate that, if we had to leave Cuba, we came to the United States of America, which is the *best* country in the world. It's not perfect, but there's no perfect country. That's what being an American means: I'm a citizen of the best country in the world.

Some of those uprooted and brought to the US before adulthood have coped with a sense of loss—of family or country or a way of life.[51]

Victoria Montoro Zamorano
SOUTH MIAMI, FLORIDA

After an initial stay in Miami, Vicki went to boarding school in New York, near her physician father, stepmother, and two siblings. Her mother Albertina O'Farrill was imprisoned in 1966, along with Polita and Ramón "Mongo" Grau, for helping children leave through Operation Pedro Pan and helping others to escape.

We stopped receiving letters from her, but we assumed there was no post between Cuba and the US. My dad and stepmom decided not to tell us about it because they thought it would be temporary. We had Cuban friends, but they didn't talk about it. I didn't find out that my mother was in prison for two years, just to show you how sheltered we were.

My mother was *very* social. She was *very* intelligent. She saw herself as a political figure. My dad was a hands-on father. She was not. Her social life was the diplomats. Occasionally I run into people who say, "Your mother saved my life, or my son's life, in the trunk of her car. She took us into a party at the Netherlands embassy and saved our lives." That's what she was doing.

She married her sweetheart from before my dad. He had just been released out of prison, so they were being watched. My mother could talk herself out of anything. I think that's why she went to prison, because she thought it would never happen to her—and if it did, she could talk herself out of it. I am convinced to this day that she thought she was untouchable. My mom and her husband were arrested at two in the morning. They were married six months, then they *both* went to prison. He was sentenced to twelve, she was sentenced to twenty years of prison plus twenty years of house arrest, so her sentence was forty years.

My mother was altruistic. If you and I were facing some guy who was being politically, unjustly persecuted, and we could hide him, I'm sure I would do it. I'm sure you would do it too. It's human nature to want to do that. She got involved in that. Maybe it was to keep herself busy because her whole life had changed so much: her children were gone, her family was gone, her friends were gone. So why did she get involved? It's natural to want to help. Selfishly, as a kid, I didn't perceive it that way. I'm a mom, and I would never leave my kids for *anything*, not even for another guy. But she disconnected completely from us.

She was forty-two when she went to jail, or something like that, and when she comes out, she's like fifty-nine.[‡] It's a huge difference in a woman's life. The changes physically are humongous. She had gone from this perfect society lady, with these glorious gowns and huge parties, to a very militant person. That shocked me. That was not the mother I remembered.

When my mother got out of Cuba, she was constantly being interviewed on Radio Martí and Radio Mambí.[§] The first time she was on some channel, she said the embargo should be lifted, that she believed it only helped the government as an

---

‡ Albertina O'Farrill was one of the political prisoners freed in 1979 after the regime's negotiations with the Carter Administration and *el diálogo* or "the dialogue" between Fidel and seventy-five exile leaders.

§ Radio Martí is operated by the US government and broadcasts to Cuba in Spanish. Radio Mambí is a Spanish-language commercial radio station in Miami that also broadcasts to Cuba.

excuse to do whatever they wanted. She started getting death threats. Someone put a bomb in the radio station where this had played. She asked to come back on the show two weeks later, and she said, "I left Cuba, and I fought so hard to have the ability to think and to speak freely. I come here and find it's just as bad. I don't want to talk to any of you ever again," and left the show. That's the way she felt. Because that's exactly how it was.

She wrote a book. She gave me the first copy that came off the press. For about six months, I didn't want to read it. I finally went to the beach and read it. I read it with the expectation that I was going to find out what made her give up her children for a political cause. But instead, it was a social book, the parties in Europe with the king and queen of Spain and the king of Italy. Very little on the arrest, very little on the trial, and nothing on the years in prison. It took me like four hours, crying the whole time, then I put it away and never looked at it again. Did it explain anything to me? No.

Neither one of us wanted to talk about it. In fact, I feel guilty because there were so many occasions when she was honored for the Peter Pan kids. I didn't want to see the Peter Pan kids. I resented all fourteen thousand of them, until I embraced them at the end of her life. And forget my sister and brother. We never went to any of the places when she was being honored. And she didn't ask us. It was like two separate lives.

Maribel Pérez Henley

MIAMI, FLORIDA

After graduating from Miami Springs High School, Maribel handled mortgages and real estate closings at a bank. Then she got a job at a law firm. She married, divorced, and raised two daughters. She remembers living in Mariel with her grandparents, parents, and extended family.

So much has been lost of our family ways that we're never going to get back.

The Cuban lifestyle of Cuba was a close-knit family, a lot of people coming in and out of your house, always trying to help another person. The Cuban lifestyle here is very different. We call before we come to somebody's house. We maybe don't see people for a long time. Nobody wants to step up and help the other person in the family. It's the culture here in the United States.

The elders were the ones who held it together, and now they're almost gone. One of the things that held this family together was my mom. Once my mom passed away, that was it. It's not only me because I've talked to friends of mine. What's left is Facebook friends. It's very sad. You realize: I'm alone.

I liked the way that we lived our lives in Cuba. I would have enjoyed being in my country and living there and being a Cuban there—not that I don't appreciate what I have now. But I would have enjoyed it if I had been able to live a normal life in Cuba with freedom and some sort of democracy. It's a beautiful place; I like the people. But things changed.

As they look back, the early Cuban refugees reflect on the sacrifices made for them. Some now see parents and others with an understanding and compassion that came with maturity.

Carlos Alvarez

TALLAHASSEE, FLORIDA

Carlos finished at the University of Florida as a consensus All-American wide receiver. He was drafted by the NFL's Dallas Cowboys in 1972 but did not sign a contract because knee injuries had slowed him. He went to law school then entered private practice. He still marvels at his parents' courage in coming to America and raising four children with their modest dress shop.

My dad was determined that we were going to become Americans from the start. And I tell you, that was a huge—I tell—you know, I so admire my dad, but—[Carlos pauses to control his emotions.]

It's okay. He sounds like he was very far-sighted and had great vision.

Yep. [Carlos pauses again.]

Very together.

Yep. [Another pause.]

I didn't know some of the risks that were taken. I'm just amazed now.

I never had a discussion with my dad as to his thinking at the time. My dad died way too young. He died of a sudden heart attack in '73. I would love to have had these discussions with him. You and I can appreciate having a thirteen-year-old, a twelve-year-old, a ten-year-old, and a five-year-old who are depending on you, risking everything to get out and then starting new, knowing that you are going to lose your profession and everything else, leaving it behind. That's what my dad did.

He took a vacation for one week toward the end. All that other time he was working or doing something for us. My mom just worked her butt off. She went from having her dresses made to making dresses. And I never heard my mom complain. Ever.

Diana Sawaya-Crane
TALLAHASSEE, FLORIDA

Diana and her sister were enrolled at St. Petersburg Junior College, staying with an aunt and uncle, when their parents came to the US in 1971 after twelve years of exile in Venezuela. They settled in Tampa.

Though they were able to make a living here, things were not easy. Dad was sixty years old when he came, and Mom was fifty-eight. While they both studied English, they did not speak it fluently. Dad opened a jewelry store in Tampa. It was 1971, at the height of the recession. The business was not doing well, so he closed the store. He ended up working as a security guard and then at an electric utility company.

Mom tried to get her doctorate degrees accepted by the Florida Department of Education. They said, "Oh, they are only equivalent to bachelor's degrees." She was offered a job teaching at a college somewhere up north. She didn't want to move. She got a job as a seamstress.

So for them, it was a *horrible* situation. They sacrificed everything for us and for what they believed would be a better life for all of us. They didn't say much about it. Just move forward, that's what I was taught. Don't look back. Go forward. My mother was always telling us, "You have to be the best in school. You have to show them that Cubans are smart, that they can do any job they want to do."

In my mother's last year of life—she died when she was ninety—she had a lot to say, that she may have made the wrong decision in moving to the United States. She was frustrated by her inability to communicate in English at her educational level. She felt that it adversely affected not only her work prospects, but also her relationships with English speakers, including members of the family.

She grieved for the life she thought our family could have had in Cuba if Castro had not come to power. She wondered what life would have been like had we stayed in Venezuela. But what would have happened? Look at Venezuela now. It's been going downhill for years.[¶] I have the feeling that Dad was conflicted. He may not have

---

¶ Under the strongmen Hugo Chavez and Nicolás Maduro, Venezuela's economy for years has been in a downward spiral with hyperinflation. More than five million Venezuelans have left their country as refugees.

wanted to move. On the other hand, he shared Mom's desire to be close to his and her family in the United States.

They wanted us to live the American Dream.

Some Cuban Americans who came in the early waves wonder about their identity and the frailty of memory. They want to understand what happened in Cuba and who they are.[52] For them the reckoning can best be achieved by returning to their island birthplace, ninety miles and a lifetime away.[53]

Mercedes Wangüemert-Peña

AUSTIN, TEXAS

Mercedes followed the example of her father, an artist, activist, and martyr in the revolt against Batista. She quit college in California and moved to South Texas in 1970 to work for three years with the political party La Raza Unida after it won political control in the town of Crystal City, an important civil rights battleground for Mexican Americans. She married the artist Amado Peña and had two children before the marriage ended. In 1979 Mercedes went back to Cuba to see her grandfather, the journalist Luís Wangüemert.

He wanted to do everything he used to do with me, and I wanted to do everything. We went to the Floridita and drank daiquiris. We went to the Hotel Nacional and had drinks. We went to a domino game. My grandfather had a library that was about ten thousand books. We had long conversations about his books. He was happy to see that I had read a whole bunch of them.

What made me go back? Oh, my God, I'd been wanting to go back. It was a physical need. The closest influence in my life had been my grandfather, and I had absolutely no contact with him. I had never been close to my mom, much less my stepfather. I was much closer to my grandparents, and I didn't have them anymore. I had nothing.

I went by myself for one week in January 1979, then I went back in June 1979 with the Brigada Antonio Maceo. I was with them, but I wasn't "with" them. They were going to see factories, mental hospitals, the glories of the revolution. I only joined them for certain activities, like lectures. The rest of the time I was at my grandfather's house with my kids. I went in June and came back in September because school had started for the kids.

The third trip was in December 1979. I moved back for a year with my children. I was the first person to be allowed to move back to Cuba, to be repatriated they called it. I was told that by Carlos Rafael Rodriguez.** This was when my name still opened the door because my father had died in the revolution. I don't think I would be alive if I hadn't done that because I was a very conflicted person. There were so many unfinished things for me in Cuba. I didn't know about myself. The best way I can describe it is that we're all like a puzzle. There are all sorts of little pieces, and they fit together, and we become one. I had pieces missing. Some of them I didn't even know were missing.

It was great. My best friend was still my best friend. I was sleeping in my old bed. My kids were sleeping in my dad's and my uncle's beds. I climbed the mango tree that I had climbed when I was a kid. My kids were going to the same school I had gone to, and that my parents had gone to. My kids were four and six. They loved it. They had a bunch of cousins. All the kids were out in the street playing baseball. I got to work at an arts and crafts center, helping my father's fellow painters that I knew as a kid.

I had felt so uprooted, looking for a place that was mine. I got my roots back.

It was difficult. There were shortages. For the boys, getting their food was hard. You had to watch what you said. Everybody kept telling me, "Close your mouth!" Physical stuff was hard, but the spiritual and the emotional were easy, and it was very good for me.

My younger son was born with a lot of health problems. When I first thought about going to Cuba, I talked to the pediatric surgeons, and they said, "Sure, no problem." You know how Cubans are. But the first time he got really sick in Cuba, nobody would see him. My boss's husband was the minister of health, and he told me, "Get out of here." I told my boss that I'm trying to figure out how to do this, and she calls me to her office about half an hour later and says, "Raúl says that he has a plane ready to take you to the United States." I go, "I don't know Raúl." She goes, "But he knows *you*." I said, "No, no, no!"

My grandfather died three days after I left. He had started getting Alzheimer's, but he made an incredible push to remain—whatever you call it. His health had been failing. Toward the end, every once in a while he was still lucid, and we would have

---

** Carlos Rafael Rodriguez, a longtime communist leader, joined Castro's guerrillas in the Sierra Maestra in late 1958. A key Castro confidant, he served the revolution in high-ranking positions, including deputy president, until 1997.

all those talks that I wanted to have with him, and he wanted to have with me. I think what killed him was that I left. My father was his favorite son. I was his first grandchild. He lost me all those years, and then he got me back. When I wasn't around, there was nothing for him.

Crystal City was pivotal in my life. It made me understand the revolutionary process, about all the things that can happen in a revolution, how people can get hurt without anybody meaning to. Some people win, some people lose. It's bound to hurt some people. So I was able to accept what had happened to me. In Cuba I was able to see the good things that the revolution had done and cherish them. I turned a blind eye to all the other stuff that I saw. You say, Well, that's the price.

Finally, I had to admit that Fidel was as bad as everybody said he was.

Mario Cartaya
FORT LAUDERDALE, FLORIDA

After he earned degrees in architecture and building construction from the University of Florida, Mario worked in Houston but then returned to South Florida to be near his family. He married, started a family, and opened his own architectural firm in Fort Lauderdale.

We read a lot about the Jewish diaspora, but the Cuban experience is also a diaspora. I've met Cubans in Egypt, Switzerland, Jordan, Vietnam, and Hungary. The doctor in Point Barrow, the northernmost point of Alaska, was a Cuban guy from Miami. The Jews got reunited in a sliver of land that they call home. Heck, the Jews even made peace with the Germans. We haven't. The Cuban diaspora is Cubans all over the world not able to make peace. And not just peace with Cuba, peace with our past, even peace with each other. We still have these giant walls that separate us.

All of us Cubans have scars that we buried—all of us. Many of us don't want to explore that pain, and you see that reflected in the hate that you hear out of some Cuban Americans. I think that comes not from being mean but from repressed emotions and pain. They don't have the courage to revisit their subconscious to find the peace inside. It took me years to find that courage. I had to go to Cuba to make my peace.

I went to Cuba in 2016 for the first time in fifty-six years. Part of me felt like I was being a traitor to my dad, returning to the land he was forced to leave. I can't tell you how scared I was, but I can tell you that it was the right thing to do. When you've been here as long as I have, and when you came at an early age, you begin to doubt your memories. I proved to myself that my memories are true.

I visited the homes that I left. I went to the cemetery where they buried my grandparents. I remember asking my friends who went with me, "Give me a few moments alone." I began talking with my grandfather, my grandmother, my uncle, and my aunt, who are all buried in the same plot, telling them, I have never forgotten you. I heard my family. I began crying, I mean *boohoo* crying, the kind of crying that comes from the pit of your stomach, from deep within your soul. The only other time I've ever cried like that was when my father died.

When I composed myself, I stayed there, kneeling and praying. I found myself thinking, Why did I cry so *hard?* And then I realized: I had never cried before over my grandfather's death. I was asked not to by my father, for my mother.

Everyone treated me so wonderfully. Everywhere I went people called me a brother. People welcomed me back. People understood my pain, and I understood their pain. They lost their families that left the country. My going back was hope for them that *their* families would come back as well one day. So that pain, that subconscious where we bury those things that we don't want to revisit, isn't just with Cuban exiles, it's with the island Cubans as well. We have that in common. It's a sad truth. When they were calling me "brother," that's exactly what they meant. That thought had never dawned on me.

I came back a different person. My memories had returned. The darkness in my soul had faced the sunlight. My fears proved to be nothing to worry about. My past faced me, I saw myself. I found the other part of me. I felt healed. I was no longer a Cuban American or an American Cuban. I stopped being that. My identity was no longer hyphenated. I was an American, *and* I was a Cuban. I had become both.

To be able to know both parts of me, feel them, and be fully integrated in them is a gift. I am an American, *and* I am a Cuban. I belong in both places: to be in Cuba and feel like I never left, and to live in America and know that *this* is my home.

EPILOGUE

The arrival of the early Cuban refugees was one of the most skillfully managed immigration crises in the nation's history.[1] Political turmoil and economic privation in the Caribbean Basin and Latin America later brought many more to our shores.[2] The rich wanted a safe place to park assets, protected by the rule of law; the humble wanted to build new lives and earn money to send home.[3] The Cubans were among the first.

Their rapid success was due to an unusual convergence of favorable conditions, some by chance, but some from deliberate policy choices made in Washington: the large number of educated refugees from Cuba's upper and middle classes; preferential treatment under US immigration and naturalization laws; the fact that almost all were considered White in race-conscious America; and bountiful government aid. This vibrant refugee community had the added advantage of being centered in Miami, a rising city at a world crossroads where the economy needed to be reinvented. With the globalization of trade on the horizon and Florida becoming the largest presidential swing state, these circumstances—coupled with the early Cuban refugees' celebrated drive—made it possible for them to build new lives and to change America. And yet their success obscures the fact that many more working-class and poor Cubans came later and now live in the US in modest circumstances.[4]

I hope this book helps to preserve the story of the Cubans who came to this country from 1959 through 1973. It's an important story to keep in mind during a roiling national debate about immigration because it demonstrates how refugees can strengthen America if we let them. More work is needed to record the memories of those in the diaspora, such as Cubans of color and those of Chinese and Jewish descent. Fortunately, some of that work is under way.[5] So this book is not the whole story, but it is part of the story.

Some historians believe that masses of Cubans would have migrated to the US even without the Cuban Revolution. They point to the island's growing population and stagnant economy in the fifties, middle-class living standards that began to slip, and the allure of America just ninety miles away.[6] Monsignor Bryan Walsh thought Cubans would have flocked to Miami no matter who ruled in Havana.[7] Bob Graham agrees: "If everything else stayed the same but Castro was eliminated from the equation, they would have come, but it would have been for different reasons. They would be seeking economic opportunity."[8] Fidel's revolution and the welcome mat laid out by four American presidents accelerated those historic forces.

To be sure, accepting more than 600,000 Cuban refugees from 1959 through 1973 was not without controversy, especially in Florida. Many in Miami pressed for aggressive resettlement because they feared the arriving Cubans would radically change their languorous city.[9] As the years passed, despite resettlement, the Cubans did exactly that, in ways no one could have foreseen.[10] They made their mark in all walks of American life.

Even the government's assistance program for the early Cuban refugees left a legacy beyond helping them. The Cuban Children's Program marked the start of the government's commitment to care for unaccompanied refugee children.[11] It pioneered interracial foster home placements and developed cost-accounting practices that were replicated nationwide.[12] An initiative to prepare single Cuban mothers to enter the workforce became a template for other public assistance programs of that era. The massive influx of Spanish-speaking children into Miami's public schools prompted government and foundation grants that created the nation's first bilingual education program. Cuban Loans empowered young exiles to build and lead.[13] These were some of the unexpected benefits of the decision to help the early Cuban refugees.

Many issues in today's angry immigration debate in our country are similar to issues presented by the early Cuban refugees: "chain migration," refugees taking jobs from needy Americans, "anchor babies," refugee children in the government's care, family reunification, "dreamers," and multitudes of migrants without a path to citizenship. These issues about contemporary refugees resonate with Cuban Americans. Or should.

American attitudes toward refugees have always been shaped by the nation's political moods. In the late nineteenth and early twentieth centuries those already in the US pushed hard to keep out Jews, Italians, and others from eastern and southern Europe.[14] Their efforts culminated in rigid "national origins" quotas enacted by the Congress in 1921 and 1924. The discriminatory quotas applied to immigrants and refugees alike.[15] Beset by the Depression, the US turned away European refugees during the thirties except for a relative handful who fit into the quotas, condemning untold numbers to Nazi death camps.[16]

After World War II, as if shamed, the Congress enacted laws in 1948 and 1950 to admit, by borrowing against future annual quotas, more than 400,000 displaced persons from war-ravaged Europe.[17] Another 200,000 visas outside the quotas were authorized by the Refugee Relief Act of 1953.[18] The government made liberal use of the parole authority to let in undocumented refugees fleeing communist regimes—Hungarians, Czechs, Poles, Soviets, Chinese, Vietnamese, Cambodians, and, of course, Cubans.[19] It did so smartly, with security reviews and border control, the committed support of relatives already here, reliance on public and private resources, and in some cases investments in the newcomers to prepare them to contribute to American society.

Country-by-country quotas were repealed when the Congress passed and President Johnson signed the Immigration and Nationality Act of 1965.[20] Among other things, it replaced them with an overall quota for immigrants from the Eastern Hemisphere and for the first time a quota for those from the Western Hemisphere.[21] No more than 20,000 immigration visas could be issued annually to those from a single country.[22] Cuban exiles getting a green card under the Cuban Adjustment Act were counted against their native island's share of the Western Hemisphere quota. This policy created a bottleneck that caused delays in their naturalization—and their right to vote in American elections—so in 1976 the Ford Administration exempted Cuban exiles from the quota.[23] It was another election-year example of Washington's favoritism for them.

The nation's ad hoc approach to its recurring refugee crises gave way to a more coherent policy in the Refugee Act of 1980.[24] The Congress adopted an ideologically neutral standard for refugee status to replace the anticommunism that previously motivated national refugee policy.[25] Following the lead of the United Nations, the Congress defined a refugee as one who cannot return to his or her homeland due to "persecution or a well-founded fear of persecution on account of race, religion, nationality, membership in a particular social group, or political opinion[.]"[26] Today the Department of Homeland Security confers refugee status on applicants after rigorous overseas interviews and security screening.[27] People who arrive at a port of entry without a visa may ask for asylum, an adjudicatory process in which only 15 percent of asylum requests were granted in fiscal year 2019 compared to all the requests submitted.[28] As immigration became a hot-button issue in the US, annual refugee admissions and asylum grants fell from 208,220 in 1980 to 76,203 in 2019.[29]

Some services like those provided for the early Cubans are still available for refugees and asylees, albeit in truncated form. The Refugee Act of 1980 created the Office of Refugee Resettlement (ORR) in the Department of Health and Human Services to oversee assistance to refugees admitted into the US. ORR provides time-limited subsistence income and medical care for needy refugees as well as funding English classes, subsidies for public schools that enroll refugee children, and reimbursement for the care of unaccompanied refugee children, typically by grants to states or private providers.[30]

Cuban migrants still have one unique benefit, in theory: if they enter and reside in the US for a year and a day, they may claim a green card under the Cuban Adjustment Act, which is still on the books, a relic that has outlived its Cold War purpose. But with the border effectively closed to them by rescission of the wet-foot, dry-foot policy, gaining entry without a visa to claim that benefit is the challenge.[31] Cubans are no longer most-favored immigrants. They are treated like everyone else. Even as President Donald J. Trump deplored Havana's human rights record, he deported Cubans in unprecedented numbers back to one of the most insular and controlled societies on the planet.[32]

It is a state of affairs very different from what the early Cuban refugees remember. Perhaps not individually, but as a group who lived through events that others can barely comprehend, they remember. Because for them memory is the foundation of identity.[33]

They remember a lush but bedeviled island ninety miles and a lifetime away. Batista's khaki-wearing political police beating and murdering dissidents, and the bombings timed to go off with the nine-o-clock *cañonazo* at La Cabaña. The smashing of parking meters with baseball bats. Fidel parading triumphantly down Havana's Malecón and pledging a new beginning, one devoted to José Martí's beloved *patria*, the ideal to free their island from foreign domination and to pursue the general welfare—"with all, and for the good of all"—an ideal still not realized.[34]

They remember Fidel's G-2 political police, the *milicianos'* roadblocks, and the Committees for the Defense of the Revolution that informed on neighbors. The luckless exile invasion sponsored by the US. The work camps in the countryside that were the price for an exit permit. Being searched in the Havana airport's glass-enclosed *la pecera* or the ferry terminal or the Varadero airport before boarding a Freedom Flight. The arrival, most with only a few items of clothing, in Key West or Miami or New York or San Juan or Madrid or Caracas or Kingston or some other place of refuge. The separation from parents and loved ones. Fathers and mothers toiling at menial jobs, waiting for the return that never came or for relatives who never left.

They remember the Spam, the blocks of cheese, and the monthly subsistence checks from the government that seem like a pittance today but meant everything then. The signs on apartment buildings that read "No Pets, No Kids, No Cubans." The taunts of "spic." Translating for parents and grandparents who never learned serviceable English. Small shops with Spanish names that sprouted on Calle Ocho or Bergenline Avenue. The Jews who embraced them from a sense of kinship not so long after the Holocaust. The Cuban Loans. They remember.

This is the history, and these are the memories—these and many others—that they carry with them all these years later: of a home they left temporarily but ultimately forever, of sadness and regret but also gratitude and hope, of lives from a different time and place left behind, and of lives created in a new home ninety miles and a lifetime away.

ABBREVIATIONS

CRP   Cuban Refugee Program established by President Kennedy in 1961

El Refugio   Cuban Refugee Emergency Center in Miami

DRE   Directorio Revolucionario Estudiantil, Student Revolutionary Directorate, an underground group that resisted the dictator Fulgencio Batista

G-2   Castro regime's political police

M-26-7   Movimiento de 26 de Julio, or July 26th Movement, the guerrilla movement established by Fidel Castro in 1955

MOU   Memorandum of Understanding between Cuba and the US, dated November 6, 1965, to create the Freedom Flights from 1965 to 1973

OAS   Organization of American States

ORR   Office of Refugee Resettlement of the Department of Health and Human Services

SIM   Servicio de Inteligencia Militar, the Batista regime's political police

ACKNOWLEDGMENTS

In *The Unwomanly Face of War: An Oral History of World War II*, Svetlana Alexievich calls her narrators "extraordinary storytellers" and says of them: "There are pages in their lives that can rival the best pages of the classics." I know what she means. This book is the result of a collaboration with many who are not named as authors but who made the book possible by sharing their memories. So first I thank my fifty-four narrators. To my great regret, I could not include in the manuscript as much as I wanted from each one. Many narrators helped me get interviews with others or loaned me family photographs for this book. For that I also express my gratitude.

For help in finding these "extraordinary storytellers," my thanks to Celene Almagro, David Armstrong, Slater Bayliss, Sally Bradshaw, Carlton Carl, Betty Castor, Mike "Miguelito" Collazo, Alfredo José Estrada, Liana Fernandez Fox, the late Dotty Griffith, Ana and Raúl Mármol, Daniel F. Martell, Juan C. Mendieta, James F. Murley, John Pope, Wayne Rich, Robert M. Rhodes, Judith C. Russell, Francis C. Skilling, Sebastian Spreng, and Armando M. Tabernilla.

Margaret A. "Peggy" Rolando of Coral Gables deserves a shout-out for introducing me to friends who gave me interviews or other help and for routinely offering accommodations at "Casa Rolando." The wine and conversation, of course, were always excellent. John M. Belohlavek and Susan Teets Turner of Tampa helped me make valuable connections and let me bunk in their garage apartment. I am grateful for their help, encouragement, and many years of friendship.

It wasn't possible to interview everyone on my prospect list, but I got introductions, suggestions, or other help from Jane Adams, Sam Bell, Kathy Betancourt, Michael Busha, Kathy Castor, Lorraine Cichowski, Tami F. Conetta, Gerald B. Cope, Idalberto "Bert" de Armas, Miguel de la O, Bonnie Erbé, Carol

Lees Gregg, Amelia Rea Maguire, James and Deborah Manuel, Mel Martinez, Stevan Northcutt, Mario Trueba, Cynthia S. Tunnicliff, Randall Vitale, Robert Volpe, and Wendy Walker. I had fruitful conversations with people whose stories are not in the book. Thanks to Hilda Gomez Gilchrist, the late Gustavo Godoy, and Raoul Lavin for their reminiscences. The late José Pujal told me disturbing stories about his years as one of Castro's political prisoners. I honor his sacrifices.

Thomas J. Aglio gave me a copy of his memoir about administering Camp St. John for teenage boys brought to the United States by Operation Pedro Pan. Gary R. Mormino loaned me research files. Luis C. Morse gave me a treasured copy of the May 10, 1961, issue of *Life* magazine with an account of the Bay of Pigs invasion in which he participated. Stephen N. Zack and Julian C. Juergensmeyer sent background materials on the University of Florida's Cuban American Lawyers Program. My thanks to all of them.

Special thanks to Luis Cruz Azaceta for graciously granting permission to use his 1993 self-portrait, *Man Holding His Country*. It's a knowing depiction of how my Cuban American narrators should be seen.

At the University of Miami's Cuban Heritage Collection (CHC), Director Elizabeth Cerejido and Archivist Amanda Moreno helped me locate important materials. Archivist Koichi Tasa found gems in UM's University Archives. I was pleased when the CHC asked to be the repository for my interview recordings and work papers, ensuring public access to my narrators' complete transcripts at www.library.miami.edu/chc/.

Judith C. Russell, dean of libraries at the University of Florida, opened doors for me in Gainesville. Archivist Peggy McBride and librarian Steve Hersh helped locate historic materials. At the Florida Supreme Court, Communications Director Craig Waters tracked down old records. Thanks also to the staff at Florida State University's Robert Manning Strozier Library in Tallahassee.

Archivist Brian McNerney welcomed me to the storied Reading Room of the Lyndon B. Johnson Presidential Library at the University of Texas at Austin and made my research there efficient and fruitful. Thanks also to Jenna de Graffenried, Lara Hall, and Scott Seely. At the Barry University Archives and Special Collections in Miami Shores, Manager Ximena Valdivia unearthed materials about the Catholic Church's almost-forgotten evacuation of Cuban children to Spain and then the US during the late sixties.

As a first-time author, I got a critical eye on portions of the manuscript, and in many cases advice on how to navigate around the shoals of the publishing world, from John M. Belohlavek, A. R. "Dick" Elam, David Finkel, Randy Fitzgerald, Julie Hauserman, Wayne S. Kabak, Martin Merzer, Ross E. Milloy, Gary R. Mormino, Rich Oppel, Neil Skene, Leslie Powell Skilling, and Victor Andres Triay. For encouraging words when I needed them, thanks to Carlos Eire, Mitchell Kaplan, Cristina Nosti, Susan Rabiner, and Jan Jarboe Russell.

Professor Samuel Freedman of Columbia University's Graduate School of Journalism got me off on the right foot at his 2015 book-writing seminar for alumni. Director Stephen M. Sloan and the staff at Baylor University's Institute for Oral History initiated me into the practice of oral history through online workshops in 2016 and 2019. Rebecca Dominguez translated an article from a Madrid magazine about unaccompanied Cuban children who came to the US by way of Spain. Dave Barfield prepared the map of Cuba, and Ron Sachs introduced us. Mary Beth Tyson furnished the author photograph. Mim Eisenberg, Barbara H. Jardee, and Ken Walden transcribed the interviews. My thanks to them as well.

Interim Editor-in-Chief Stephanye Hunter wooed me to the University of Florida Press and held my hand as the book came together. Her guidance was always thoughtful and constructive. The outside experts she chose to review the manuscript recommended changes that greatly strengthened it. Thanks also to Sally Antrobus, Eleanor Deumens, Rachel Doll, Ale Gasso, Romi Gutierrez, Jenna Kolesari, and Rachel Welton.

I began this project in 2015 while in full-time practice at my law firm, Hopping Green & Sams of Tallahassee, and I took "of counsel" status in 2018 so I could finish it. Throughout, I had the unstinting support of my colleagues. Thanks in particular to Kim Hancock, Gary K. Hunter, Felicia Kitzmiller, Marisol Roberts, and Kathy Scott.

I had constant support and encouragement from family and friends. My greatest thanks are for my wife, Vicki Weber. She cannibalized our household account to pay for my reporting trips, transcripts, office supplies, and piles of books. She was always an encouraging critic. At the dinner table one night, she said, "Just remember, the dedication for this book needs to be: 'To Vicki, dead or alive,'" to which I added, "preferably alive." It became a running joke.

Thank you, Vicki, for all you did to make this book possible, and for everything else in the beautiful life we share.

NOTES

INTRODUCTION

1. Carlos Alvarez, interviewed by the author in Tallahassee, Florida, November 16, 2016.
2. "HMS Northway (F-142)," NavSource Naval History (website), Photographic Archive of the U.S. Navy, Amphibious Photo Archive, http://www.navsource.org/archives/10/12/1211.htm.
3. "West India Lists Ferries for Sale," *New York Times*, June 2, 1961.
4. "Havana Passenger and Automobile Ferry," November 1, 1956, NavSource Naval History (website), https://www.navsource.org/archives/10/12/10121110.jpg (sales brochure for West India Fruit & Steamship Co., Inc.).
5. "HMS Northway (F-142)" and "Havana Passenger and Automobile Ferry," November 1, 1956, NavSource Naval History (website), https://www.navsource.org/archives/10/12/10121110.jpg (sales brochure for West India Fruit & Steamship Co., Inc).
6. Hemingway, "Great Blue River," in *By-Line*, 404.
7. "Ferry to Havana Ends Run," *New York Times*, November 2, 1960.

CHAPTER 1. HOME

1. Scarpaci, Segre, and Coyula, *Havana*, 93.
2. Gott, *New History*, 165.
3. Perrottet, *¡Cuba Libre!* 24; DePalma, *Cubans: Ordinary Lives*, 49.
4. Thomas, *Cuba*, 1103–4.
5. Pérez, *Becoming Cuban*, 452–55, 461, 450.
6. Scarpaci, Segre, and Coyula, *Havana*, 101.
7. Moruzzi, *Before Castro*, 148–50.
8. Gott, *New History*, 114.
9. Scarpaci, Segre, and Coyula, *Havana*, 89.
10. Gott, *New History*, 126.
11. Thomas, "U.S. and Castro," 27.
12. Hansen, *Guantánamo*, 25–26.
13. Thomas, *Cuba*, 88; Pérez, *Ties of Intimacy*, 59–63.
14. Pérez, *Ties of Intimacy*, 34, 37–39, 44, 46–47, 50–54.
15. Gott, *New History*, 97–104.
16. Morris, *Rise of Roosevelt*, 681–88.
17. Pérez, *Ties of Intimacy*, 97.

18. Pérez, *Ties of Intimacy*, 97–98, 111.

19. Pérez, *Becoming Cuban*, 117–21.

20. Thomas, *Cuba*, 403.

21. Pérez, *Structure*, 121–22.

22. Gott, *New History*, 111; Thomas, *Cuba*, 605–25.

23. Tony Perrottet, "When Americans Loved Fidel Castro," *New York Times*, January 24, 2019.

24. Pérez, *Becoming Cuban*, 105–09; Gott, *New History*, 115.

25. Pérez, *Ties of Intimacy*, 117–21.

26. Mace, "Currency, Credit, Crises," 231–34.

27. Pérez, *Ties of Intimacy*, 130–33.

28. Pérez, *Ties of Intimacy*, 71–72; Wood, "'Gators Making Merry," 76–79.

29. Deere, "Here Come the Yankees!" 730, 744.

30. Pérez, *Ties of Intimacy*, 136–37.

31. Pérez, *Ties of Intimacy*, 140–42.

32. English, *Nocturne*, 10–15.

33. Thomas, *Cuba*, 1102.

34. Pérez, *Ties of Intimacy*, 207–9.

35. Duany, "Postrevolution Exodus."

36. Duany, "Postrevolution Exodus."

37. Gott, *New History*, 6–9, 118–19, 126–27.

38. Gott, *New History*, 44–48.

39. Thomas, *Cuba*, 168–70.

40. Thomas, *Cuba*, 184–89, 497, 540–41.

41. Young, "Globalization and the Border Wall," in *Deportation*, 54–59.

42. Duany, "Postrevolution Exodus."

43. Gott, *New History*, 118–19; Aja, *Forgotten Cubans*, 38.

44. Pedraza, *Disaffection*, 155.

45. Gjelten, *Bacardi*, 77.

46. Pérez, *Structure*, 75–77, 128.

47. Pérez, *Becoming Cuban*, 322–23.

48. Thomas, *Cuba*, 516

49. Gott, *New History*, 118–19.

50. Gott, *New History*, 120–23.

51. Thomas, *Cuba*, 523–24.

52. Thomas, *Cuba*, 1120–21.

53. Pérez, *Becoming Cuban*, 323–24, 270.

54. Thomas, *Cuba*, 1117, 1111.

55. Gott, *New History*, 29–30.

56. Pérez, *Becoming Cuban*, 325–27.

57. Scarpaci, Segre, and Coyula, *Havana*, 78.

58. Thomas, *Cuba*, 1096.

59. Scarpaci, Segre, and Coyula, *Havana*, 96, 78–79.

60. Estrada, *Autobiography*, 92–93.

61. Thomas, *Cuba*, 1101.

62. Pedraza, *Disaffection*, 248–49.

63. Scarpaci, Segre, and Coyula, *Havana*, 86–88, 99, 214.

64. English, *Nocturne*, x–xiii.

65. Moruzzi, *Before Castro*, 81–89.

66. Horst, "Sleeping on the Ashes," 33–35, 130–31, 205–11, 215–18.

67. Scarpaci, Segre, and Coyula, *Havana*, 94.

68. Thomas, *Cuba*, 1099.

69. Scarpaci, Segre, and Coyula, *Havana*, 100.

70. Gott, *New History*, 165.

71. Thomas, *Cuba*, 1095–96.

72. Scarpaci, Segre, and Coyula, *Havana*, 94–95.

73. Thomas, *Cuba*, 720.

74. Hansen, *Young Castro*, 152.

75. Torres, *Apple*, 38; Thomas, *Cuba*, 1104.

76. Pérez, *Becoming Cuban*, 400.

77. Scarpaci, Segre, and Coyula, *Havana*, 116.

78. Pérez, *Becoming Cuban*, 400.

79. Scarpaci, Segre, and Coyula, *Havana*, 116–17.

80. Pérez, *Becoming Cuban*, 407–9.

81. Thomas, *Cuba*, 1510 ("Cuban Presidents" table).

82. "Cubans Overjoyed as Mendieta Rules," *New York Times*, January 19, 1934; J. D. Phillips, "Mendieta Accepts Cuban Presidency; Takes Oath Today," *New York Times*, January 18, 1934.

83. Clark, "Exodus," 46.

84. Gott, *New History*, 137–43.

85. Gjelten, *Bacardi*, 124–25.

86. Thomas, *Cuba*, 719–20.

87. Gjelten, *Bacardi*, 133–35; Thomas, *Cuba*, 722.

88. "Dictator with the People," *Time*, April 21, 1952, 43–44.

89. Thomas, *Cuba*, 757–58.

90. "Dictator with the People," *Time*, April 21, 1952, 43–44.

CHAPTER 2. AFTER THE COUP

1. "Revolution at Dawn," *Time*, March 17, 1952, 36.

2. Gott, *New History*, 146.

3. Domínguez, "Batista Regime," in *Sultanistic Regimes*, 124; net present value calculation via www.in2013dollars.com (accessed February 25, 2021).

4. "Winner Take All," *Time*, March 24, 1952, 38; Thomas, *Cuba*, 790–91; Domínguez, "Batista Regime," in *Sultanistic Regimes*, 120–21; R. Hart Phillips, "Cuba Recovering After Revolution," *New York Times*, March 12, 1952.

5. "Strong Man's Law," *Time*, April 14, 1952, 39.

6. Thomas, *Cuba*, 786.

7. Office of Historian, Dept. of State, *Foreign Relations, 1952–54*, 871 (Document 327, Memorandum by the Secretary of State to the President, March 24, 1952); "Batista's Cuban Rule Is Recognized by U.S.," *New York Times*, March 28, 1952.

8. Pérez, *Becoming Cuban*, 448.

9. Thomas, *Cuba*, 781–82.

10. "Revolt by Television," *Time*, September 1, 1952, 26.

11. Perrottet, *¡Cuba Libre!* 40–43.

12. Thomas, *Cuba*, 803, 807–11.

13. Hansen, *Young Castro*, xvi, 208–9.

14. Hansen, *Young Castro*, 157–58; Thomas, *Cuba*, 824–29, 835.

15. Hansen, *Young Castro*, 173–79.

16. Gott, *New History*, 149–51; Hansen, *Young Castro*, xiii, 250.

17. Perrottet, *¡Cuba Libre!* 61–62.

18. "One-Man Race," *Time*, November 8, 1954, 40.

19. Pedraza, *Disaffection*, 44, 73–74.

20. "Forgive & Forget," *Time*, May 2, 1955, 39.

21. Hansen, *Young Castro*, 262, 277.

22. Thomas, *Cuba*, 888–89; Perrottet, *¡Cuba Libre!* 76.

23. Hansen, *Young Castro*, 306–9, 166.

24. "Cuba Wipes Out Invaders; Leader Among 40 Dead," *New York Times*, December 3, 1956.

25. Hansen, *Young Castro*, 314–17; Hansen, *Guantánamo*, xiv.

26. "Creeping Revolt," *Time*, January 7, 1957, 33.

27. Thomas, *Cuba*, 925.

28. "Creeping Revolt," *Time*, January 7, 1957, 33.

29. "Running-Sore Revolt," *Time*, February 25, 1957, 43.

30. "Creeping Revolt," *Time*, January 7, 1957, 33.

31. Thomas, *Cuba*, 870–71.

32. Herbert L. Matthews, "Surface Calm Hid Cuba Discontent," *New York Times*, March 14, 1957.

33. Hansen, *Young Castro*, 279.

34. Hansen, *Young Castro*, 295.

35. Thomas, *Cuba*, 919–22.

36. DePalma, *Man Who Invented Fidel*, 5, 83–85, 158–59, 275–76.

37. Herbert L. Matthews, "Now Castro Faces the Harder Fight," *New York Times Magazine*, March 8, 1959, 22.

38. Herbert L. Matthews, "Cuban Rebel Is Visited in Hideout," *New York Times*, February 24, 1957; Gott, *New History*, 158.

39. Domínguez, "Batista Regime," in *Sultanistic Regimes*, 129.

40. "Moscow's Man in Havana," *Time*, April 27, 1962, 35.

41. Thomas, *Cuba*, 920; Domínguez, "Batista Regime," in *Sultanistic Regimes*, 127.

42. Norman Lewis, "Cuban Interlude," *New Yorker*, May 3, 1958, 77; "Fidel Castro's Mistake," *New York Times*, October 28, 1958.

43. Thomas, *Cuba*, 925–31.

44. Estrada, *Autobiography*, 217–18.

45. Gott, *New History*, 160.

46. "Not Afraid to Die," *Time*, March 25, 1957, 36.

47. Thomas, *Cuba*, 930–32.

48. Sweig, *Inside*, 2, 12.

49. Gott, *New History*, 157.

50. Hansen, *Young Castro*, 331.

51. Perrottet, *¡Cuba Libre!* 160–61.

52. Thomas, *Cuba*, 957–59, 1100.

53. Perrottet, *¡Cuba Libre!* 162.

54. Domínguez, "Batista Regime," in *Sultanistic Regimes*, 125.

55. English, *Nocturne*, 164, 302.

56. Thomas, *Cuba*, 1068–69.

57. "A Game of Casino," *Time*, January 20, 1958, 32.

58. English, *Nocturne*, 132–33.

59. Perrottet, *¡Cuba Libre!* 283–84.

60. Gjelten, *Bacardi*, 193–95.

61. Rathbone, *Sugar King*, 13.

62. "The First Year of Rebellion," *Time*, December 9, 1957, 44.

63. Sweig, *Inside*, 24, 77–81, 89–90, 126–33.

64. "Career Rebel," *Time*, July 8, 1957, 20; "This Man Castro," *Time*, April 14, 1958, 35.

65. "Career Rebel," *Time*, July 8, 1957, 20; Fidel Castro, "Why We Fight," *Coronet*, February 1958, 85.

66. Thomas, *Cuba*, 954–55.

67. Sweig, *Inside*, 122.

68. Gott, *New History*, 160

69. "Dignified Plea," *Time*, September 20, 1954, 45; Thomas, *Cuba*, 985–86.

70. "Less Than Total War," *Time*, April 14, 1958, 35.

71. Thomas, *Cuba*, 992–94.

72. Sweig, *Inside*, 54.

73. "Women of the Rebellion," *Time*, January 19, 1959.

74. Hansen, *Young Castro*, 395, 384–86.

75. Pérez, *Structure*, 204–06.

76. Sweig, *Inside*, 178–80.

77. Hansen, *Young Castro*, 395, 384–85, 386.

78. Domínguez, "Batista Regime" in *Sultanistic Regimes*, 129.

79. Perrottet, *¡Cuba Libre!* 204.

80. Thomas, *Cuba*, 1005–11, 1020.

81. "Into the Third Year," *Time*, December 1, 1958, 32.

82. Hansen, *Young Castro*, 390–91.

83. Domínguez, "Batista Regime," in *Sultanistic Regimes*, 130.

84. Greene, *Our Man*, 21.

85. Office of Historian, Dept. of State, *Foreign Relations, 1958–60*, 30 (Document 18, Despatch from the Consulate at Santiago de Cuba by Oscar H. Guerra, February 21, 1958).

86. Hansen, *Young Castro*, 360.

87. Thomas, *Cuba*, 1015–16.

88. Hansen, *Young Castro*, 391–92; Thomas, "U.S. and Castro," 30.

89. "End of a War," *Time*, January 12, 1959, 32.

90. Thomas, *Cuba*, 1027; "End of a War," *Time*, January 12, 1959, 32.

91. Perrottet, *¡Cuba Libre!* 309.

92. E. W. Kenworthy, "United States Foresees No Obstacle to Early Recognition of the Castro Regime," *New York Times*, January 3, 1959.

93. R. Hart Phillips, "Urrutia Will Let 300 Foes Depart," *New York Times*, January 8, 1959.

94. R. Hart Phillips, "Castro Names President as Rebels Enter Havana; Street Clashes Continue," *New York Times*, January 3, 1959.

95. Herbert L. Matthews, "Rioters Mob and Loot in Havana," *New York Times*, January 2, 1959.

96. Thomas, *Cuba*, 1022–23.

97. Perrottet, *¡Cuba Libre!* 310–12.

98. "Mobs Pillage Havana; Castro to Take Over?" *Miami Herald*, January 2, 1959.

99. Gott, *New History*, 165.

100. Sweig, *Inside*, 179–80.

101. Thomas, *Cuba*, 1033.

102. Pérez, *Structure,* 210; Perrottet, *¡Cuba Libre!* 315–16.

103. Thomas, *Cuba*, 1033.

104. Pérez, *Structure*, 214.

105. R. Hart Phillips, "Havana Welcomes Castro at End of Triumphal Trip," *New York Times*, January 9, 1959.

106. R. Hart Phillips, "Havana Welcomes Castro at End of Triumphal Trip," *New York Times*, January 9, 1959; Pérez, *Structure*, 225.

107. Perrottet, ¡Cuba Libre! 323.

108. "Cuban Students Yield Their Arms," *New York Times*, January 11, 1959.

109. Perrottet, ¡Cuba Libre! 323.

CHAPTER 3. LEAVING CUBA

1. Perrottet, ¡Cuba Libre! 291, 309.

2. "All Quiet in East, Raul Castro Says," *New York Times*, January 8, 1959.

3. "The Vengeful Visionary," *Time*, January 26, 1959, 40.

4. Gjelten, *Bacardi*, 207.

5. Domínguez, "Batista Regime," in *Sultanistic Regimes*, 127–28.

6. "Jubilation & Revenge," *Time*, January 19, 1959, 35; "End of a War," *Time*, January 12, 1959, 32.

7. Thomas, *Cuba*, 1044.

8. E. W. Kenworthy, "Castro Declares Regime Is Free of Red Influence," *New York Times*, April 18, 1959.

9. Thomas, "U.S. and Castro," 30; Sweig, *Inside*, 180–81.

10. R. Hart Phillips, "Urrutia Takes Up Duties in Havana; Names a Premier," *New York Times*, January 6, 1959; "Castro Takes Over," *Time*, February 23, 1959, 37.

11. Thomas, *Cuba*, 1196–97.

12. Gott, *New History*, 170; "The First 100 Days," *Time*, April 20, 1959, 42.

13. Tad Szulc, "Red Influence Growing in Cuba Behind Façade of the Revolution," *New York Times*, August 2, 1960; Thomas, *Cuba*, 1193.

14. John Lardner, "The Ordeal of Fidel Castro," *New Yorker*, February 21, 1959, 121.

15. "The Other Face," *Time*, April 27, 1959, 27; "Humanist Abroad," *Time*, May 4, 1959, 27.

16. LeoGrande and Kornbluh, *Back Channel*, 15.

17. Tony Perrottet, "Chanting Crowds and Camo Chic," *New York Times*, April 16, 2019.

18. Thomas, *Cuba*, 1210.

19. Lindesay Parrott, "Castro Defends Election Delay," *New York Times*, April 23, 1959.

20. "The Other Face," *Time*, April 27, 1959, 27.

21. Lindesay Parrott, "Castro Defends Election Delay," *New York Times*, April 23, 1959.

22. R. Hart Phillips, "Castro Calling Halt in Military Trials," *New York Times*, May 12, 1959.

23. "Castro Cuts Up Plantations, Parcels Land to Peasants," *Miami Herald*, May 19, 1959.

24. "Confiscation!" *Time*, June 1, 1959, 34; Allison, "Cuba's Seizures," 49.

25. R. Hart Phillips, "Cubans Grumble Over Shortages," *New York Times*, June 15, 1961.

26. Thomas, "U.S. and Castro," 32.

27. Gott, *New History*, 180.

28. Thomas, *Cuba*, 1244–45, 1255–56.

29. R. Hart Phillips, "Ex-Castro Aide Draws 20 Years," *New York Times*, December 16, 1959.

30. "To the Wall!" *Time*, November 9, 1959.

31. R. Hart Phillips, "5 Ministers Quit Cabinet in Cuba," *New York Times*, June 12, 1959.

32. Thomas, *Cuba*, 1232–34.

33. Thomas, *Cuba*, 1252.

34. "Back on Post," *Time*, March 28, 1960, 38.

35. "Opinion of the Week: At Home and Abroad," *New York Times*, July 24, 1960.

36. Thomas, *Cuba*, 1228–29; "Enemies Underground," *Time*, October 26, 1959, 39.

37. "Growing Troubles," *Time*, October 17, 1960, 42.

38. Thomas, *Cuba*, 1321.

39. "Red All the Way," *Time*, October 10, 1960, 45.

40. "Castro's Growing Arms," *Time*, November 14, 1960, 37.

41. Allison, "Cuba's Seizures," 49.

42. "Clarified & Defined," *Time,* February 22, 1960, 40; Allison, "Cuba's Seizures," 49; Thomas, *Cuba,* 1284, 1288.

43. "Coping with Castro," *Time*, July 18, 1960, 26.

44. R. Hart Phillips, "Cuba Nationalizes Banks and All Major Companies; U.S. Indicts Castro in U.N.," *New York Times*, October 15, 1960.

45. E. W. Kenworthy, "U.S. Puts Embargo on Goods to Cuba; Curbs Ship Deals," *New York Times*, October 20, 1960.

46. R. Hart Phillips, "Castro Seizes 166 U.S. Concerns; Americans to Shun Cuba Sugar," *New York Times*, October 26, 1960.

47. "Johnson Signs Bill to Aid Americans in Claims on Cuba," *New York Times*, October 18, 1964.

48. "The Breaking Point," *Time*, January 13, 1961, 29.

49. Richard Eder, "Cuba Shuts Borders to Exchange Pesos for New Currency," *New York Times*, August 6, 1961.

50. "Keeping Them Poor," *Time*, August 18, 1961, 31.

51. "Certain Deficiencies," *Time*, September 1, 1961, 29.

52. "Castro Is Rationing Basic Cuban Foods," *New York Times,* March 13, 1962.

53. Thomas, *Cuba*, 1297, 1333.

54. Thomas, *Cuba*, 1096.

55. Clark, "Exodus," 80.

56. "New Travel Curbs Bemoaned in Cuba," *New York Times*, December 19, 1959.

57. "Exodus," *Time*, August 22, 1960, 30.

58. Anillo-Badia, "Outstanding Claims," 86 (citing Interior Ministry Resolution No. 454 of September 29, 1961, and Law No. 989 of December 5, 1961).

59. "Crises: Phony & Real," *Time*, November 14, 1960, 36.

60. "Twice Around the World," *Time*, August 4, 1961, 37.

61. Triay, *Fleeing Castro*, 72–73.

62. R. Hart Phillips, "100 Face Death in Trials About to Begin at Havana," *New York Times*, January 15, 1959.

63. Pedraza, *Political Disaffection*, 156–58.

64. Boswell and Curtis, *Cuban-American Experience*, 47.

65. Duany, "Postrevolution Exodus."

66. Pérez, *Ties of Intimacy*, 64; Mohl, "Port of Miami," in *Forgotten Doors*, 86.

67. Allman, *City of the Future*, 160.

68. Mormino and Pozzetta, *Ybor City*, 64–67.

69. Mohl, "Port of Miami," in *Forgotten Doors*, 86.

70. Mormino, *Land of Sunshine*, 17.

71. Clark, "Exodus," 46.

CHAPTER 4. FIRST WAVE

1. Thomas, "Cuban Refugees," 46.

2. *Cuban Refugee Hearings*, 1961, 210 (Statement of James L. Hennessy, Executive Assistant to the Commissioner, Immigration and Naturalization Service).

3. Juanita Greene, "Wide Political Gaps, Money Divide Miami's Cuba Exiles," *Miami Herald*, December 3, 1960.

4. Clark, "Exodus," 74.

5. García, *Havana USA*, 16.

6. *Cuban Refugee Hearings*, 1961, 206 (Statement of Robert F. Hale, Director, Visa Office, Department of State).

7. Clark, "Exodus," 82.

8. *Cuban Refugee Hearings*, 1961, 210–11 (Statement of James L. Hennessy, Executive Assistant to the Commissioner, Immigration and Naturalization Service).

9. Kurzban, *Critical Analysis*, 871–72 and n30.

10. Cox and Rodríguez, *President and Immigration*, 502.

11. Clark, "Exodus," 73.

12. Woytych, "Cuban Refugee," 19; Cuban Adjustment Act of 1966, Pub. L. No. 89–732, 80 Stat. 1161 (codified as amended at 8 U.S.C. §1255 (2020)).

13. Boswell and Curtis, *Cuban-American Experience*, 46 (Table 3.3).

14. Mitchell, "Cuban Refugee Program," 8, 5.

15. Tebeau, *History of Florida*, 287, 383–87, 431–34.

16. García, *Havana USA*, 16.

17. Pan American World Airways, System Timetable (Spring and Summer), April 28, 1957, 42, online at Airline Timetable Images, http://www.timetableimages.com/ttimages/pa.htm.

18. Mohl, "Port of Miami," in *Forgotten Doors*, 88.

19. Agnes Ash, "Havana Reborn in a Corner of Miami," *New York Times*, December 18, 1966.

20. García, *Havana USA*, 86.

21. Sicius, "Miami Diocese," 40; E. V. W. Jones, "Ike Releases Million to Aid Cuban Exiles," *Miami Herald*, December 3, 1960.

22. Mitchell, "Cuban Refugee Program," 3–4.

23. Mormino, *Land of Sunshine*, 286.

24. García, *Havana USA*, 21.

25. Comptroller General, *Analysis of Federal Expenditures*, 24.

26. "Cuban Refugee Tower Named as Historic Site," *New York Times*, October 7, 1979.

27. Mitchell, "Cuban Refugee Program," 3.

28. Thomas, "Cuban Refugees," 50–52.

29. Mitchell, "Cuban Refugee Program," 6.

30. Thomas, "Cuban Refugees," 52.

31. Clark, "Exodus," 77–78.

32. "The New Exodus," *Time*, August 18, 1961, 33.

33. Loewen, *Sundown Towns*, 6–7.

34. George, "Colored Town," 435.

35. Rothstein, *Color of Law*, 44–45; Mohl, "Whitening Miami," 320.

36. *Buchanan v. Warley*, 245 U.S. 60 (1917); Rothstein, *Color of Law*, 45–48.

37. Mohl, "Whitening Miami," 329–30; *State v. Wilson*, 25 So. 2d 860 (Fla. 1946).

38. Rothstein, *Color of Law*, 52–53.

39. Mohl, "Whitening Miami," 324–28.

40. Rothstein, *Color of Law*, 63–67, 70–75.

41. Mohl, "Whitening Miami," 321–22.

42. Loewen, *Sundown Towns*, 4–7.

43. Loewen, *Sundown Towns*, 71, 78; Allman, *City of the Future*, 147.

44. Loewen, *Sundown Towns*, 339.

45. Boswell and Curtis, *Cuban-American Experience*, 103.

46. "Miami Perturbed by Cuba Refugees," *New York Times*, October 21, 1961.

47. Juanita Greene, "Jobless American Citizens Resent Hiring of Cuban Refugees at Low Pay," *Miami Herald*, December 2, 1960.

48. R. Hart Phillips, "Miami Is Going Latin as Cubans Make Their Effect Felt in City," *New York Times*, March 18, 1962.

49. Maria Torres, "Cuban Exiles Are Not a Bit Golden," *Chicago Tribune*, November 15, 1986.

50. Aja, *Forgotten Cubans*, 7–8.

51. Boswell and Curtis, *Cuban-American Experience*, 103; Danielle Clealand, "Undoing the Invisibility of Blackness in Miami," *Black Latinas Know Collective* (blog), undated, http://www.blacklatinasknow.org/post/undoing-the-invisibility-of-blackness-in-miami (accessed June 8, 2021).

52. Pedraza, *Disaffection*, 159.

53. Juanita Greene, "Wide Political Gaps, Money Divide Miami's Cuba Exiles," *Miami Herald*, December 3, 1960.

54. "They Would Be Free," *Time*, December 12, 1960, 32–33.

55. Dom Bonafede, "Anti-Castro Exiles Wreck Cuba Consulate," *Miami Herald*, October 14, 1960.

56. Sicius, "Miami Diocese," 52.

57. Gellman, "*St. Louis* Tragedy," 151–56.

58. Thomas, "Cuban Refugees," 50.

59. Joseph Carter, "2 Airlines Halt Runs to Havana," *New York Times*, October 24, 1962; García, *Havana USA*, 13.

60. Pérez, *Becoming Cuban*, 500–01.

CHAPTER 5. CHILDREN WITHOUT PARENTS

1. Thomas, *Cuba*, 1271.

2. Torres, *Apple*, 89–90.

3. Clark, "Exodus," 78; "And Now the Children?" *Time*, October 6, 1961, 41.

4. R. Hart Phillips, "'Castro Freed Cuba from U.S.' Is 'Correct' Answer in Havana," *New York Times*, June 8, 1960.

5. Torres, *Apple,* 111.

6. Triay, *Fleeing Castro*, 5–6.

7. Torres, *Apple*, 67.

8. "And Now the Children?" *Time*, October 6, 1961, 41; Pedraza, *Disaffection*, 81.

9. Triay, *Fleeing Castro*, 16.

10. Cauce, "Fifty Years Later," 93–94.

11. Torres, *Apple*, 60–61.

12. Triay, *Fleeing Castro*, 16–17.

13. Torres, *Apple*, 66.

14. Triay, *Fleeing Castro*, 16–17.

15. Walsh, "Refugee Children," 397–98.

16. Torres, *Apple*, 67–68.

17. Torres, *Apple*, 56–57, 60–62.

18. Walsh, "Refugee Children," 395–96.

19. Sicius, "Miami Diocese," 45.

20. Oettinger, "Services," 380.

21. Walsh, "Refugee Children," 383.

22. Torres, *Apple*, 148.

23. Oettinger, "Services," 379–80.

24. John W. Finney, "President Orders Cuba Refugee Aid," *New York Times*, February 4, 1961.

25. Walsh, "Refugee Children," 396–97.

26. Triay, *Fleeing Castro*, 53.

27. Torres, *Apple*, 148.

28. Oettinger, "Services," 381.

29. Tad Szulc, "Red Influence Growing in Cuba Behind the Façade of the Revolution," *New York Times*, August 2, 1960.

30. "The Archbishop Speaks," *Time*, May 30, 1960, 24.

31. "Bishop of Havana Decries the Methods of Totalitarianism," *New York Times*, June 3, 1960.

32. R. Hart Phillips, "Prelates Reject Castro's Attacks," *New York Times*, December 4, 1960.

33. Sicius, "Miami Diocese," 40.

34. Max Frankel, "Castro Pledges Purge of Judges," *New York Times*, December 18, 1960.

35. Sam Pope Brewer, "Cuba Deporting Foreign Clergy," *New York Times*, May 8, 1961.

36. Richard Eder, "Havana Deports 135 Priests and Accused Bishop to Spain," *New York Times*, September 18, 1961.

37. Triay, *Bay of Pigs*, 15.

38. Clemente C. Amázaga and Eloísa Echazábal, "Unaccompanied Cuban Children's Program Florida Camps and Group Homes 1960 Through 1978," Pedropan.org (website), http://pedropanexodus.com/wp-content/uploads/2015/11/255585261-florida-Camps-and-Group-Homes-1-1.pdf.

39. Walsh, "Refugee Children," 404–06.

40. Walsh, "Cultural Identity," 3.

41. Triay, *Fleeing Castro*, 22.

42. Walsh, "Refugee Children," 401–2.

43. Triay, *Fleeing Castro*, 33–35.

44. Torres, *Apple*, 76; Triay, *Fleeing Castro*, 34.

45. Triay, *Fleeing Castro*, 23–24.

46. Triay, *Fleeing Castro*, 35–37.

47. Torres, *Apple*, 133–37.

48. Thomas, "U.S.A.," 10.

49. Luisa Yanez, "The Prince of Pedro Pan," *Miami Herald*, May 17, 2009.

50. "Cuban Children Helped in Florida," *New York Times*, May 27, 1962.

51. Walsh, "Refugee Children," 412–13.

52. Gene Miller, "'Peter Pan' Means Real Life to Some Kids," *Miami Herald*, March 9, 1962.

53. Torres, *Apple*, 9, 267.

54. Children's Bureau, *Children in Exile*, 6.

55. Triay, *Fleeing Castro*, 103; Torres, *Apple*, 162–71.

56. Triay, *Fleeing Castro*, 87.

57. Children's Bureau, *Children in Exile*, 8; Triay, *Fleeing Castro*, 70–73.

58. Triay, *Fleeing Castro*, 68.

59. Walsh, "Refugee Children," 412–13.

60. Cauce, "Fifty Years Later," 99.

61. Torres, *Apple*, 187.

62. Triay, *Fleeing Castro*, 53.

63. Triay, *Fleeing Castro*, 33–34.

64. Torres, *Apple*, 241–43.

65. "Cuban Children Helped in Florida," *New York Times*, May 27, 1962.

66. Torres, *Apple*, 243–46.

67. Pedraza, *Disaffection*, 286–91.

CHAPTER 6. NO RETURN

1. Triay, *Bay of Pigs*, 8.

2. Smith, *Eisenhower*, 621–27.

3. Smith, *Eisenhower*, 627–32.

4. Triay, *Bay of Pigs*, 11, 38

5. Rasenberger, *Brilliant Disaster*, 137.

6. Thomas, *Cuba*, 1301.

7. Pedraza, *Disaffection*, 95.

8. Rasenberger, *Brilliant Disaster*, 118–19, 125–38.

9. Thomas, *Cuba*, 1369; Pfeiffer, *Bay of Pigs I*, 182–83.

10. Triay, *Bay of Pigs*, 38–40.

11. Rasenberger, *Brilliant Disaster*, 227–29.

12. Thomas, *Cuba*, 1307–8.

13. Rasenberger, *Brilliant Disaster*, 140; Triay, *Bay of Pigs*, 41, 13.

14. Thomas, *Cuba*, 1362.

15. Triay, *Bay of Pigs*, 41.

16. Thomas, *Cuba*, 1301.

17. Thomas, *Cuba*, 1304–05; García, *Havana USA*, 31–32.

18. "The Underground," *Time*, January 27, 1961, 26; Rasenberger, *Brilliant Disaster*, 383.

19. "The Massacre," *Time*, April 28, 1961, 22.

20. Gott, *New History*, 193.

21. Triay, *Bay of Pigs*, 44–45.

22. "Castro's Triumph," *Time*, May 5, 1961, 32.

23. Rasenberger, *Brilliant Disaster*, 185; Thomas, *Cuba*, 1355

24. Pfeiffer, *Bay of Pigs I*, 211–12, 300.

25. "Castro's Triumph," *Time*, May 5, 1961, 32.

26. Rasenberger, *Brilliant Disaster*, 230–32.

27. Rasenberger, *Brilliant Disaster*, 236.

28. Pfeiffer, *Bay of Pigs I*, 265–72.

29. E. W. Kenworthy, "President Bars Using U.S. Force to Oust Castro," *New York Times*, April 13, 1961; Thomas, *Cuba*, 1310.

30. Triay, *Bay of Pigs*, 45–46.

31. Thomas, *Cuba*, 1355–56, 1369.

32. Rasenberger, *Brilliant Disaster*, 237.

33. Thomas, *Cuba*, 1364.

34. Pfeiffer, *Bay of Pigs I*, 298.

35. Triay, *Bay of Pigs*, 78.

36. Thomas, *Cuba*, 1367–68.

37. Triay, *Bay of Pigs*, 75.

38. Rasenberger, *Brilliant Disaster*, 282–86, 299; Triay, *Bay of Pigs*, 82.

39. Rasenberger, *Brilliant Disaster*, 321–23.

40. Triay, *Bay of Pigs*, 39.

41. John Dille, "With a Quiet Curse It Began," *Life*, May 10, 1961, 25.

42. Pedraza, *Disaffection*, 95.

43. Thomas, *Cuba*, 1370–71.

44. Rasenberger, *Brilliant Disaster*, 338–41, 353.

45. Pfeiffer, *Bay of Pigs III*, 149; Mimi Whitefield, "Unveiled CIA Report Reveals Internal Warfare over Blame for Bay of Pigs Failure," *Miami Herald*, November 9, 2016.

46. "Transcript of the President's News Conference on World and Domestic Affairs," *New York Times*, April 22, 1961.

47. "Outward Bound," *Time*, May 19, 1961, 34.

48. "Propaganda Backfire," *Time*, May 26, 1961, 28; Triay, *Bay of Pigs*, 133.

49. LeoGrande and Kornbluh, *Back Channel*, 48; "Propaganda Backfire," *Time*, May 26, 1961, 28.

50. Damon Stetson, "U.S. Tractor Unit Reports Failure; Rebukes Castro," *New York Times*, June 24, 1961.

51. Thomas, *Cuba*, 1385 n1.

52. Rasenberger, *Brilliant Disaster*, 357.

53. Triay, *Bay of Pigs*, 134–36.

54. Rasenberger, *Brilliant Disaster*, 358–59.

55. "On the Block," *Time*, April 20, 1962, 45.

56. Luis C. Morse, interviewed by the author at Miami, Florida, January 9, 2018.

57. Rasenberger, *Brilliant Disaster*, 352.

58. Didion, *Miami*, 88–90.

59. Thomas, *Cuba*, 1400, 1403–5, 1411–14; Gott, *New History*, 207.

60. R. Hart Phillips, "Exiles in Miami Voice Discontent," *New York Times*, October 29, 1962.

61. Rasenberger, *Brilliant Disaster*, 368–75.

62. "Cuban Prisoners Land in Florida; Ransom Is Paid," *New York Times*, December 24, 1962.

63. "Ransomed Captives Vow Return to Topple Castro," *New York Times*, December 26, 1962.

64. Triay, *Bay of Pigs*, 137.

65. Erneido A. Oliva, "Why Did the Assault Brigade 2506 Give Its Flag to President Kennedy for Safekeeping?" *Cuban-American Military Council* (website), accessed January 31, 2020, http://camco-cuba.org/2004-05/BRIGADEFLAG.html.

66. Tom Wicker, "Kennedy's Speech Stirs Cuba Exiles," *New York Times*, December 30, 1962.

67. "President Orders a Total Embargo on Cuban Imports," *New York Times*, February 4, 1962.

68. Henry Raymont, "U.S. Tightening Ban on Travel to Cuba," *New York Times*, July 3, 1963.

69. Hedrick Smith, "U.S. Freezes Cuban Assets in Move to Bar Subversion," *New York Times*, July 9, 1963.

70. "Travel Now—Pay Later," *Time*, July 12, 1963, 43.

71. "Refugee Bargain with Cubans Ends," *New York Times*, July 4, 1963.

72. "150,000 Cubans Reported Ready to Flee to U.S.," *New York Times*, December 4, 1962.

73. "Airline Service Is Castro's Price to Free Emigrés," *New York Times*, December 31, 1962.

74. Clark, "Exodus," 74 (Table 3).

75. "The Raiders," *Time*, September 21, 1962, 34.

76. Gott, *New History*, 208–9.

77. "U.S. Curbs Miami Exiles to Prevent Raids on Cuba," *New York Times*, April 1, 1963.

78. "Cuban Exile Chief Quits with Attack on Kennedy," *New York Times*, April 19, 1963.

79. LeoGrande and Kornbluh, *Back Channel*, 60–70.

80. Dallek, *Unfinished Life*, 661–63.

81. LeoGrande and Kornbluh, *Back Channel*, 64 (citing Memorandum for the Record, Subject: *Mr. Donovan's Trip to Cuba*, from Gordon Chase, March 4, 1963, The National Security Archive, "Kennedy Sought Dialogue with Cuba," accessed January 31, 2020, https://nsarchive2.gwu.edu/NSAEBB103/NSAEBB103/630304.pdf.

82. "Text of President's Address to Press Association," *New York Times*, November 19, 1963.

83. Jean Daniel, "Unofficial Envoy: An Historic Report from Two Capitals," *New Republic*, December 14, 1963, 16.

84. Jean Daniel, "When Castro Heard the News," *New Republic*, December 7, 1963, 7.

85. Triay, *Bay of Pigs*, 137.

CHAPTER 7. *LA REVOLUCIÓN*

1. Thomas, *Cuba*, 1312–13.

2. "Castro Rules Out Elections in Cuba," *New York Times*, May 2, 1961; "Tropical Red Square," *Time*, January 12, 1962, 32.

3. R. Hart Phillips, "Cuba to Develop Along Red Lines," *New York Times*, May 1, 1961.

4. "End of the Capitalists," *Time*, April 19, 1968, 36.

5. Pedraza, *Disaffection*, 122.

6. Scarpaci, Segre, and Coyula, *Havana*, 138–39.

7. "The Petrified Forest," *Time*, October 8, 1965, 39; Richard Eder, "Cuba Lives by Castro's Moods," *New York Times Magazine*, July 26, 1964, 47.

8. "Fidel's New People," *Time*, August 2, 1968, 29.

9. Thomas, *Cuba*, 1335–36; Pedraza, *Disaffection*, 122.

10. "The Petrified Forest," *Time*, October 8, 1965, 38; "Salt in the Sugar," *Time*, June 18, 1965, 35.

11. "Exporter of Communism," *Time*, August 6, 1965, 36.

12. Pedraza, *Disaffection*, 74.

13. Thomas, *Cuba*, 1321–32.

14. "The Petrified Forest," *Time*, October 8, 1965, 38–39.

15. Triay, *Fleeing Castro*, 41, 43.

16. Rainsford, *Our Woman*, 137–38.

17. Marino Gomez-Santos, "Niños Cubanos en España," *ABC*, January 12, 1969, 43 (translated from the Spanish by Rebecca Dominguez, Tucson, Arizona), http://hemeroteca.abc.es/nav/Navigate.exe/hemeroteca/madrid/abc/1969/01/12/043.html.

18. Clark, "Exodus," 135–36.

19. Marino Gomez-Santos, "Niños Cubanos en España," *ABC*, January 12, 1969, 43 (translated from the Spanish by Rebecca Dominguez, Tucson, Arizona), http://hemeroteca.abc.es/nav/Navigate.exe/hemeroteca/madrid/abc/1969/01/12/043.html.

20. "Cuban Children Arriving from Spain" (memo), Monsignor Bryan O. Walsh to Bishop Coleman F. Carroll, January 26, 1968, 2, Operation Pedro Pan—Unaccompanied Cuban Children Records, Barry Archives.

21. "Cuban Child Program in New Phase," press release, May 31, 1969, Operation Pedro Pan—Unaccompanied Cuban Children Records, Barry Archives.

22. Operation Pedro Pan Group, Inc., Facebook, March 16, 2013, https://www.facebook.com/OPPGI/posts/between-1965-and-1969-anywhere-between-3000-and-5000-cuban-children-mostly-teen-/456757744394452/; "Cuban Children Arriving from Spain" (memo), Monsignor Bryan O. Walsh to Bishop Coleman F. Carroll, January 26, 1968, 2, Operation Pedro Pan—Unaccompanied Cuban Children Records, Barry Archives.

23. Office of Historian, Dept. of State, *Foreign Relations, 1964–68*, 592 (Document 240, Verbal Message from Cuban Prime Minister Fidel Castro to President Johnson, February 12, 1964).

24. LeoGrande and Kornbluh, *Back Channel*, 83–103.

25. "Stop & Stop Now!" *Time*, July 31, 1964, 32.

26. "Cuban Refugees in the United States" (memo), Gordon Chase to Mr. Redmon, April 9, 1965, "Country File–Cuba–Refugees," NSF, box 30, LBJ Library.

27. "5 Elude Security, Escape to Gitmo," *Miami Herald*, October 29, 1965.

28. Hansen, *Guantánamo*, 266–67.

29. "The Petrified Forest," *Time*, October 8, 1965, 36–37.

30. Clark, "Exodus," 74 (Table 3).

31. Cass, "Cuban Exodus," 49.

32. Clark, "Exodus," 85; Gott, *New History*, 219–25, 256–60.

33. "Refugees Gather in Cuban Village," *New York Times*, October 14, 1965.

34. "Exodus," *Newsweek*, October 11, 1965.

35. Cass, "Cuban Exodus," 50–51.

36. Richard Eder, "Crowded Shed in a Cuban Fishing Village Is a Cold War Gateway to U.S.," *New York Times*, October 23, 1965; "Cuba Port Teems with Small Craft," *New York Times*, October 18, 1965.

37. Cass, "Cuban Exodus," 52–53.

38. LeoGrande and Kornbluh, *Back Channel*, 105.

39. "President Opens Door to Refugees from Cuba, Signs Immigration Law," *Miami Herald*, October 4, 1965.

40. LeoGrande and Kornbluh, *Back Channel*, 105–7.

41. "Statement by the President on the Agreement Covering Movement of Cuban Refugees to the United States," White House Press Release, November 6, 1965, 1, 5, text of MOU, Statements of Lyndon Baines Johnson, box 167, LBJ Library.

42. Richard Eder, "U.S. and Castro Agree to Start Refugee Airlift," *New York Times*, November 7, 1965.

43. Clark, "Exodus," 88–89.

44. Cass, "Cuban Exodus," 55.

45. Martin Waldron, "Cuba Air Exodus on as 75 Exiles Arrive," *New York Times*, December 2, 1965.

46. Roberto Fabricio, "261,000 Rode Flights to Freedom," *Miami Herald*, April 7, 1973.

47. "Statement by the President on the Agreement Covering Movement of Cuban Refugees to the United States," White House Press Release, November 6, 1965, 2–3, text of MOU, Statements of Lyndon Baines Johnson, box 167, LBJ Library.

48. Don Bohning, "Havana to Resume Refugee Airlift 'Soon,'" *Miami Herald*, December 1, 1972.

49. Richard Eder, "U.S. and Castro Agree to Start Refugee Airlift," *New York Times*, November 7, 1965.

50. Facts About the Family Reunion Phase of the Cuban Refugee Program (March 1967), "Cuban Refugee Program, Airlift (English printed materials), 1965–1969," folder 48, box 3, Cuban Refugee Center Records, UM CHC.

51. Mary Louise Wilkinson, "The Quiet Exodus," *Boston Globe*, April 10, 1966.

52. Clark, "Exodus," 92–94.

53. Frank Solar, "Cuban Airlift Starting Fourth Year," *Miami Herald*, December 2, 1968.

54. Cuban Refugees, 27–28, The Department of Justice During the Administration of President Lyndon B. Johnson, November 1963–January 1969, "Volume IX, Immigration and Naturalization, Part XIII, Immigration and Naturalization Service, [1 of 2]," Administrative Histories, box 8, LBJ Library.

55. Clark, "Exodus," 83–84.

56. "U.S. Eases Visa Rule on Cubans in Mexico," *New York Times*, July 26, 1966.

57. Clark, "Exodus," 133–36; "Cubans Receive Little Aid in Long Madrid Stopover," *Miami Herald*, November 28, 1972.

58. Roberto Fabricio, "For a Few Stranded Cubans, U.S. Can Bypass Red Tape," *Miami Herald*, November 28, 1972; Roberto Fabricio, "Stranded in Spain, Cuban Refugees Wait and Hope," *Miami Herald*, November 26, 1972.

59. Henry Giniger, "U.S. Opens Doors to More Cubans," *New York Times*, April 15, 1974; Clark, *Why?* 19.

60. George A. Volsky, "Cuba Reassessing Refugee Airlift," *New York Times*, December 6, 1970, 25.

61. Roberto Fabricio, "Many Missed Last Flight to Freedom Out of Cuba," *Miami Herald*, April 7, 1973.

CHAPTER 8. SECOND WAVE

1. "Fidel: Cubans Can Go to 'Yankee Paradise,'" *Miami Herald*, September 29, 1965; Don Bohning, "All Lines to Cuba Are Busy," *Miami Herald*, October 8, 1965.

2. "Fisherman Says U.S. 'Ruins' His Business," *Miami Herald*, October 29, 1965.

3. Cass, "Cuban Exodus," 51–52.

4. Gertrude Samuels, "Why Castro Exports Cubans," *New York Times Magazine*, November 7, 1965, 129–30.

5. Gary Blonston and Lee Winfrey, "Aid Center to Prepare for Influx," *Miami Herald*, October 4, 1965; "U.S. Plans Cuban Airlift to Bring 200 Here Daily," *Miami Herald*, October 27, 1965.

6. Don Bohning, "Freedom House Set Up to Aid Cuban Exiles," *Miami Herald*, October 21, 1965.

7. Don Bohning, "Helter-Skelter Evacuation May Be Straightened Out," *Miami Herald*, October 24, 1965.

8. Lee Winfrey, "100,000 to Fly Here in U.S.-Cuba Pact," *Miami Herald*, November 7, 1965.

9. Richard Eder, "U.S. and Castro Agree to Start Refugee Airlift," *New York Times*, November 7, 1965.

10. Clark, "Exodus," 97.

11. "More Refugees, More Blackmail," *Time*, October 29, 1965, 43.

12. Juanita Greene, "Miami Fears Effects of Cuban Influx," *Miami Herald*, October 5, 1965.

13. "Awaiting the New Refugee Wave," *Miami Herald*, October 29, 1965; Jack Kofoed, "Miami Already Has Too Many Refugees," *Miami Herald*, October 5, 1965.

14. "Johnson Is Sending Mission on Cubans," *New York Times*, October 30, 1965.

15. Lee Winfrey and Don Bohning, "80 Pct. of Incoming Exiles to Move Out Within 3 Days," *Miami Herald*, October 26, 1965.

16. Federal Task Force, *Report to the President*, 3–4.

17. Bret Collier, "Cuban Refugee Airlift Operates Slowly but Smoothly," *Christian Science Monitor*, August 17, 1966.

18. Woytych, "Cuban Refugee," 16.

19. Carlos Martinez, "Refugees Would Rather Stay in Miami, but Will Move On," *Miami Herald*, October 19, 1965.

20. "Cuban Refugee Center Gears for 800 a Week," *Washington Evening Star*, November 29, 1965.

21. Lee Winfrey and Don Bohning, "80 Pct. of Incoming Exiles to Move Out Within 3 Days," *Miami Herald*, October 26, 1965.

22. Mary Louise Wilkinson, "The Quiet Exodus," *Boston Globe*, April 10, 1966.

23. Comptroller General, *Analysis of Federal Expenditures to Aid Cuban Refugees*, 24–27.

24. Pedraza, *Disaffection*, 82.

25. Cauce, "Fifty Years Later," 98.

26. Torres, *Apple*, 268.

27. García, *Havana USA*, 39; "Cuban Refugee Arrivals," *Miami Herald*, June 6, 1968.

28. "Cuban Airlift: Major Events in Its History," *Miami Herald*, September 1, 1971.

29. "3 Negroes Killed in New Miami Riot," *New York Times*, August 9, 1968; "We Should Reconsider Value of Cuban Airlift," *Miami Herald*, December 5, 1968.

30. "Cuban Airlift Simply U.S. Aid to Castro," *Miami Herald*, February 11, 1970.

31. "It's Time to Ground the Airlift from Cuba," *Miami Herald*, February 18, 1969.

32. Pete Laine, "Proposal to Halt Cuban Airlift Withdrawn," *Miami Herald*, June 30, 1971.

33. Pete Laine, "Cuban Airlift Is Saved from Immediate Cutoff," *Miami Herald*, July 17, 1971; Henry Raymont, "Administration Seeking to Bar Cuts in Cuban Refugee Funds," *New York Times*, July 10, 1970.

34. Moore, *Refugee Resettlement Programs and Policies*, 27 (Table V); net present value calculation via www.in2013dollars.com (accessed April 2, 2019).

35. Gott, *New History*, 214.

36. Roberto Fabricio, "261,000 Rode Flights to Freedom," *Miami Herald*, April 7, 1973.

37. Clark, "Exodus," 226.

38. García, *Havana USA*, 43–44.

39. Clark, "Exodus," 238 (Table 19).

40. Aja, *Forgotten Cubans*, 41.

41. Susan Jacoby, "Miami *sí*, Cuba *no*," *New York Times Magazine*, September 29, 1974, 103.

42. Iver Peterson, "The Long War in Vietnam: A History," *New York Times*, May 1, 1975.

43. Roberto Fabricio, "Many Missed Last Flight to Freedom Out of Cuba," *Miami Herald*, April 7, 1973.

44. Clark, "Exodus," 74 (Table 3).

CHAPTER 9 SETTLED IN AMERICA

1. García, *Havana USA*, 26–27.

2. Thomas, "U.S.A.," 14.

3. Thomas, "Cuban Refugees," 54.

4. Ch. 72–125, Laws of Florida, 1972 Fla. Laws 1198 (codified as amended at §455.10, Fla. Stat. (2020)); Ch. 77–255, Laws of Florida, 1977 Fla. Laws 39 (codified as amended at §455.11, Fla. Stat. (2020)).

5. *Cuban Refugee Hearings*, 1966, 103 (Statement of Ellen Winston, Commissioner of Welfare, Department of Health, Education, and Welfare).

6. Kirkpatrick, "Federal Student Loans," 84.

7. Memo, Mike Feldman to Lee C. White, Special Counsel, June 29, 1964, "ND 19–2/CO," National Security–Defense, EX ND 19 / Korean War, NSF, box 418, LBJ Library.

8. Memo, Wilfred H. Rommel to the President, *Enrolled Bill HR 15183–Cuban refugees*, October 29, 1966, 2, "P.L. 89–732," Reports on Enrolled Legislation, box 45, LBJ Library.

9. Cuban Refugees, 29, The Department of Justice During the Administration of President Lyndon B. Johnson, November 1963–January 1969, "Volume IX, Immigration and Naturalization, Part XIII, Immigration and Naturalization Service [1 of 2]," Administrative Histories, box 8, LBJ Library.

10. "Cuban Refugees Seek New Status," *New York Times*, November 15, 1966.

11. Cuban Adjustment Act of 1966, Pub. L. No. 89–732, 80 Stat. 1161 (codified as amended at 8 U.S.C. §1255 (2020)).

12. Refugee Act of 1980, Pub. L. No. 96–212, 94 Stat. 108.

13. García, *Havana USA*, 42.

14. Woytych, "Cuban Refugee," 19.

15. García, *Havana USA*, 113.

16. García, *Havana USA*, 28.

17. *In re: Proposed Amendment to Article IV, Section 22, Rules of the Supreme Court Relating to the Admission to the Bar*, No. 43,040 (Fla. Order entered July 31, 1973), 5, 2.

18. *In re Florida Board of Bar Examiners: Amendment to Article III, Section 19*, 284 So. 2d 697 (Fla. 1973).

19. Memo, Dean J. R. Julin to Vice President Harold Hansen, October 27, 1975, Papers of Robert Q. Marston, UF Libraries; "Cubans Denied Special Law Exams," *Miami Herald*, June 27, 1976; *In re Petition of Cuban-American Lawyers Program*, 367 So. 2d 218 (Fla. 1979), denying dispensation to Cuban refugee bar applicants.

20. García, *Havana USA*, 89.

21. Rumbaut, "Ages, Life Stages," 165–67.

22. Jon Nordheimer, "Cuban Exiles, Too, Are Troubled by Generation Gap," *New York Times*, April 16, 1971.

23. Pedraza, *Disaffection*, 139–45.

24. Torres, *Apple*, 219–20.

25. Rieff, *The Exile*, 26.

26. Mitchell, "Cuban Refugee Program," 8; Kirkpatrick, "Federal Student Loans," 84–85, 90.

27. Kirkpatrick, "Federal Student Loans," 85.

28. The United States Loan Program for Cuban Students (US Office of Education circular), "CRC–Loan Program for Cuban Students / Documents," folder 258, box 13, Cuban Refugee Center Records, UM CHC.

29. Get Ready for College and Go (US Office of Education brochure), 1965, "National Defense Student Loan Program [1 of 3]," Federal Records: Department of Health, Education, and Welfare, 1963–69, box 123, LBJ Library.

30. "53,000 in Schools; College Loans Easy," *Miami Herald*, July 13, 1971.

31. Alfonso A. Narvaez, "50,000 Cubans Add Prosperity and Problems to Jersey," *New York Times*, November 24, 1970.

32. R. Hart Phillips, "Cuban Exiles Growing Sugar Cane in Florida," *New York Times*, January 19, 1962.

33. "Cuban Labor Fueling Growth of Miami's Busy Garment Industry," *New York Times*, November 19, 1967.

34. Rieff, *Going to Miami*, 144.

35. Pérez, *Becoming Cuban*, 502.

36. "Bank for Cubans Opened in Miami," *New York Times*, May 17, 1974.

37. Portes and Armony, *Global Edge*, 104.

38. Aja, *Forgotten Cubans*, 32.

39. Portes and Stepick, *City on the Edge*, 46, 182.

40. Portes and Armony, *Global Edge*, 67.

41. Antón and Hernández, *Cubans in America*, 185.

42. Susan Jacoby, "Miami *sí*, Cuba *no*," *New York Times Magazine*, September 29, 1974, 28.

43. Antón and Hernández, *Cubans in America*, 186.

44. Pérez, *Becoming Cuban*, 502.

45. Allman, *City of the Future,* 300–1.

46. "$2,000,000 Is Left to Cuba Art Fund," *New York Times*, May 29, 1957.

47. García, *Havana USA*, 120–21.

48. Joseph F. Sullivan, "Cubans Identified as Main Supplier of Cocaine Here," *New York Times,* December 19, 1973.

49. García, *Havana USA*, 141–42.

50. Guy Gugliotta and Helga Silva, "Secrets, Strife Led to Cuban Dialogue," *Miami Herald*, April 9, 1979; García, *Havana USA*, 48–51.

51. Robert D. McFadden, "Cuban Refugee Leader Slain in Union City," *New York Times*, November 26, 1979.

52. Fabiola Santiago, "When Stations Talk, Listeners Act," *Miami Herald*, June 22, 1986.

53. García, *Havana USA*, 143–44.

54. "Bilingual Elections Due in 464 Counties Under Voting Act," *New York Times*, August 28, 1975.

55. "Latinization of the Miami Area Is Showing No Signs of Abating," *New York Times*, April 18, 1973.

56. "Cubans' Vote Felt in Miami Election," *New York Times*, November 18, 1973.

57. Fredric Tasker, "Anti-Bilingualism Amendment Approved in Dade County," *Miami Herald*, November 5, 1980.

58. Portes and Armony, *Global Edge*, 10.

59. García, *Havana USA*, 84.

60. Jonathan Blitzer, "So Goes the Nation," *New Yorker*, September 25, 2019, 20.

61. Triay, *Mariel*, 23–26, 28–29.

62. Gott, *New History*, 266–69.

63. García, *Voices*, 3–5.

64. Allman, *City of the Future*, 27.

65. García, *Havana USA*, 63.

66. García, *Havana USA*, 67–70.

67. Portes and Armony, *Global Edge*, 104.

68. Pedraza, *Disaffection*, 152–54.

69. García, *Havana USA*, 64–65.

CHAPTER 10. HOME

1. Portes and Armony, *Global Edge*, 104.

2. García, *Havana USA*, 60–61; DePalma, *Cubans: Ordinary Lives*, 214.

3. Mormino, *Land of Sunshine*, 288–89.

4. Pedraza, *Disaffection*, 179–80.

5. García, *Havana USA*, 74, 79–80.

6. Note, *Cuban Adjustment Act*, 907. *See* 8 U.S.C. §1158(b)(1) (2020), referencing 8 U.S.C. §1101(a) (42).

7. Julie Hirschfield Davis and Frances Robles, "Obama Ends Exemption for Cubans Who Arrive Without Visas," *New York Times*, January 12, 2017.

8. Gott, *New History*, 214.

9. Duany, "Postrevolution Exodus."

10. Portes and Armony, *Global Edge*, 111.

11. Mormino, *Land of Sunshine*, 288; Portes and Armony, *Global Edge*, 102, 110 (Table 5).

12. Boswell and Curtis, *Cuban-American Experience*, 67.

13. García, *Havana USA*, 84.

14. Mormino, *Land of Sunshine*, 290–91 (Table 6).

15. Portes and Armony, *Global Edge*, 29–38, 24.

16. Allman, *City of the Future*, 148.

17. García, *Dreaming*, 60.

18. McHugh, Miyares, and Skop, "Magnetism," 507–9, 516.

19. Luisa Yanez and Elaine de Valle, "A Bittersweet Celebration for Cuban Exiles," *Miami Herald*, May 21, 2002.

20. Pérez, *Becoming Cuban*, 501–3.

21. Antón and Hernández, *Cubans in America*, 213–15.

22. McHugh, Miyares, and Skop, "Magnetism," 510, 507.

23. Duany, "Postrevolution Exodus"; Noe-Bustamante, Flores, and Shah, "Facts on Hispanics of Cuban Origin," 3.

24. García, *Havana USA*, 83–84.

25. Gott, *New History*, 310.

26. Rick Bragg, "Cuban Boy Seized by U.S. Agents and Reunited with His Father," *New York Times*, April 23, 2000.

27. Pedraza, *Disaffection*, 286.

28. David Gonzalez with Lizette Alvarez, "Justices Allow Cuban Boy to Fly Home," *New York Times*, June 29, 2000.

29. Juan Forer and Felicity Barringer, "Police Fire Tear Gas as Hundreds of Angry Protesters Take to the Streets in Miami," *New York Times*, April 23, 2000.

30. Juan Forero, "Little Havana Locks Its Doors in Quiet Protest," *New York Times*, April 26, 2000.

31. William Schneider, "Elián González Defeated Al Gore," *Atlantic*, May 2, 2001, https://www.theatlantic.com/politics/archive/2001/05/elian-gonzalez-defeated-al-gore/377714/.

32. Linda Greenhouse, "Bush Prevails," *New York Times*, December 13, 2000; Todd S. Purdom, "Bush Is Declared Winner in Florida, but Gore Vows to Contest Results," *New York Times*, November 27, 2000.

33. Martinez and Verdeja, "Elián," in *Epic Journey*, 199–200.

34. Rick Bragg, "Castro Emerges as Conflict's Clear Winner," *New York Times*, April 27, 2000.

35. David Rieff, "The Exiles' Last Hurrah," *New York Times*, April 2, 2000.

36. Juan Forero, "In Miami, Some Cuban-Americans Take Less Popular Views," *New York Times*, April 28, 2000.

37. Comparison of state-by-state totals in the Electoral College for presidential elections from 1980 through 2020 on 270towin.com (website), accessed December 27, 2020, https://www.270towin.com/historical-presidential-elections/.

38. Mormino, *Land of Sunshine*, 182–83.

39. Nijman, "Globalization," 166–67.

40. Portes and Armony, *Global Edge*, 146–47.

41. Nijman, "Globalization," 174.

42. Jon Lee Anderson, "The Cuba Play," *New Yorker*, October 3, 2016, 51.

43. "Americans Now Free to Travel Anywhere," *New York Times*, March 19, 1977; Graham Hovey, "U.S. Will Allow Citizens to Spend Dollars in Cuba," *New York Times*, March 26, 1977.

44. Barbara Crossette, "U.S., Linking Cuba to 'Violence,' Blocks Tourist and Business Trips," *New York Times*, April 20, 1982; Frank Bruni, "Bush Administration Showing Willingness to Enforce Law on Visiting Cuba," *New York Times*, August 5, 2001; John Wagner and Karen DeYoung, "Trump Announces Revisions to Parts of Obama's Cuba Policy," *Washington Post*, June 16, 2017.

45. Christopher Marquis, "Despite U.S. Restrictions Against Cuba, Door Opens Wider for Visits by Americans," *New York Times*, June 19, 2000; Carol E. Lee and Felicia Schwartz, "Obama Eases Restrictions on Trade, Travel to Cuba," *Wall Street Journal*, March 15, 2016.

46. Sullivan, *Issues for 111th Congress*, 17–26.

47. Dirk Johnson, "Children of 'Operation Pedro Pan' Recall Painful Separations from Parents," *New York Times,* April 22, 2000.

48. "2003 Winners," National Book Foundation (website), accessed May 11, 2020, https://www.nationalbook.org/awards-prizes/national-book-awards-2003/.

49. Cauce, "Fifty Years Later," 98–99.

50. Triay, *Fleeing Castro*, 72–74, 96–98.

51. García, *Havana USA*, 112.

52. Ronald Smothers, "Cuban Exiles Visiting Home Find Identity," *New York Times*, February 14, 1978.

53. Portes and Armony, *Global Edge*, 50.

EPILOGUE

1. Allman, *City of the Future*, 290.

2. Portes and Armony, *Global Edge*, 47–48.

3. Nijman, "Globalization," 168; Portes and Armony, *Global Edge*, 107–08.

4. Pedraza, "Manifold Migrations," 316–17.

5. "Black Migration into a White City: Power, Privilege and Exclusion in Miami (With Devyn

Spence Benson)," Danielle Pilar Clealand, PhD, accessed June 8, 2021, http://www.danielleclealand.com/research/.

6. Pérez, *Becoming Cuban*, 468, 450–51.

7. Allman, *City of the Future*, 282–83.

8. Bob Graham, interviewed by the author at Miami Lakes, Florida, October 15, 2018.

9. García, *Havana USA*, 39–40.

10. Gott, *New History*, 215.

11. Triay, *Fleeing Castro*, 50–51.

12. Oettinger, "Services," 384.

13. García, *Havana USA*, 42, 89, 28.

14. David C. Atkinson, "What History Can Tell Us About the Fallout from Restricting Immigration," *Time*, February 3, 2017, https://time.com/4659392/history-fallout-restricting-immigration/.

15. LeMaster and Zall, *Compassion Fatigue*, 450.

16. Okrent, *Guarded Gate*, 391–93.

17. Yang, *One Mighty Tide*, 139 (citing Displaced Persons Act of 1948, Pub. L. No. 80–774, 62 Stat. 1009, amended by Pub. L. No. 81–555, 64 Stat. 219).

18. Refugee Relief Act of 1953, Pub. L. No. 83–203, 66 Stat. 174.

19. Anker and Posner, *Forty Year Crisis*, 14–15, 21, 30–31.

20. Immigration and Nationality Act of 1965, Pub. L. No. 89–236, 79 Stat. 911 (codified as amended 8 U.S.C. §1101 *et seq.* (2020)).

21. Memo, Phillip S. Hughes to the President, *Enrolled Bill HR 2580–Immigration reform* (October 1, 1965), 2, "P.L. 89–236," Reports on Enrolled Legislation, box 27, LBJ Library.

22. Yang, *One Mighty Tide*, 259.

23. "Applications for Visas Expedited for Cuban Refugees Already Here," *New York Times*, September 20, 1976.

24. Refugee Act of 1980, Pub. L. No. 96–212, 94 Stat. 108.

25. Anker and Posner, *Forty Year Crisis*, 11–12 (citing Refugee Act of 1980, Pub. L. No. 96–212, 94 Stat. 108).

26. LeMaster and Zall, *Compassion Fatigue*, 455–57 (citing 8 U.S.C. §1101(a)(42) (2020)).

27. Baugh, *2019 Annual Report*, 2–3.

28. Baugh, *2019 Annual Report*, 1, 7–8.

29. Dept. of State, *Proposed Refugee Admissions 2021*, 9.

30. Administration for Children and Families, *2017 ORR Annual Report*, 4 (Table 1).

31. Julie Hirschfield Davis and Frances Robles, "Obama Ends Exemption for Cubans Who Arrive Without Visas," *New York Times*, January 12, 2017.

32. Molly O'Toole, "Trump Condemns Cuba but Closes the Door to Many Trying to Flee," *Los Angeles Times*, July 30, 2019; DePalma, *Cubans: Ordinary Lives*, 331.

33. Lillian Guerra, "Fear and Loathing in Havana and Miami," *New York Times*, February 17, 2020.

34. Pérez, *Structure*, 281.

BIBLIOGRAPHY

Books, journal articles, unpublished papers, and government publications listed here are identified in the notes by the author's surname and a short-form title, as shown in brackets after each entry. Newspaper articles, magazine pieces, statutes, blogs, and websites are cited in full in the notes. Archival records are cited in full with a short form reference to the archive as shown in brackets below.

ARCHIVES

Archives and Special Collections, Monsignor William Barry Memorial Library, Barry University, Miami Shores, Florida. [Barry Archives]

Cuban Heritage Collection, Otto G. Richter Library, University of Miami, Coral Gables, Florida. [UM CHC]

Lyndon B. Johnson Presidential Library, University of Texas at Austin, Austin, Texas. [LBJ Library]

Special and Area Studies Collections, George A. Smathers Libraries, University of Florida, Gainesville, Florida. [UF Libraries]

BOOKS, JOURNAL ARTICLES, AND UNPUBLISHED MATERIAL

Aja, Alan A. *Miami's Forgotten Cubans: Race, Racialization, and the Miami Afro-Cuban Experience.* New York: Palgrave MacMillan, 2016. [Aja, *Forgotten Cubans*]

Alexievich, Svetlana. *The Unwomanly Face of War: An Oral History of Women in World War II.* Translated by Richard Pevear and Larissa Volokhonsky. New York: Random House, 2017.

Allison, Richard C. "Cuba's Seizures of American Business." *American Bar Association Journal* 47, no. 1 (January 1961). [Allison, "Cuba's Seizures"]

Allman, T. D. *Miami: City of the Future.* Rev. ed. Gainesville: University Press of Florida, 2013. [Allman, *City of the Future*]

Anillo-Badia, Rolando. "Outstanding Claims to Expropriated Property in Cuba." In *2011 Annual Proceedings of the Association for the Study of the Cuban Economy* (2011) (https://www.ascecuba.org/c/wp-content/uploads/2014/09/v21-anillo.pdf). [Anillo-Badia, "Outstanding Claims"]

Anker, Deborah E., and Michael H. Posner. *The Forty Year Crisis: A Legislative History of the Refugee Act of 1980,* 19 San Diego L. Rev. 9 (1981) (https://digital.sandiego.edu/sdlr/vol19/iss1/3/). [Anker and Posner, *Forty Year Crisis*]

Antón, Alex, and Roger E. Hernández. *Cubans in America: A Vibrant History of a People in Exile.* New York: Kensington Books, 2002. [Antón and Hernández, *Cubans in America*]

Boswell, Thomas D., and James R. Curtis. *The Cuban-American Experience*. Totawa, NJ: Rowman & Allanheld, 1983. [Boswell and Curtis, *Cuban-American Experience*]

Cass, William F., Captain, US Coast Guard. "Cuban Exodus." *US Naval Institute Proceedings* 92, no. 6 (June 1966). [Cass, "Cuban Exodus"]

Cauce, Rita M. "Operation Pedro Pan: Fifty Years Later." *Tequesta: The Journal of HistoryMiami Museum* 72 (2012). [Cauce, "Fifty Years Later"]

Clark, Juan M. "The Exodus from Revolutionary Cuba (1959–1974): A Sociological Analysis." PhD diss., University of Florida, 1975 (http://www.latinamericanstudies.org/book/Clark-PhD-1975.pdf). [Clark, "Exodus"]

——. *Why? The Cuban Exodus: Background, Evolution and Impact in U.S.A.* Miami: Union of Cubans in Exile, 1977. [Clark, *Why?*]

Cox, Adam B., and Cristina M. Rodríguez, *The President and Immigration Law*, 119 Yale L. J. 458 (2009). [Cox and Rodríguez, *President and Immigration*]

Dallek, Robert. *An Unfinished Life: John F. Kennedy, 1917–1963*. Boston: Little, Brown & Company, 2003. [Dallek, *Unfinished Life*]

Deere, Carmen Diana. "Here Come the Yankees! The Rise and Decline of American Colonies in Cuba, 1898–1930." *Hispanic American Historical Review* 78, no. 4 (November 1998). [Deere, "Here Come the Yankees!"]

DePalma, Anthony. *The Cubans: Ordinary Lives in Extraordinary Times*. New York: Viking, 2020. [DePalma, *Cubans: Ordinary Lives*]

——. *The Man Who Invented Fidel: Castro, Cuba, and Herbert L. Matthews of the New York Times*. New York: Public Affairs, 2006. [DePalma, *Man Who Invented Fidel*]

Didion, Joan. *Miami*. New York: Vintage International, 1998. [Didion, *Miami*]

Domínguez, Jorge I. "The Batista Regime in Cuba." In *Sultanistic Regimes*, edited by H. E. Chehabi and Juan I. Linz, chap. 5. Baltimore: Johns Hopkins University Press, 1998. [Dominguez, "Batista Regime," in *Sultanistic Regimes*]

Duany, Jorge. "Cuban Migration: A Postrevolution Exodus Ebbs and Flows." *Online Journal of the Migration Policy Institute* (website), July 6, 2017, https://www.migrationpolicy.org/article/cuban-migration-postrevolution-exodus-ebbs-and-flows. [Duany, "Postrevolution Exodus"]

English, T. J. *Havana Nocturne: How the Mob Owned Cuba . . . and Then Lost It to the Revolution*. New York: Harper, 2008. [English, *Nocturne*]

Estrada, Alfredo José. *Havana: Autobiography of a City*. New York: Palgrave MacMillan, 2007. [Estrada, *Autobiography*]

García, Cristina. *Dreaming in Cuban*. New York: Ballantine Books, 1992. [García, *Dreaming*]

García, José Manuel. *Voices from Mariel: Oral Histories of the 1980 Cuban Boatlift*. Gainesville: University Press of Florida, 2008. [García, *Voices*]

García, María Cristina. *Havana USA: Cuban Exiles and Cuban Americans in South Florida, 1959–1994*. Berkeley: University of California Press, 1996. [García, *Havana USA*]

Gellman, Irwin F. "The *St. Louis* Tragedy." *American Jewish Historical Quarterly* 61, no. 2 (December 1971). [Gellman, "*St. Louis* Tragedy"]

George, Paul S. "Colored Town: Miami's Black Community, 1896–1930." *Florida Historical Quarterly* 56, no. 4 (April 1978). [George, "Colored Town"]

Gjelten, Tom. *Bacardi and the Long Fight for Cuba: The Biography of a Cause*. New York: Penguin Books, 2009. [Gjelten, *Bacardi*]

Gott, Richard. *Cuba: A New History*. New Haven: Yale University Press, 2004. [Gott, *New History*]

Greene, Graham. *Our Man in Havana*. New York: Penguin Group, 2007. [Greene, *Our Man*]

Hansen, Jonathan M. *Guantánamo: An American History*. New York: Hill and Wang, 2011. [Hansen, *Guantánamo*]

———. *Young Castro: The Making of a Revolutionary*. New York: Simon & Schuster, 2019. [Hansen, *Young Castro*]

Hemingway, Ernest. "The Great Blue River," originally published in *Holiday* magazine, 1949. In *By-Line: Ernest Hemingway, Selected Articles and Dispatches of Four Decades*, edited by William White, 403–16. Trade paperback ed. New York: Scribner, 2003. [Hemingway, "Great Blue River," in *By-Line*]

Horst, Jesse Lewis. "Sleeping on the Ashes: Slum Clearance in Havana in an Age of Revolution, 1930–65." PhD diss., University of Pittsburgh, 2016 (http://d-scholarship.pitt.edu/29364/). [Horst, "Sleeping on the Ashes"]

Kirkpatrick, John I. "A Study of Federal Student Loan Programs." New York: College Entrance Examination Board, 1968 (https://eric.ed.gov/?id=ED125397). [Kirkpatrick, "Federal Student Loans"]

Kurzban, Ira J. *A Critical Analysis of Refugee Law*, 36 U. Miami L. Rev. 865 (1982). [Kurzban, *Critical Analysis*]

LeMaster, Roger J., and Barnaby Zall. *Compassion Fatigue: The Expansion of Refugee Admissions to the United States*, 6 B.C. Int'l & Comp. L. Rev. 447 (1983). [LeMaster and Zall, *Compassion Fatigue*]

LeoGrande, William M., and Peter Kornbluh. *Back Channel to Cuba: The Hidden History of Negotiations Between Washington and Havana*. Updated ed. Chapel Hill: University of North Carolina Press, 2015. [LeoGrande and Kornbluh, *Back Channel*]

Loewen, James W. *Sundown Towns: A Hidden Dimension of American Racism*. New York: New Press, 2018. [Loewen, *Sundown Towns*]

Mace, Lesley. "Currency, Credit, Crises, and Cuba: The Fed's Early History in Florida." *Florida Historical Quarterly* 94, no. 2 (Fall 2015). [Mace, "Currency, Credit, Crises"]

Martinez, Guillermo, and Sam Verdeja. "Elián." In *Cubans: An Epic Journey*, edited by Sam Verdeja and Guillermo Martinez, chap. 13. St. Louis: Reedy Press, 2011. [Martinez and Verdeja, "Elián," in *Epic Journey*]

———. "The First Exiles." In *Cubans: An Epic Journey*, edited by Sam Verdeja and Guillermo Martinez, chap. 4. St. Louis: Reedy Press, 2011. [Martinez and Verdeja, "First Exiles," in *Epic Journey*]

McHugh, Kevin E., Ines M. Miyares, and Emily H. Skop. "The Magnetism of Miami: Segmented Paths in Cuban Migration." *Geographical Review* 87, no. 4 (October 1997). [McHugh, Miyares, and Skop, "Magnetism"]

Mohl, Raymond A. "Whitening Miami: Race, Housing, and Government Policy in Twentieth-Century Dade County." *Florida Historical Quarterly* 79, no. 3 (Winter 2001). [Mohl, "Whitening Miami"]

———. "Immigration through the Port of Miami." In *Forgotten Doors: The Other Ports of Entry to the United States*, edited by M. Mark Stolarik, chap. 4. Philadelphia: Balch Institute Press, 1988. [Mohl, "Port of Miami," in *Forgotten Doors*]

Mormino, Gary R. *Land of Sunshine, State of Dreams: A Social History of Modern Florida*. Gainesville: University Press of Florida, 2005. [Mormino, *Land of Sunshine*]

Mormino, Gary R., and George E. Pozzetta. *The Immigrant World of Ybor City: Italians and Their Latin Neighbors in Tampa, 1885–1985*. Gainesville: University Press of Florida, 1998. [Mormino and Pozzetta, *Ybor City*]

Morris, Edmund. *The Rise of Theodore Roosevelt*. New York: Modern Library, 2001. [Morris, *Rise of Roosevelt*]

Moruzzi, Peter. *Havana Before Castro: When Cuba Was a Tropical Playground*. Salt Lake City: Gibbs Smith, 2008. [Moruzzi, *Before Castro*]

Nijman, Jan. "Globalization to a Latin Beat: The Miami Growth Machine." *Annals of the American Association of Policy and Social Science* 551, no. 1 (May 1997). [Nijman, "Globalization"]

Noe-Bustamante, Luis, Antonio Flores, and Sono Shah. "Facts on Hispanics of Cuban Origin in the United States, 2017." Washington: Pew Research Center, September 16, 2019 (https://www.pewresearch.org/hispanic/fact-sheet/u-s-hispanics-on-cuban-origin-latinos/). [Noe-Bustamante, Flores, and Shah, "Facts on Hispanics of Cuban Origin"]

Note. *The Cuban Adjustment Act of 1966: Mirando a través de los ojos de Don Quijote y Sancho Panza*, 114 Harv. L. Rev. 902 (2001). [Note, *Cuban Adjustment Act*]

Oettinger, Katherine Brownell. "Services to Unaccompanied Cuban Refugee Children in the United States." *Social Service Review* 36, no. 4 (December 1962). [Oettinger, "Services"]

Okrent, Daniel. *The Guarded Gate: Bigotry, Eugenics, and the Law That Kept Two Generations of Jews, Italians, and Other European Immigrants Out of America*. New York: Scribner, 2019. [Okrent, *Guarded Gate*]

Pedraza, Silvia. "Cuba's Refugees: Manifold Migrations." *1995 Annual Proceedings of the Association for the Study of the Cuban Economy*, 1995, (https://www.ascecuba.org/c/wp-content/uploads/2014/09/v05-FILE26.pdf). [Pedraza, "Manifold Migrations"]

———. *Political Disaffection in Cuba's Revolution and Exodus*. New York: Cambridge University Press, 2007. [Pedraza, *Disaffection*]

Pérez, Louis A. Jr., *Cuba and the United States: Ties of Singular Intimacy*. 3rd ed. Athens: University of Georgia Press, 2003. [Pérez, *Ties of Intimacy*]

———. *On Becoming Cuban: Identity, Nationality, and Culture*. Paperback ed. Chapel Hill: University of North Carolina Press, 2008. [Pérez, *Becoming Cuban*]

———. *The Structure of Cuban History: Meanings and Purpose of the Past*. Chapel Hill: University of North Carolina Press, 2013. [Pérez, *Structure*]

Perrottet, Tony. ¡Cuba *Libre! Che, Fidel, and the Improbable Revolution That Changed World History*. New York: Blue Rider Press, 2019. [Perrottet, ¡Cuba *Libre!*]

Portes, Alejandro, and Ariel C. Armony. *The Global Edge: Miami in the Twenty-First Century*. Berkeley: University of California Press, 2018. [Portes and Armony, *Global Edge*]

Portes, Alejandro, and Alex Stepick. *City on the Edge: The Transformation of Miami*. Berkeley: University of California Press, 1994. [Portes and Stepick, *City on the Edge*]

Rainsford, Sarah. *Our Woman in Havana: Reporting Castro's Cuba*. London: Oneworld Publications, 2018. [Rainsford, *Our Woman*]

Rasenberger, Jim. *The Brilliant Disaster: JFK, Castro, and America's Doomed Invasion of Cuba's Bay of Pigs*. New York: Scribner, 2012. [Rasenberger, *Brilliant Disaster*]

Rathbone, John Paul. *The Sugar King of Havana: The Rise and Fall of Julio Lobo, Cuba's Last Tycoon*. New York: Penguin Books, 2011. [Rathbone, *Sugar King*]

Rieff, David. *The Exile: Cuba in the Heart of Miami*. New York: Simon & Schuster, 1993. [Rieff, *The Exile*]

———. *Going to Miami: Exiles, Tourists, and Refugees in the New America*. Boston: Little, Brown and Company, 1987. [Rieff, *Going to Miami*]

Rothstein, Richard. *The Color of Law: A Forgotten History of How Our Government Segregated America*. New York: Liveright Publishing Corporation, 2018. [Rothstein, *Color of Law*]

Rumbaut, Rubén G. "Ages, Life Stages, and Generational Cohorts: Decomposing the Immigrant First and Second Generations in the United State." *International Migration Review* 38, no. 3 (Fall 2004). [Rumbaut, "Ages, Life Stages"]

Scarpaci, Joseph L., Roberto Segre, and Mario Coyula. *Havana: Two Faces of the Antillean Metropolis*. Rev. ed. Chapel Hill: University of North Carolina Press, 2002. [Scarpaci, Segre, and Coyula, *Havana*]

Sicius, Francis J. "The Miami Diocese and the Cuban Refugee Crisis of 1960–1961." *Tequesta* 61 (2001). [Sicius, "Miami Diocese"]

Smith, Jean Edward. *Eisenhower in War and Peace*. New York: Random House, 2012. [Smith, *Eisenhower*]

Sweig, Julia E. *Inside the Cuban Revolution: Fidel Castro and the Urban Underground*. Cambridge: Harvard University Press, 2002. [Sweig, *Inside*]

Tebeau, Charlton W. *A History of Florida*. Coral Gables: University of Miami Press, 1971. [Tebeau, *History of Florida*]

Terkel, Studs. *The Studs Terkel Reader: My American Century.* New York: New Press, 1997.

Thomas, Hugh. *Cuba: The Pursuit of Freedom.* New York: Harper & Row, 1971. [Thomas, *Cuba*]

———. "The U.S. and Fidel Castro, 1959–1962." *American Heritage* 29, no. 6 (October–November 1978). [Thomas, "U.S. and Castro"]

Thomas, John F. "Cuban Refugees in the United States." *International Migration Review* 1, no. 2 (Spring 1967). [Thomas, "Cuban Refugees"]

———. "U.S.A. as a Country of First Asylum." *International Migration* 3, no. 1–2 (January 1965). [Thomas, "U.S.A."]

Torres, María de los Ángeles. *The Lost Apple: Operation Pedro Pan, Cuban Children in the U.S., and the Promise of a Better Future.* Boston: Beacon Press, 2003. [Torres, *Apple*]

Triay, Victor Andrés. *Bay of Pigs: An Oral History of Brigade 2506.* Gainesville: University Press of Florida, 2001. [Triay, *Bay of Pigs*]

———. *Fleeing Castro: Operation Pedro Pan and the Cuban Children's Program.* Gainesville: University Press of Florida, 1998. [Triay, *Fleeing Castro*]

———. *The Mariel Boatlift: A Cuban-American Journey.* Gainesville: University of Florida Press, 2019. [Triay, *Mariel*]

Walsh, Bryan O. "Cuban Refugee Children." *Journal of Inter-american Studies and World Affairs* 13 no. 3–4 (July–October 1971). [Walsh, "Refuge Children"]

———. "Cultural Identity and Mental Health Factors Among Cuban Unaccompanied Minors." Paper presented at annual meeting of the American Anthropological Association, Los Angeles, CA, December 4, 1981. https://dloc.com/AA00054479/00001/pdf. [Walsh, "Cultural Identity"]

Wood, Michael T. "'Gators Making Merry in Cuba: The University of Florida Football Team in Havana, December 1912." *Florida Historical Quarterly* 92, no. 1 (Summer 2015). [Wood, "'Gators Making Merry"]

Yang, Jia Lynn. *One Mighty and Irresistible Tide: The Epic Struggle Over American Immigration, 1924–1965.* New York: W. W. Norton & Company, 2020. [Yang, *One Mighty Tide*]

Young, Elliott. "Globalization and the Border Wall: Transnational Policing Regimes in North America, 1890s to the Present." In *Deportation in the Americas: Histories of Exclusion and Resistance*, edited by Kenyon Zimmer and Cristina Salinas, chap. 2. College Station: Texas A&M University Press, 2018. [Young, "Globalization and the Border Wall," in *Deportation*]

GOVERNMENT PUBLICATIONS

Administration for Children and Families, Department of Health and Human Services. *Annual Report to Congress Office of Refugee Resettlement Fiscal Year 2017* (2017). [Administration for Children and Families, *2017 ORR Annual Report*]

Baugh, Ryan, Office of Immigration Statistics, Department of Homeland Security. *Annual Flow Report Refugees and Asylees: 2019* (September 2020). [Baugh, *2019 Annual Report*]

Children's Bureau, Department of Health, Education and Welfare. *Cuba's Children in Exile: The Story of the Unaccompanied Cuban Refugee Children's Program* (1967). "Cuban Refugee Program," WHCF, EX CO 55, box 25, LBJ Library. [Children's Bureau, *Children in Exile*]

Comptroller General. *Report to the Subcommittee to Investigate Problems Connected with Refugees and Escapees, Committee on the Judiciary, U.S. Senate: Analysis of Federal Expenditures to Aid Cuban Refugees*, B-164031 (3) (1971). [Comptroller General, *Analysis of Federal Expenditures*]

Cuban Refugee Problems: Hearings before the Subcommittee to Investigate Problems Connected with Refugees and Escapees of the Committee on the Judiciary, U.S. Senate, 87th Congress (1961). [*Cuban Refuge Hearings*, 1961]

Cuban Refugee Problems: Hearings before the Subcommittee to Investigate Problems Connected with Refu-

gees and Escapees of the Committee on the Judiciary, U.S. Senate, 89th Congress (1966) [Cuban Refugee Hearings, 1966]

Department of State, *Report to Congress on Proposed Refugee Admissions for Fiscal Year 2021* (https://www.state.gov/wp-content/uploads/2020/10/FY21-USRAP-Report-to-Congress-FINAL-for-WEBSITE-102220-508.pdf). [Dept. of State, *Proposed Refugee Admissions 2021*]

Federal Task Force for Greater Miami, *Report to the President*, attached to Memo, Secretary Gardener to the President (June 29, 1966), "Federal Task Force on Greater Miami-Cuban Refugee Problem, June 29, 1966," Office Files of Douglas Cater, box 95, LBJ Library. [Federal Task Force, *Report to the President*]

Mitchell, William L. "The Cuban Refugee Program." *Social Security Bulletin* 25, no. 3 (March 1962). [Mitchell, "Cuban Refugee Program"]

Moore, Charlotte J., Congressional Research Service, Library of Congress. *Review of U.S. Refugee Resettlement Programs and Policies*, SN-052–070–05409–3 (1980). [Moore, *Refugee Resettlement Programs and Policies*]

Office of the Historian, Department of State, *Foreign Relations of the United States, 1952–1954*, vol. 4. N. Stephen Kane and William F. Sanford Jr., eds. Washington: Government Printing Office, 1983 (https://history.state.gov/historicaldocuments/frus1952-54v04/d327). [Office of Historian, Dept. of State, *Foreign Relations, 1952–54*]

——. *Foreign Relations of the United States, 1958–1960*, vol. 6. John P. Glennon, ed. Washington: Government Printing Office, 1983 (https://history.state.gov/historicaldocuments/frus1958-60v06/d18). [Office of Historian, Dept. of State, *Foreign Relations, 1958–60*]

——. *Foreign Relations of the United States, 1964–1968*, vol. 32. Daniel Lawler and Carolyn Yee, eds. Washington: Government Printing Office, 2005 (https://history.state.gov/historicaldocuments/frus1964-68v32). [Office of Historian, Dept. of State, *Foreign Relations, 1964–68*].

Pfeiffer, Jack B. Central Intelligence Agency, *Official History of the Bay of Pigs Operation I: Air Operations, March 1960–April 1961* (September 1979) (https://cia.gov/library/readingroom/docs/bop-vol1-part1.pdf, https://cia.gov/library/readingroom/docs/bop-vol1-part2.pdf, https://cia.gov/library/readingroom/docs/bop-vol1-part3.pdf). [Pfeiffer, *Bay of Pigs I*]

——. *Official History of the Bay of Pigs Operation III: Evolution of CIA's Anti-Castro Policies, 1959–January 1961* (December 1979) (https://cia.gov/library/readingroom/docs/bop-vol3.pdf). [Pfeiffer, *Bay of Pigs III*]

Sullivan, Mark P., Congressional Research Service, Library of Congress. *Cuba: Issues for the 111th Congress*, R40193 (2011). [Sullivan, *Issues for 111th Congress*]

Woytych, Robert L. "The Cuban Refugee," *I and N Reporter*, October 1967, p. 16 (Department of Justice, Immigration and Naturalization Service publication). "Papers of the Department of Health, Education, and Welfare, Cuban Refugee Program," WHCF, EX CO 55, box 25, LBJ Library. [Woytych, "Cuban Refugee"]

INTERVIEWS BY THE AUTHOR

Complete interview transcripts are available at the University of Miami's Cuban Heritage Collection. Visit www.library.miami.edu/chc/.

Aglio, Thomas J.–Winter Park, FL, June 1, 2018.

Alderman, Silvia Morell–Tallahassee, FL, February 11 and May 27, 2017.

Alvarez, Arelis Duran–Miami Beach, FL, May 28, 2019.

Alvarez, Carlos–Tallahassee, FL, November 16, 2016, and February 27, 2017.

Alvarez, Luis M.–Miami Beach, FL, May 28, 2019.

Calvet, Cesar E.–Orlando, FL, September 21, 2017, and March 8, 2019.

Cano, Margarita Fernández–Miami, FL, October 18, 2018.

Cardenas, Alberto R. "Al"–Miami, FL, May 29, 2019.

Cartaya, Mario–Fort Lauderdale, FL, July 19, 2017.

Castillo, Angel Jr.–Coral Gables, FL, May 19, 2017.

Castillo, Gabriel (aka Gaby Gabriel)–Miami, FL, July 22, 2017.

Cepero, Justo Luis–Tampa, FL, June 5, 2018.

Collazo, Mercedes Fernandez–Tampa, FL, September 19, 2017.

Collazo, Miguel "Mike"–Tampa, FL, September 20, 2017.

Cruz Azaceta, Luis–New Orleans, LA, January 25, 2020.

Cueto, Emilio–Gainesville, FL, January 6, 2019.

Duany, Andrés M.–Miami, FL, June 6, 2017.

Duany, Jorge M.–Miami, FL, May 30, 2019.

Echazábal, Eloísa M.–Miami, FL, December 18, 2017.

Fernandez, Rafael E. "Ralph"–Tampa, FL, September 20, 2017.

Fernandez, Ricardo "Rick"–Tallahassee, FL, November 10, 2016, and March 17, 2017.

Flores, Isaac M. "Ike"–Orlando, FL, November 21, 2016, and April 26, 2017.

Freyre, Pedro A.–Miami, FL, July 21, 2017.

Garcia, Tere Castellanos–Miami, FL, May 16, 2017.

García Orta, Paulina (aka Paulina Rodriguez-Muro)–Miami, FL, October 18, 2018.

George, Paul S.–Miami, FL, May 17, 2017.

González, Romualdo "Romi"–New Orleans, LA, December 4, 2017.

Graham, Bob–Miami Lakes, FL, October 15, 2018.

Henley, Maribel Pérez–Miami, FL, February 17, 2020.

Henriques, Adolfo–Coral Gables, FL, May 18, 2017.

Hodges, Ana Cowley–Houston, TX, February 6, 2018.

Hoffman, Isis Rivero–Key Biscayne, FL, October 17, 2018.

Juergensmeyer, Julian C.–Atlanta, GA, June 8, 2017.

Laurencio, Hector (née Hector Garcia)–Coral Gables, FL, May 20, 2017.

Laurencio, Maria Galatas–Coral Gables, FL, June 6, 2017.

Mármol, Guillermo G. "Gil"–Dallas, TX, December 28, 2017.

Márquez, Myriam–Miami, FL, May 28, 2019.

Martell, Henry (née Enrique Martell)–Coral Gables, FL, October 16, 2018.

Miyar, Marijean Collado–Coral Gables, FL, July 21, 2017.

Morales, Ricardo "Dick" Jr.–Jacksonville, FL, May 30, 2017.

Mormino, Gary R.–Tampa, FL, September 21, 2017.

Morse, Luis C.–Miami, FL, January 9, 2018.

Padrón, Eduardo J.–Miami, FL, May 16, 2017.

Pérez-de Cobos, Edmundo–Coral Gables, FL, May 18, 2017.

Rodriguez, Nestor A.–Miami, FL, May 19, 2017.

Roiz, Carmen Leiva–Miami, FL, October 16, 2018.

Sawaya-Crane, Diana–Tallahassee, FL, June 21, 2017, and February 26, 2018.

Tabernilla, Hilda Molina–Palm Beach, FL, June 29, 2017.

Valiente, Jose E.–Tampa, FL, September 19, 2017.

Valls, Julieta Navarrete–South Miami, FL, July 20, 2017.

Villalobos, Jose A.–Miami, FL, July 11, 2017.

Villamil, Marielena Alejo–Coral Gables, FL, January 9, 2018.

Wangüemert-Peña, Mercedes–Austin, TX, December 28, 2016, January 1, and October 12, 2017.

Zamorano, Victoria Montoro–South Miami, FL, October 17, 2018.

INDEX

elected president, 78; isolation policy of, 151–52; Missile Crisis and, 149, 154; Operation Mongoose and, 147, 152; overtures from Castro, 154; restricting raiders, 152–53

Kennedy Administration, 117, 152

Key West, 72

Key West ferry, 1–3, 12, 59, 76, 257

La Cabaña, 28, 37, 53, 141, 159, 166, 256

Lansky, Meyer, 38–39

La pecera, 68–69, 71, 116, 122–23, 130, 256–57

La Raza Unida, 249

La Sagüesera. *See* Miami, Florida (La Sagüesera)

Laurencio, Hector (*née* Hector García), xxiii, 121–23, 237

Laurencio, Maria Galatas, xxiii, 46–47, 68, 84–85, 139–40, 241

Ley de peligrosidad, 224

Liberty City. *See* Miami (Liberty City)

Little Havana. *See* Miami (Little Havana)

Lobo, Julio, 38–39, 73

Maceo, Antonio, 15, 41–42

Machado, Gerardo, 7, 11, 231

Madrid, Spain, 87, 172–73

Mariel Boatlift: beginning of, 223–24; criminals and mental patients, 224–25; schism with early refugees, 226–28

Mármol, Guillermo G. "Gil," xxiii, 49, 65–66, 107, 235

Márquez, Myriam, xxiii, 57, 193–94, 240–41

Martell, Henry (*née* Enrique Martell), xxiii, 44–45, 123–24, 215–16

Martí, José, 4, 41–42, 51, 256

Martínez, Melquíades "Mel," 129, 129n

Martínez Ybor, Vicente, xvii, 72

Matos, Huber, 58

Matthews, Herbert, 34–35

Metropolitan Museum of Art, 220

Mexico, 32, 164, 172

Miami, Florida: bilingual education, 206, 254; comparison to other Cuban enclaves, 232–33; Cuban American businesses, 100, 214–17; early years, 82, 89; La Sagüesera, 82, 100n; Latin Americans attracted to, 228, 238, 253; Liberty City, 89; Little Havana, 82–83, 153, 234; Public Library, 218–19; racial discrimination in, 89, 94, 117; refugee influx, 82–83, 89, 94, 181, 228, 231, 254; refugees shunned, 78, 94–95, 117; reminiscent of Cuba, 210, 231; return of resettled exiles, 228, 231, 233; social and civic organizations, 220; transformation, 82–83, 94, 214–15, 222–23, 234–38, 253–54; violence by exiles, 221

Miami Beach, Florida, 83, 89, 100–101, 118–19, 228

Miami Herald, 130, 181, 193, 195

Miami-Dade Community College. *See* Miami Dade College

Miami-Dade County, 230, 238

Miami Dade College, 153, 202, 214, 229–30

Migration accords of 1995, 226

Milicianos. See Cuba (revolutionary) (*milicianos*)

Miller, Gene, 130

Missile Crisis, 73, 88, 132, 149, 154–55

Miyar, Marijean Collado, xxiii, 11–12, 81–82, 103, 228–29

Moncada Barracks, 31

Morales, Ricardo "Dick," Jr., xxiii, 5–6, 47–48

Mormino, Gary R., xxiii, 237–38

Morse, Luis C., xxiv, 61–62, 136–37, 143–48

Movimiento de 26 de Julio (M-26-7), 32, 33, 36, 42, 46

MS *St. Louis*, 96

Neiman Marcus, 114–15

New Jersey, 91, 185

New Orleans, Louisiana, 2, 40, 45, 112

New York, 91–92, 96, 130, 185–87, 229

New York Times, 34

Nixon, Richard M., 55

Nixon Administration, 195–96

Obama, Barack, 227, 237, 241

O'Farrill, Albertina, xvii, 45–46, 125, 160, 244–46

Union City, New Jersey, 91, 185, 214, 231–32
United Nations, 255
United States: asylum in, 255–56; Cuban tourists in, 6, 9, 12; Cubans educated in before 1959, 5–6, 8–9; diplomatic relations with Cuba severed, 64, 79; domination of Cuba by, 4, 9; embassy of, 115, 174; Federal Reserve, 9; higher education in, 191, 195, 202–3, 212–15, 217 (*see also* Cuban Refugee Program [CRP] [Cuban Loans]); immigration laws of, 254–56; intervention in War of Independence, 7; isolation policy of, 63–65, 151–52, 158, 160, 163; Joint Chiefs of Staff, 135, 143; military occupation of Cuba, 7, 9, 15, 41–42; normalization of relations with Cuba, 226, 237, 241; opposed to Castro, 42, 112, 115, 135, 163, 168; parole into, 79–80, 121, 172; public works by, 7; religious faiths transplanted from, 9–10; Small Business Administration, 215; State Department, 79, 121, 161, 168, 172; Supreme Court of, 89, 234; tourism from, 4, 9; troops dispatched by, 7, 15; visa waivers, 79, 121, 132; wet-foot, dry-foot policy, 226, 256
University of Florida, 203–5, 209, 214
University of Havana, 29, 34, 44–45, 55, 61–62
University of Miami, 147, 203–5, 228
Urrutia, Manuel, 48, 55, 60

Valdés, Ramiro, 140, 165
Valiente, Jose E., xxv, 21–22, 88–89, *104*, 213
Valls, Julieta Navarrete, xxv, 40, 114–15, 242–43
Varadero, 78, *103*, *108*, 165, 170, 176–77
Vedado district, 10, 20, 37
Venezuela, 70, 147–48, 248
Vibora district, 14
Villalobos, Jose A., xxv, 60–61, 138–39
Villamil, Marielena Alejo, xxv, 19–21, 58–59, 76–77, *105*, 155, 232–33
Voting Rights Act of 1965, 221

Waiting for Snow in Havana, 243
Walsh, Bryan, 115, 118–19, 121, 128, 254
Wangüemert-Peña, Mercedes, xxv, 14–15, 35–36, 66–67, 99–101, *108*, 154, 249–51
Ward-Garcia Line, 140–41
Windward Passage, 7
Wood, Leonard, 8, 15

Ybor City. *See* Tampa, Florida: Ybor City
Yucatán Channel, 7

Zamorano, Victoria Montoro, xxv, 45–46, 124–25, 244–46
Zapata Swamp (Ciénaga de Zapata). *See* Bay of Pigs (Bahia de Cochinos)
Zig-Zag, 81

A graduate of the University of Texas at Austin and the Columbia Journalism School, David Powell worked as a reporter for ten years, most of that with the Associated Press in New York, Miami, and Tallahassee. After earning a law degree from Florida State University, he practiced law for thirty years. In his work he met many Cuban Americans and was moved by the stories of their lives. He began recording interviews about their memories in 2016, first in Florida and then elsewhere. In 2021 the University of Miami acquired his interview recordings, transcripts, and work papers for its Cuban Heritage Collection. He and his wife reside in Tallahassee, Florida.